EDUCATION IN A COMPETITIVE AND GLOBALIZING WORLD

CURRICULUM REFORM IN CHINA: CHANGES AND CHALLENGES

Education in a Competitive and Globalizing World

Additional books in this series can be found on Nova's website under the Series tab.

Additional E-books in this series can be found on Nova's website under the E-books tab.

China in the 21st Century

Additional books in this series can be found on Nova's website under the Series tab.

Additional E-books in this series can be found on Nova's website under the E-books tab.

EDUCATION IN A COMPETITIVE AND GLOBALIZING WORLD

CURRICULUM REFORM IN CHINA: CHANGES AND CHALLENGES

HONG-BIAO YIN
AND
JOHN CHI-KIN LEE
EDITORS

Nova Science Publishers, Inc.
New York

Copyright © 2012 by Nova Science Publishers, Inc.

All rights reserved. No part of this book may be reproduced, stored in a retrieval system or transmitted in any form or by any means: electronic, electrostatic, magnetic, tape, mechanical photocopying, recording or otherwise without the written permission of the Publisher.

For permission to use material from this book please contact us:
Telephone 631-231-7269; Fax 631-231-8175
Web Site: http://www.novapublishers.com

NOTICE TO THE READER

The Publisher has taken reasonable care in the preparation of this book, but makes no expressed or implied warranty of any kind and assumes no responsibility for any errors or omissions. No liability is assumed for incidental or consequential damages in connection with or arising out of information contained in this book. The Publisher shall not be liable for any special, consequential, or exemplary damages resulting, in whole or in part, from the readers' use of, or reliance upon, this material. Any parts of this book based on government reports are so indicated and copyright is claimed for those parts to the extent applicable to compilations of such works.

Independent verification should be sought for any data, advice or recommendations contained in this book. In addition, no responsibility is assumed by the publisher for any injury and/or damage to persons or property arising from any methods, products, instructions, ideas or otherwise contained in this publication.

This publication is designed to provide accurate and authoritative information with regard to the subject matter covered herein. It is sold with the clear understanding that the Publisher is not engaged in rendering legal or any other professional services. If legal or any other expert assistance is required, the services of a competent person should be sought. FROM A DECLARATION OF PARTICIPANTS JOINTLY ADOPTED BY A COMMITTEE OF THE AMERICAN BAR ASSOCIATION AND A COMMITTEE OF PUBLISHERS.

Additional color graphics may be available in the e-book version of this book.

Library of Congress Cataloging-in-Publication Data

Curriculum reform in China : changes and challenges / editors, Hong-Biao Yin, John Chi-Kin Lee.
    p. cm.
 Includes index.
 ISBN 978-1-61470-943-5 (hardcover)
 1. Curriculum planning--China. 2. Curriculum change--China. 3. Education--Curricula--China.
I. Yin, Hong-Biao. II. Li, Zijian, 1960-
 LB2806.15.C882 2011
 375'.0010951--dc23
               2011028896

Published by Nova Science Publishers, Inc. †New York

CONTENTS

Preface		**vii**
Contributors		**xiii**

Part I. Introduction

Chapter 1	China's National Curriculum Reform in the Global Era *Hong-Biao Yin and John Chi-Kin Lee*	**1**

Part II. The Context of the Reform

Chapter 2	Changing Concepts and Practices of Curriculum in China *Janette Ryan*	**13**
Chapter 3	Curriculum Making in the New Curriculum Reform: Structure, Process and Meaning *Zongyi Deng*	**31**
Chapter 4	Leading Curriculum Reform in China: Principals in the Middle *Haiyan Qian and Allan Walker*	**47**
Chapter 5	Conditions for Successful Reforms: Characteristics of the Organisation and Culture in Chinese Schools in a Global Context *Jessica Harris, Yong Zhao and Brian J. Caldwell*	**61**

Part III. Change Implementation in Subject Areas

Chapter 6	Mathematics Curriculum Reform in China: Latest Developments and Challenges *Rui Ding and Ngai-Ying Wong*	**81**
Chapter 7	Chemistry Curriculum Reform in China: Policy and Practice *Bing Wei*	**95**
Chapter 8	Integrated Science Reform in China *Shuang Zhang*	**111**
Chapter 9	Transforming Citizenship Education in Social Studies Curriculum of Primary Schools: A Textbook Analysis *Wenlan Wang, John Chi-Kin Lee and Hong-Biao Yin*	**123**

Chapter 10	Curriculum Reform of Moral Education in High Schools in China *J. Mark Halstead and Chuanyan Zhu*	**137**
Chapter 11	Toward a Competence-Based Vocational Senior Secondary English Curriculum *Wen Zhao and David Coniam*	**155**
Chapter 12	Chinese Senior Secondary Elective Courses and College Entrance Examination Systems: Non-, Dual-, or Multi-Streaming? *Shengyao Feng*	**169**

Part IV. Teacher Professional Development in Curriculum Reform

Chapter 13	Emotion as a Lens to Understand Teacher Development in Curriculum Reform *Hong-Biao Yin, John Chi-Kin Lee and Edmond Hau-Fai Law*	**185**
Chapter 14	Belief as the Prerequisite to Action: Curriculum Reform and the Transformation of Teaching Conceptions in Rural China *Tanja Sargent*	**203**
Chapter 15	Teacher Learning through Teaching Reflection in the Context of Curriculum Reform *Mingren Zhao*	**225**
Chapter 16	Qualities of Good Teachers in China: A Comparative Perspective *Shujie Liu and Lingqi Meng*	**237**
Index		**253**

PREFACE

Curriculum reform has played a central role in the educational changes in contemporary China. The government of the People's Republic of China, being at the center of the centralized educational administration system, assumes the responsibility for designing and organizing the systemic reform initiatives. This is especially the case for what has been happening since the end of 1990s. At the turn of the new millennium, the Chinese government initiated the new round of national curriculum reform (NCR) for basic education which is also the eighth round of nation-wide curriculum reform since the founding of the Peoples' Republic of China. This book will give insightful information on the state of educational programs in China's immediate future and written by many educators in China's learning system.

Chapter 1 – Entering the new millennium, the Ministry of Education of the People's Republic of China initiated a new round of national curriculum reform for basic education which continues until today. In this chapter, we try to locate China's national curriculum reform in the context of globalization, and briefly discuss the framework behind the chapters and importance of this volume.

Chapter 2 – The scale and depth of China's current curriculum reform program, China's eight since 1949, mean that it is the most radical and far-reaching. It envisages sustained and enduring reform of all aspects of school curriculum policy, management, administration and resources, teaching and learning and assessment practices. The reform has drawn from China's own educational traditions as well as from the experiences of education systems worldwide. It has thus resulted in 'hybrid' forms of curriculum practice, where outside experience has been drawn upon, but has been implemented and organised in 'Chinese' ways and on a vast scale. The reform has been the subject of much discussion and even conflict and resistance, as well as much enthusiasm and dedication, but has undoubtedly resulted in significant change. This change has been patchy, but the magnitude and speed of the reform and associated changes have been achieved at a much faster pace and on a larger scale than has previously been achieved in other contexts. The changes to teachers' pedagogical and conceptual understandings and practices in many areas in little over a decade in China have taken over 30 years to achieve in other educational systems. This chapter documents these changes and the various structures and processes that have been put in place to achieve them and provides examples of some of the ways that teachers working in teacher professional learning communities have implemented these changes. It points to the importance of teacher research and professional development and a collaborative support network for teachers for achieving innovative and sustainable change to teachers' research and teaching practices and consequently students' learning in China.

Chapter 3 – This chapter deals with the mechanism of curriculum making in the new curriculum reform. It analyzes the structure, process and meaning of curriculum making at the national, local, school and classroom levels. The chapter shows that the experience of China's curriculum reform instantiates a larger institutional and organizational process of curriculum making in the international arena. It concludes by addressing the complexity and challenges involved in using state-based curriculum making as an instrument for the reform.

Chapter 4 – The curriculum reform in China presents radical changes not only to how and what students learn, but also to how principals lead, relationships within the school and connections with governments and parents. The purpose of the chapter is to present a snapshot of some of the struggles faced by secondary school principals in Shanghai during their implementation of the curriculum reform. Based on the empirical evidence, this chapter attempts to explain, from the principals' perspectives, why they fail to perform the expected "curriculum leader" role. The explanation is presented in the form of three propositions. They include the important principal role to win resources, the dominant expectation to produce good performance on exams and the pressure of culturally and structurally engrained relationships. The chapter ends with the discussion of some implications for leadership to enhance learning in the future.

Chapter 5 – Reforms to the basic education system in China have reflected an increasing awareness of and openness to new ideas from the global education sphere. Many of the concepts involved in the development and implementation of these reforms, including adopting holistic perspectives of student development; decentralising school governance to facilitate local decision-making to address local needs; and, an increased focus on practical, lifelong learning for all involved in schools, have been promoted in research and policies throughout the world. While working within this global context, the system of schooling in China has retained a unique character that is quite different from education in the West. Drawing on an international project on school transformation, this chapter aims to examine how five secondary schools in Chongqing, a municipality in Southwestern China, have harnessed and aligned their resources to provide effective school governance following the curriculum reforms. Furthermore, the chapter will examine the similarities and differences between the organisational structures and cultures of these schools in China and successful schools in Australia, England, Finland, Wales and the United States.

Chapter 6 – In this chapter, we will offer a full picture of the most recent developments of the Chinese mathematics curriculum reform, including its background, goal, implementation and debates that arose. Factors leading to the success of curriculum reform will be discussed. They include political and economic factor, examination culture, social participation, textbook development and teacher preparation. We believe that all these events will not inspire mathematics education but curriculum innovations in general.

Chapter 7 - Since the start of the new millennium, the chemistry curriculum at the level of the secondary school in China has experienced a dramatic change. This chapter reviews the current school chemistry curriculum reform in China in both policy and practice with particular focus on these issues: science curriculum policy, the official chemistry curriculum standards, chemistry textbooks, and curriculum implementation. The changes, both positive and negative, from these two perspectives are analyzed and critically commented upon. The data examined for this chapter mainly came from official documents, research studies, and internally circulated documents. In the last part of this chapter, the problems and challenges identified in the current chemistry curriculum reform have been discussed within the perspective of Confucian cultural tradition.

Chapter 8 – This chapter is about the policy and implementation of integrated science curricula at junior secondary schools in Mainland China. Adopting the framework of John Goodlad's (1979) three levels of curriculum, i.e., intended curriculum, implemented curriculum and attained curriculum, this chapter mainly addresses the intended and implemetented integrated science curricula. It is divided into three parts. First, it provides an overview of the integrated science curricula in China based on related curriculum policy documents. Second, it reports the findings of a research attempting to reconstruct the experiences of teachers in two junior secondary schools who have been involved in implementing the integrated science curricula for six years. Finally, it discusses the implications of the research findings for the future development of integrated science.

Chapter 9 – Citizenship education is an emerging area of study in Mainland China. In this chapter, two sets of social studies textbooks are compared and analyzed to find any transformation of citizenship education in primary schools under the current China' NCR. Based on a frequency comparison and content analysis of these textbooks, results show that citizenship education in social studies curriculum has undergone dramatic transformations, including the depoliticisation of social studies curriculum and the significant increase in content of citizenship education, increase of diverse elements of citizenship education, and the changing nature of content and pedagogies of citizenship education. However, the new social studies curriculum still adopts a relatively passive, obligation-based approach to citizenship education. This chapter concludes that there is still a need to enhance citizenship education in Mainland China.

Chapter 10 – The complexity of Moral Education (deyu in Chinese) is illustrated both by the breadth of content of the subject, which combines character education and personal and social development (including mental and physical health) with the academic study of politics, economics, law, ethics and philosophy, and also by the diversity of influences on contemporary Chinese values, which include the socialist, collectivist and patriotic values associated with the ideology of communism, traditional values such as Confucian teaching and contemporary social and economic values that are to some extent influenced by western materialism and individualism. The curriculum reforms seek to bring coherence to this complexity by encouraging teachers responsible for Moral Education to meet the needs of contemporary China by using modern theories and approaches to create future citizens of the highest moral calibre who retain their ideological and political commitments. The chapter reviews existing research on the impact of the reforms and then presents the findings of the authors' own research which examines school responses to the reforms in more detail, focusing on teachers' practice and students' attitudes. A clear tension emerges between the replacement of the old textbooks with their outdated material and the retention of the old system of university entrance examinations which inhibit the full implementation of the reforms. A further tension exists between the natural tendency of teachers to be authoritarian and dominate the whole instruction process and the intention of the reforms to make learning more autonomous and student-centred. These tensions may partly be resolved by more in-service training for teachers, but it is also important that Moral Education should remain in touch with the actual values students are developing in their own lives.

Chapter 11 – Vocational education (VE) in Mainland China has been undergoing curriculum reform since the new millennium, in tandem with reforms in primary, junior and senior secondary education and higher education. This chapter begins with an introduction of the three types of post-secondary vocational schools in Mainland China, with a focus on vocational senior secondary schools. The chapter then describes the vocational senior secondary English curriculums issued since the late 1980s, in particular the 2000 National Vocational English Syllabus (NVES) and the 2009 NVES. The chapter finally presents a detailed description of the competence-based 2009 NVES, with a critical analysis of its two competence dimensions — the level of scales on the vertical dimension and the descriptive scheme on the horizontal dimension. The purpose of the chapter has been to provide a critical overview of the current competence-based vocational senior secondary English curriculum in Mainland China.

Chapter 12 – In 2003, China's Ministry of Education (MOE) issued the General Senior Secondary School Curriculum Program (Experimental version) which puts forward the idea of potential college-major oriented elective courses. From 2006 onwards, the four pilot provinces or autonomous regions began to promulgate successively their college entrance examination programs, paying no attention to the major-oriented elective courses. In 2010, the MOE issued the National Outline for Medium and Long-term Education Reform and Development (2010-2020), with an emphasis on the dominant position of fostering and assessing comprehensive capacities of students. Clearly, there exist inherent contradictions and conflicts among those documents and policies. It is argued in this chapter that the most preferred option in Mainland China should be "multi-streaming" by which is meant there is major-based curriculum differentiation which flexibly provides elective courses according to the potential college-majors. This chapter suggests that such a multi-streaming option is in line with international trends and also has strong theoretical foundations.

Chapter 13 – Teacher emotion provides a lens, through which we can understand the characteristics of teacher development in large-scale educational change. However, compared with the rich exploration of teachers' emotional geographies in the West, only a few studies have adopted Hargreaves' emotional geographies to analyze human interactions in education in Chinese societies. This chapter aims at exploring the nature of emotions felt by teachers in their interactions with teacher trainers during a period of the national curriculum reform in Mainland China. Three kinds of emotional geographies were evident: professional, political, and moral. The implications for teacher emotion research and teacher development in curriculum reform are discussed.

Chapter 14 – The Chinese New Curriculum reforms that began in primary schools in 2001 aim for the transformation of teachers' beliefs as the prerequisite to the transformation of teaching practices from traditional teacher-centered approaches to more progressive student-centered approaches. This chapter draws on classroom observation and in-depth interview data to investigate the relationship between the New Curriculum reform implementation and the beliefs about teaching and learning held by primary school teachers in rural northwest China. My findings suggest that teachers who are more familiar with, and have more positive attitudes about, the New Curriculum reforms also have more "progressive" beliefs about teaching.

Chapter 15 – State-sponsored teacher training for the New Curriculum reforms has often been based on "deficit approaches" leaving teachers as passive participants in the process. This is ironic given that the theoretical core of the New Curriculum is based on constructivism and progressivism. School-based teaching reflection, on the other hand, can be situational and target-oriented. In this chapter, the reflection and learning of teachers with different levels of teaching competence are examined. Findings suggest that teaching reflections vary significantly by teaching competence. Teachers with average teaching competence usually learn superficially from reflection following a "point-by-point summary", producing gradual teacher change. Veteran teachers achieve authentic learning by reflection based on "systematic inquiry", resulting in a fundamental teacher change. However, when teachers doubt the value of curriculum reform, following any reflection, they prefer not to express their doubts in case it is viewed as a lack of commitment to the reform, thus diminishing public discussion of problems and reducing constructive critical reflection and action.

Chapter 16 – Since the 1920's many researchers have conducted studies exploring the qualities of good teachers. However, a limited number of empirical studies have been conducted in the People's Republic of China (hereafter called China). The current study has two objectives. The first one aimed to compare a good teacher's characteristics in China and the USA. To achieve this, qualitative data of a good teacher's characteristics were collected in China. The results obtained from China were then compared to those reported in the USA. The second objective was to test whether or not there are differences among teachers', students' and parents' perceptions of a good teacher's characteristics in China. To achieve this, questionnaires were administered, and then statistical analyses were conducted. The qualitative data analyses have revealed four themes about the characteristics of good Chinese teachers: teacher ethics, professional skills, professional development, and students' test scores. This study helps readers better understand good teachers in a Chinese context and provides a framework for future comparative study between China and the USA regarding the qualities of good teachers.

CONTRIBUTORS

Brian J. Caldwell is Managing Director and Principal Consultant at Educational Transformations Pty Ltd in Australia and Associate Director of the Specialist Schools and Academies Trust in England, providing support for its international arm – International Networking for Educational Transformation (iNet). From 1998 to 2004 he served as Dean of Education at the University of Melbourne where he is currently Professorial Fellow. His international work over the last 25 years includes more than 500 presentations, projects and other professional assignments in or for 40 countries. His most recent books are *Why not the Best Schools* (2008) with Jessica Harris, *Our School Our Future* (2010) with David Loader, and *Changing Schools in an Era of Globalization* (2011) with John Chi-Kin Lee.

David Coniam is a professor and chair of the Department of Curriculum and Instruction at The Chinese University of Hong Kong, where he is a teacher educator, working with ESL teachers in Hong Kong secondary schools. His main publication and research interests are in language teaching methodology, language assessment, computer assisted language learning and computational and corpus linguistics.

Zongyi Deng is an associate professor in Nanyang Technological University and former associate professor at the University of Hong Kong (HKU). He is currently an associate editor of *Journal of Curriculum Studies* (*JCS*). Recent publications appear in *The Sage Handbook of Curriculum and Instruction*, *International Encyclopedia of Education*, *Curriculum Inquiry*, and *JCS*.

Rui Ding is a lecturer in the Department of Curriculum and Instruction, School of Educational Science, Northeast Normal University in China. Her publications focus on mathematics curriculum reform and classroom environment.

Shengyao Feng is a professor in the Department of Curriculum and Instruction at the South China Normal University, Guangzhou, China. He is a committee member of Chinese National Association for Curriculum Studies. His research interests include curriculum reform, college entrance examination and comparative education. He is the author of *Curriculum Practices in the Four Asian Dragons* (1998, in Chinese), and edited *Curriculum Reform: China and the World* (2004, in Chinese).

J. Mark Halstead is a research professor and formerly Head of Department of Community and International Education at the University of Huddersfield, UK, with responsibility for the university's education courses in Beijing and Guangzhou. He has previously worked at the universities of Plymouth, Oxford and Cambridge. He has written widely on educational values, spiritual and moral education, comparative education and multicultural education. His collaborative publications include *The Common School and the Comprehensive Ideal* (Wiley-Blackwell, 2008), *Citizenship and Moral Education* (Routledge, 2006), *Values in Sex Education: from principles to practice* (Routledge-Falmer, 2003), *Education in Morality* (Routledge, 1999) and *Values in Education and Education in Values* (Falmer Press, 1996).

Jessica Harris is Postdoctoral Research Fellow in the School of Education, University of Queensland, Australia. Her research interests include international and comparative education, globalization and education, education policy and governance, social capital in education, Ethnomethodology and Conversation Analysis. Her most recent book is *Why not the Best Schools* (2008) with Brian J. Caldwell.

Edmond Hau-Fai Law is Associate Professor in the Department of Curriculum and Instruction at The Hong Kong Institute of Education. He specializes in curriculum and leadership studies, language in education and socio-cultural and discourse approaches to the study of curriculum. His publications have appeared in journals such as *Educational Management Administration and Leadership*, *The Curriculum Journal*, and *Curriculum and Teaching*. His most recent book is *Schools as Curriculum Agencies: Asian and European Perspectives on School-Based Curriculum Development* (Sense Publishers, The Netherlands, 2010) with Nienke Nieveen.

John Chi-Kin Lee is Vice President (Academic) and Chair Professor of Curriculum and Instruction in the Hong Kong Institute of Education and former Dean of Education, The Chinese University of Hong Kong (2003-2010). He is the regional editor (Asia) of *Education Research and Evaluation* and associate editor of *Teachers and Teaching*. In addition to more than twenty books as well as 150 journal articles and book chapters, his recent co-edited books are *New Understandings of Teacher's Work: Emotions and Educational Change* (with Chris Day, Springer) and *Changing Schools in an Era of Globalization* (with Brian Caldwell, Routledge).

Shujie Liu is an assistant professor in the Department of Educational Studies and Research, the College of Education and Psychology, the University of Southern Mississippi, USA. Her research has focused primarily on comparative study of education and examination of psychometric properties. In comparative educational study, the emphasis is in the fields of school/teacher effectiveness, teacher evaluation, and student academic achievement/self concept. Her research has been published in a range of international journals, including *School Effectiveness and School Improvement*, *Educational Psychology*, and *Educational Assessment, Evaluation and Accountability*.

Lingqi Meng is an assistant professor in the Division of Humanities, Arts, and Social Sciences, Pennsylvania State University (Berks Campus), USA. His research focus is comparative math education. His current research interest is to use TIMSS data to conduct research and to establish cultural models for comparative educational study.

Haiyan Qian is an assistant professor in the Institute of Higher Education, Fudan University at Shanghai, China. She is currently also a post-doctoral fellow at the Asia Pacific Centre of Leadership and Change at the Hong Kong Institute of Education. Her research interests include educational leadership and education change in China.

Janette Ryan is Director of the UK Higher Education Academy *Teaching International Students* Project, a Research Associate of the China Centre at the University of Oxford, Visiting Professor at the Centre for Academic Practice and Internationalisation at Leeds

Metropolitan University and an adjunct lecturer in the Faculty of Education at Monash University Australia. Her publications include *China's Higher Education Reform and Internationalisation* (Routledge, 2011), *Education Reform in China* (Routledge, 2011) and *International Education and the Chinese Learner* (co-edited with Gordon Slethaug, Hong Kong University Press, 2010).

Tanja Sargent is an assistant professor in the Educational Theory, Policy and Administration department at Rutgers Graduate School of Education in New Jersey, USA. Her publications have focused on teacher professional development and the implementation of education reforms in China and have appeared in journals such as the *Journal of Teacher Education, Comparative Education Review* and *Modern China*.

Allan Walker is the Joseph Lau Chair Professor of International Educational Leadership, Chair of the Department of Educational Policy and Leadership and Director of the Asia Pacific Centre of Leadership and Change at the Hong Kong Institute of Education. He was previously Chair Professor of Educational Administration and Policy at the Chinese University of Hong Kong and has worked at universities in Singapore and Australia. He has worked extensively through East and South East Asia and written extensively on school leadership, leadership development, the influence of culture on leadership and organizational behavior and education reform across the region.

Wenlan Wang is an associate professor of the Department of Curriculum and Instruction at the South China Normal University, Guangzhou, China. Her main publication and research interests are in citizenship education, curriculum studies, and teaching and learning of social studies. She is the author of *A Study of Citizenship Education in Social Studies Curriculum* (2006, in Chinese).

Bing Wei is an associate professor in the Faculty of Education, University of Macau. His research interests include social contexts of science curriculum, scientific literacy, history and philosophy of science and science teaching, and science teacher development. He has published papers on science/chemistry curriculum in China in *Science Education, International Journal of Science Education, Research in Science Education*. He also wrote chapters in *Internationalisation and Globalisation in Mathematics and Science Education* (Springer, 2007), *Handbook of Research in Science Education Research in Asia* (Sense Publishers, 2010).

Ngai-Ying Wong is a professor in the Department of Curriculum and Instruction at The Chinese University of Hong Kong, where he is the chair of the Board of Undergraduate Studies and the programme director of the Master of Science in Mathematics Education. He is the member of mathematics committees in both Hong Kong Examinations and Assessment Authority and Curriculum Development Council. He is also the founding president of Hong Kong Association for Mathematics Education. His research interests include mathematics curriculum reform, conceptions of mathematics, *bianshi* teaching, Confucian Cultural Heritage Learner's phenomena and student activities.

Hong-Biao Yin is an assistant professor in the Department of Curriculum and Instruction, Faculty of Education, The Chinese University of Hong Kong, Hong Kong SAR, China. His publications focus on curriculum change and implementation, teacher emotion, teacher development, and student motivation and appear in a range of journals, including *Journal of Educational Change, Teaching and Teacher Education, Curriculum and Teaching*, and *Educational Psychology*. He also coauthored *Curriculum Change: Theory and Practice* (2008, in Chinese) with John Chi-Kin Lee.

Shuang Zhang is an assistant professor in the General Education Office at The Hong Kong Institute of Education, Hong Kong SAR, China. Her research interests focus on integrated curriculum, teacher belief and curriculum change.

Mingren Zhao is an associate professor in the Faculty of Education and Vice-director of the Center for Teacher Education Research at the Northwest Normal University, Lanzhou, China. His publications focus on teaching reflection, teacher learning, teacher education policy and educational change.

Wen Zhao is a professor of Foreign Studies College at Northeastern University and a member of the Advisory Committee of College English Teaching of the Ministry of Education of Mainland China. Her research interests include the English curriculum and instruction, computer assisted language learning and corpus linguistics.

Yong Zhao is President Chair and Associate Dean for Global Education at the College of Education, University of Oregon. Previously he was University Distinguished Professor in the Department of Counselling, Educational Psychology, and Special Education at the College of Education, Michigan State University, where he also served as the founding director of the Center for Teaching and Technology, executive director of the Confucius Institute, as well as the US-China Center for Research on Educational Excellence. He is a fellow of the International Academy for Education. His research interests include computer gaming and education, diffusion of innovations, teacher adoption of technology, computer-assisted language learning, globalization and education, and international and comparative education. His recent publications include *Catching Up or Leading the Way: American Education in the Age of Globalization* (ASCD, 2009) and *Handbook of Asian Education* (Routledge, 2011).

Chuanyan Zhu has recently completed her PhD in the School of Education and Professional Development at the University of Huddersfield, UK. Her PhD thesis is on *Students' Understanding of Values Diversity: An Examination of the Process and Outcomes of Values Communication in English Lessons in a High School in Mainland China*. In collaboration with J. Mark Halstead, she published "Personal autonomy as an element in Chinese educational reform" in *Asia Pacific Journal of Education* (2009). She has also published articles in *Mass Communication Research* (Taiwan) and other Chinese journals.

PART I. INTRODUCTION

In: Curriculum Reform in China
Editors: Hong-Biao Yin and John Chi-Kin Lee

ISBN 978-1-61470-943-5
© 2012 Nova Science Publishers, Inc.

Chapter 1

CHINA'S NATIONAL CURRICULUM REFORM IN THE GLOBAL ERA

Hong-Biao Yin and John Chi-Kin Lee

ABSTRACT

Entering the new millennium, the Ministry of Education of the People's Republic of China initiated a new round of national curriculum reform for basic education which continues until today. In this chapter, we try to locate China's national curriculum reform in the context of globalization, and briefly discuss the framework behind the chapters and importance of this volume.

THE DEVELOPMENT OF THE NATIONAL CURRICULUM REFORM IN CHINA

Curriculum reform has played a central role in the educational changes in contemporary China[1]. The government of the People's Republic of China, being at the center of the centralized educational administration system, assumes the responsibility for designing and organizing the systemic reform initiatives (Zhao and Qiu, 2010). This is especially the case for what has been happening since the end of 1990s. At the turn of the new millennium, the Chinese government initiated the new round of national curriculum reform (NCR) for basic education[2] which is also the eighth round of nation-wide curriculum reform since the founding of the Peoples' Republic of China. In December 1998, the Ministry of Education (MOE) issued the *Action Plan toward the Revitalization of Education in the Twenty-first Century*, suggesting a further education reform in response to the challenges of cultivating creative talents and well-rounded citizens for the 21st century:

---

[1] Unless otherwise specified, "China" refers to the Chinese mainland in this book.
[2] It is also called "the new curriculum reform" in China.

Currently, and in the near future, the lack of creative talent capable of international leadership is the greatest restriction to our nation's creative ability and competitiveness.... The revitalization of our nation's education is an objective requirement for the realization of the goals of socialist modernization and the great renaissance of the Chinese nation (MOE, 1998).

In June 1999, the State Council, the top administrative organ in China, promulgated the *Decisions of the Party Central Committee and the State Council on Deepening Reform in Education and Developing Quality-oriented Education in an All-round Way*, deciding to initiate a new round of NCR covering all aspects of the curriculum system including goals, content, structure, etc.:

(Article 14) Readjusting and reforming the system, structure and contents of curricula, establishing new curricula system for basic education, and adopting curricula at national, local and school levels. Something has to be done to revamp those curricula that place so much undue emphasis on the integrity of various disciplines of learning that they have become divorced from the times, social development and the practical situations of students. No time shall be lost to devise mechanisms for upgrading the teaching content and increasing the comprehensibility and practicality of the lessons; due attention must be paid to laboratory teaching and to the cultivation of students' actual operational abilities (The State Council, 1999).

In June 2001, the blueprint of this NCR, i.e., the *Guideline on Basic Education Curriculum Reform (Experimental Draft)*, was published by the Ministry of Education. It stated that the new curriculum system covers all three stages of basic education, i.e., preschool education, compulsory education (Grade 1-9) and the general senior secondary education (Grade 10-12), and described the plan for the reform as nine aspects, namely reform goals, curriculum structure, curriculum standards, teaching and learning, the development of teaching materials, curriculum evaluation, curriculum management, teacher training and the organization of the curriculum reform. The basic education curriculum reform aims to cultivate among students, spirits of patriotism, collectivism and love for socialism as well as the inheritance and carrying forward of the fine Chinese traditions. In addition, students are encouraged to develop an innovative spirit, actual operational abilities, and acquire literacy in science and arts together with an environmental awareness (Lee et al., 2011).

Specifically, the *Guideline* defined the six goals of the curriculum reform as follows (MOE, 2001):

- to change the emphasis in past curricula from simply knowledge transmission, and stress the process of learning;
- to change the discipline-centered curriculum structure, and make it integrated and adaptable to the various needs of pupils in different regions;
- to renew the "difficult, complicated, prejudiced, and out-dated" curriculum content, and strengthen the relevance of curricula to students' lives, society, and the development of science and technology;
- to change the emphasis of teaching and curriculum implementation from rote and drill, to place more emphasis on active learning and inquiry ability;

- to change the emphasis of curriculum assessment on selection functions, and stress the function of assessment in promoting the development of students, teachers, and schools; and

- to replace the centralized curriculum management with a three-tier system of national, local, and school curriculum management to make the curricula adaptable to local areas, schools, and students.

In September 2001, the NCR for compulsory education (Grade 1-9) was put into practice in 38 experimental areas selected from the entire nation. By September 2007, all 31 provinces, municipalities, and autonomous regions in Mainland China had adopted the new curriculum for compulsory education. For senior secondary education, the Ministry of Education issued the *Curriculum Guideline for General Senior Secondary School (Experimental draft)* and new curriculum standards for fifteen subjects in March 2003. Since September 2004, the curriculum reform at the stage of senior secondary education has been implemented in four selected provinces (i.e., Guangdong, Shandong, Hainan and Ningxia) and has gradually been extended to other provinces. By September 2010, 30 of the 31 provinces, autonomous regions and municipalities on the Chinese mainland have adopted the new senior secondary curriculum[3], and the other province, Guangxi, is expected to implement the curriculum reform from the start of the school year 2011-2012.

To date, this round of NCR, has, depending on location, been implementing for ten years. Although it is still too early to make a final judgment on its influence, the available evidence shows that the reform has brought some positive changes to educational practice. As summarized by Zhu Mu-ju (2007), the Director-General of the National Centre for School Curriculum and Textbook Development and the chief designer of the NCR, the changes brought by the new curriculum aiming at transcending "subject-centeredness" include: (a) revising academic courses and connecting them to student experience and social development; (b) adding integrated practice activity courses; (c) diversifying curriculum with locality- and school-based courses; and (d) providing elective courses to all students. Feng (2006) also concluded that there were four positive outcomes of the reform as follows: (a) the administrative style of government has to a greater or lesser degree, changed and decentralized; (b) the ratios of local and school curricula have been increased in the three-tier system consisting of national, local and school curricula; (c) innovative approaches in teacher development have been introduced, such as "expert teacher studio" and school-based teaching research; and (d) a positive tendency highlighting teaching reflection is emerging in the learning and teaching process.

In Guan and Meng's (2007) review paper, they observed eight changes in practice, including (a) the establishment of the three-level curriculum management mechanism; (b) more flexible requirements for schools, teachers and students; (c) a more diverse curriculum structure containing required courses, elective courses and integrated practice activity courses; (d) the development of teachers' professional competence by teacher training in line with the reform; (e) the adoption of a student-centered teaching approach; (f) the adoption of

---

[3] Shanghai is included too. However, Shanghai is an independent experimental area of curriculum reform which was set up by the Ministry of Education in the late-1980s. In Shanghai, the second term of basic education curriculum reform has been initiated since 1998, and the curriculum reform of senior secondary education has been implemented since 2004. The reform initiatives in Shanghai are similar to those of the national curriculum reform.

developmental evaluation which caters for learners' diversity better; (g) the wider use of technology and techniques in the teaching process; and (h) the enhancement of skills education which helps students master more life or work related skills.

However, implementing such an NCR in China is by no means a smooth process without problems. To ensure the implementation of the reform, practitioners in schools and administrative sectors have to shoulder a huge amount of hard work and cope with the limitations from the actual conditions (Liu and Qi, 2005; Yin and Lee, 2008a). For example, how to apply innovative teaching methods such as cooperative or inquiry-based learning in a classroom of more than fifty students? How to improve the professional development of over 10 million classroom teachers nation-wide and help them know how to use various teaching strategies and assessment methods? With the implementation of the reform, debates on the reform emerged and gradually intensified, such as "what should be the theoretical base of China's national curriculum reform" and "how should we balance the relationship between inheriting our Chinese traditions and learning from the West". In these debates, one side considered that the reform imported too many ideas and practices from the West which are unsuitable in the context of China while the other side thought China's education had to learn from the West to catch up with the rapid world developments; one side upheld the Marxist epistemology and all-round development theory as the foundation of the reform, while the other suggested updating or reinterpretation of the connotation of these Marxist viewpoints was necessary in the current global context. These debates reflected the dilemmas in which all stakeholders, including researchers, subject experts, policy makers, teacher educators and practitioners, faced in the reform. In Yin and Lee's (2008b) study, they summarized four tensions impacting the implementation of the reform: the cultural tension between the new pedagogical culture advocated by the reform and the cultural traditions in China; the professional tension between the requirements on teachers' competence and the professional support for them; the institutional tension between the reform requirements and the local policy environment; and the resource tension between the high resource expectation on schools and the actual conditions which exist. Zhong Qi-quan (2006), an influential professor at East China Normal University and the leader of the "National Consultant Team on Basic Education Curriculum Reform", pointed out there are three bottle-necks causing the problems and confusion in the reform, namely the lack of support from the changes of national-level college entrance examination system, the lack of education legislation to support the reform, and the lack of research into teachers to facilitate teacher growth and development in the reform. In short, China's NCR is still striving to overcome the various constraints and dilemmas, and produce desirable fundamental transformations for the schooling system.

THE GLOBAL WAVE OF LARGE-SCALE REFORM SINCE THE MID-1990S

Today, "there is no greater context for educational change than that of globalization, nor no grander way of conceptualizing what educational change is about" (Well et al., 1998, p. 322). Put simply, globalization means "time-space compression" (Harvey, 1989). In the field of education, globalization often refers to reforms, structures and policies that transcend national borders (Astiz, Wiseman, and Baker, 2002). It has been widely discussed the profound influence of globalization, a tendency deriving from the field of economy and technology, on educational policies and reforms across the world (Angus, 2004; Atweh and Clarkson, 2002; Carnoy and Rhoten, 2002; Dale and Robertson, 2002; Monkman and Baird, 2002; Mundy, 2005; Naidoo, Singh, and Sanagavarapu, 2007; Vongalis-Macrow, 2009). One salient effect of globalization is that various countries have tended to organize fundamental and systemic rather than merely incremental, piecemeal educational or curriculum reforms during the past decade (Waks, 2003).

Seen from a global perspective, the NCR in China is bound up with the global wave of large-scale reform in many Asian countries since the mid-1990s (Kennedy and Lee, 2008). At the beginning of the new millennium, Fullan (2000) keenly observed that a growing intensity in the efforts at large-scale reform has been witnessed globally at the end of 1990s, which he named as "the return of large-scale reform". These reform initiatives are recognized by their efforts to bring quality improvement of the whole school system as well as their large scale. England's *National Language and Numeracy Strategy* in 1997 is one significant example. A decade later, Fullan (2009) came back to this issue again and confirmed that large-scale reform has already come of age. After the mid-1990s, quite a number of States initiated national or territory-wide educational reforms which leading to simultaneous transformations at school, district and national levels. The global wave of large-scale reform is mirrored in many educational or curriculum reforms in various countries and areas: besides England's *National Language and Numeracy Strategy*, can be seen the series of educational reforms following George Bush's *No Child Left Behind* in 2002 and Barak Obama's *Race to the Top* in 2009 in the United States, Norway's national curriculum reforms of compulsory education in 1997 and 2006; Finland's national reforms of core curriculum for basic education in 1994 and 2004; the national curriculum reforms in Korea and Singapore, both of which were launched in 1997; and Japan's national curriculum reforms in 1998 and 2008. Very recently – in March 2010, Australia issued its first national curriculum plan for the four subjects English, mathematics, science and history. China's NCR is also one of them, illustrating that China has also responded to the global tendency of "the return of large-scale reform" since mid-1990s.

As described by Monkman and Baird (2002, p.497), "like beauty, the significance of globalization is in the eye of the beholder". In some writers' views, globalization is a transnational trend toward which educators in individual countries should be very cautious, because the standards, regimes and regulations that come to be adopted by many countries are made by Western countries according to their own values and interests (Naidoo et al., 2007). Therefore, globalization, from a socio-cultural perspective, often implies the international dissemination of some Western ideologies, such as marketization, entrepreneurialism, new managerialism, and rigid accountability structures (Angus, 2004; Vongalis-Macrow, 2009). In Dimmock and Walker's (2000) definition, globalization often causes the export of theory, policy and practice from some systems, usually the developed Anglo-American world, and their import into others, particularly non-Western and developing countries. As a result of the mechanism of transplantation or importation, globalization increases homogeneity among the reform initiatives in various countries. This kind of homogeneity can be easily found in the global wave of large-scale reform from the mid-1990s. In the reform policies and initiatives in these various countries, many innovative ideas and practices were similarly advocated, including decentralization, accountability, constructivism, curriculum integration, self-regulated and inquiry-based learning, and the cultivation of generic skills such as cooperation, communication and critical thinking, etc. – many of them also exist in China's NCR, resulting in a process of educational isomorphism within and around the world (Carnoy and Rhoten, 2002). In this process of educational isomorphism, the cultural and educational traditions in local countries are adapted and marginalized to some extent, sometimes leading to dramatic conflict between the local traditions and the newly arrived "exotic" educational ideas and practices. The debates and tensions in China's NCR exactly reflect the conflicts between the two sides.

However, in some others' eyes, globalization, particularly the economic perspective, does not necessarily produce homogeneity and simple isomorphism. It creates heterogeneity through local adaptation or the process of hybridization, too (Carnoy and Rhoten, 2002; Dale and Robertson, 2002; Green, 1999; Monkman and Baird, 2002). For example, Dale and Robertson's (2002) examination of three regional organizations, i.e., the European Union (EU), the North American Free Trade Area (NAFTA), and the Asia Pacific Economic Conference (APEC), found that these regional organizations play different mediating roles in the process of globalization. Though there is an increasingly globally structured agenda for education, there is as yet little increasing convergence of national practices or policies. In Astiz and his colleagues' (2002) study that qualitatively examines four nations and quantitatively examines 39 nations, they found that these nations respond to the decentralization of curricular control in different ways, leading to a mixing of centralized and decentralized models of curricular administration in national educational systems. These findings highlighted the significance of local context and adaptation resulting from traditions, cultural imperatives, historical legacy, and national political circumstances that have the potential to produce cross-national variation in reform policies and initiatives (Astiz et al., 2002). After comparing the educational reforms in European and Asian states, Green (1999) suggested that even thought there is considerable convergence at the level of policy rhetoric and reform objectives, "there is less evidence of any systemic convergence at the level of structures and processes in different countries. National education systems, though more international, are far from disappearing" (p. 69).

These studies contain encouraging messages for China' NCR. As mentioned above, the NCR in China adopted many seemingly "Anglo-American" ideas and policies, such as decentralization, curriculum integration, constructivist teaching, inquiry-based learning, formative assessment, cultivation of generic skills, etc., which caused heated debates on the nature and theoretical base of the reform. In spite of this, the reform process was not just a simple "copy and paste" exercise. On the contrary, some recent studies indicated that China's NCR distinctly differentiates from the reform initiatives in other countries. For example, when comparing of educational trends in China and the United States, Preus (2007) found that to meet the demands of globalization, Chinese education is becoming increasingly decentralized and learner-centered, which is precisely the opposite direction to that of recent reforms in the United States. Specifically, the reform in China moved the Chinese education system toward decentralization of basic education and a "quality-oriented" education with an emphasis on learner-cenetred methods, while the reform in the United States made the education system more centralized, "test-oriented" and placed more emphasis on the method of direct instruction. Halpin's (2010) recent comparison of the national curriculum reforms in China and England found similar contrasting directions, too. For instance, China's NCR emphasizes the importance of local implementation, inviting teachers to play a crucial role in interpreting at the local school sites, a broad centrally determined curricular framework, including modes of formative student assessment. In contrast, England's national curriculum reform chiefly requires schools to teach centrally prescribed subject-derived curricular content, the learning of which is periodically monitored through teacher administered pre-specified standardized tests. Moreover, in a recent comparison between education reforms in China and the Russian Federation after the 1980s – though it is more about reforms of the administrative and financial system rather than reforms of curriculum and teaching, Baskan and Erduran (2009) concluded that although the two countries were similar in ideological background and reform objectives, their routes towards reforming education were quite different, mainly because of the differences in their political and economic situations.

In the special issue of *Asia Pacific Journal of Education* (Vol. 29, No. 4, 2009) on basic education in China, the guest editors suggested viewing the basic education reform in China after 1997 as "globalization with Chinese characteristics" (Liu and Fang, 2009) mimicking Deng Xiaoping's "socialism with Chinese characteristics". We completely agree with them about this claim. China's NCR is trying to create more diversity and difference through the local adaptation by administrators, educators and students, even though it does follow a convergent educational reform agenda in this global era.

A BRIEF OUTLINE OF THIS VOLUME

With the rapid development of China's economy and political influence, more and more books and journal papers have recently been published about China's education system. However, there is a still a scarcity of scholarly books about the NCR in China, the most systemic, fundamental, and large-scale reform in recent years. To facilitate scholarly discussion on leading, implementing and understanding the NCR in China, we initiated this book which brings together distinguished scholars from around the world who share a common interest in research into curriculum reform and implementation.

The book comprises sixteen chapters organized into four sections. In this chapter which includes the introductory section of the book, we attempt to give an overview of China's NCR to the readers by briefly outlining its origin, process and global context. In the second section which contains four chapters, the authors focus on discussion of the contextual factors of the NCR in China at the national and local levels. In Chapter 2, Janette Ryan reviews the reform policy of NCR and its changes, highlighting the importance and prospect of Learning and Development Community in China. In Chapter 3, Zongyi Deng summarizes the curriculum making mechanisms of NCR, and reveals the institutional and cultural constraints of curriculum development in China. In Chapter 4, Haiyan Qian and Allan Walker sketch a picture of the challenges faced by principals in China as leaders of the new curriculum, showing that substantive changes in student learning may take some time. In Chapter 5, adopting a global perspective, Jessica Harris, Yong Zhao, and Brian J. Caldwell describe the characteristics of the organization and culture in Chinese schools, and provide some examples of successful schools in China.

In the third section consisting of seven chapters, the authors describe the change implementation in particular subjects or areas. In Chapter 6, Rui Ding and Ngai-Ying Wong introduce the mathematics curriculum reform in China, and summarize several factors leading to the success of curriculum reform which may be valuable reference for other countries. In

Chapter 7, Bing Wei outlines the chemistry curriculum reform in China, revealing the existence of an examination culture and the gap between intended and implemented curricula. In Chapter 8, Shuang Zhang analyzes the policy and implementation of integrated science curricula, highlighting the significance of understanding teachers' dilemmas for effective reform. In Chapter 9, Wenlan Wang, John Chi-Kin Lee, and Hong-Biao Yin describe the changes to citizenship education in social studies curricula, suggesting a need for further exploration and experimentation with citizenship education in China. In Chapter 10, J. Mark Halsted and Chuanyan Zhu discuss the curriculum reform of moral education in high schools, emphasizing the value of in-service training for moral education teachers in China. In Chapter 11, Wen Zhao and David Coniam describe the changes of English curriculum in vocational senior secondary schools, providing a critical overview of the current competence-based vocational English curriculum in China. In Chapter 12, based on an analysis of senior secondary elective courses and the college entrance examination system, Shengyao Feng argues that a "multi-streaming" approach should be adopted in the NCR.

The fourth and final section focuses on the fit of teacher professional development within the reform and comprises four chapters. In Chapter 13, Hong-Biao Yin, John Chi-Kin Lee, and Edmond Hau-Fai Law analyze teacher development through the lens of emotional geographies, suggesting that teacher trainers in the context of curriculum reform should be seen as learners as well as trainers. In Chapter 14, Tanja Sargent investigates the relationship between the reform implementation and the beliefs about teaching and learning held by teachers in rural China, and underlines the change of teacher belief as the prerequisite to their action in reform. In Chapter 15, Mingren Zhao summarizes the types of teaching reflection and presents the impact of different types of teaching reflection on teacher learning in the context of curriculum reform. In Chapter 16, Shujie Liu and Lingqi Meng explore the qualities of good Chinese teachers, and provide a framework for future comparative study of China and the USA regarding the qualities of good teachers.

This volume aims not only at identifying changes and challenges in China's NCR but also at facilitating advanced research on curriculum reform and implementation in China. In addition, it is hoped that having examined the current practices of curriculum reform and implementation, researchers and educators will be able to reconstruct change theories and models that are rooted in Chinese cultural traditions and education values. Consequently, the spirit of China's NCR will be brought to life, and the quality of everyone's education system may be enhanced.

REFERENCES

Angus, L. (2004). Globalization and educational change: Bringing about the reshaping and re-norming of practice. *Journal of Educational Policy, 19*(1), 23-41.

Astiz, M. F., Wiseman, A. W., and Baker, D. P. (2002). Slouching towards decentralization: Consequences of globalization for curricular control in national education systems. *Comparative Education Review, 46*(1), 66-88.

Atweh, B., and Clarkson, P. (2002). Globalized curriculum or global approach to curriculum reform in mathematics education. *Asia Pacific Education Review, 3*(2), 160-167.

Baskan, G. A., and Erduran, Y. (2009). Reforming education in developing economies of the world: Major issues of educational reform in China and Russian Federation. *Procedia Social and Behavioral Sciences*, *1*(1), 347-357.

Carnoy, M., and Rhoten, D. (2002). What does globalization mean for educational change? A comparative approach. *Comparative Education Review*, *46*(1), 1-9.

Dale, R., and Robertson, S. L. (2002). The varying effects of regional organizations as subjects of globalization of education. *Comparative Education Review*, *46*(1), 10-36.

Dimmock, C., and Walker, A. (2000). Globalisation and societal culture: Redefining schooling and school leadership in the twenty-first century. *Compare*, *30*(3), 303-312.

Feng, D. (2006). China's recent curriculum reform: Progress and problems. *Planning and Changing*, *31*(1/2), 131-144.

Fullan, M. (2000). The return of large-scale reform. *Journal of Educational Change*, *1*(1), 5-28.

Fullan, M. (2009). Large-scale reform comes of age. *Journal of Educational Change*, *10*(2-3), 101-113.

Green, A. (1999). Education and globalization in Europe and East Asia: Convergent and divergent trends. *Journal of Educational Policy*, *14*(1), 55-71.

Guan, Q., and Meng, W. (2007). China's new national curriculum reform: Innovation, challenges and strategies. *Frontiers of Education in China*, *2*(4), 579-604.

Halpin, D. (2010). National curriculum reform in China and England: Origins, character and comparison. *Frontiers of Education in China*, *5*(2), 258-269.

Harvey, D. (1989). *The condition of postmodernity*. Oxford: Blackwell.

Kennedy, K. J., and Lee, J. C. K. (2008). *The changing role of schools in Asian societies: Schools for the knowledge society*. New York/London: Routledge.

Lee, J. C. K., Loc, N., So, K., Subramanism, R., Yen, P., and Yin, H. B. (2011). Curriculum and assessment. In Y. Zhao, J. Lei, G. Li, M. F. He, K. Okano, G. David, R., Hema, and M. Nagwa (Eds.), *Handbook of Asian education: A cultural perspective* (pp. 29-50). New York: Routledge.

Liu, P., and Qi, C. (2005). Reform in the curriculum of basic education in the People's Republic of China: Pedagogy, application, and learners. *International Journal of Educational Reform*, *14*(1), 35-44.

Liu, Y., and Fang, Y. (2009). Basic education reform in China: Globalization with Chinese characteristics. *Asia Pacific Journal of Education*, *29*(4), 407-412.

Ministry of Education (1998). *Action plan toward the revitalization of education in the twenty-first century* (*mianxiang ershiyi shiji jiaoyu zhenxing xingdong jihua*). Beijing: Ministry of Education. (in Chinese).

Monkman, K., and Baird, M. (2002). Educational change in the context of globalization. *Comparative Education Review*, *46*(4), 497-508.

Mundy, K. (2005). Globalization and educational change: New policy worlds. In N. Bascia, A. Cumming, A. Datnow, K. Leithwood and D. Livingstone (Eds.), *International handbook of educational policy* (pp. 3-17). Dordrecht: Springer.

Naidoo, L., Singh, M. and Sanagavarapu, P. (2007). Globalisation, westernisation and Sino-Australian educational reform. *Transnational Curriculum Inquiry*, *4*(1). Retrieved 25 March 25 2009 from http://nitinat.library.ubc.ca/ojs/index.php/tci.

Preus, B. (2007). Educational trends in China and the United States: Proverbial pendulum or potential for balance. *Phi Delta Kappan*, *89*(2), 115-118.

The State Council (1999). *Decisions of the party central committee and the state council on deepening reform in education and developing quality-oriented education in an all-round way* (*zhonggong zhongyang guowuyuan guanyu shenhua jyu gaige quanmian tuijin suzhi jyu de jueding*). Beijing: Ministry of Education. (in Chinese).

Vongalis-Macrow, A., (2009). The simplicity of educational reforms: Defining globalization and reframing educational policies during the 1990s. *International Journal of Educational Policies*, 3(2), 62-80.

Waks, L. J. (2003). How globalization can cause fundamental curriculum change: An American perspective. *Journal of Educational Change*, 4(4), 383-418.

Wells, A. S., Carnochan, S., Slayton, J., Allen, R. L., and Vasudeva, A. (1998). Globalization and educational change. In A. Hargreaves, A., Lieberman, M. Fullan and D. Hopkins (Eds.), *International handbook of educational change* (pp. 322-348). Dordrecht: Kluwer Academic Publishers.

Yin, H., and Lee, J. C. K. (2008a), *Curriculum change: Theory and practice*. Taipei: Higher Education Publishing. (in Chinese).

Yin, H. B., and Lee, J. C. K. (2008b). Analyzing the tensions in curriculum reform: Roots, types, and coping strategies. *Exploring Education Development*, (24), 49-54. (in Chinese).

Zhao, Y., and Qiu, W. (2010). China as a case study of systemic educational reform. In A. Hargreaves, A., Lieberman, M. Fullan and D. Hopkins (Eds.), *Second international handbook of educational change* (pp. 349-361). Dordrecht: Springer Science + Business Media B.V.

Zhong, Q. (2006). Curriculum reform in China: Challenges and reflections. *Frontiers of Education in China*, 1(3), 370-382.

Zhu, M. (2007). Recent Chinese experiences in curriculum reform. *Prospects*, 37(2), 223-235.

PART II. THE CONTEXT OF THE REFORM

In: Curriculum Reform in China
Editors: Hong-Biao Yin and John Chi-Kin Lee

ISBN 978-1-61470-943-5
© 2012 Nova Science Publishers, Inc.

Chapter 2

CHANGING CONCEPTS AND PRACTICES OF CURRICULUM IN CHINA[4]

Janette Ryan

ABSTRACT

The scale and depth of China's current curriculum reform program, China's eight since 1949, mean that it is the most radical and far-reaching. It envisages sustained and enduring reform of all aspects of school curriculum policy, management, administration and resources, teaching and learning and assessment practices. The reform has drawn from China's own educational traditions as well as from the experiences of education systems worldwide. It has thus resulted in 'hybrid' forms of curriculum practice, where outside experience has been drawn upon, but has been implemented and organised in 'Chinese' ways and on a vast scale. The reform has been the subject of much discussion and even conflict and resistance, as well as much enthusiasm and dedication, but has undoubtedly resulted in significant change. This change has been patchy, but the magnitude and speed of the reform and associated changes have been achieved at a much faster pace and on a larger scale than has previously been achieved in other contexts. The changes to teachers' pedagogical and conceptual understandings and practices in many areas in little over a decade in China have taken over 30 years to achieve in other educational systems. This chapter documents these changes and the various structures and processes that have been put in place to achieve them and provides examples of some of the ways that teachers working in teacher professional learning communities have implemented these changes. It points to the importance of teacher research and professional development and a collaborative support network for teachers for achieving innovative and sustainable change to teachers' research and teaching practices and consequently students' learning in China.

---

[4] The university members of the LDC project referred to in this chapter are Dr Changyun Kang, Beijing Normal University, Professor Gaalen Erickson, University of British Columbia, and Drs Ian Mitchell and Janette Ryan, Monash University.

INTRODUCTION

A decade ago China launched its eighth curriculum reform since the founding of the People's Republic of China. Following the 'opening up' and reform era over the last thirty years, there has been considerable reform to China's social and economic fabric, but much less attention to the educational arena where reform of the basic education curriculum has been much slower. Nevertheless, the scope and pace of change since the announcement of the curriculum reform program in 1999 has been just as ambitious and extensive.

The current curriculum reform covers every aspect of basic education (Kindergarten to Year 12). The reform program is wide-ranging and encompasses curriculum aims, structure, content, delivery, assessment and administration. It has entailed a move from the 'two basics' (knowledge and skills) to 'quality education' and the promotion of new and innovative teaching and learning concepts and approaches. This involves a move away from behaviourist to social constructivist theories of education, from teacher-directed to student-centred learning, and towards the development of autonomous and collaborative learners (Paine and Fang, 2006; Ryan, Kang, Mitchell and Erickson, 2009; Zhong, 2006; Zhu, 2005; Zhu and Kang, 2002). The reform has had implications for related areas such as teacher education and teachers' professional development. The depth and breadth of the reform mean that substantial changes are required to teachers' pedagogy and this has highlighted the need for professional development support for both new and experienced teachers (Guan and Meng, 2007; Paine and Fang, 2006; Robinson and Yi, 2007; Ryan, Kang, Mitchell and Erickson, 2009). To support this reform, the Ministry of Education (MOE) established 18 Research Centres for Basic Education Curriculum Reform at several universities and institutes across China to act as a bridge between academic research and teaching practice to develop in-service teacher professional development. Some of these teacher professional development activities are documented and discussed in this chapter, which relate to an international crosscultural research project between teacher leaders and practitioners in several provinces across China and academic researchers in China, Australia and Canada, and describe how they are working to implement the aims of the new curriculum reform.

Given the wide-ranging nature of the proposed reform and the fundamental changes required as a result, those most closely involved with the reform policy recognised early the need for careful research and consultation. This has occurred through a series of stages designed as cycles of research, consultation, review and consolidation for first the primary sector and then secondary education. These stages progressively considered issues of ideology and planning; design, experimentation and implementation; and reflection, evaluation and then re-design and implementation. A description of the aims and processes involved in each of these stages is first given to provide the context for the later discussion of the various challenges involved in the reform as well as examples of the strategies being pursued by teachers, school leaders and university researchers.

BACKGROUND

The curriculum reform program began in 1996 and has involved five distinct stages (see Liu and Kang , 2011, for further details of each of these stages):

Stage 1: Curriculum ideology and planning (1996-1998)

In the initial stage of the reform program, the MOE organised a survey of compulsory education curriculum (covering the first nine years of schooling) by experts from six key 'normal' (i.e., specialist Education) universities in 1996. It examined curriculum goals, teaching content, approaches to teaching and learning, and examination and assessment issues. The survey uncovered outmoded educational concepts and curriculum content and a lack of connection with contemporary theories of child development and learning (Liu and Kang , 2011; Zhu, 2005; Zhu and Kang, 2002). School curricula lacked relevance for students, inhibited engagement and creativity and were over-burdensome in workload and examination and selection pressures. A program of research was subsequently carried out into curriculum change in other countries including the UK, US, Canada, Germany, Japan, Australia, Korea, Russia, Sweden, India, Brazil and Egypt as well as Hong Kong and Taiwan. Extensive consultations were carried out across China on the values and vision needed to underpin the reform and this in turn prompted various research initiatives culminating in a blueprint outlining the values, aims and timetable of the proposed reform (see below).

Stage 2: Design, dissemination and experimental stage of the curriculum documents (1999-2001)

In 1999, the MOE published the *Confronting the Twenty-first Century Education Rejuvenation Action Plan* which provided the initial framework for the reform program. A team comprising over forty experts from universities, local administration bureaus, and principal and teacher representatives held a series of seminars and consultations on the reform proposals as well as on rural curriculum reform, curriculum support policies and subject curriculum standards. Following the subsequent publication of the *Basic Education Curriculum Reform Program Application, Adjudication and Administration Details* and *Curriculum Reform Basic Education Project Outlines*, forty research projects by universities, research institutes and provincial administration bureaus were commissioned which covered the national standards, local curriculum administration and development, school curriculum administration, processes for assessment, curriculum and textbook assessment, and teacher research and training. Feedback from local teachers was sought through MOE-commissioned local education bureaus within Guangdong, Guangxi, Fujian, Jiangsu, Liaoning, Hebei and Hubei Provinces and regionally through Southwest Normal University, Northwest Normal University and Fujian Normal University. The new curriculum was officially launched with the release of the *Guidelines on Basic Education Curriculum Reform* (*jichu jiaoyu kecheng gaige gangyao*) published by the MOE in 2001.These guidelines underpinned the next stages of curriculum design, experimentation and implementation. Their aim was to outline minimum standards and articulate the transformation of curriculum to ensure a focus on the individual student and their intellectual development, creativity, analysis and problem-solving abilities, and skills of communication and collaboration.

The major aims of the reform were identified in the Guidelines:

- Changing the teaching and learning focus from the 'two basics' (basic knowledge and basic skills) to broader overall aims including active learning, and developing appropriate attitudes and values;
- Developing a new balanced and comprehensive curriculum structure that has a better balance of teaching hours for different subjects and that caters for the needs of the students with diverse background in diverse regions;

- Changing from an overemphasis on knowledge from textbooks to a greater focus on linking the students' learning with real life and the development of modern society, science and technology;
- Changing the traditional pedagogy, advocating students' more active and engaging learning, and nurturing their ability in the areas of sharing, cooperation and communication;
- Establishing an assessment system that promotes students' all-round development as well as teacher's professional development;
- Implementing a three-level curriculum administration system that involves coordination and communication structures between and among national, local and school levels.

In early 2001, 38 experimental districts were identified and professional development was provided for all administrators, teacher researchers, principals and teachers involved in the pilot work (Zhu, 2005; Zhu and Kang, 2002).

This stage of the reform program was an important one for its later success. It involved a recognition by those involved that a major challenge in such a wide-ranging reform would be how to maintain fidelity (Fullan, 1991) between the stated 'ideal' curriculum and the actual, 'enacted' curriculum in the classroom (Marsh and Willis, 1999) and to avoid passive outward compliance. Those involved recognised the importance of a shared vision of curriculum reform (Smith and Lovat, 2003), the need for 'mutual adaptation and accommodation', the challenges involved in creating motivation, initiative and creativity at the level of teachers and schools, and the need for teacher professional development and the redesign of teacher training. Seminars were organised where participants were encouraged to consider and share local knowledge, issues and contexts as well as China's cultural and intellectual traditions in designing strategies to implement the new curriculum.

Stage 3: Compulsory education curriculum pilot and finalisation of the senior high school curriculum program (2001-2004)

The new curriculum standards for compulsory education (Grades 1 to 9) were issued in 2001 and introduced in a pilot school district in each provincial city in the 38 experimental districts. By 2003, 1,072 more counties across the country had introduced the new curriculum. By 2005, every initial grade of primary and middle school was required to begin using the new curriculum. The new senior high school curriculum standards were introduced in 2003 for Grades 10 to 12 and in 2004 the new senior high school curriculum was piloted in four provinces across the country. The senior high school reforms were designed to give students more choice of subjects and electives, encourage school-based curriculum development and move away from subject-based teaching to the teaching of more generic academic skills such as inquiry, problem-based, cooperative and collaborative learning.

An important feature of this phase of the reform program was the introduction of a system of teacher professional development that combined teacher research with school-based inquiry. This was supported by expert teams from over 17 universities that visited each of the pilot districts and worked with teachers to interpret the new curriculum and update their educational theories and philosophies (although this work was not always successful, see later discussion). The expert teams helped to establish teacher research mechanisms based on school and classroom practice and integrated with curriculum reform and teacher development, often through school-based or networks of professional learning communities (see below). It was recognised that the practice of individual reflection, peer communication and support, professional learning and innovation is a valuable tool for teachers trying to improve their professional development and address their own teaching and learning concerns in their own contexts. It had become clear that simply relying on training initial pre-service teachers would never solve the overall needs for teachers' professional development.

Stage 4: Finalisation of compulsory education curriculum, nation-wide implementation and the new senior high school curriculum pilot (2004-2007)

The new compulsory education curriculum was put into effect nation-wide in 2004 and had been fully implemented for the first cohort of middle school graduates. By 2005 the entering grades in primary and middle schools were all required to study the new curriculum and the new high school entrance examination was introduced in 17 pilot districts. This raised questions about how the high school entrance examinations could better reflect the new subject standards and demonstrate students' learning and development under the new curriculum. The first senior high school graduates under the new curriculum took the university entrance examination in 2007.

Surveys during this period showed that, despite much debate and some criticisms in several areas (in particular in Mathematics, see Liu and Kang, 2011) the new curriculum had been generally positively received and had resulted in improved student motivation and engagement and teacher enthusiasm (Guan and Meng, 2007; Liu and Kang, 2011; Zhong, 2006). This phase saw the introduction in high schools of wider subject choices and curriculum models, alternative methods of assessment such as learning portfolios (see Guo, 2007), and more-locally relevant education resources and teaching and learning practices. This phase also saw the introduction of a more systematic approach to professional support for teachers nation-wide through research seminars and online resources for teachers. Many school-based professional learning communities (see later) provided local and peer support for teacher change and development as well as a move towards school-based curriculum development (Zhong, 2006).

Stage 5: Reflection, reinterpretation and further implementation (August 2007 to the present)

The new senior high school curriculum was implemented in 2007 and 2008 in ten provinces and in Beijing, and province-wide in Shandong. It has since been extended to 25 provinces with the aim of full implementation by 2010. One of the most contentious areas under the new curriculum program has been its alignment with university entrance examinations and the assessment of learning under the new curriculum (Guan and Meng, 2007). Substantial progress is being made in this regard however. Pilot work is continuing on the alignment of the university entrance in Shandong, Guangdong, Hainan and Ningxia Provinces. Under new guidelines issued by the MOE in 2008, local education authorities have been asked to expedite the reform of the high school curriculum to align university entrance examinations, school tests and quality assurance of school-based testing.

Evaluations of the new curriculum program were conducted in 2001, 2003 and 2005 and these identified a number of significant issues and continuing challenges. These include differences in needs and resources between city and rural areas; a shortage of curriculum and financial resources; and teaching practices still focused on textbooks and reliance on rote recall. The lack of professional development support for teachers; continuing overcrowding in classrooms; and increased teaching workloads pointed to continuing pressures on teachers. These issues are discussed in further detail in the section below.

In May 2010, the Government released the second draft of its 10 year blueprint for education for public discussion (Ministry of Education, 2010). On its release, Premier Wen Jiabao stated that education was a national priority and called for an improvement in its quality, an increase in investment in education, a reduction in the differences between cities and rural areas and, interestingly, a reduction in the 'burden' of schooling for children (Standing Committee of the State Council, 2010). Both Premier Wen and President Hu have both in very recent times stated that the improvement of education in China is a pressing national priority and have signaled the Government's intention to further deepen the reforms.

DISCUSSION

Despite initial resistance and contestation, overall there has been general acceptance of the aims of the new curriculum (Guan and Meng, 2007; Liu and Kang, 2011; Zhong, 2009). Bringing about teacher change has been one of the most difficult areas in the successful implementation of the aims of the reform program. The survey findings referred to above in particular point to the importance of providing more resources for teachers' professional development but there have been substantial improvements in this area. According to Liu and Kang (2011), two of the key national organisers of the curriculum reform program:

> In districts and schools where the new curriculum has been solidly implemented, it is clear that, compared with school life of five or ten years ago, the new curriculum has provided real change in schools, classrooms and amongst teachers and students. Relationships between teachers and students are more harmonious, the classroom atmosphere is more democratic, students are treated with more respect, and the curriculum content has moved closer to students' own experiences. Knowledge acquisition is no longer the only goal of learning. The initiative and enthusiasm of schools and teachers have been further motivated by the unprecedented improvement in teachers' professional development (p. 38).

Zhong (2006) believes that the changes brought about by the curriculum reform program are irreversible as the restrictions felt by teachers through the exam-oriented curricula have produced a strong desire for change amongst teachers as they have felt alienated and constrained by this system. Guan and Meng (2007) similarly argue that the depth of the changes has become apparent and comment that even the use of grades and scores is becoming less common:

> Never before have so much interest and enthusiasm of students been seen. Students' creativity and broad knowledge, especially active motivation have been enhanced. The student-centered instruction conveys many advantages of cooperative learning, research-based learning, engagement and involvement. Classroom instruction is no longer boring. And students' comprehensive quality has been improved. (p. 597)

There is still much work to be done in terms of teachers' practices. In reviewing achievements to date against the original goals of the program, Liu and Kang (2011) remark that 'it is hard not to feel despondent'. Old attitudes and values linger, drill work is still common, examination marks continue to be dominant, and the numbers of teachers effectively implementing the new approaches is still relatively low. Nevertheless, there are significant pockets of real and substantial change, as documented later in this section. Liu and Kang point to the significance of the very existence of the debate around educational values and practices, and they remain optimistic about the potential for real change:

> In recent years, the debates around curriculum reform, in particular the different and even opposing voices among the reform processes that are being enforced by the government, are in fact the hallmarks of social progress and intellectual prosperity... more importantly, our government, academics and the media need to learn how to jointly build an academic and education culture that is democratic, open, scientific, equal, dialogic and consultative. This is not only the main pursuit of this round of curriculum reform; it will also have profound historic implications for the nation's rejuvenation, economic progress and academic prosperity as well as for the healthy growth of individuals within it. (Kang and Liu, 2011, p. 39)

Continuing discussion and debates prompted by the new curriculum have foregrounded fundamental issues in education. This includes issues such as the purposes of education; its contribution to national prosperity and individuals' personal development; the balance between intellectual heritage and innovation, and national and international perspectives and localised concerns; public versus private education; the needs of developed urban societies and less developed rural communities; transmission-based versus inquiry-based learning; and the role of teachers and their relationships with students. In recent years, the Chinese Government has re-stated its support for the curriculum reform program. The Chinese Communist Party's 17th Congress report in 2007 called for 'updating education concepts, deepening reforms in the areas of teaching content and approaches, examinations and recruitment mechanisms and the quality assessment system'. At a conference on national education in Beijing in July 2010, President Hu Jintao called for the deepening of the curriculum reform program and for education to become a national priority (Global Times, 26 July 2010) following the release in May of the second draft of the 10 year blueprint for education.

As outlined above, however, the curriculum reform program faces continuing issues and difficulties which are discussed below. These include resistance to curriculum and pedagogical change and 'foreign imports'; lack of professional development support for teachers; a shortage of curriculum and financial resources; differences in needs and resources between the city and rural areas; continuing overcrowding in classrooms; and increased teaching workloads.

Resistance to Change

The scope and depth of change required under the new curriculum were perhaps initially underestimated by those involved and they didn't anticipate the level of resistance that the reforms would encounter (Guan and Meng, 2007; Ryan, Kang, Mitchell and Erickson, 2009; Paine and Fang, 2006; Zhong, 2006). The scale of the proposed changes has posed major challenges for all levels of participants, most notably school administrators and teachers, especially in terms of unfamiliar concepts of teaching and learning and the practical difficulties that arise for teachers in putting these new ideas and concepts into practice. The various challenges entailed in the reform program are outlined by Li Yuping, a key organiser of the LDC project described later in this chapter and a former school principal and district education consultant:

> When the curriculum reform was implemented, it was met with all kinds of resistance and created conflicts that we could never have imagined. For example, teachers were confronted with specific teaching and learning problems emerging in their classroom that they didn't know how to deal with. A new inquiry system to support the teachers to implement the new curriculum was needed. (Li, in Liu, Li and Kang, 2009)

Zhong (2006) argues that it was not the curriculum reform itself that led to the conflicts and tensions but rather 'lay in the old systems and mechanisms and were precipitated by the reform' (p. 371). Deeply rooted values and beliefs still play a role in influencing teachers' beliefs about knowledge and learning and these in turn influence ideas about the role of the teacher and concepts of the 'ideal' student. Even teachers willing to change struggle with these deeply held beliefs often rooted in Confucianism and Confucian education ideals. As Liu Keqin, a key leader in the curriculum reform program and a member of the National 1-6 Mathematics Curriculum Standards Development Group (also Principal of Beijing Zhongguancun Number 4 School, one of the most active in implementing the new curriculum) states:

> Chinese teachers have been heavily influenced by Confucianism and these cultural influences on them are very strong. It's called 'Honouring the teacher'; getting children to listen to the teacher, and thinking that children who listen to the teacher are good students... But now, we want to learn more about how to respect other people, and that means helping children to become more mature and more independent of teachers, how to become more self-confident. So the first thing that teachers need to do is to treat children as equals, in the way that they talk with them and the ways that they work with them; they need to listen carefully to what children are saying to them. (Interview with Principal Liu, Beijing, March 2007).

Teacher Professional Development

The pivotal role of teachers in the effective implementation of the new curriculum and the need for deep conceptual change amongst teachers was recognised early (Zhu, 2002) but in the beginning the curriculum reform program was dominated by a government-orientated and 'top-down' approach. Such an ambitious reform could never be easy to achieve and events have revealed some problems with the initial, top down strategies for implementation, especially in terms of promoting the necessary professional development for teachers to implement new concepts of teaching and learning. The MOE did advocate school-based teaching research in an attempt to address the shortcomings of a purely top-down implementation model. In practice, however, the executive model emerged as the initial primary vehicle for change. As has been the case in other systems seeking curriculum and teacher change (Erickson, Mitchell, Kang and Ryan, 2008), it became clear that teachers play a crucial role in the implementation of curriculum reform and the importance of teacher research and professional development and peer support to underpin and drive this was recognised. The need for improved teacher education and teacher development to support the reform process was officially recognised in China's 11th 5 Year Plan (2006-2010).

There have been numerous attempts over the past five to ten years to improve teacher professional development (see, for example, Paine, Fang and Wilson, 2003 and Paine and Fang, 2006) and to experiment with new curriculum development approaches such as school-based curriculum reform (Xu, 2008). While teachers are generally supportive of the goals of the reform, they can find it difficult to implement (Ma and Kang, 2007; Ma, Yin, Tang and Liu, 2009; Zhong, 2006). Ma and Kang (2007) argue that long-term, multi-leveled teacher training is required for such an immense curriculum reform while Yu and Kang (2003) advocate models based on classroom problems and classroom-based teacher inquiry. Several such approaches exist through professional learning communities (PLCs) of teachers (Hannum and Park, 2007; Paine and Fang, 2007; Ryan, Kang, Mitchell and Erickson, 2009; Sargent and Hannum, 2008) and examples of approaches to teacher research-based models of curriculum change are discussed below. School-based teacher professional development has long been a feature of teacher work in China, often carried out thorough professional learning communities (*jiaoyanzu*). These activities generally involve the observation of other teachers' classes and subsequent debrief and observation of model lessons (similar to the 'lesson study' method also found in Japan). Teachers in China regularly open their classroom for observation and critique by other teachers, a feature that is rare in Western systems.

As has been shown elsewhere, 'top down' curriculum reform (through the development of system-wide policies and procedures) often has only limited effect (Fullan, 2001). It can be resisted by teachers unless they are able to see the value of changing their teaching practices, receive personal and practical support in how to develop and implement new approaches, and receive support and recognition for their efforts. As mentioned above, one of the ways developed to counter the 'top down' nature of the reform was through the development of professional learning communities. PLCs have been shown to be an effective method of promoting deep and sustained teacher development (Borko, 2004; Fullan, 2001; York-Barr and Duke, 2004). PLCs build on the existing models of school-based teacher professional development but instead focus on teacher research as a vehicle for teacher autonomy in deciding which aspects of their practice they wish to improve. According to Li (2009, p. 31), an organiser of the LDC project described below. "We realize that this kind of traditional 'top down' copying model does not work in practice. Instead, we now emphasize effective teacher inquiry as a means of developing effective teaching strategies".

Lack of Resources

The lack of financial and curriculum resources continues to be a problem in many areas. In schools in well-resourced areas such as Beijing, the standards of facilities are excellent and class sizes are generally small, but in other areas especially rural areas in provinces such as Inner Mongolia (Liu, Li and Kang, 2009) and Gansu (Sargent and Hannum, 2008) class sizes are still often very large. Sargent and Hannum's (2008) study of PLCs in schools in rural Gansu Province found that PLCs operate even within remote areas but that they are constrained by a lack of finances, support systems and leadership. Observations of many lessons in overcrowded classrooms show however that innovative and engaging teaching and learning can occur when teachers are actively working to improve their practice (Liu, Li and Kang, 2009; Ryan, Kang, Mitchell and Erickson, 2009).

The insufficiency of new curriculum resources has been identified as one of the most important barriers to the implementation of the curriculum reform (Ma, Yin, Tang and Liu, 2009; Zhu, 2005). The universities involved in curriculum reform nationally, especially Beijing Normal University (see Kang, Erickson, Ryan and Mitchell, 2009; and Erickson, Kang, Mitchell, Ryan, Liu and Li, 2007) and East China Normal University in Shanghai (see, for example, Zheng, 2009), have been working to address this need and have already developed a number of new, innovative and creative curriculum resources for early childhood, primary and secondary levels which are aligned with concepts such as inquiry learning, experiential learning, problem solving and collaborative learning.

Uneven Progress between City and Rural Areas

Progress on implementing the new curriculum and the provision of education resources generally remains uneven, with poor and inadequate conditions existing in rural areas (Hu, 2003; Postiglione, 2006; Shi, 2006; Wong, 2009a, 2009b).

As control of educational administration and funding has moved away from the central government, there are vast differences in expenditure on education within provinces (Hannum and Park, 2007; Wong, 2009a) and even among districts, with significant discrepancies between developed coastal areas and cities such as Beijing, Shanghai and Guangzhou and the poor and remote areas in the Northwest and Southwest and in some central provinces (Wong, 2009a).

Implementation of the curriculum reforms in the rural areas has been problematic. This is due to several issues including the difficulty in training and retaining teachers to work in areas where conditions are harsh especially in isolated or nomadic areas such as rural Gansu (Robinson, 2008) or Tibet (Postiglione, 2006).

Several recent government initiatives aim to improve the qualifications of teachers and the professionalisation of teaching in poorer and more remote areas (Robinson and Yi, 2007; Postiglione, 2006). The central government has allocated more resources to remote areas in the western and central regions of China through extra resources and subsidies (Tan, 2009; Wong, 2009a, 2009b; World Bank, 2008). Government funding to education more generally has greatly increased over the past three to four years and most of this expenditure has been on improving the qualifications, status and pay of teachers (Robinson and Yi, 2007; Wong 2009a, 2009b).

Despite the lack of financial and other resources, there has been some excellent work by teachers in remote areas such as rural Gansu (Sargent and Hannum, 2008) and in through the LDC project in Inner Mongolia and more recently in Xinjiang. These initiatives demonstrate that despite various difficulties those involved are committed to the aims of the new curriculum, are enthusiastic about changing their practices and are proud of their achievements (Guo, 2007; Li, 2009: Li and Gao, 2007; Sargent and Hannum, 2008; Wang, 2006; Wang and Wang, 2007).

Changing Concepts and Teaching Practices: The Learning and Development Community Project

The lack of research on teachers has been identified as one of the 'bottlenecks' that has inhibited the effective implementation of the curriculum reform (Zhong, 2006). Zhong (2006) argues that although the concepts of 'teachers as researchers', action research and research into practice is common elsewhere such approaches are rare in China. In Canada and Australia, the use of professional learning communities and the effectiveness of teacher research for enduring change has been recognised (Borko, 2004; Erickson, Mitchell, Minnes, Brandes and Mitchell, 2005; Fullan, 2001; York-Barr and Duke, 2004). As part of the international research conducted in Stage 1 of the curriculum reform program which identified such models as potentially useful in implementing the kinds of teacher change envisaged in China, a professional learning community called the *Learning and Development Community* (LDC) was established by organisers of the curriculum reform program Kang Changyun and Liu Keqin. The project began in 2005 at one school in Beijing and has since spread to several provinces including Guangdong, Shandong, Inner Mongolia and Xinjiang, with the ultimate aim of establishing 'base' schools which will network with other schools across their regions.

The LDC project has moved away from the conventional teacher professional development model in China of 'master' lessons, lesson observation and critique (Paine and Fang, 2006) to an inquiry-based model. Rather than learning from 'experts' or 'model' practice, the project supports teachers in their own research and development:

> A teacher cannot just accept and adopt another teacher's teaching strategies into their own practice without a reflective and inquiry process. We realise that this kind of traditional 'top-down' copying model will not work in practice. Instead we begin to emphasise a proper way of effective teacher inquiry with a focus on effective teaching strategy development. (Li, 2009, p. 31)

The LDC project is supported by district personnel and a team of researchers and academics from China, Canada and Australia. University academics from all three countries work with school and district leaders but the LDC project and its activities are driven by the teachers themselves. The project involves networks of teachers working collaboratively through inquiry learning. In this model, those supporting the teachers do not see themselves as 'experts' but rather as critical friends:

> None of the members of the research team see themselves as 'experts', but rather see our role as simply to put forward suggestions about trying different approaches, because ultimately the strength of the education reforms has to come from the teachers themselves. (Liu, 2009, p. 20)

The LDC project is a 'bottom up' initiative where teachers carry out their own research to improve their teaching and curriculum practices. It works through a cycle of action amongst participants, working with colleagues and university academics as 'critical friends', and then reflection on action and further action. Its success to date has been built on mutual respect for individuals and local contexts and open dialogue amongst participants. LDC members share their insights and findings; observe and provide feedback to colleagues; open their classrooms to outside observers (including parents); and discuss issues such as lesson review and evaluation at staff meetings. Teachers share their challenges, ideas and successes amongst 'nested circles' of teacher/school/district/academic communities. These 'nested circles' exist at the local school level, between schools at the district level, and then across districts and provinces at the national level. The international research team connects these at the international level by sharing and discussing ideas about effective curriculum and pedagogical practices in other contexts.

Regular contact is maintained between all of the levels of the LDC project. The international team members have made regular visits between China, Canada and Australia and interacted with teachers, schools, district administrators and academics across China, sharing relevant experiences from Western cultures, and jointly analysing data from observations of teaching and participation in the LDC activities. Teams of teachers have also made exchange visits between countries. As the networks grow members are increasingly using electronic forms of communication such as Internet forums and teacher blogs. Regular national conferences are held and members have published their findings in both Chinese and English language publications and have presented their work at national and international conferences in China, the US and the UK. These presentations have been on a diverse range of new pedagogical approaches such as professional portfolio development (Liu, Li and Kang, 2009); collective lesson preparation and debriefing (Li and Gao, 2007); small group work and peer assessment (Wang and Wang, 2007); student portfolios (Guo, 2007); and the creation of online communities of teachers (Li and Li, 2007). Many of the teachers have written their own accounts of their research and their experimentation with new teaching and learning concepts. These include improving group work through peer leadership (Hua, 2009), sharing intellectual control of the class with students (Hua and Mitchell, 2009), encouraging students to challenge the teacher's knowledge (Hua, 2009a), conducting pre- and post-testing of students' learning concepts (Li, Wang and Li, 2009), using students' drawings and ideas to drive a lesson (Liu, 2009), peer assessment and joint work in student workbooks (Wang, 2009) and including parents in lessons and inviting them to observe lessons and give feedback (Hua, 2009b). Although many of these lessons do involve 'Western' concepts such as collaborative learning and small group work, they also include innovative elements that are not found in Western systems such as inviting critique from parents and the use of formal, quantitative research methods to evaluate the results of a lesson. The strategies and projects developed by the teachers empower them to adapt their teaching to the new curriculum reform in their own contexts and in response to their own concerns. From observation of many of these lessons, it is clear that they would be considered innovative and engaging in any system.

'Borrowing' from the West or Reciprocal Learning?

In the first stage of the curriculum reform program there was a concerted effort to learn from the experiences of other countries and these efforts have led to the adoption and adaptation of many foreign or 'Western' concepts of education and 'hybrid' approaches to teaching and learning practices. This has not been without contestation. The need for caution in applying 'Western' teaching and learning ideas, without consideration of local contexts and existing knowledge and expertise, has rightly been voiced by many Chinese educationalists (Guan and Meng, 2007; Hu, 2002; Jiang, 2005) especially when conditions such as overcrowded classrooms make the implementation of more student-centred approaches a challenge. As demonstrated by the teachers in the LDC project described above, these do not necessarily create a barrier to innovative and creative approaches but local contexts and conditions do need to be respected and taken into consideration by those most closely involved. Guan and Meng (2007) believe that many of the tensions that have arisen from the reforms is due to the uncritical introduction of Western (they refer to 'American') practices. Beijing Normal University academic Professor Gu Mingyuan, a widely respected 'elder statesman' of Chinese education, argues however that such cross-cultural 'borrowings' are part of the dynamic of cultural transformation:

> Cultural traditions are dynamic and ever developing. To carry forward Chinese culture does not mean that we have to say no to foreign cultures. On the contrary, if China wants to have its own national culture developed, it has to constantly absorb foreign cultures. However, we have to make wise choices (Gu, 2001, p. 105) .

In the LDC project, there has been a concern to avoid the imposition of externally imposed, 'Western' ideas of curriculum reform implementation. The LDC model seeks to avoid imposing 'top down' (from outside the school) or culturally inappropriate models (from outside China) by sharing and applying some of the lessons learnt by teachers researching their own practice elsewhere. Rather than a simple 'borrowing' of ideas from West to East, there has been a cross-fertilisation of ideas between East and West. Experience over the course of the project since 2004 has shown that many of the challenges that teachers face in China are similar to those experienced by their counterparts in Canada and Australia and that many of the teachers' ideas about strategies 'cross the cultural divide'. These include practical difficulties such as effective group work, collaborative learning and stimulating students' engagement and creativity while maintaining an orderly and purposeful classroom (Ryan, Kang, Mitchell and Erickson, 2009).

CONCLUSION

The aims of the curriculum reform program though ambitious have been achieved in many areas and this progress augurs well for the work to come. The initial groundwork has begun to bear fruit and the collaborations between teachers and researchers in projects such as the LDC one show that there can be benefits far beyond those originally envisaged as teachers and schools continue to work enthusiastically and are re-energised. They share their concerns and difficulties as well as their ideas and strategies and are showing the way to others who wish to transform their practice and improve the learning of their students. One of the unexpected findings of the international dimension of the LDC project was that that there are common concerns shared by teachers across vastly different cultural and geographical contexts. Although many of the new teaching and learning concepts were initially unfamiliar to the LDC teachers, the experience of those involved in this project over several years has shown that many of the ideas and practices of teachers elsewhere resonated with the Chinese teachers. Sometimes these were similar to things that they had already been doing but were named or enacted differently.

An unexpected outcome of the LDC project has been the opportunity for two-way learning as teachers in other countries have benefitted from the experiences of the teacher researchers in China (see for example PEEL Seeds, 2010). Reciprocal visits of LDC teachers and researchers between China, Canada and Australia which have included demonstration lessons, workshops and shared debriefings in each context have resulted in much 'two-way' learning. The Canadian and Australian teachers and researchers have been impressed by the open and frank ways that the Chinese educationalists provide peer feedback on teaching as well as the enthusiasm and commitment shown by the Chinese teachers to radically reforming their practices (see for example, PEEL Seeds 2009 and 2010). Although teaching and learning is heavily socially and culturally situated, there are elements that resonate across cultures and demonstrate the mobility of ideas (Erickson, Mitchell, Kang and Ryan, 2008). Moreover, the diversity of schools and teachers involved in countries as geographically vast as China, Canada and Australia has shown that there are often more commonalities than differences between cultures and that there is often more diversity to be found *within* cultures than *between* them (Ryan and Louie, 2007). Rather than seeing ideas about teaching and learning as being confined to cultural or national boundaries, Kang Changyun (in Kang, Erickson, Ryan and Mitchell, 2009), believes that ideas about effective teaching and learning 'are the common treasures of humanity'.

Much is still to be done but the work of teachers in China cited here shows that teaching and learning concepts and practices are changing, often rapidly and radically, and this change is on a steady upward trajectory. The prospects for the future look very promising. Models such as the successful and growing LDC project demonstrate that effective and sustainable curriculum reform can be built through collaborative models that give consideration to local contexts and individual teacher agency. The LDC project has shown that this approach is most successful when it recognises the importance of local contexts and individuals; is underpinned by commitment from teachers, leadership from school principals, and support from district and regional governments and university academics; and when partnerships and relationships (local, national and international) are constructed through mutual respect and genuine dialogue. Such approaches not only lead to learning in local and national contexts but can lead to cross-cultural understanding and the generation of new types of knowledge internationally in a more interconnected and global world.

REFERENCES

Borko, H. (2004). Professional development and teacher learning: Mapping the terrain. *Educational Researcher, 33*(8), 3-15.

Erickson, G., Kang, C. Y., Mitchell, I., Ryan, J., Liu, K. Q., and Li, Y. P. (2007, November). *The role of teacher professional learning communities in China's curriculum reform.* Paper presented at the 3rd Innovation and International Forum on Teacher Education Conference, Shanghai, China. (in Chinese and English).

Erickson, G., Mitchell, I., Kang, C. Y., and Ryan, J. (2008). Role of teacher research and cross-cultural collaboration in the context of curriculum reform in China. In A. Samaras,

C. Beck, A. Freese, and C. Kosnik (Eds.), *Learning communities in practice* (pp. 179-191). Netherlands: Springer.

Erickson, G., Mitchell, I., Minnes, C., Brandes, G., and Mitchell, J. (2005). Collaborative teacher learning: Findings from two professional development projects. *Teaching and Teacher Education*, *21*(7), 787-798.

Fullan, M. (1991). *The new meaning of educational change*. New York: Teachers College Press.

Fullan, M. (2001). *Leading in a culture of change*. San Francisco: Jossey-Bass.

Global Times. (2010, July 26). *President Hu Jintao stresses education development*. Retrieved 26 July 2010 from http://china.globaltimes.cn/chinanews/2010-07/551899. html.

Gu, M. Y. (2001). *Education in China and abroad: Perspectives of a lifetime in comparative education*. Hong Kong: Comparative Education Centre, The University of Hong Kong.

Guan, Q., and Meng, W. J. (2007). China's new national curriculum: Innovation, challenges and Strategies. *Frontiers in Education in China*, *2*(4), 579-603.

Guo, X. Y. (2007, November). *Developing a portfolio project in a reading and writing classroom with my students* (*he haizimen yiqi jian dangandai*). Paper presented at the 3rd Innovation and International Forum on Teacher Education Conference, Shanghai, China. (in Chinese)

Hannum, E., and Park, A. (2007). *Education and reform in China*. Abingdon, Oxon: Routledge.

Hua, Y. H. (2009a). An unsuccessful class. *PEEL Seeds*, *106*, 13-15. Melbourne, PEEL (Project for the Enhancement of Effective Learning).

Hua, Y. H. (2009b). Setting up three dimensional classrooms. *PEEL Seeds, 106,* 18-19. Melbourne, PEEL (Project for the Enhancement of Effective Learning).

Hua, Y. H., and Mitchell, I. (2009). Exploring fingerprints in a Year 3 Science lesson: A conversation between a Chinese teacher and an Australian observer. *PEEL Seeds*, *106*, 15-18. Melbourne, PEEL (Project for the Enhancement of Effective Learning).

Hu, G. W. (2002). Potential cultural resistance to pedagogical imports: The case of communicative language teaching in China. *Language, Culture and Curriculum*, *15*(2), 93-105.

Hu, G. W. (2003). English language teaching in China: Regional differences and contributing factors. *Journal of Multicultural and Multilingual Development*, *24*(4), 290-318.

Jiang, K. (2005). The centre-periphery model and cross-national educational transfer: The influence of the US on teaching reform in China's universities. *Asia Pacific Journal of Education*, *25*(2), 227-239.

Kang, C. Y., Erickson, G., Ryan, J., and Mitchell, I. (Forthcoming). Constructing a cross-cultural teacher Professional Learning Community in the context of China's basic education curriculum. In J. Ryan (Ed.), *Education reform in China*. London: Routledge.

Kang, C. Y., Erickson, G., Ryan, J., and Mitchell, I. (2009, March). *China's educational reform programme: International research collaboration and cross cultural learning*. Paper presented at the China's Education Reform: Radical Shifts and their Implications Conference, University of Oxford, Oxford.

Li, X. Y., Wang, C. S., and Li, Y. P. (2009). Pre-view for thinking. *PEEL Seeds*, *106*, 34-38. Melbourne, PEEL (Project for the Enhancement of Effective Learning).

Li, Y. P. (2009). The learning and development community in China. *PEEL Seeds*, *106*, 30-33. Melbourne, PEEL (Project for the Enhancement of Effective Learning).

Li, Y. Y., and Gao, X. Z. (2007, November). *Collaborative reflection on our school-based inquiry journey*. Paper presented at the 3rd Innovation and International Forum on Teacher Education Conference, Shanghai, China. (in Chinese).

Li, D. H., and Li, Z. H. (2007, November). *Complicity and collective improvisation in school-based teacher inquiry (Jingxin cehua - youxiao yajiu)*. Paper presented at the 3rd Innovation and International Forum on Teacher Education Conference, Shanghai, China. (in Chinese).

Liu, J., and Kang, C. Y. (2011). Reflection in action: Ongoing K-12 curriculum reform in China. In J. Ryan (Ed.), *Education reform in China* (pp. 21-40). London: Routledge.

Liu, K. Q. (2006). *Engaged education*. Beijing: Beijing Normal University Press. (in Chinese).

Liu, K. Q. (2009). Establishing Learning Development Communities at Beijing Number 4 School. *PEEL Seeds*, *106*, 17-20. Melbourne, PEEL (Project for the Enhancement of Effective Learning).

Liu, K. Q., Li, Y. P., and Kang, C. Y. (2009, March). *Collaborative narration: Our story in a crosscultural professional learning community*. Paper presented at the China's Education Reform: Radical Shifts and their Implications Conference, University of Oxford, Oxford.

Ma Y. P., and Kang, C. Y. (2007). *The implementation and assessment of China's ongoing curriculum*. Presentation in University of British Colombia, China.

Ma, Y. P., and Tang, L. F. (2002) The implementation of the new curriculum: The status quo and countermeasures (xinkecheng shishide xianzhuang yu duice – Bufen shiyanqu pinggu jieguode fensi yu sikao). *Journal of Northeast Normal University*, (5), 124-129. (in Chinese).

Ma, Y. P., Yin, H. B., Tang, L. F., and Liu, L. Y. (2009). Teacher receptivity to system-wide curriculum reform in the initiation stage: a Chinese perspective. *Asia Pacific Education Review*, *10*(3), 423-432.

Marsh, C. J., and Willis, G. (1999). *Curriculum: Alternative approaches, ongoing issues*. Upper Saddle River, NJ; Columbus, OH: Prentice Hall, Inc.

Ministry of Education (MOE). (2010). *China's middle and longer term curriculum reform and development implementation plan: Second round call for public comment* (*Guojia zhong he changqi gaige he fazhan guihua gangyao: Dierlun gongkai zhengqiu yi jian*). Retrieved 7 September 2010 from http://www.moe.edu.cn/edoas/website18/zhuanti/2010zqyj/zqyjg.htm.

Mitchell, I., Ryan, J., Kang, C. Y., and Erickson, G. (2007, April). *Role of teacher research and cross-cultural collaboration in the context of curriculum reform in China*. Paper presented at the International Conference on Teacher Research, Chicago.

Paine, L., and Fang, Y. P. (2006). Reform as hybrid model of teaching and teacher development in China. *International Journal of Education Research*, *45*, 279-289.

Paine, L., and Fang, Y. P. (2007). Challenges in reforming professional development. In E. Hannum and A. Park (Eds.). *Education and Reform in China* (pp. 173-190). Oxford: Routledge.

Paine, L., Fang, Y. P., and Wilson, S. (2003). Reform as hybrid model of teaching and teacher education. *International Journal of Educational Research*, *45*(4/5), 279-289.

PEEL Seeds. (2009). Chinese education. *PEEL Seeds*, *106*.

PEEL Seeds. (2010). China revisited. *PEEL Seeds, 107.*

Postiglione, G. (2006). *Education and social change in China: Inequality in a market economy.* New York: M. E. Sharpe Inc.

Robinson, B. (2008). Using distance education and ICT to improve access, equity and the quality in rural teachers' professional development in western China. *International Review of Research in Open and Distance Learning, 9*(1), 1-17.

Robinson, B., and Yi, W. W. (2007). The role and status of non-governmental ('daike') teachers in China's rural education. *International Journal of Educational Development, 28*(1), 35-54.

Ryan, J., Kang, C. Y., Mitchell, I., and Erickson, G. (2009). China's basic education reform: An account of an international collaborative research and development project. *Asia Pacific Journal of Education, 29*(4), 427-441.

Ryan, J., and Louie, K. (2007). False dichotomy? 'Western' and 'Eastern' concepts of scholarship and learning. *Educational Philosophy and Theory, 39*(4), 404-417.

Sargent, T., and Hannum, E. (2008, December). *Doing more with less: Teacher professional learning communities in resource-constrained primary schools in rural China.* Paper presented at the Conference on Poverty, Education, and Health in Rural China, University of Oxford, Oxford.

Shi, L. J. (2006). The successors to Confucianism or a new generation? A questionnaire study on Chinese students' culture of learning English. *Language, Culture and Curriculum, 19*(1), 122-147.

Smith, D., and Lovat, T. (2003). *Curriculum action on reflection* (4th ed.). Tuggerah, NSW: Social Science Press.

Standing Committee of the State Council (2010). *Long term education reform and development programs.* Retrieved 7 September 2010 from http://www. prcgov.org/ 2010-05/12/content_9840333.htm.

Tan, Y. (2009). *More university spots go to poor.* China Daily, 17 July 2009.

Wang, F. L. (2006, August). *Developing strategies collaboratively with my students* (*celüe banhe wode xuesheng gongtong chengzhang*). Paper presented at the Towards Excellence: Learning Development Community Annual Conference, Beijing, China.

Wang, F. L. (2009). Developing teacher strategies which promote the development of teachers and students. *PEEL Seeds, 106,* 33-34.

Wang, L. X. and Wang, F. L. (2007, November). *Stories from our teaching strategies room* (*celüeshi de gushi*). Paper presented at the 3rd Innovation and International Forum on Teacher Education Conference, Shanghai, China. (in Chinese).

Wong, C. (2009a, March). *The challenge of providing free education in rural China: A glimpse from the southwestern provinces.* Paper presented at the China's Education Reform: Radical Shifts and their Implications Conference, University of Oxford, Oxford.

Wong, C. (2009b, May). *China's public service delivery system.* Paper presented at the Colloquium on Building a Harmonious Society in China: Reducing Poverty and Improving Public Services, University of Oxford, Oxford.

World Bank (2008). *China: Public Services for building the new socialist countryside* (*gaishan nongcun gonggong fuwue*). Beijing: CITIC Press. (in Chinese).

Xu, Y. Z. (2008, October). *School-based teacher development through a school-university collaborative project.* Paper presented at the Asia-Pacific Conference on International Education, Shanghai, China.

York-Barr, J., and Duke, K. (2004). What do we know about teacher leadership? Findings from two decades of scholarship. *Review of Educational Research, 74*(3), 255-316.

Yu, W. S., and Kang C. Y. (2003). The meaning of ongoing China's curriculum reform project. *Journal of the Chinese Society of Education*, (11), 16-21. (in Chinese).

Zheng, X. H. (2009, March). *Life science curriculum in Shanghai middle schools.* Paper presented at the China's Education Reform: Radical Shifts and their Implications Conference, University of Oxford, Oxford.

Zhong, Q. Q. (2006). Curriculum reform in China: Challenges and reflections. *Frontiers of Education in China, 1*(3), 370-382.

Zhu, M. J. (2005, October). *A report on the current state of the basic education reform in China.* Presentation at the Conference on University, Schools and Government in educational reform: International Perspectives, Beijing, China.

Zhu, M. J., and Kang, C. Y. (2002). *Approaching the New Curriculum: Dialogues with curriculum participants.* Beijing: Beijing Normal University Press. (in Chinese).

In: Curriculum Reform in China
Editors: Hong-Biao Yin and John Chi-Kin Lee

ISBN 978-1-61470-943-5
© 2012 Nova Science Publishers, Inc.

Chapter 3

CURRICULUM MAKING IN THE NEW CURRICULUM REFORM: STRUCTURE, PROCESS AND MEANING

Zongyi Deng

ABSTRACT

This chapter deals with the mechanism of curriculum making in the new curriculum reform. It analyzes the structure, process and meaning of curriculum making at the national, local, school and classroom levels. The chapter shows that the experience of China's curriculum reform instantiates a larger institutional and organizational process of curriculum making in the international arena. It concludes by addressing the complexity and challenges involved in using state-based curriculum making as an instrument for the reform.

The beginning of the 21st century saw many countries (e.g., China, Singapore, and Norway) embarking on curriculum reform as a response to the challenges of globalization. They were engaged in the endeavor of state-based curriculum making (or remaking)—including curriculum planning, development and implementation—an undertaking that involves articulating a reform vision and goals, translating the vision and goals into the official curriculum, and implementing the curriculum in schools and classrooms. Many governments have developed and institutionalized structures and processes that regulate and support curriculum making activities for curriculum reform according to their distinct social, cultural and economic conditions (Rosemund, 2000).

This chapter deals with the *mechanism* of curriculum making in China's new curriculum reform, that is, with the *structure* and *process* that the Chinese government has put in place to regulate and support curriculum planning, development and implementation in the reform movement. The new curriculum reform was initiated in 2001, which represented a national response in the education arena to the challenges of globalization and to the rapid developments and changes in China's social, economic and political context over the past twenty years. The reform vision is encapsulated in the notion of *quality education* (*suzhi jiaoyu*)—a term that is used to stress the importance of helping *all* students achieve broad and balanced moral, intellectual, physical and aesthetic development in order to meet the needs of the nation in the 21st century (Dello-Iacovo, 2009). This signals a radical departure from examination-oriented education that has plagued students and teachers in China for many decades. The government has formulated a new national curriculum structure, curriculum standards, and regulations concerning curriculum implementation, curriculum evaluation, teacher education and professional development which together are supposed to steer classroom teaching toward a kind that is in line with the vision of quality education. To facilitate and support the reform movement, the government has put in place a tripartite system of curriculum administration that distributes responsibilities for curriculum making among the state, localities and schools.

The chapter analyzes the *structure* and *process* of curriculum making which are embedded in and shaped by the three-tiered system of curriculum administration. By way of a curriculum making framework (Doyle 1992a, 1992b), it discusses what curriculum making entails at the national, local, school, and classroom levels. The chapter concludes by addressing the complexity and challenges involved in state-based curriculum making as an instrument for the new curriculum reform.

THE STRUCTURE OF CURRICULUM MAKING

In dictionaries the term *curriculum* is relatively simple, referring to programs, courses of study, textbooks, and syllabuses. But the term is rather complex and highly contentious in academic literature (see Jackson, 1992). In public and political arena the term is inextricably associated with the notion of education. All public and political discourses concerning education and educational policies ultimately become *curricular* (Connelly and Xu, 2011). Further, curriculum exists in many levels, policy, program, school/classroom (Connelly and Connelly, 2008). Over thirty years ago, Goodlad and associates (1979) argued that curriculum is "made" in different locales or places: in state departments of education, in local school boards, in schools, and in classrooms. They wrote:

> Curriculum planning goes on wherever there are people responsible for, or seeking to plan, an educational program. When state legislators pass laws regarding the teaching of the dangers of drug abuse, the inclusion of physical education, or requirements outlining the time to be spent on given subjects, they are engaging in curriculum planning. When local school boards, decree that reading will be taught according to a hierarchy of specific behavioral objectives, they are involved in curriculum planning. When school staff decides to use television broadcasts as a basis for interesting students in current events, they are engaged in curriculum planning. When individual teachers decide to use selected library books for enriching language arts offerings, they are involved in curriculum planning. (Goodlad and associates, 1979, pp. 27- 28)

State departments of education, local school boards and schools constitute the U.S. system of curriculum administration that regulates and structures curriculum making activities. In that system curriculum making is largely localized; curriculum planning and development are largely the business of local schools and school boards, and the federal government and states do not have much control over what is taught in schools (Cohen and Spillane, 1992).

The perspective of Goodlad and associates, albeit articulated in the U.S., is useful for describing how curriculum making is regulated and structured in China. Like in the U.S., the curriculum in China is made in different places: in the Ministry of Education (MOE), in provincial or municipal departments of education, and in schools and classrooms. Unlike in the U.S., curriculum planning and development in China are centralized at the Ministry in Beijing and geographically distributed to provincial or municipal departments and schools— during the new curriculum reform movement.

The adoption of the tripartite system of curriculum administration has created a new structure of curriculum making. According to the new structure, there are three levels of curriculum making, the national, the local, and the school, each of which involves a particular group of players, with clearly-defined roles and responsibilities.

- At the national level, the key players include ministers and officers at the Ministry. Their main responsibilities include: articulating the vision of quality education and defining its nature and basic tasks; developing national curriculum standards in view of the vision; stipulating types of curriculum and ratio at different grade levels; developing criteria and guidelines for compiling and developing curriculum materials; formulating or reformulating the assessment and evaluation system; and formulating policies of curriculum management and development.
- At the local level, the key players are leaders and officers in a particular provincial or municipal department of education. Their main responsibility include: formulating plans to implement the national curriculum for their province or municipality in view of their distinct local needs; and developing locally-based curricula according to the particular geographic, cultural and economic conditions of the province or municipality.
- At the school level, the key players are classroom teachers and school leaders. Their main responsibilities include implementing the national and local curricula. In addition, working within the framework of the national and local curricula, they are required to plan and develop specific courses or select courses based upon their school traditions and strengths, student interests and needs. In other words, they are to participate in what is called school-based curriculum development (SBCD) (MOE, 1999, 2001).

The curriculum planning and development activities of these three groups yield three distinct kinds of curriculum, the *national curriculum* (curriculum structure, programs and subjects developed by the Ministry), the *local curriculum* (special courses developed by local departments of education), and the *school curriculum* (special courses developed by individual schools) (MOE, 2001).

This is a sharp contrast to the structure of curriculum making in China before the new curriculum reform. For many decades, curriculum planning and development were exclusively the business of the central government, and local governments and schools were primarily responsible for implementing the curriculum handed down from the central government, without freedom to develop locally or school-based courses. Consequently, such a top-down structure created a highly-centralized and uniform national curriculum that, many have argued, was incapable of meeting the diverse needs of China—a populous, multi-ethnic, multi-cultural nation with very uneven economic, social, and educational developments in differing provinces and municipalities. The current three-tiered system of curriculum administration is designed to meet such diverse and complex needs in the nation. To a certain extent, it allows centralization to be reduced in a way that the power and authority over curriculum planning and development are shared among the central government, local governments and schools. In addition, it allows a certain degree of adaptation at local and school levels during the implementation process, therefore enhancing the adaptability of the national curriculum to the varied needs and situations of provinces or municipalities, local districts and schools (Zhu, 2007). Through establishing the tripartite system of curriculum administration, the Ministry ascribes more active roles for provinces/municipalities and schools in curriculum planning, development and implementation.

I now turn to another aspect of the mechanism—i.e., the *process* through which the curriculum reform was envisioned, planned, and implemented in schools and classrooms.

THE PROCESS OF CURRICULUM MAKING

As indicated earlier, in curriculum reform the *process* of curriculum making involves formulating a reform vision and goals, translating the vision and goals into curriculum structures, programs and courses of study, and implementing reform-induced changes in schools and classrooms. This is a very complex undertaking requiring coordination and cooperation among different groups of players across the entire school system. How such a process unfolds has to do with how curriculum making is structured or organized in the school system which, in turn, has to do with the system of curriculum administration.

Congruent with the three-tiered system of curriculum administration, curriculum making in the new curriculum reform was initiated and coordinated by the central government, and progressively proceeded with support and involvement of professionals and stakeholders at the provincial/municipal and school levels. The government first articulated a reform vision and goals and developed a new curriculum framework and sets of curriculum standards. The framework and standards were then progressively introduced to a handful of schools and districts selected in different provinces and municipalities across China for initial implementation or field-tests. Experiences and ideas gained from those pilot schools and districts were then disseminated to other schools and districts. There are three phrases of making the new curriculum: (1) planning and development, (2) initial implementation, and (3) full implementation.

Planning and Development

Three key events characterize the planning and development phase: a national survey, an initial drafting of a curriculum reform framework and curriculum standards, and the official release of the framework, curriculum standards and related documents.

- During 1996-1998 the Ministry conducted a national survey to ascertain the current issues and problems confronting the education system. The survey sample consisted of 16000 students and 2000 teachers and principals in 9 provinces and municipalities across the nation.
- In 1999 an expert group was formed to deliberate on the vision and aims of the new curriculum and to draft a reform guiding framework. The group consisted of ministry officers, educational theorists, curriculum specialists, subject matter experts, and school teachers. Meanwhile, the Ministry was engaged in the task of developing curriculum standards for 18 school subjects, reviewing and revising textbooks and teacher guides according to the standards.
- In June 2001 the Ministry issued the *Guidelines on Basic Education Curriculum Reform (Experimental)* containing the reform framework which outlines fundamental and systemic changes in the system.[5] In addition, the Ministry released 22 curriculum standards for compulsory education (grades 1-9), 16 curriculum standards for regular senior high schools (grades 10-12), and a document concerning revamping the evaluation and assessment system for middle and primary schools (Zhu, 2007; also Feng, 2006; Guan and Meng, 2007).

Initial Implementation

The initial implementation phase can be characterized in terms of progressive adoption and refinement. The Ministry started with identifying a pilot district in each province and municipality to pilot the new curriculum. The experimentation was then extended to other districts after the curriculum was revised and refined based on what were learned from the implementation in the pilot districts. The acquired experience, understanding and insight were shared among other districts. Here are four important signposts during the initial implementation journey:

- In 2001 38 districts in 27 provinces and municipalities were designated as national experimental areas for curriculum reform.
- In 2002, more than 500 districts in all provinces across China were chosen as provincial experimental areas.
- In 2003, on the basis of experimental results and feedbacks, the Ministry revised all curriculum standards, student textbooks and teacher guides.
- In fall 2004 the Ministry issued the curriculum standards of all school subjects and related documents for compulsory education (Grade 1 to 9) (Guan and Meng, 2007; Zhu, 2006).

---

[5] The framework includes eight essential components: (1) purposes and objectives, (2) curriculum structure, (3) curriculum standards, (4) learning and teaching process, (5) development of instructional materials, (6) curriculum evaluation, (7) teacher education and development, and (8) implementation of curriculum reform (MOE, 2001).

Full Implementation

Full implementation came into force during 2004 and 2005. In 2004 there were 65 to 70 percent of students in the whole nation using the new curriculum. By fall 2005, all elementary and secondary schools had taken up the new curriculum at the starting grade levels (Guan and Meng, 2007). The implementation has continued since, until the new curriculum was adopted across entire China (Feng, 2006).

Throughout the implementation process a wide range of support has been provided to teachers, primarily by means of teacher professional development. The government has implemented what is called the "Continuous Education Project" which aims at systematically training or retraining the entire population of teachers. A variety of professional development opportunities—including short courses, seminars, school-based workshops, summer programs, etc.—has been introduced to equip teachers to teach the new curriculum (see Xu, 2009).

Taken as a whole, the making of the new curriculum involves a ten-year progressive, step-by-step, and evolutionary process. It is very unlike the conventional direct implementation depicted in the literature—characterized as an execution of the reform blue print set by a central government. The Ministry believes that the simplistic view of direct implementation is no longer adequate in view of the complex situations of China at a time of rapid change. The process of curriculum making in China's new curriculum reform presents a striking contrast with the one in the UK curriculum reform in 2000s, where the new national curriculum was "quickly" handed down to schools and teachers by the government for implementation. The new curriculum reform in China, Halpin's (2010) observed, entails a journey where the government "were working with key stake holders over an extended period to create and establish one" (p. 258).

MAKING THE NEW CURRICULUM: WHAT DOES IT MEAN?

Tyler's (1949) *Basic Principles of Curriculum and Instruction* is often used by reformers and educators to justify a prescriptive way of thinking about standard-setting and curriculum making. It prescribes the following four questions as fundamental to the work of curriculum making:

1. What educational purposes should the school seek to attain?
2. What educational experiences can be provided that are likely to attain these purposes?
3. How can these educational experiences be effectively organized?
4. How can we determine whether these purposes are being attained?

This way of thinking about curriculum making, Westbury (2008) argued, is "idealistic" and rather than "realistic" because Tyler Rationale does not describe what curriculum developers actually do when engaged in curriculum making.

What does it mean to participate in curriculum making at the national, local, and school levels? In the preceding section I have described three different groups of key players involved in shaping or reshaping the curriculum across the system in terms of roles and responsibilities. Now I describe what they actually do by way of a curriculum making framework developed by Doyle (1992a, 1992d) and Westbury (2000)—a perspective that focuses on the kind of activities and discourse involved in making the curriculum.

Curriculum making, broadly construed, operates across three distinct domains or contexts, namely *policy*, *programmatic* and *classroom*, each of which is associated with a particular kind of curricular discourse and/or activity.

- In the policy or institutional arena, curriculum making centers on policies and discourses at the intersection between schooling, culture, and society. It embodies a conception of what schooling should be with respect to the society and culture. Curriculum-making at this level "typifies" what is desirable in social and cultural orders, what is to be valued and sought after by members of a society or nation (Doyle, 1992a, 1992b).
- In the programmatic domain, curriculum making centers on translating the aims, ideals, and expectations at the policy level into an operational framework that provides the ultimate base for the work of schools and classrooms. It transforms the abstract curriculum (aims, ideals, and expectations) at into school subjects, programmes, or courses of study embodied in curriculum documents and materials provided to a system of schools. The process of constructing a school subject or a course of study involves "framing a set of arguments that rationalize the selection and arrangement of content [knowledge, skills, and dispositions] and the transformation of that content" for school and classroom use (Doyle, 1992b, p. 71).
- In the classroom context, curriculum making centers on the pedagogical interpretation of the programmatic curriculum by a teacher. It involves transforming the programmatic curriculum embodied in curriculum documents and materials into the classroom curriculum characterized by a cluster of events—jointly developed by the teacher and a group of students within a particular classroom (Doyle, 1992a, 1992b). Classroom curriculum making involves further elaboration of the programmatic curriculum, making it connect with the experience, interests, and the capacities of students (Westbury, 2000).

These three domains of curriculum making provide a useful frame of reference for understanding the kind of curriculum work conducted at the national, local, school, and classroom levels. I will show that the national, local and school curriculum making operate across the policy and programmatic domains, and in classroom, teachers need to be viewed curriculum makers in implementing the new curriculum.

Policy Curriculum Making

Curriculum making in the policy arena is the province of the central government represented by the Ministry. It involves articulating the aims and vision of schooling as well as formulating the reasons or rationales for the aims and vision. The ultimate goal of quality education is to help students achieve broad and balanced moral, intellectual, physical and aesthetic development and a high level of character building. More specifically, the aims of quality education include:

- enabling the development of a new, well-educated, idealistic, moral and patriotic generation who will love socialism and inherit and cherish Chinese tradition;
- helping students develop an awareness of socialist democracy and laws as well as respect for state laws and social norms;
- helping students cultivate desirable worldview, values and attitudes;
- helping students develop a sense of social responsibility;
- helping students developing an innovative spirit, practical skills, a knowledge base of sciences and humanities, and an awareness of environmental protection issues; and
- helping students develop good physical health and psychological qualities, healthy aesthetical tastes and lifestyles. (MOE, 2001)

Underlying the aims of quality education are three kinds of discourse—economic, political, and educational—that provide justifications and rationales for the new curriculum. The economic discourse foregrounds the emergence of a global economy and the rapid economic developments of China (e.g., the establishment of a market economy, the entry into the World Trade Organization, etc.), pointing to the need for a creative, innovative, and self-motivated future work force. The political discourse highlights the new social and political conditions of China (e.g., a move towards decentralization in governance, the emergence of a legal system of education, and the implementation of nine-year compulsory education), arguing for a new national curriculum that is more responsive and adaptable to the changing diverse social and economic needs of the nation (Feng 2006; Huang, 2004). The educational discourse critically questions the predominance of examination-oriented education, and in so doing, calls for a kind of student-oriented education that centres on developing well-rounded individuals (Liu and Qi, 2005). These discourses provide support for a vision of schooling in which the curriculum needs to be:

> conducive to the universalizing of nine-year compulsory education, be attainable for the overwhelming majority of the students, embody the basic requirements for citizenship, and be focused on fostering the students' motivation and ability to undertake lifelong learning. Under the prerequisite that all students should achieve the basic requirements, the curriculum for regular senior middle school has been arranged in several optional levels to give students more choices and development opportunities, and to lay a solid foundation for them to cultivate competencies in life skills, hands-on practice and creativity. (Zhu, 2007, p. 224; also MOE, 2001)

In other words, curriculum making at the national level provides the "institutional frame" of decisions on curricular changes and the discourses that give legitimacy to those decisions (Mosenmund, 2007). It conveys the vision and expectations that the government has for the "inner work" of schooling across the school system (Westbury, 2008). The vision, expectations and discourses in turn provide an important frame of reference for subsequent programmatic curriculum making.

Programmatic Curriculum Making

Programmatic curriculum making is largely a national undertaking carried out by the Ministry. However, certain responsibilities are delegated to local provinces, municipalities and schools. The three-tiered system of curriculum administration gives meaning and shape to the discourses and activities of making the programmatic curriculum at the national, local and school level.

At the national level, the task of programmatic curriculum making entails translating the vision, aims and expectations of quality education into a *curriculum structure* (consisting of various domains and related school subjects or programs) and *curriculum standards* that are the ultimate basis for the national system of schooling, together with a set of *enabling conditions* about classroom teaching, curriculum evaluation, teacher education and professional development. The new curriculum structure divides the school timetable of nine-year compulsory education into five domains: (1) academic learning (history, geography, science, Chinese, mathematics and foreign languages) (53 percent), (2) moral education (8.5 percent), (3) arts and music (10 percent), (4) physical education and health (10.5 percent), and (5) integrated studies and elective subjects (community service, information technology, inquiry/project-based learning, and vocational and technical education) (18 percent). The new curriculum is enlarged and enriched by incorporating a significant ratio of integrated practical activity and elective subjects (Zhu, 2007). Conventional academic subjects are retained in the curriculum, after being pruned of complicated, difficult and out-dated elements.

The new curriculum standards consist of statements of what students should know and be able do in different school subjects over the course of schooling, with respect to three dimensions of content: (1) knowledge and basic skills; (2) attitudes and values; (3) competencies in application and problem solving (MOE, 2001). Three sets of curriculum standards are created for elementary, junior high, and senior high schools respectively. For a school subject like science, the construction of curriculum standards entails interpreting and theorizing the content in a way that links the content backward to the policy purposes of the school subject (e.g., developing competencies) and forward to the (enacted) curriculum in schools and classrooms (see Deng, 2010). It is intended to facilitate the use of constructivist approaches to classroom teaching, encouraging inquiry learning, cooperative learning, experiential learning, critical thinking and creativity. The introduction of curriculum standards also signals a shift from the past emphasis on knowledge transmission to a broader stress on the development of competencies, attitudes and values in students.

Furthermore, programmatic curriculum making involves outlining a set of conditions or regulations that are necessary for implementing quality education in schools and classrooms—pertaining to classroom teaching, curriculum evaluation, and teacher education and professional development—conditions that purport to provide support for classroom teachers in the implementation process (see MOE 2001).

In short, at the national or ministerial level, the task of programmatic curriculum making is to articulate a curriculum structure and curriculum standards, alongside a set of enabling conditions, which serve to steer or prescribe the curriculum or forms of teaching and learning in schools and classrooms. It spells out what the schools should be teaching at various grade levels, how that teaching should be categorized and sequenced in terms of "domains," "subjects" and "courses," as well as how teaching should be undertaken (Westbury, 2010).

At the local (provincial and municipal) level, educational officers in a provincial or municipal department of education participate in programmatic curriculum making through articulating an operational plan for implementing the new curriculum according to the special situations and needs of the province or municipality. They work out how best to reinterpret the new national curriculum, meshing it sensitively with local situations and needs. In addition, working within the national curriculum framework, they develop locally-based courses (15% of the curriculum) that reflect the history, culture and economy of the province or municipality.

Likewise, at the school level, teachers and school leaders participate in programmatic curriculum making through school-based curriculum development. Apart from implementing the national and local curricula, they are expected to explore and select appropriate curriculum resources according to the school context, developing school-based courses (5 percent of the curriculum) relevant to students' interests and backgrounds.

Overall, within the three-tried system of curriculum administration, locally and school-based curriculum developments are organizational strategies employed by the Ministry to engage provincial/municipal officials, school leaders and classroom teachers in the task of enhancing the responsiveness and adaptability of the national curriculum to the diverse local situations, issues and concerns. Locally and school-based courses are supposed to provide students with opportunities to study what has happened in their homeland through courses that are not included in state-mandated curriculum—courses that address local social, economic and cultural issues and traditions. Zhu (2007) offered the following examples:

> A course on grafting technology of watermelon seedlings devised by a rural school in Ning'an County, Heilongjiang Province, enabled local farmers to increase earnings from watermelon planting and sales. A history course offered by schools in Mengjin County, Henan Province, re-examined the history course on why the city of Kaifeng turned from a booming city into a pile of underground ruins during the Northern Song Dynasty (A.D. 960–1127). A course adopted by schools in Quanzhou, Fujian Province, examined that City's historical contributions as the starting point of the celebrated seaward Silk Road during the heyday of the Tang Dynasty (A.D. 618–907). (p. 229).

Teachers as Curriculum Makers

Classrooms teachers are the ones ultimately responsible for carrying out the new curriculum in classroom. In the new curriculum reform teachers are construed as not passive curriculum implementers *but* active curriculum makers. They are supposed to interpret and transform the new curriculum into activities or events in which students actively participate in questioning, exploring, and constructing knowledge (MOE, 2001). Teachers are supposed to engage students in cooperative, experiential, meaningful and reflective learning, enabling them "to have dialogues with the objective world, with other people and themselves" (Zhong, 2006, p. 378), and helping them develop competencies, positive values and attitudes.

A classroom teacher is a curriculum maker also in the sense that he or she interprets and transforms the new curriculum using his or her personal practical knowledge, in consideration of curriculum commonplaces—the teacher or self, students, subject matter, and milieu (see Clandinin and Connelly, 1992; Connelly and Clandinin, 1988). This process is shaped by various school local factors—others teacher, students, school principals, parents, etc.. However, the interpretation and transformation necessarily reflect a teacher's understanding of the potential of the new curriculum contained in curriculum documents and materials. Working within an organizational framework of public schooling, classroom teachers are the "intermediaries" between the policy/programmatic curriculum and the classroom curriculum (Reid, 2006).

The above discussion shows the different functions of curriculum making in the policy, programmatic, and classroom arenas, as well as the institutional differences between the Ministry, and local departments of education, schools and classrooms—in terms of curriculum tasks, responsibilities and concerns. The Ministry, local departments of education, schools and classroom teachers are engaged in three different curriculum making tasks, each of which is characterized by a distinct kind of curricular discourse and practice. Different players at different levels bring to bear their distinct ideologies, beliefs and concerns on their curriculum making task.

CONCLUSION

I have discussed the mechanism of curriculum making in the new curriculum reform through analyzing the structure, process and meaning of curriculum making at the national, local, school and classroom levels. The analysis supports certain general assertions about state-based curriculum making in the context of a worldwide emergence of curriculum reform over the last two decades.[6] The idea of state-based curriculum making "captures a wide-ranging set of activities and processes emerging within webs of societal and cultural ideologies and symbols, politics and organized interest groups, organizational and administrative structures and processes, and local understandings, beliefs and practices"(Westbury, 2008, p. 50). As a reform instrument, state-based curriculum making is rooted in a government's awareness of its own development and internal and external situations. In responding to the new development and new situations, a government establishes and institutionalizes a structure and process that channel a reform vision and expectations into the official curriculum and into schools and classrooms (Rosenmund, 2000). The structure and process of curriculum making are embedded in and shaped by the political, administrative and educational infrastructures of a country (Rosenmund, 2007). In other words, China's reform experience can be viewed as an instantiation of a larger institutional and organizational process of curriculum making in the international arena.

Further, the case of curriculum reform in China exemplifies a typical way of using curriculum making as an instrument by the state to manage and regulate the work of schooling—a method that has been widely employed by many countries across the world. As Westbury (2008) observed, through developing national curriculum standards, a government projects to schools a range of authoritative formal decisions about and expectations for what schools teach, how that teaching should be undertaken. Those decisions are linked with textbook approval and adoption, teacher preparation and professional development, assessment and evaluation. Spaces that have not been available for locally and school-based

---

[6] For example, the introduction of British National Curriculum, of American states' standards, and of the new curriculum frame and guidelines in Norway.

curriculum development are made available. In short, the case of China typifies an international pattern of curriculum making.

The new curriculum reform in China bears resemblance to the systemic reform (also called *standards-based reform*) in the US in the late 1980s and early 1990s as well. There are three integral components embodied in the US reform: (1) establishing challenging academic standards for what all students need to know and be able to do; (2) aligning policies—such as examination, teacher professional development—and accountability programs to the standards; and (3) restructuring the governance system to delegate to districts and schools the responsibilities for developing specific approaches that meet the standards (Goertz et al., 1995). Unlike the US reform, the new curriculum reform in China stresses *holistic* rather than ambitious academic standards. Nonetheless, it is *systemic* in that the reform requires educational changes to be integrated around a set of curriculum standards or outcomes, an alignment among various parts of the education system (textbook development, teacher professional development, etc.), and some form of decentralization that empowers educators and leaders at the local levels to make independent decisions. Policymakers and reformers in China seem to have learned or adopted ideas from the US standards-based reform. In fact, as many have pointed out (e.g., Zhang, 2005; Jiang and Lu, 2005), the constructivist assumptions about knowledge, teaching and learning that underpin the kind of teaching practice envisioned in the new curriculum reform are adopted from the US reform.

How successful is the instrument of state-based curriculum making in the new curriculum reform? Success inside the classroom is still not very evident. Today classroom practice remains largely unchanged; it continued to be driven by examination preparation. As Zhao (2007) observed,

> According to a recent national study by the Ministry of Education, although many educators seem to have accepted the concept of "quality education" and some teachers have changed their teaching practices, by and large the focus on the whole child remains lip service. "Quality education is loudly spoken, but test-oriented education gets the real attention," notes the report. As a result, competition among students remains fierce, schools and teachers continue to teach to the test at the expense of students' physical and mental health, test preparation overrides national curriculum requirements, and some schools resort to militaristic ways of managing their students. Under intense pressure, students spend all their time and energy on schoolwork. (p. 73)

The experience seems to conform a decade of research in the US that classroom practice is resistant to change (e.g., Cohen and Ball, 1990a, 1990b; Cuban, 1993). As indicated by Zhao (2007), the extant assessment and examination system militates against the new curriculum reform. High-stakes examinations powerfully steer teachers to teach to tests rather than to the broad aims of quality education, hence narrowing the overall curriculum experience in classroom. When adopting the ideas of standards-based reform from the US, policy-makers and reformers in China did not seem to have fully recognized the constraint on curriculum reform imposed by the existing examination and assessment system. In other words, they seemed to have overlooked the precondition of alignment of curriculum standards with assessment/examination policies entailed in a systemic reform. In the US school system high-stakes examinations are literally nonexistent. Tests and examinations in general are not directly (or only loosely) tied to the intended curriculum, and are not used for selection purposes (Cohen and Spillane, 1992).

Another important constraint—that has not received sufficient attention from Chinese policy-makers and reformers—has to do with the entrenched cultural beliefs about the nature of knowledge, teaching and learning held by Chinese teachers. Partly due to the pervasive examination culture, Chinese teachers tend to view knowledge as a body of facts, concepts and principles contained in officially-approved textbooks, upon which students are tested during examination. Accordingly, they are inclined to define teaching in terms of giving out or imparting knowledge codified in school textbooks, and learning in terms of acquiring, memorizing and practising this knowledge (c.f., Waktin and Biggs, 2001). These beliefs seemingly contradict constructivist assumptions about knowledge, teaching and learning. Yet they are so widespread that they steer their thinking toward the traditional kind of teaching practice (Cuban, 1993). Therefore, to propose that teachers shift from traditional practice to the new practice envisioned in the curriculum reform is a proposal that they fundamentally transform their cultural beliefs about nature of knowledge, teaching and learning. Yet changes in teachers' beliefs are extremely difficult because they often challenge the core value held by teachers (Fullan and Stiegelbauer, 1991). This was also a challenge faced by American policymakers and reformers when implementing standards-based reform (see Cohen and Ball, 1990a, 1990b; Cohen and Spillane, 1992).

In short, when learning or borrowing the policy practice of standards-based reform from the US, China reformers and curriculum makers did not sufficiently analyze the constraints imposed by the institutional and cultural context of schooling on the new curriculum reform. Without such an analysis and without introducing necessary modifications and changes, policy learning would become primarily "policy copying" (Mok, 2007). Classroom practice remains largely unchanged because the reform clashes with the high-stakes examination and assessment system, and with teachers' cultural beliefs and assumptions.

There is an urgent need to fundamentally reform the high-stakes assessment and examination system—particularly college entrance exams—if state-based curriculum making is to render significant changes in classroom practice. State-based curriculum making, teachers' professional development, and the assessment/examination system are among the instruments of systemic reform that are used to change classroom practice. These various instruments need to work together in a way that supports, rather than hinders, the implementation of quality education in schools and classrooms.

Furthermore, curriculum making at the national and provincial levels depends, for its effect, on classroom teachers who, as mentioned before, are ultimately responsible for carrying out the new curriculum in their classrooms. Providing teachers with extensive opportunities to learn what they need to know in the light of the complex demands of implementation and engaging them in such learning are crucial for changing classroom practice. In particular, they need opportunities to re-examine their instructional beliefs and assumptions. Only then will they be able to undergo changes in their instructional beliefs (Cohen and Barnes, 1993). Furthermore, the professional learning opportunities for teaching, Cohen and Hill (2001) argue, need to be grounded in classroom practice, allowing teachers to seriously study the new curriculum and related student work.

Last but not least, state-based curriculum making is embedded in and shaped by the "multiple layers of contexts" (Talbert and McLaughlin, 1993) —including students, parents, teachers, schools, local culture, local departments of education, the Ministry, and so forth. The new curriculum reform thus needs to be viewed as a national enterprise, one in which the national, local and school leaders have as much to learn as classroom teachers. Parents and local community leaders have a lot to learn as well, if they are to embrace and support a new paradigm of education (c.f., Cohen and Spillane, 1992).

REFERENCES

Clandinin, D. J., and Connelly, F. M. (1992). Teacher as curriculum maker. In P. W. Jackson (Ed.), *Handbook of research in curriculum* (pp. 402-435). New York: Macmillan.

Cohen, D. K., and Ball, B. L. (1990a). Policy and practice: An overview. *Educational Evaluation and Policy Analysis, 12*(3), 233-239.

Cohen, D. K., and Ball, B. L. (1990b). Policy and practice: A commentary. *Educational Evaluation and Policy Analysis, 12*(3), 331-338.

Cohen, D. K., and Spillane, J. P. (1992). Policy and practice: The relations between governance and instruction. *Review of research in education, 18*, 3-49.

Cohen. D. K., and Barnes, C. A. (1993). Conclusion: A new pedagogy for policy? In D. Cohen, M. McLaughlin, and J. Talbert (Eds.), *Teaching for understanding: Challenges for policy and practice* (pp. 240-275). San Francisco, CA: Jossey-Bass.

Cohen, D. K., and Hill, H. C. (2001). *Learning policy: When state education reform works.* New Haven, CT: Yale University Press.

Connelly, F. M., and Clandinin, D. J. (1988). Teachers as curriculum planners: Narratives of experience. New York: Teachers College Press.

Connelly, F. M., and Connelly, G. (2009). The syllabus: Policy instrument and practical curriculum guide. In A. Luke, K. Weir, A. Woods and M. Moroney (Eds.), *Development of a set of principles to guide a P-12 syllabus framework: A report to the Queensland Studies Authority* (pp. 128-139). Brisbane, Australia: Queensland University of Technology.

Connelly, F. M., and Xu, S. (2011). Curriculum and curriculum studies. In J. Arthur and A. Peterson (Eds.), *The Routledge companion to education.* New York: Routledge. (Forthcoming)

Cuban, L. (1993). *How teachers taught: Constancy and change in American classrooms, 1890- 1990.* New York: Teachers College Press.

Dello-Iacovo, B. (2009). Curriculum reform and "quality education" in China: An overview. *International Journal of Educational Development, 29*, 241-249.

Deng, Z. (2010). Scientific literacy: Content and curriculum making. In C. Linder, L. Östman, Roberts, D. A., P.-O., Wickman, G. Erickson, and A. MacKinnon (Eds.), *Exploring the landscapes of scientific literacy* (pp. 45-56). New York: Routledge.

Doyle, W. (1992a). Curriculum and pedagogy. In P. W. Jackson (Ed.), *Handbook of research on curriculum* (pp. 486-516). New York: Macmillan.

Doyle, W. (1992b). Constructing curriculum in the classroom. In F. K. Oser, A. Dick and J. Patry (Eds.), *Effective and responsible teaching: The new syntheses* (pp. 66-79). San Francisco: Jossey-Bass Publishers.

Feng, D. (2006). China's recent curriculum reform: Progress and problems. *Planning and Changing, 37* (1/2), 131-144.

Fullan, M. G., and Stiegelbauer, S. (1991). *The new meaning of educational change.* New York, NY: Teachers College Press.

Goertz, M. E., Floden, R. E. and O'Day, J. (1996). *Studies of education reform: Systemic reform,* Washington, DC: U.S. Government Printing Office.

Goodlad, J. I., and associates (1979). *Curriculum inquiry: The study of curriculum practice.* New York: McGraw-Hill.

Guan, Q., and Meng, W. (2007) China's new national curriculum reform: Innovation, challenges and strategies. *Frontiers of Education in China, 2* (4), 579-604.

Halpin, D. (2010). National curriculum reform in China and England: Origins, character and comparison. *Frontiers of Education in China, 5*(2), 258-269.

Huang, F. (2004). Curriculum reform in contemporary China: seven goals and six strategies. *Journal of Curriculum Studies, 36* (1), 101-115.

Jackson, P. W. (2002). Conceptions of curriculum and curriculum specialists. In P. W. Jackson (Ed.), *Handbook of research on curriculum* (pp. 3-40). New York: Macmillan.

Liu, P., and Qi, C. (2005). Reform in the curriculum of basic education in the People's Republic of China: Pedagogy, application, and learners. *International Journal of Educational Reform, 14* (1), 35-44.

Mok, K. H. (2007). Questing for internationalization of universities in Asia: Critical reflections. *Journal of Studies in International Education, 11* (3/4), 433-454.

McLaughlin, M. W., and Talbert, J. E. (1993). Introduction: New vision of teaching. In D. Cohen, M. McLaughlin and J. Talbert (Eds.), *Teaching for understanding: Challenges for policy and practice* (pp. 1-10). San Francisco: Jossey-Bass.

Ministry of Education. (1999). Decision to further educational systemic reform and promote quality oriented education (*guanyu shenhua jiaoyu tizhi gaige quanmian tuijin suzhi jiaoyu de jueding*). Beijing: Ministry of Education.

Ministry of Education (2001). Programme on the reform of the basic education curriculum (Experimental) (*jichu jiaoyu kecheng gaige gangyao [Shixing]*). Beijing: Ministry of Education.

Reid, W. A. (2006). *The pursuit of curriculum: schooling and the public interest.* Greenwich, CT: Information Publishing.

Rosenmund, M. (2000). Approaches to international comparative research on curricula and curriculum-making processes. *Journal of Curriculum Studies, 32*(5), 599-606.

Rosenmund, M. (2007). The current discourse on curriculum change: A comparative analysis of national reports on education. In A. Benavot and C. Braslavsky (Eds.), *School knowledge in comparative and historical Perspective: Changing curricula in primary and secondary education.* (pp. 173-194). CERC Studies in Comparative Education, No 19. Hong Kong: University of Hong Kong, Comparative Education Research Centre.

Talbert, J. E., and McLaughlin, M. W. (1993). Understanding teaching in context. In D. Cohen, M. McLaughlin, and J. Talbert (Eds.), *Teaching for understanding: Challenges for policy and practice* (pp. 167-206). San Francisco: Jossey-Bass.

Tyler, R. W. (1949). *Basic principles of curriculum and instruction.* Chicago: University of Chicago Press.

Watkins, D. A., and Biggs, J. B. (2001). *Teaching the Chinese learner: Psychological and pedagogical perspective.* Hong Kong; Melbourne: Comparative Education Research Centre, The University of Hong Kong; Australian Council for Educational Research.

Westbury, I. (2000). Teaching as a reflective practice: What might didaktik teach curriculum. In I. Westbury, S. Hopmann and K. Riquarts (Eds.), *Teaching as a reflective practice: The German Didaktik tradition* (pp. 15-39). Mahwah, NJ: Lawrence Erlbaum Associates.

Westbury, I. (2008). The making of formal curricula: Why do states make curricula, and how? In F. M. Connelly, M. F. He and J. Phillion (Eds.), *Sage handbook of curriculum and instruction* (pp. 45-65). Thousand Oaks, CA: Sage.

Westbury, I. (2010). *Introduction.* Unpublished manuscript.

Xu, Y. (2009). School-based teacher development through a school-university collaborative project: A case study of a recent initiative in China. *Journal of Curriculum Studies, 41*(1), 49-66.

Jiang, S. D., and Lu, H. W. (2005) Constructivism and new ideas of classroom teaching. *Journal of Chongqing College of Education, 18*(2), 70-73. (in Chinese).

Zhang, J. (2005). New basic education reform is not a Copernican revolution. *Contemporary Educational Science*, (13), 14-16. (in Chinese).

Zhao, Y. (2007). China and the whole child. *Educational Leadership, 64*(8), 70-73.

Zhong, Q. (2006). Curriculum reform in China. *Frontiers of Education in China, 1*(3), 370-382.

Zhu, M. (2007). Recent Chinese experiences in curriculum reform. *Prospects, 37*(2), 223-235.

In: Curriculum Reform in China
Editors: Hong-Biao Yin and John Chi-Kin Lee

ISBN 978-1-61470-943-5
© 2012 Nova Science Publishers, Inc.

Chapter 4

LEADING CURRICULUM REFORM IN CHINA: PRINCIPALS IN THE MIDDLE[7]

Haiyan Qian and Allan Walker

ABSTRACT

The curriculum reform in China presents radical changes not only to how and what students learn, but also to how principals lead, relationships within the school and connections with governments and parents. The purpose of the chapter is to present a snapshot of some of the struggles faced by secondary school principals in Shanghai during their implementation of the curriculum reform. Based on the empirical evidence, this chapter attempts to explain, from the principals' perspectives, why they fail to perform the expected "curriculum leader" role. The explanation is presented in the form of three propositions. They include the important principal role to win resources, the dominant expectation to produce good performance on exams and the pressure of culturally and structurally engrained relationships. The chapter ends with the discussion of some implications for leadership to enhance learning in the future.

Curriculum reform in China is seen as the pathway to changing the ways students are prepared for the 21st Century. Since its introduction almost a decade ago, the "new curriculum" reform in China has consumed much of the energy and time of school principals (Chen, 2007; Zhong and Yue, 2006). The fundamentals of the reform present radical changes not only to how and what students learn, but also to how principals lead, relationships within the school and connections with governments and parents. In many cases, the attempted implementation of the reform has trapped schools and school leaders between meeting the demands of the established system, such as performance on national exams, and those of the new curriculum, such as a greater emphasis on creativity and inquiry (Tao, 2006).

The purpose of this chapter is to present a snapshot of some of the struggles faced by secondary school principals in Shanghai as they attempt to implement curriculum reform.

---

[7] Parts of this chapter are taken from Walker, A., Qian, H. Y., & Zhang, S. (2011). Secondary school principals in curriculum reform: Victims or accomplices? *Frontiers of Education in China*, 6(3).

Shanghai schools have been at the forefront of curriculum reform in China but, at least according to recent government reviews, have largely failed to make the reforms work (Luo, 2010). Few studies have attempted to investigate this issue from the perspective of the principals themselves. Without a deeper understanding of what is happening at the school level, it is unlikely that intervention for improvement can be made meaningful.

This chapter has three main sections. The first section sketches a fairly broad picture of curriculum reform and its challenges to school principals in China. The section also sketches the literature that discusses school principals under curriculum reform. The second section introduces a study conducted in Shanghai with a group of senior secondary school principals that was designed to uncover their experiences with curriculum reform. This study provides empirical evidence as to how principals interpret the reforms in their schools. The research findings provide empirical evidence relating to the concerns and struggles of principals that have been discussed in the literature. In the form of three propositions this section attempts to explain, from the principals' perspectives, why they fail to perform the expected "curriculum leader" role. The third section discusses some implications for leadership to enhance learning in the future.

THE CONTEXT

China has a millennia-long tradition of valuing formally-examined student outcomes above all else. The lingering influence of the Imperial Examination[8] and its descendant – the National College Entrance Exam (colloquially referred to as the High Exam) – continues to equate student learning with excellent results on standardized examinations. The obsession with exam performance in China has, over the last decade, been given serious consideration by the National Government.

Over the last decade the Central government has moved to de-emphasize the all-consuming "High Exam" focus. Initiative and creativity are considered to be more essential at the national level for increased global competitiveness. Thus, the government policy-makers attempted to modify the exam-oriented education system in order to promote holistic student development. Towards this end, a series of policy initiatives have been released since the turn of the new century. One of the most high-profile of these was the New Curriculum Reform which was launched in 2001 (Zhong, 2006).

Curriculum reform was proposed as the key strategy to promote higher quality education in China. The New Curriculum aims squarely at changing beliefs about, and approaches to, teaching and learning. It focuses on the cultivation of students' moral development, innovative spirit, critical thinking and practical abilities. The reform began by establishing new criteria for elementary and secondary school curricula, standards for syllabi and the content of textbooks. The reform also established a system whereby the curriculum was managed simultaneously at the central, local and school levels. As a form of decentralization this called on schools, cities, districts and provinces to design school-based curricula that accounted for local needs.

---

[8] The Imperial Examination System lasted in China for 1300 years - from its founding during the Sui Dynasty in 605 to its abolition near the end of Qing Dynasty in 1905. The examinations determined who among the population would be permitted to enter the state's bureaucracy.

Shanghai has led the way in this regard and much of its curriculum reform even predates that of Central policy makers. Shanghai initiated its stage-1 curriculum reform as early as 1988 while the stage-2 reform was launched in 1998. After years of experiments, all the senior secondary schools in Shanghai joined the new curriculum scheme in 2006. The new curriculum comprised three categories of courses: basic, extended and research courses (Shanghai Education Commission, 2004). While the basic courses mainly remained as the exam subjects within the national framework, individual schools were delegated responsibility to design and organize the extended and research courses. Each school established a curriculum reform team headed by the principal.

The curriculum reform challenges principals to assume more responsibility as curriculum and instructional leaders. This is not easy for principals who have been accustomed to leading based on clear orders assigned from the top, who have internalized the languages of "effective instruction" instead of "curriculum design," and who have seen exam results as the single most important criterion for school quality. Thus, when normative demands for high exam results meet new, more pedagogically emancipatory policy requirements, how principals interpret and manage the conflicting demands begins to spin.

However, few studies have illuminated the principals' worklives under curriculum reform. An examination of the literature detects some problems. One major issue is a marked lack of empirical studies in the discourse of Chinese educational leadership. Education research relies overwhelmingly on the traditional Chinese way of argumentation (Yang, 2005). Many falsely-labelled research papers are simply an explanation or illustration of some policies or personal reflections, which are lacking theoretical contribution and are short of tight logical reasoning (T. Wang, 2004; Yang, 2005). For example, in the first volume of *Educational Administration Review in China* (*zhongguo jiaoyu guanli pinglun*, a new journal that claims to improve the knowledge base of school administration in China), only 3 out of 19 papers are based on empirical data (Chu, 2003).

Existing "research" tends to take two forms. One form is to provide prescriptive suggestions telling principals what they should be and do. For example, a large proportion of such literature is reform-oriented. Researchers comment on the qualities and attitudes which principals need to have towards the goal of the successful implementation of a certain reform initiative. In a paper which addresses the leadership qualities needed to face the challenge of the new curriculum reform, Zhou (2006) proposes that principals should be able to take the following thirteen roles: a caring teacher, a tolerant friend, a trusted supervisor, a highly disciplined person, a cooperative team-member, a fire-fighter, a flexible leader, a servant, a learner, a researcher, an optimistic person, an innovator, and a practitioner. In a sense, researchers aim to tease out some forms of idealized practices that principals can adopt as reference points. However, these prescriptions, as handed to principals, are not usually based on the specific school realities and tend to be far too lofty for principals to address the realities of schools.

The other main form of "research" touches upon the actual reality and discusses the issues and problems that concern principals. Much of the writing comprising this literature uses limited first-hand observation and interview data. Such papers usually begin with words such as these: "I have visited a school and talked to the principal…," or "I have some friends who are principals and they told me…." However, the data are not collected or analysed within the accepted convention; thus they cannot be deemed as empirical studies. Given the diffuse sources informing this mainly anecdotal work, they provide sharply different stories from the prescriptive research: stories of daily realities, dilemmas, concerns and problems facing principals. For example, Zhang and Gu (2005) discussed some major concerns of principals such as worrying about financial responsibility, pressure for better exam performance and the need to fulfill *"guanxi"* obligations.

Thus the question is: does empirical research also support these findings? What meanings do principals themselves attach to the curriculum reform? What struggles and dilemmas do principals face when they cope with the curriculum reform? There is a need to conduct more systematic empirical studies in order to probe into Chinese principals' worklives. The next section will present the major findings of an empirical study conducted in Shanghai. A significant portion of empirical evidence in the study seemed to support the general observations of principals' struggles as identified in the earlier literature.

STRUGGLES OF PRINCIPALS UNDER CURRICULUM REFORM

This section first briefly sketches the study conducted in Shanghai (Qian, 2009). Pertinent findings will then be presented in the form of three propositions in order to analyse the roles of the principals as they struggle with the curriculum reform.

The broader study aimed to understand how principals perceive and enact their leadership for learning in the current reform context in Mainland China. The reform context covered the three important policy initiatives currently being implemented in China, i.e., reform of the school review system, personnel reform, and curriculum reform. This chapter focuses on data relating to how principals interpret and implement the curriculum reform.

The Study

The study investigated the lived experiences of eleven secondary school principals in Shanghai as they sought to lead their schools within a context of ongoing education reform. In-depth interviews formed the major data-collection technique. All interviews were conducted in Shanghai schools in 2007 and 2008.

Purposive sampling was used to select participants. All participants were selected from secondary school principals. The High Exam is the point at which many debates over school curriculum and review policies converge. Due to the pressure of the High Exam, the work lives of secondary school principals and teachers are particularly fraught with tensions and dilemmas (Yin and Lee, 2008). Thus, the study focused on the senior secondary school level.

The major purpose of the study was to solicit principals' own interpretations and comments on the ongoing reform environment, and curriculum reform in particular. Many common interpretations emerging from the study provided empirical support to the struggles and concerns of principals which were teased out in the earlier literature (e.g., Zhang and Gu, 2005).

Emerging Propositions on Principals' Struggles

There appear to be three main realities of a principal's job which interfere with the efficacious implementation of curriculum reform. These realities have structural, cultural and relational faces. They can be captured in three propositions which are presented below and then teased out in greater detail.

1. Principals' time and energy are consumed by identifying and collecting resources for their schools. This detracts from time and energy available for focusing on the curriculum reform.
2. Despite the formal focus on successful curriculum reform, society as a whole continues to place its dominant expectations on performance on the High Exam.
3. Culturally and structurally engrained hierarchical relationships continue to determine what principals value and do. The messages carried through these relationships often run contrary to the rhetoric of the curriculum reform.

Proposition 1. Principals' time and energy are consumed by identifying and collecting resources for their school. This detracts from the time and energy available for focusing on the curriculum reform.

Chinese principals are concerned about financial responsibility. Principals appear to be worried about insufficient funding to support the development of their schools and to motivate teachers to do a better job. The capability to make more money for schools seems to have become a must for principals today. Principals have to, in their own words, "'beg for alms'" (*huayuan*) from various sources such as the local government, local enterprises, and parents (Zhang and Gu, 2005). Seeking financial support calls for principals' creativity. They have to lobby local education authorities to give their schools greater quotas to admit self-paying students (*zexiao sheng*), to seek donations from local enterprises and parents, or to engage in business activities such as renting their classrooms to all kinds of informal schools (Lin, 2000; Zhang and Gu, 2005). Seeking financial help consumes much of the principals' time and distorts their attention from teaching and learning. This often results in principals' personal and professional dilemmas.

In our study, principals also indicated that they had to put much of their time and energy into acquiring resources from outside of schools instead of monitoring teaching and learning within schools. Their logic for this was simple – teachers are the school's most important resource; in order to attract, keep and motivate them, a school needs money to reward them. Therefore, finding money is paramount. As Principal L said,

> "Nowadays people flow to places and work units that provide higher incomes. This is a consequence brought on by marketization."

Principal T explained that teachers also took their own financial welfare into careful account when they evaluated a principal.

> "Teachers definitely [take the income they can get at the school into consideration] when they evaluate a principal. For example, if I gave each teacher a 500 *yuan* bonus as a celebration for, let's say, International Labour Day last year, then they would expect me to

give them more this year. When I first came to the school, some teachers said 'here comes a new principal. Then how about giving each teacher 1000 *yuan* as a gift for the first meeting?' We have nearly 170 staff members. If I distribute 1000 *yuan* to each of them, what will be the total sum? You see, you cannot avoid talking about money. "

Thus, principals seemed to assume personal responsibility for taking care of teachers as soon as they became principals, just because that was what they were supposed to do. For example, as Principal X reflected:

"If I were not a principal, I would not have to worry about the financial issues. I would expect my principal to give me money. However, since I have taken the position of the principal, that means others will count on me to give them money. Then I have to get more money from different sources. So I have to please others and ask them to donate, instead of assuming for myself a superior role of an intellectual."

Thus, to please the major source of school resources – the government - many principals admitted that they had to spend considerable time attending meetings organized by various government departments. Principal J claimed that he had to devote at least one and a half days a week to attending meetings. Principal L said that few principals could continue to teach because of these interruptions.

"Since I became a principal, I have not conducted any serious teaching. There is no way for me to teach a major subject [Chinese, in his case]. If I teach a major subject, that means five to six teaching hours for one class. However, how can I have this amount of time? Time has to be devoted to attending meetings. If I did teach a major subject, students and parents would complain. It will happen that in the time slots I am scheduled to teach, I receive a conference notice and have to ask for leave. [As I cannot ensure the teaching time], I cannot teach any major subjects."

Even though the government remained the most important source of funding, principals knew they had to obtain additional resources from other sources. On top of regular recurrent funding (distributed on the basis of student numbers), the government had additional funds to allocate to schools in need. Whether a school had access to this money seemed dependent mainly on the competence of principals to persuade and make good relationships with the government. As Principal X said, the key was to make your superiors believe that your school was worthy of extra investment.

"The government will invest in a school that is worthy of the money. You cannot wait for the government to invest; instead you need to arouse their investment desires. For example, you can invite the government officials to come when your school has some celebrations or activities. When your school receives visits or inspections from the municipal government, you have to do your best because it concerns the face (public representation) of your direct leaders, the district government officials."

On top of "spare" government funds, principals actively tapped different channels for money. For example, although Principal T's school was under district administration, it was located geographically in a town (a smaller unit under the governance of the district). On just the third day of his principalship, he went to visit the township government officials. In return, they gave the school 50,000 *yuan*. This was seen as part of a reciprocal relationship. Principal T's visit showed his respect for the office and made the officials feel they had a face (*mianzi*). The money was given in recognition of this new relationship.

Thus, winning financial resources became one of the principals' top concerns. Consequently much of their time was distracted from school curriculum and instruction.

Proposition 2. Despite the formal focus on successful curriculum reform, society as a whole continues to place its dominant expectations on performance on the High Exam.

Winning financial resources is not the single detractor of principals' attention. What concerns principals most are students' academic results and school leavers' destinations. These have been the concerns of school principals in China for many years, even before the structural reform took place. However, the coupling of the increasing competition among schools, the financial stringency and the advocacy for quality education and curriculum reform has resulted in an increasingly complicated issue. Today, the success of a secondary school, at least in the eyes of parents and the public, is still judged by the college entrance examination results and the number of students who are admitted to universities. Academic results are also related to schools' financial well-being. Schools with higher admission rates are more likely to get financial support from local governments, parents and local enterprises, and *vice versa* (Zhang and Gu, 2005).

Given these considerations, it is not surprising that ensuring a high admission rate to universities is the top priority in many schools (Liu, 2005). To attract more students of quality, schools nowadays engage in all kinds of marketing strategies such as media advertisements, open days, home visits, and bonus awards (M. Wang, 2005; Zhang and Gu, 2005). In terms of teaching content, many schools also seem to reach a consensus that "what to be examined is what is to be taught in schools" (*ibid.*). This apparently contradicts the ethos of the new curriculum reform. Facing the dilemma, many schools prepare two sets of timetables and syllables. One set, attuned to entrance examinations, is actually adopted in schools, while the other is reserved for external assessment to show that the school is implementing the new curriculum reform (*ibid.*).

Our study showed that principals in Shanghai were not significantly different. The principals suggested that the main reason that the curriculum reform could not shift the emphasis from basic courses was because the examination system remained unchanged; the High Exam remains the single most important predictor of success. They explained that society as a whole, parents and superintendents, continued to judge schools in terms of their performance on the High Exam. Principals were very clear about this. Principal L condensed the Principals' feelings as follows:

> "The only criterion the society values in a high school is how many students can go to college. The school superintendents also view the school in this way. Thus, it is meaningless talking about [promoting all-round development] and cultivating more Lu Ban (a famous craftsman in ancient China) among students. One hundred Lu Ban cannot compare with a *zhuangyuan* (the person who achieves the highest score) in the High Exam."

Thus, although the curriculum reform aimed to change the teaching and learning "'process" by adding extended and research courses, it did not touch upon the "'outcome," that is, the exam system. As a result, many principals felt puzzled and uneasy about their role, especially as leaders of learning. Principal Y adopted a metaphor of "'balloon blowing" to the situation:

"We are blowing up a balloon…We put a lot of elements into the balloon and expect them to have some chemical reactions. .. We want students and teachers to be more active in the classrooms. We add in research courses and extensive courses. Then, what happens? We find the outlet of the balloon is the same and the evaluation criterion has not changed. People start to lose confidence in the curriculum reform. We are blowing up the balloon, but there are no other outlets. Many people, including principals, cannot understand it."

The confusion faced by principals, as they were torn between orthodoxy and policy rhetoric, was apparent at all levels. On the one hand, the principals saw clearly that the "real" success criteria remained unchanged and they were thus unwilling to risk shifting emphasis away from the High Exam. For example, Principals G and X frequently used the term "'bottom-line" to refer to the High Exam. In their opinions, if a school relaxed its focus on the High Exam, it would weaken its very foundation. On the other hand, the principals were also aware that they were expected to implement the new reform. Their perspective was that as a national reform it had to be implemented to demonstrate their loyalty to the government. For example, principals were interested in participating in the "research and extensive course design" competitions organized by governments of various levels. As Principal G explained, the research and extensive courses were like the frontiers that a school needed to explore because they could become a school "brand," and thereby boost their reputation. As such, the research and extensive courses were regarded as accessories that could be used for the purpose of advertising. In this case, the effectiveness of the new extended and research courses was questionable.

Proposition 3. Culturally and structurally engrained hierarchical relationships continue to determine what principals value and do. The messages carried through these relationships often run contrary to the rhetoric of the curriculum reform.

Guanxi is another key concern of principals. One consensus among principals is that establishing and maintaining *guanxi* (connections and good relationships) with important school stakeholders and other influential figures is important. As one school principal stated, "if you have *guanxi* [with those influential people], then nothing matters; if you don't, then everything matters" (Zhang and Gu, 2005). Good relationships with local government agencies can provide schools with all kinds of benefits, including financial support. The other side of the coin is that principals often get caught in the relationship network (*guanxi wang*) and, as a result, their decision-making autonomy is influenced by the hierarchical connections to accede to their superiors' wishes.

Our study also showed that maintaining good relationships, or *guanxi*, with the government was remarkably important to the principals. Principals were very conscious of their roles as state employees, and their accountability to, and their dependence on, the various government agencies. Principals' career progressions largely (and indeed, maintenance) depended on the government. As Principal J reflected:

"Principals are appointed by the government, thus we are required to be accountable to our superiors. We need to exert our rights according to the requirements of the state and the government. This is irrefutable."

Consequently, principals lacked autonomy and had little room for innovation. As Principal L commented:

"There are a lot of pre-conditions to make a school better. One important condition is the autonomy of the principal. However, what autonomy do we have? Everything has been tightly regulated. If you do something your superiors do not endorse, then you risk losing your position as a principal."

This lack of autonomy and the accompanying dependence on the government subjugated principals to a role "beneath" the government officials – rather than allowing them to be independent professionals. As principals understood their position was "beneath" the government officials, the vertical loyalty to superiors appeared to be taken for granted. As a result, most principals would not "make a fuss" or strive to establish their identity as independent professionals. As Principal J explained:

"It seems that principals never really think about whether it should be the principal or the government to be held accountable for the school. They do not think there is a need to think about this problem. They believe that it is a way of being responsible for the school by doing whatever they are required to do by the higher governments."

If principals did not view themselves as independent professionals, it was impossible for them to seriously use the power devolved to them to defend what was good for students in the long term. This happened when principals were granted the power to modify the curriculum. They still tended to choose to read and follow the stances of their superiors.

Findings from this study showed clearly that principals believed that although government agencies openly advocated the curriculum reform, in private they sent clear messages that schools were expected to achieve consistently good results in the High Exam and that this was the priority. Principal U provided further evidence of the ambiguous attitude of the local government. He recounted how, in the month of April, the district bureau had summoned all the high school principals and asked them to put the High Exam (scheduled in June) as their top priority. In the meeting, the district bureau even suggested that principals move their working desks to the Senior Three Teachers' Office. In other words, principals were expected to actively encourage teachers to focus strictly on improving better student exam scores and to monitor this carefully.

Consequently, principals mimicked the government stance. While not loosening the focus on exams, principals endorsed the curriculum reform in public. Achievements in areas defined by curriculum reform were always highlighted on school websites. Likewise, school publicity material devoted page after page to the *extended* and *research* courses designed by the schools. The articles, written by principals themselves, often listed the new school curriculum as an important achievement. In all, the principals deemed it "'clever" to demonstrate their adherence to the policy. Principal T's words reflect this:

"In this respect, I will not contradict the municipal education bureau. I am clever. There is nothing to bargain or discuss, because we are a public school. I just need to combine my interpretation with the policy during the process of implementation."

Thus, despite open support for the curriculum reform, real stories from schools paint a different picture. Although principals were rhetorically given the power to redesign and manage teaching and learning programmes, they had to use this power in a context that continued to value exam results over "student development." As a result, principals demonstrated a clear sense of priority in their daily work. They hesitated to use the curriculum power devolved to them and therefore drove few genuine changes in learning design and/or pedagogies. Their logic was remarkably pragmatic and followed a relatively simple logic. First, High Exam results are widely known by the public, and failure in the Exam disappoints and alienates parents and district education officials. Second, the *extended* and *research* courses demanded by reforms were not examinable, so that the outcomes of the courses were unlikely to be detected, at least in the short term. Therefore, the wisest path was to openly preach the virtues of the new curriculum but to keep the real emphasis on the High Exam. As Principal Y said, "you may find that the curriculum reform is haunted by various deceptions."

In general, Chinese principals' work was fraught with confusion and tension. The coupling of the traditional exam culture and *guanxi* obligations left them uncertain about what tack to take in terms of improving genuine student learning. The next section discusses the implications of the findings.

IMPLICATIONS AND CONCLUSION

The study showed principals today were driven by societal and (hidden) systemic considerations to prioritise and gear their leadership toward formal, measurable exam outcomes rather than less measurable reform-espoused outcomes. This situation carries at least three implications for leadership for curriculum change in Chinese schools, as well as in other countries aiming to make improvements around student learning.

1. School leaders can promote successful curriculum change only when learning goals are clearly and explicitly defined. Darling-Hammond and Ifill-Lynch (2006) explain, "struggling learners benefit when learning goals and the desired quality of learning products are public and explicit" (p. 13). Chinese principals, however, are often faced with ambiguous student learning goals that are defined by different people and on different occasions. It is undoubtedly difficult for them to promote authentic student learning in their schools. But is it impossible?

2. When there are multiple, complex and compelling internal and external forces demanding a school's attention, it is often the leadership shown by principals that can make a difference. Multiple studies (e.g., Leithwood et al., 2006; Militello et al., 2009) have shown that successful schools can harness these forces instead of allowing them to define their schools. A successful principal needs to know which forces are in play and how to respond to them. A successful principal will make the effort to ensure the alignment between personal, school and societal purposes of school leadership and to leverage all available forces to serve student learning. Can principals forge better alignment between apparently conflicting demands?

3. To harness the contradictory forces of reform and tradition and reinvent schools as dynamic entities, each school has to engage in learning. Learning should not only focus on the student and classroom levels, it should be prevalent across organizational levels. Studies (e.g. Hallinger and Heck, 1996, Leithwood et al., 2006) show that a principal's influence on student learning tends to be exercised indirectly through the conditions they create and manage. Thus, principals should enable and support teacher learning and ensure they continue to learn themselves. In other words, a leader engages in an ongoing, collective inquiry with others, particularly teachers, to promote student learning (Militello et al., 2009; Robinson, 2008). For example, when teachers are confronted by new instructional and pedagogical requirements while exam pressures endure, this can be used as an opportunity for professional debate and discussion to take place on how apparently contradictory forces can be usefully reconciled for the benefit of students, or how schools can internally align curriculum, instruction and assessment. The bottom line is that, even though the context may confuse and frustrate, successful curriculum leaders should try to overcome this within their schools. There is always some room for principals to negotiate approaches to student learning, which may involve, for example, focusing on student-based learning and holistic development in the first two years of senior high school and then devoting the final year to exam performance. Can principals use their position to drive change *within* their schools or clusters of schools?

In this chapter, we have attempted to sketch a picture of the challenges principals in China face as leaders of the new curriculum. The resulting picture has generally been portrayed as one of confusion and frustration as a result of trying to serve too many masters. However, as time goes by, the picture may not be as bleak as the one we have painted. Some positive signs are emerging as principals interact with the curriculum reforms.

The first of these is that the reform has challenged the dominant mindset which positions exams at the centre of student learning. Through being forced to confront the reform demands and different conceptualisations of student learning, change is influencing leadership by stealth. Concepts such as inquiry-based learning, integrated courses, creative thinking and holistic learning are now part of principals' language and, as such, have entered education discourse. The trick now is to convert this discourse into action and cultural change.

It may be that principals and teachers are presently working their way through the initial emotion-loaded phase of change and that real progress lies beneath this state of flux (Yin, 2008). Authentic change in schools is inevitably a slow process, and this is especially so when it challenges cultures that are so deeply embedded in the educative psyche. Time will tell, but it may be that the reforms currently making life so uncomfortable for many school leaders will result in more positive learning experiences for students in China.

REFERENCES

Chen, M. H. (2007). The anxieties facing principals in exerting curriculum leadership (xiaozhang kecheng lingdao de kunrao). *Shanghai Education*, (11B), 2-3. (in Chinese).

Cheung, M. B., and Walker, A. (2006). Inner words and outer limits: the formation of beginning school principals in Hong Kong. *Journal of Educational Administration*, *44*(4), 389- 407.

Chu, H. (2003). *Educational administration review [Vol. 1]* (*zhongguo jiaoyu guanli pinglun [diyi juan]*). Beijing: Educational Science Publisher. (in Chinese).

Darling-Hammond, L., and Ifill-Lynch, O. (2006). If they'd only do their work! *Educational Leadership*, *63*(5), 8-13.

Gu, M. Y. (2006). An analysis of the impact of traditional Chinese culture on Chinese education. *Frontiers of Education in China*, *2*, 169-90.

Hallinger, P., and Heck, R. (1996). The principal's role in school effectiveness: A review of methodological issues, 1980-1995. In K. Leithwood, J. Chapman, D. Corson, P. Hallinger and A. Weaver-Hart (Eds.), *International handbook of educational leadership and administration* (pp. 723-84). New York: Kluwer.

Leithwood, L., Day, C., Sammons, P., Harris, P., and Hopkins, D. (2006). *Seven strong claims about successful school leadership*. Nottingham, UK: National College of School Leadership.

Lin, J. (2000). Reform in primary and secondary school administration. In C. Dimmock and A. Walker (Eds.), *Future school administration: Western and Asian perspectives* (pp. 291-310). Hong Kong: The Chinese University Press.

Liu, X. (2005). Some thoughts on secondary and primary school principal responsibility system (dui zhongxiaoxue xiaozhang fuzezhi de sikao). *Ningxia Education*, (Supplementary), 7-8. (in Chinese).

Luo, Y. J. (2010). How many obstacles will curriculum reform meet (kegai haiyao guo jidaokan), *Shanghai Education*, (5), 18-20. (In Chinese).

Mao, L. (1984). *History of Chinese education* (*zhongguo jiaoyushi jianbian*). Beijing: Education Science Publisher. (in Chinese).

Militello, M., Rallis, S. F., and Goldring, E. B. (2009). *Leading with inquiry and action: How principals improve teaching and learning*. Thousand Oaks, CA: Corwin.

Qian, H. Y. (2009). The secondary school principalship in China: Leading at the cusp of change. Unpublished PhD thesis, The Chinese University of Hong Kong, Hong Kong.

Robinson, V. M. J. (2008). Forging the links between distributed leadership and educational outcomes. *Journal of Educational Administration*, *46*(2), 241-256.

Shanghai Education Commission (2004). *Opinions on promoting the stage-2 curriculum reform in primary and secondary schools (and kindergartens) in Shanghai.*

Shanghai Education Commission (2006). *Opinions of Shanghai education examination academic on 2006 high school entrance examinations and enrollment).*

Silins, H., and Mulford, B. (2002). *Leadership and school results: Second international handbook of educational leadership and administration*. Dordrecht, The Netherlands: Kluwer.

Sunoo, H. H. (1985). *China of Confucius: A critical interpretation*. Virginia Beach, VA: Heritage Research House, Inc.

Tao, X. P. (2006). *Promote the learning-centred school development and fasten the pace of teacher professionalisation* (*yi xuexi qiu fazhan, jiaokuai jiaoshi zhuanyehua bufa, tuidong xuexiao jiaoyu de neihan fazhan*). Keynote address at the Eighteenth National Conference of Chinese Education Association. Retrieved from http://www.xdxx.com. cn/show.aspx?id=1019andcid=17.

Wang, T. (2004). Understanding Chinese educational leaders' conceptions of learning and leadership in an international education context. Unpublished PhD thesis, The University of Canberra, Australia.

Wang, M. (2005). *Postponing publication of junior school leaving exam results: Competition for good students* (*tuichi gongbu zhongkao chengji: shengyuan zhengduozhan beihou cang yinyou*). Retrieved from http://education.163.com/05/ 0825/09/1S097F4U00290060.html.

Yang, R. (2005, April). *Education policy research in the People's Republic of China.* Paper presented to the Australia Association for Education Cairns Focus Conference, James Cook University, Cairns.

Yin, H. B. (2008). A study of teacher emotion: The context and framework (jiaoshi qingxu yanjiu: fazhan mailuo yu gainian kuangjia). *Global Education, 37*(4), 77-82. (in Chinese).

Yin, H. B., and Lee, J. C. K. (2008). An analysis of the tensions of Curriculum Reform: Source, types and solutions (kecheng gaige zhangli fenxi: genyuan, leixing yu xiaojie). *Exploring Educational Development*, (24), 49-54. (in Chinese).

Zhang, G., and Gu, C. (2005). Ten major concerns of Chinese principals (zhongguo xiaozhang shida yousilu). *The 21st Century Principals, 3*, 18-39. (in Chinese).

Zhong, Q. Q. (2006). Curriculum reform in China: Challenges and reflections. *Frontiers of Education in China, 1*(3), 370-382.

Zhong, Q. Q., and Yue, G. D. (2006). Curriculum leadership at the school level: Essence, power, responsibility and difficulties (xuexiao cengmian de kecheng lingdao: neihan, quanxian, zeren he kunjing). *Global Education, 35*(3), 7-14. (in Chinese).

Zhou, R. (2006). *Thirteen roles of good principals in the context of new curriculum reform* (*xinkegai beijing xia haoxiaozhang de shisanzhong juese*). Retrieved from http://edu. people.com.cn/GB/1055/4080384.html.

In: Curriculum Reform in China
Editors: Hong-Biao Yin and John Chi-Kin Lee

ISBN 978-1-61470-943-5
© 2012 Nova Science Publishers, Inc.

Chapter 5

CONDITIONS FOR SUCCESSFUL REFORMS: CHARACTERISTICS OF THE ORGANISATION AND CULTURE IN CHINESE SCHOOLS IN A GLOBAL CONTEXT

Jessica Harris, Yong Zhao and Brian J. Caldwell

ABSTRACT

Reforms to the basic education system in China have reflected an increasing awareness of and openness to new ideas from the global education sphere. Many of the concepts involved in the development and implementation of these reforms, including adopting holistic perspectives of student development; decentralising school governance to facilitate local decision-making to address local needs; and, an increased focus on practical, lifelong learning for all involved in schools, have been promoted in research and policies throughout the world. While working within this global context, the system of schooling in China has retained a unique character that is quite different from education in the West. Drawing on an international project on school transformation, this chapter aims to examine how five secondary schools in Chongqing, a municipality in Southwestern China, have harnessed and aligned their resources to provide effective school governance following the curriculum reforms. Furthermore, the chapter will examine the similarities and differences between the organisational structures and cultures of these schools in China and successful schools in Australia, England, Finland, Wales and the United States.

INTRODUCTION

Educators and policy-makers throughout the world are operating in a new environment. School systems of the past are no longer sufficient to prepare the students of today to participate in a globalised workforce and equip them with skills to work in the 21st Century. Educators, policy-makers and system leaders are thus looking to research and information from within and beyond national boundaries in order to shape reforms that will support student learning now and in the future. The organisation, culture and practices within schools that are recognised as supporting 'high performance' can offer unique insights into approaches that can be used by a system to effectively prepare students for lifelong learning. Research into how success is achieved within a system from the ground up provides a complementary perspective to the work, which looks beyond the boundaries of the system.

Significant increases in international comparative research have given educators, researchers and policy-makers greater understanding of the differences between school systems and also the shared characteristics that are evident in high performing school systems in different parts of the world. As in many other countries, those working in or for the education system in China have shown a growing awareness and openness to ideas, policies and practices that reflect research and educational movements from the global context (Halstead and Zhu, 2009; Niu, 2009). One of the most significant concerns about the increasing internationalisation of education in China, however, is that some international approaches do not pay adequate attention to issues of the complex organisation and cultures within the schools and school systems (Wang, 2007).

A number of the issues, ideas and approaches advocated in the international education field have been reflected in the Chinese national curriculum reforms. Responses to these national curriculum reforms, however, have resulted in changes that are unique to China and, importantly, to their local contexts (Harris, Zhao, and Caldwell, 2009). For instance, there has been international support for the implementation of student-centred, holistic approaches to schooling in order to prepare students to work in the 'knowledge economy' (Zhao, 2007). These approaches have been highlighted in China as part of debates around national examinations and the need to cultivate creativity (Guan and Meng, 2007; Zhao, 2009). Schools have further adapted these ideas and approaches to develop and deliver distinctive programs for their students. In this way, characteristics of school organisations can highlight unique features of their local, systemic and national contexts as well as reflect characteristics and trends that are evident beyond these boundaries.

In this chapter, we draw on findings from an international comparative study that examined the ways in which secondary schools in six countries harnessed their resources to support their transformation. Resources are defined broadly as forms of capital: intellectual, financial, social and spiritual capital. We describe the ways in which five successful secondary schools in Chongqing, a municipality in Southwestern China, strengthened and utilised each of the four forms of capital to develop strong school governance processes following significant changes in education in China. Particular reference is made to the similarities and differences in of the organisation, culture and governance of these secondary schools in Chongqing and schools in five other countries (Caldwell and Harris, 2008). The aim of this study was to develop a model that could adapt to identify features of specific school contexts. In addition to identifying a range of common elements in the approaches used by schools in these six countries, the project found that each school had developed their own unique strategies to strengthen and align the four forms of capital. As such, the strategies used by the five schools in Chongqing differed significantly according to their local needs and could not be claimed to be representative of approaches that may be used in other school contexts in China.

SCHOOLS

This chapter draws on the International Project to Frame the Transformation of Schools (IPFTS) (Caldwell and Harris, 2008). This project was an international collaborative effort, led by Melbourne-based Educational Transformations Pty Ltd, with financial support from the former Department of Education, Science and Training (DEST) of the Australian (Commonwealth) Government and the former Department of Education, Lifelong Learning and Skills (DELLS) of the Welsh Assembly Government. The project was undertaken in collaboration with a number of international partners, including the US-China Center for Research on Excellence in Education, based at Michigan State University (US) and Beijing Normal University (China); the University of Wales Institute, Cardiff (UWIC); SENTE – the Research Unit for Urban and Regional Development Studies, at the University of Tampere, Finland; and International Networking for Educational Transformation (iNet) of the Specialist Schools and Academies Trust (SSAT), England.

The primary aim of the IPFTS was to examine how successful secondary schools in six countries aligned and harnessed their resources to achieve transformation. The definition of transformation used for the purpose of this project was 'change... that is significant, systematic and sustained, resulting in high levels of achievement for all students in all settings' (Caldwell, 2006, p.27). In order to achieve the goal of transformation, schools draw on and align resources, namely financial, intellectual, social and spiritual capitals, as illustrated by the model in Figure 1. Caldwell and Spinks (2008) proposed that these four forms of capital are vital to the transformation process. They indicated that each of these forms of capital should be strengthened and aligned through school governance in order to support the needs of all students in their goal of achieving success.

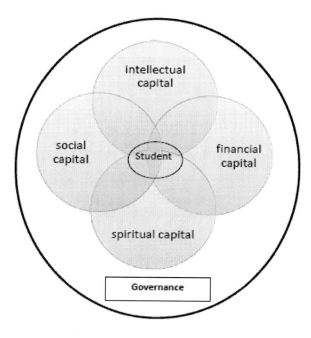

Figure 1. A model to frame the transformation of schools (adapted from Caldwell and Harris, 2008; Caldwell and Spinks, 2008).

METHODOLOGY

The IPFTS was carried out in two stages, involving the development and validation of the model in examining school governance processes. The first stage brought together extensive research from literature, workshops and seminars. Insights into school transformation were drawn from workshops and seminars with approximately 2500 school and school system leaders in 11 countries between 2004 and 2007. The input from these leaders were analysed and collated to create sample indicators of effective approaches to using and developing intellectual, social, spiritual and financial capitals through school governance. These sample indicators of effective provided a framework for the second stage of the project.

The second stage of the IPFTS aimed to validate these sample indicators through the examination of whether and where the indicators of effective practice were actually being used in schools around the globe. To enable this examination, Educational Transformations and international research partners conducted case studies of five secondary schools in each of the six countries: Australia, China, England, Finland, the United States and Wales. The case studies in China took place within the municipality of Chongqing and were led by Professor Yong Zhao from the US-China Center for Research in Educational Excellence (Zhao et al., 2008).

In order to identify five secondary schools that were recognised as supporting student success, each of the research teams within the six countries was asked to draw on their own or other expert knowledge of the relevant school systems. The schools that were selected had either made significant progress towards achieving transformation, had recently achieved their success or had maintained a high level of performance over a significant period of time. The five schools in Chongqing fell in the latter category, maintaining high levels of student achievement and strong reputations throughout reforms within the system.

The sample indicators of effective approaches for schools to strengthen and align the four forms of capital and governance were provided to the international research partners to frame their case studies in each setting. 10 sample indicators were provided for each form of capital and for governance, resulting in a total of 50 sample indicators. Researchers worked with the leaders and staff of each school to identify and describe the approaches that each school had adopted for developing, harnessing and strengthening their financial, intellectual, social and spiritual capital (Caldwell and Harris, 2008). The characteristics of each school were then examined in relation to the sample indicators, to participating schools in each country, and to schools from all six countries.

REVIEW OF LITERATURE

The model (Figure 1) was initially developed in response to extensive engagement with school and school system leaders, which suggested that successful schools, particularly schools that achieved success in disadvantaged settings, had developed approaches to governance that enabled them to strengthen and align four forms of capital with a focus on improving student outcomes (Caldwell and Spinks, 2008). Research on school governance and the four forms of capital further highlight the vital roles that each aspect of the model plays in supporting school transformations. Some of this research is discussed below.

Our project examining how secondary schools harnessed and aligned their resources to achieve transformation through effective school governance structures indicated that the four forms of capital do not work in isolation. Each form of capital works in conjunction with the others to shape, support and strengthen schools approaches to securing success for students, who are at the centre of all efforts. The strong relationships, depicted in Figure 1 as overlaps between the forms of capital, were clearly evident in the study of secondary schools in China (Zhao et al., 2008), particularly in the case of their social capital. Each of the schools in Chongqing had formed relationships with other organisations, including schools, universities, businesses and other organisations. These relationships not only shaped the schools' social capital but also strengthened their intellectual capital, providing staff and students with access to knowledge and skills that may not have otherwise been available. Schools were also able to draw on the support of parents (social capital) to strengthen their financial capital, through a variety of fees.

Financial Capital

The effective use of *financial capital*, or the monetary resources available to schools, has been the source of significant interest and concern throughout the world in recent decades. Over the past decade in China, there has been growing interest in the equity and efficacy of resource distribution within and between schools (Hu, Zhang, and Liang, 2009). There is now consensus in the literature that shows that although the financial capital of schools and school systems is important, increasing funding to schools alone is unlikely to result in significant improvements in student performance (e.g., Hanushek, 2004). This finding is highlighted in the McKinsey report (Barber and Mourshed, 2007), which indicated that, between 1980 and 2005, after adjustment for inflation per capita funding for schools in the United States had increased by around 73%. Over the same period, however, student performances in national assessments have remained relatively static.

Social Capital

The notion of *social capital* has been the source of considerable educational research over the past two decades. Numerous studies have identified links between forms of social capital and a variety of student outcomes, including improved behaviour, student retention and academic performance (Harris and Goodall, 2006; Henderson and Mapp, 2002; Lumby and Foskett, 1999). While social capital has been defined in numerous ways, in sociological, economic and education research, we will be using the term social capital to refer to "the strength of formal and informal partnerships and networks involving the school, parents, community, business and industry, indeed all individuals, agencies, organisations and institutions that have the potential to support and be supported by the school" (Caldwell and Harris, 2008, p. 59). Each of the secondary schools examined in China and, indeed in all of the settings in the international project, had implemented approaches to establish and support strong links with parents, their local communities, private organisations, and other schools and education providers.

Intellectual Capital

Intellectual capital refers to the levels of knowledge and skill of all of those who work in or for the school. The knowledge and skills of teachers, in particular, are of paramount importance to the quality of a school or school system and one of the greatest sources of influence on student performance (Barber and Mourshed, 2007; Dinham, Ingvarson, and Kleinhenz, 2008; Hattie, 2007). In their comparative study of high performing school systems around the world, Barber and Mourshed's (2007) indicated that there were three primary areas that education systems needed to address in order to improve their performance. These areas included: attracting talented staff; providing support for lifelong professional learning; and encouraging teachers to focus on the development of the range of talents held by each individual child. The IPFTS case studies, particularly those from China, indicate that schools that have achieved transformation are similarly focused on these three areas.

Spiritual Capital

The term *spiritual capital* is used to refer to the idea of moral purpose and the degree of alignment between the values, attitudes and beliefs about life and learning held by the school and members of its community. In comparison with the other notions of financial, intellectual and social capital, the concept of spiritual capital has only been recently developed and is currently emerging in the fields of economics and business (Zohar and Marshall, 2004).

Shared religious beliefs comprised one of the foundations of spiritual capital for three of the 30 case study schools in the IPFTS. While the majority of the schools in this project were secular, they had still established a strong spiritual capital through the promotion of their values and beliefs, which they worked to align with those held by their local communities. The schools in Chongqing and in other countries sought not only to support their students' physical, psychological and academic development but also their moral education and the development of their values and beliefs (Harris, Zhao and Caldwell, 2009).

Governance

There has been increasing awareness of the importance of effective school governance processes over the past decade (Millikan, 2002; Caldwell and Harris, 2008). Despite the important role of governance, however, there is no consensus within the literature on its definition. Definitions of governance have traditionally been concerned with structures, processes, authorities and responsibilities. For example, Keohane and Nye (2000, p. 12) define governance as 'the processes and institutions, both formal and informal, that guide and restrain the collective activities of a group'. For the purposes of the IPFTS and for this chapter, we are defining governance as the process through which schools build their financial, intellectual, social, and spiritual capital and align them to achieve their goals.

One of the most noteworthy findings of the international project was that the governance practices in the five secondary schools in each of the six countries involved in the research shared similar characteristics. Furthermore, while involving some shared characteristics of governance, each of the schools had developed unique governance processes for strengthening, harnessing and aligning the four forms of capital that were tailored to suit the needs of their local communities. When examining the shared characteristics of the case study schools from Chongqing, for example, we found that each school demonstrated a balance of centralised and distributed governance. Although the school principal is ultimately responsible for the school, a broader team of school leaders, most frequently including deputy principals, were involved in school governance processes. Each of these five schools had developed an appropriate form of distributed leadership, enabling deputy principals to take responsibility for specific aspects of the school.

FINDINGS

In this section, we describe how the five secondary schools from China that participated in the IPFTS harnessed and aligned the four forms of capital to achieve success. Our discussion will focus on how the governance processes, policies and programs of these schools have been influenced by a range of changes, including the curriculum reforms, socio-cultural changes within China and worldwide trends in education. Particular attention will be paid to the similarities and differences between the approaches used by schools in China and the IPFTS schools from Australia, England, Finland, Wales and the United States.

Financial Capital

All schools involved in the IPFTS faced similar issues regarding their financial capital. Regardless of the setting in which they operated, these schools reported that the funding that they received from the government was not sufficient to support all the programs, facilities and opportunities they provided for their students. This observation extends Wang's (1994) claim that 'the biggest problem of the Chinese education… is the financial scarcity' (cited in Hu et al., 2009, p. 34). Schools in all six countries sought further funding to support their financial capital.

One of the main issues of school funding in China following the implementation of localised funding and a 'market' approach to schooling is the considerable variation in resourcing in different parts of the country. The diversity between regions may disadvantage some schools, particularly those in regional and remote areas of China (Yan, 2009). The Chongqing government, however, allocates significant funding to compulsory education, including 500,000 RMB (around 70,000 U.S. dollars) annually for elementary and secondary schools that face financial difficulties. Tsang (2001, p. 18) indicates that schools generally receive around 64.8 percent of their funding from the government, raising 15.5 percent of revenue from school fees. Under the 'principal responsibility system', the principal is responsible for sourcing the remaining budget, which Tsang estimated at 19.7 percent. Where possible, however, schools attempt to increase the levels of funding gained through fees and other sources.

The case study schools in Chongqing indicated that schools with higher levels of financial capital were in an advantageous position. These schools were able to allocate significant funds to employ and support high quality staff (see discussion in intellectual capital), provide better access to technology and to improve their facilities and programs. In this sense, strong financial capital offers schools the opportunity to attract more students. On the other hand, schools that are not able to supplement their government funding, 'would not be able to attract better students or teachers, much less maintain their prior status' (Delany and Paine, 1991, p. 34). As such, schools are in fierce competition for possible funding and principals have adopted entrepreneurial methods for generating external money.

Like other schools in the IPFTS, participating schools in Chongqing proved to be highly effective in harnessing and building their financial capital. One of the strategies used to build financial capital, as suggested by Tsang (2001), was charging school fees and seeking donations from parents. The excellent reputations of these schools enabled them to set informal 'donation fees', which encourage parents to donate a specific amount, and 'school choice fees' at a government approved rate for students who would like to, but may have been otherwise ineligible to, attend the school. In some cases, such as Chongqing 8th Secondary School, the funds provided by parents through fees and donations can be as high as 200 percent of the amount provided by the government.

The second strategy used by these schools to develop their financial capital involved the formation of strong links or partnerships with private organisations. The prevalence of these partnerships in the IPFTS schools highlights the innovative and entrepreneurial approaches used by schools to increase their financial capital. Chongqing Yucai Middle School, for example, adopted an innovative "half public, half self-support" approach through its partnership with a private for-profit organisation and with support from the local government. Chongqing Yucai Middle School was able to cultivate the Yucai Jingkai campus as a successful and profitable private school that is managed by the partner organisation. The private Yucai Jingkai campus, in turn, provides Chongqing Yucai Middle School with valuable financial assistance.

The principals of the five secondary schools in Chongqing worked diligently to ensure that the school's financial capital was efficiently and effectively allocated. The principal of the Chongqing 18th Middle School, for instance, uses a long-term development plan to frame his annual budget. The school leaders regularly consult with the district government to identify social trends and develop their long-term plans and develop annual budgets that address the needs and priorities of the school and the local community. Financial capital is then used to address priorities, such as the development of new facilities, including an up-to-date gymnasium and modern laboratories. The careful planning and monitoring of the annual school budgets seen in schools, like the Chongqing 18th Middle School, demonstrates the commitment of schools to effectively allocate resources. This finding challenges the assertion by Hu and colleagues (Hu et al., 2009) that:

> As non-profit organizations, schools do not have any motivation to cost accounting and cost minimization. But when deciding resources allocation, most schools will maximize their benefit as principle because of their external effects. (p. 35)

The careful management of resources by the Chongqing 18th Middle School undoubtedly provides positive 'external effects', such as attracting more students and increasing the school's intellectual capital. The capable administrative team managing this school, however, also harnesses their financial capital to ensure that they are providing a high quality, holistic education for all of their students.

Intellectual Capital

The foundation of the strong intellectual capital for each of these schools in Chongqing was attracting high-quality, talented teachers. Under the principal responsibility system, principals have gained the ability to attract and hire new teachers (Zhao et al., 2008). Reforms in the teachers' employment system from a centralised, public employment to '*jiaoshi pinren zhi* (JPZ, a free contract employment system)' (Niu, 2009, p. 7) have dramatically changed the ways in which teachers are employed and distributed throughout China. Within this devolved system, teachers are able to select the schools at which they would like to work and, conversely, schools are able to recruit specific teachers.

In addition to having the ability to advertise and select teachers, schools in China have the opportunity to negotiate salaries with individual teachers. Teachers' salaries comprise a basic salary, a payment based on their ranking level, class-hour wages and achievement bonuses. The basic salary and additional payments based on the ranking level of teachers are determined according to a framework developed by the education authorities that takes into account teachers' qualifications and prior experience. The class-hour wages and achievement bonuses, however, are determined entirely at the school level (Zhao et al., 2008). Schools with stronger financial capital are able to set these salary components at a higher rate. Schools that achieve high rankings in the *zhong kao*, the high school entrance examination and the *gao kao*, the university entrance examination, often receive additional funds from the government and other sources. This type of supplementary funding can be used to increase the salaries offered to talented teachers, including *yinjin rencai*, the 'imported expertise' of teachers recruited from other schools (Zhao et al., 2008).

As a result of this free contract system, schools with higher levels of funding, strong reputations and those located in desirable locations, are often better able to attract high quality teachers. Niu (2009) argues that this has led to the inequitable distribution of quality teachers throughout schools, including a 'regional brain drain' with teachers moving from the less developed central and western parts of China and the eastern and coastal regions. There has also been the movement of teachers from rural into urban schools.

Each of the schools in Chongqing was able to harness their resources and their strong reputations to establish themselves as attractive destinations for teachers. Additionally, these schools worked diligently to attract talented teachers by demonstrating their commitment to teaching and learning, providing excellent working conditions and supporting the ongoing professional development of their staff. Two significant approaches to professional development were highlighted within these schools, including the involvement of research in professional development and the establishment of strong teams for teaching and learning.

The promotion of using research and research-based evidence to inform and improve teachers' professional practice was a focal point of strengthening intellectual capital in the Chongqing schools. The use of research to inform educational practices has been a focus of discussion and reforms at an international level (i.e., Dinham, 2008; Groundwater-Smith, 2000; Rowe, 2004; Slavin, 2002). In China, teachers' involvement in research and curriculum development was encouraged through the curriculum reform slogan of 'Teachers as Curriculum'. While Zhong (2006) indicated that the state of teacher-led research in China required dramatic improvement, the IPFTS found that China was the only country in which all five participating schools actively promoted teachers' use of and involvement in education research. In Qinghua High school, all school decisions from whole school governance processes to classroom activities are examined and informed by research evidence (Zhao et al., 2008). Teachers in this school are also encouraged to be actively involved in research projects, either individually or as a group. Support is given for teachers to present their research at local, national and international education conferences.

The schools involved in the IPFTS in Chongqing further supported the professional learning of their teachers through the establishment of formal collaborative supports. These schools implemented structures that enabled teachers to work in small teams, organised to involve a broad range of teachers and skill levels from those with little teaching experience to 'master teachers'. Experienced 'master' teachers are offered additional remuneration or fewer teaching hours as incentives to act as mentors. Under the leadership of a senior teacher, teams work together to improve their skills and ensure that each team member maintains high quality pedagogical and content knowledge. Collaborative activities, including classroom observations, teaching demonstrations and group lesson planning, are used to support the professional development of all team members. Furthermore, the involvement of teachers with a wide variety of experience levels in each group offers new teachers with access to the expertise of those with more experience.

All of the schools involved in the IPFTS had strong collaborative and research-based approaches to the professional development of all teachers. The participating schools in Chongqing, however, offered the only examples of formalised arrangements for ongoing in-house professional development activities within the six countries. The team approaches implemented in these five schools provided ongoing support for all staff and provided exemplars of how high quality teaching could be supported within a school environment.

Social Capital

The concept of social capital for these schools in China differed from the notions held in the five Western countries involved in the IPFTS. In the West, understandings of social capital tend to concentrate on the involvement of parents and the community in school activities. The case study schools from Australia, England, Finland, Wales and the United States all actively encouraged parents and other community members to attend school events, make use of school facilities and even participate in some of the decision-making processes within the school. These types of involvement were seen to reflect the strength of the relationships between the school and these community members, which formed the basis of the schools' social capital. In China, on the other hand, parents and members of the community do not traditionally participate in school life in these ways. Some schools, like Chongqing 37th Secondary School, however, appear to be working against this tradition by encouraging parents to be involved in school decision-making processes (Zhao et al., 2008). The majority of the case study schools in Chongqing, however, seemed to hold a different view of social capital.

Rather than focusing on their direct relationships with individual members of the community, the schools in China reported that they have worked to build their social capital by developing relationships with a range of organisations, agencies and institutions. Relationships with local organisations have enabled these schools to provide students with insights into different aspects of life, such as areas of the arts, business and the military. These relationships support the schools' aims to provide a more holistic approach to education for students. Furthermore, each school indicated that they collaborate with government agencies that play an important role in schooling in China to ensure that they have a strong understanding of local developments and plans. Like all of the case study schools involved in the IPFTS, the schools in Chongqing have established close working relationships with other schools, particularly schools in their local area that their students attended previously and/or may attend in the future. Some of the schools, including Chongqing Yucai Middle School, also maintain links with schools that share the same teaching philosophy.

A characteristic shared by schools in China and internationally is that each had developed positive relationships with local universities. These schools, however, had fostered relationships that would support them in unique ways. Some of the Chinese schools, for example, reported that their links with local teacher education programs and education research institutions provided their teachers with professional development activities and the chance to collaborate in educational research. Chongqing 8th Secondary School harnesses this aspect of their social capital to extend the range of opportunities that they can offer their students. Students at this school are able to attend weekly lectures that have been arranged in conjunction with the local university, which cover a variety of topics from social issues to particular aspects of student life. Thus, Chongqing 8th Secondary School has been able to harness its social capital to provide students with local expertise.

The case studies from China highlighted the strategic approaches taken by these schools in developing their social capital to expand other forms of capital. The collaborative relationships that they have developed with universities, schools and other educational institutions enhance the schools' intellectual capital by expanding the range of learning opportunities available to both staff and students. The strong relationships with other organisations in the local area provide these school leaders with greater access to knowledge about the plans, developments and needs of their local community. This knowledge and the ability to respond to local needs can help these schools to harness their social capital and develop the 'favourable social conditions' required for the successful response to education reforms (Zhong, 2006).

Spiritual Capital

The approaches adopted by the five secondary schools in Chongqing strongly reflected the national curriculum reform's focus on holistic approaches to learning. Staff from each of these schools reported their strong conviction of the importance of educating the 'whole' student, not only academic achievement. As such, these five schools had established programs and policies to support student development in a range of areas, including students' moral education. Traditionally, teachers in China are recognised as both experts in teaching and learning and as moral agents, who can support the moral education and development of their students. Zhu (2006) indicates that for a long period, a significant portion of moral education in China had been based on political issues. The curriculum reforms, however, emphasised the potential for moral education to be incorporated more fully within the curriculum to assist teachers in preparing their students for the future. The teachers from the IPFTS case studies in Chongqing indicated that they work with students to develop their skills in terms of both academic life and moral life. They aim to develop well-rounded students, who will contribute to their communities in a variety of ways.

One of the prominent features of spiritual capital in China is the high cultural value that is placed on teaching and learning. Teachers in China are traditionally regarded as highly respected members of society. Each of the case study schools in Chongqing reported that they felt it is important to recognise and publicly reward the work of their teaching staff. The principal at Chongqing 37th Secondary School, for example, described the school's strategy to praise high quality teachers and their achievements in public, whereas any suggestions or feedback regarding teachers' work are provided individually. This strategy has assisted in creating a motivated, enthusiastic and positive environment for the teachers and their students.

One of the most marked examples of schools developing their spiritual capital was identified in Chongqing 18th Middle School. In this school, the teachers' focus on the moral education of students led to the development of a moral education program. This program, entitled the 'Six One Moral Education Programme' (Zhao, Ni, Qiu et al., 2008) is designed to support students' moral education. The program uses a range of approaches, including, online work through a dedicated Web site, one-on-one counseling and course work. Visual arts, performance and creative writing are all used in this program to support students' wellbeing, integrity and social development. Chongqing 18th Middle School reported that the Six One Moral Education Programme had been very successful and, by December 2007, had received more than 400 visiting delegations from areas including Beijing, Macau and Britain.

Governance

The decentralisation of education management, and the 'principal responsibility system' (Zhao et al., 2008) created an environment in which the leaders from each of the case study schools in China were able to implement organisational structures and processes that suited the needs of their local communities. School principals are responsible for running the school and have power and authority over teachers. Under the 'principal responsibility system', principals were given responsibility for decision-making regarding personnel, finance, teaching, and instruction (Delany and Paine, 1991). While, the principals of the schools in Chongqing maintain primary responsibility for the overall development, efficient management and success of the school, the case studies highlight that each of these principals are supported in achieving this success. The IPFTS found that schools from all six countries had some form of distributed leadership as part of their approach to governance. Although all schools in this project had embraced the concept of distributed leadership, the approaches, practices and structures for leadership were developed to address the unique needs of each school.

In Chongqing 8th Secondary school, for example, the principal is supported by two governance teams, comprising of senior-level and middle-level leaders from the school community. The senior-level governance team involves between 6 and 7 people, including the school principal, the vice principals and the representative from the Chinese Communist Party. Each member of this senior-level governance team has adopted responsibility for specific aspects of the school governance. The vice-principals are responsible for liaising with the middle-level governance team, which includes around 20–30 members from throughout the school staff and representatives from the teachers' union, and reporting back to the senior-level governance team.

Although the responsibility for decision-making ultimately lies with the principal of the Chongqing 8th Secondary school, processes have been implemented so that no final decisions are made before all objections have been heard. The governance teams not only listen to objections from the staff, objections and critiques of proposed programs and policies are actively invited. The principal reported that he believes his staff are 'experts in finding logic underlying different matters' and are, therefore, a unique source of intellectual capital that the school can harness to support its governance processes. He stated that only by discussing, disagreeing and drawing on the knowledge and skills of staff members can the governance team arrive at sound decisions that are based on strong evidence, data and logic.

Other participating Chongqing schools adopt different approaches to shared decision-making and invite the involvement of stakeholders from outside the school staff. As noted in the section on social capital, Chongqing 37th Secondary, involves parents and teachers in a number of the decision-making processes within the school. Regular meetings, involving the principal, parents and teachers, are held to discuss and make decisions regarding the school's progress. The current direction and governance of the school are the result of effective collaboration and consultation between the school leaders, administrators, teachers and parents. By lending support to the governance processes, this type of non-traditional involvement of parents in school decision-making may be seen as a method to both support and harness the social capital of the school. The parents and staff of Chongqing 37th Secondary school recognise the principal as a visionary leader, who has transformed the working environment by leading with 'humanity'.

CONCLUSION

The organisation and cultures identified in Chinese schools are different from schools in other countries, including the Western countries involved in the IPFTS. These cultural differences have meant that the concepts of intellectual, spiritual, financial and social capital have taken somewhat different meanings. It is clear, however, that each of the Chongqing case study schools is strong in all of these dimensions and that they share important commonalities with schools in the five Western countries, including supporting teachers' continued professional learning to enhance intellectual capital, adopting entrepreneurial approaches to building financial capital, developing strong relationships between the schools and external organisations as part of the school's social capital, focusing on students' well-being to improve spiritual capital, and creating distributed approaches to leadership that suit the needs of the individual schools. These commonalities suggest a shared framework for assessing school progress toward transformation and for assembling new frameworks to assist in understanding governance and leadership in schools.

Findings from the IPFTS yielded a breakthrough in understanding governance in international contexts, which, in turn, provided a breakthrough in understanding leadership. Many recent reports and recommendations on school governance suffer from a shortcoming in their preoccupation with structures, roles, responsibilities and accountabilities. Questions addressed include: 'How should parents be involved in the decision-making processes of the school?'; 'Should a school have a governing body that includes representatives of different stakeholders, and what should be the role of the principal in such an arrangement?'; 'Should the governing body set policy and approve the school budget?'; or 'How should meetings of the governing body be organised?'

Securing answers to such questions is necessary if governing arrangements are to work. These answers differ from country to country and often differ from school to school within each country. While these may be necessary tasks, however, they are far from sufficient. A breakthrough in understanding arises from adopting a broader view of governance as the process through which the school builds its intellectual, social, financial and spiritual capital and aligns them to achieve its goals. The IPFTS demonstrated that this view of governance holds up across the six international settings.

Different models of governance are emerging. Those in the five schools in China were summarised in this paper. In England, new arrangements include federations of two or more schools as well as academies. In Canada and the United States there are charter schools. These involve new structures, roles, responsibilities, accountabilities and funding arrangements. While comprising a small minority of all schools, they constitute a break from more than a century of standard approaches to the governance of education in the public sector. The IPFTS found that, while there is no one best way as far as governance is concerned, all approaches have one thing in common: Each is attempting to get the best configuration of arrangements to build intellectual, social, spiritual and financial capital and align them to achieve the goals of the school, which, in most instances, is to secure success for all students. Transformation may occur when success calls for significant, systematic and sustained change.

REFERENCES

Barber, M., and Mourshed, M. (2007). *How the world's best performing school systems come out on top.* London: McKinsey and Company.

Bolman, L., and Deal, T. (2003). *Reframing organizations: Artistry, choice and leadership* (3rd ed.). San Francisco: Jossey-Bass.

Caldwell, B. J. (2006). *Re-imagining educational leadership.* Camberwell, Melbourne, Australia: ACER Press.

Caldwell, B. J. and Harris, J. (2008). *Why not the best schools?* Camberwell, Melbourne, Australia: ACER Press.

Caldwell, B. J., and Spinks, J. (2008). *Raising the stakes: From improvement to transformation in the reform of schools.* London: Routledge.

Chan, K. K. D., and Mok, (2001). The resurgence of private education in post-Mao China: Problems and prospects. In G. Peterson, R. Hayhoe, and Y. L. Lu (Eds.), *Culture and identity in twentieth-century China* (pp. 297-313). Ann Arbor: University of Michigan Press.

Cheng, Y. C. (2005). New paradigm of school leadership. In Y. C. Cheng (Ed.), *New paradigm for re-engineering education: Globalization, localization and individualization* (pp. 213-242). Dordrecht, Netherlands: Springer.

Clarke, D., Emanuelsson, J. , Jablonka, E., and Mok, I. A. C. (2006). *Making connections: Comparing mathematics classrooms around the world.* Rotterdam, Netherlands: Sense Publishers.

Delany, B., and Paine, L. (1991). Shifting patterns of authority in Chinese schools. *Comparative Education Review, 35*(1), 23-42.

Department of Children, Schools and Family (2008, June 18). *Seventy-nine new specialist schools announced* [Press release]. Retrieved 30 March 2009 from http://www.dcsf. gov.uk/pns/DisplayPN.cgi?pn_id = 2008_0118.

Dinham, S. (2008). *How to get your school moving and improving.* Camberwell, Melbourne, Australia: ACER Press.

Dinham, S., Ingvarson, L., and Kleinhenz, E. (2008). Investing in teacher quality: Doing what matters most. *Teaching talent: The best teachers for Australia's classrooms* (pp. 5-53). Melbourne, Australia: Business Council of Australia.

Douglas, E., and Harris, J. (2008). *Why not the best schools? The Australia report.* Camberwell, Melbourne, Australia: ACER Press.

Egan, D. (2008). *Why not the best schools? The Wales report.* Camberwell, Melbourne, Australia: ACER Press.

Epstein, I. (1982). An analysis of the Chinese national examination: The politics of curricular change. *Peabody Journal of Education, 59*(3), 180-189.

Goodfellow, M., and Walton, M. (2008). *Why not the best schools? The England report.* Camberwell, Melbourne, Australia: ACER Press.

Groundwater-Smith, S. (2000, December). *Evidence-based practice: Towards whole school improvement.* Paper presented to the annual conference of the Australian Association for Research in Education, Sydney, Australia. Retrieved 27 September 2003 from http://www.aare.edu.au/00pap/gro00303.htm.

Guan, Q., and Meng, W. (2007). China's new national curriculum reform: Innovation, challenges and strategies. *Frontiers of Education in China, 2*(4), 579-604.

Halstead, J. M., and Zhu, C. (2009). Autonomy as an element in Chinese educational reform: a case study of English lessons in a senior high school in Beijing. *Asia Pacific Journal of Education, 29*(4), 443-456.

Hanushek, E. A. (2004, August). *Some simple analytics of school quality*(National Bureau of Economic Research Working Paper 10229). Invited paper presented at the Making Schools Better Conference of the Melbourne Institute of Applied Economic and Social Research, University of Melbourne, Australia.

Harris, A., and Goodall, J. (2006). *Parental involvement in education: An overview of the literature.* Unpublished manuscript, prepared for the Specialist Schools and Academies Trust, UK.

Harris, J. (2009). Global characteristics of school transformation in China. *Asia Pacific Journal of Education, 29*(4), 413-427.

Hattie, J. (2007, August/September). *Developing potentials for learning: Evidence, assessment and progress.* Paper presented at the 12th Biennial Conference of the European Association for Research on Learning and Instruction, Budapest, Hungary.

Henderson, A. T., and Mapp, K. L. (2002). *A new wave of evidence: The impact of school, family, and community connections on student achievement.* Austin, TX: National Center for Family and Community Connections with Schools.

Hu, Y., Zhang, Z., and Liang, W. (2009). Efficiency of primary schools in Beijing, China: an evaluation by data envelopment analysis. *International Journal of Educational Management, 23*(1), 34-50.

Keohane, R. O., and Nye, J. S. (2000). Introduction. In J. S. Nye and J. D. Donahue (Eds.), *Governance in a globalizing world* (pp. 1-44). Washington D.C.: Brookings Institution.

Liu, C., Zhang, L., Luo, R., Rozelle, S., Sharbono, B., and Shi, Y. (2009). Development challenges, tuition barriers, and high school education in China. *Asia Pacific Journal of Education, 29*(4), 503-520.

Lumby, J., and Foskett, N. (1999). *Managing external relations in schools and colleges.* Thousand Oaks, CA: Sage.

Millikan, R. H. (2002). *Governance and administration of schools: The importance of stability, continuity and high quality board and school leadership.* Victoria: IARTV.

Ministry of Education (1993). *Framework for China's education reform and development (zhongguo jiaoyu gaige he fazhan gangyao).* Retrieved 21 April 2009 from http://www.moe.edu.cn/edoas/website18/level3.jsp?tablename=208andinfoid = 3334.

Ministry of Education (2007). *2006 national statistical report on educational expenditure (jiaoyubu guojia tongjiju caizhengbu guanyu 2006 nian quanguo jiaoyu jingfei zhixing qingkuang tongji gonggao).* Retrieved 21 April 2009 from http://www.moe. edu.cn/edoas/website18/30/info1203404952861630.htm.

Niu, W. (2007). Western influences on Chinese educational testing. *Comparative Education, 43*(1), 71-91.

Niu, Z. (2009). Reforms on teachers' employment system and children's rights to education in China. *International Journal of Educational Management, 23*(1), 7-18.

Rowe, K. J. (2004, August). *The importance of teaching: Ensuring better schooling by building teacher capacities that maximise the quality of teaching and learning provision – Implications of findings from emerging international and Australian evidence-based research.* Invited paper presented at the Making Schools Better Conference of the Melbourne Institute of Applied Economic and Social Research, University of Melbourne, Australia.

Saarivirta, T. (2008). *Why not the best schools? The inland report.* Camberwell, Melbourne, Australia: ACER Press.

Sergiovanni, T. J. (1984). Leadership and excellence in schooling. *Educational Leadership, 41*(5), 4-13.

Slavin, R. E. (2002). Evidence-based education policies: Transforming educational practice and research. *Educational Researcher, 31*(7), 15-21.

Tsang, M. C. (2001). School choice in the People's Republic of China. Retrieved 20 August 2010 from http://www.teacherscollege.edu/ centers/coce/pdf_files/b1.pdf.

Wang, T. (2007). Understanding Chinese educational leaders' conceptions in an international education context. *International Journal of Leadership in Education, 10*(1), 71 -88.

Yan, W., and Ehrich, L. C. (2009). Principal preparation and training: A look at China and its issues. *International Journal of Educational Management, 23*(1), 51-64.

Yang, J. (2005, August). *High school education in China: Challenges and priorities* [PowerPoint presentation]. Paper presented at the ECS National Policy Forum, Denver, Colorado.

Zhao, Y. (2009). *Catching up or leading the way: American education in the age of globalization.* Alexandria, VA: ASCD.

Zhao, Y. (2007). China and the whole child. *Educational Leadership, 64*(8), 70-73.

Zhao, Y., Ni, R., Qiu, W., Yang, W., Chen, Q., and Zhang, G. (2008). *Why not the best schools? The China report.* Camberwell, Melbourne, Australia: ACER Press.

Zhao, Y. , Ni, R. , Yang, W. , Chen, Q., and Zhang, G. (2008). *Why not the best schools? The US report.* Camberwell, Melbourne, Australia: ACER Press.

Zhong, Q. (2006). Curriculum reform in China: Challenges and reflections. *Frontiers of Education in China, 1*(3), 370-382.

Zhou, M. S. (2003). *Chinese education financing system and its challenge* (*woguo jiaoyu touzi de tedian yiji suo mianlin de wenti*). Retrieved 21 April 2009 from http://www.ep-china.net/article/economic/2003/07/20030726145020.htm.

Zhu, X. (2006). Moral education and values in curriculum reform in China. *Frontiers of Education in China, 1*(2), 191-200.

Zohar, D., and Marshall, I. (2004). *Spiritual capital: Wealth we can live by.* San Francisco: Berrett-Koehler.

PART III. CHANGE IMPLEMENTATION IN SUBJECT AREAS

In: Curriculum Reform in China
Editors: Hong-Biao Yin and John Chi-Kin Lee

ISBN 978-1-61470-943-5
© 2012 Nova Science Publishers, Inc.

Chapter 6

MATHEMATICS CURRICULUM REFORM IN CHINA: LATEST DEVELOPMENTS AND CHALLENGES

Rui Ding and Ngai-Ying Wong

ABSTRACT

In this chapter, we will offer a full picture of the most recent developments of the Chinese mathematics curriculum reform, including its background, goal, implementation and debates that arose. Factors leading to the success of curriculum reform will be discussed. They include political and economic factor, examination culture, social participation, textbook development and teacher preparation. We believe that all these events will not inspire mathematics education but curriculum innovations in general.

BACKGROUND OF THE CURRICULUM REFORM

Shortly after the Cultural Revolution in China in 1978, entrance examinations at all levels resumed. At the same time, the Ministry of Education released the new primary and secondary mathematics curricula, which the authorities stressed to have incorporated the current international trend of learning and teaching (Su and Xie, 2007). In 1986, the free education law was announced and the government started to implement the nine year free education. In response to this, the Ministry of Education worked out another mathematics teaching guide in accordance to three principles: appropriately reduce the toughness of the content; relieve the learning burden of the students; make the teaching requirements more explicit. The two basics (basic knowledge and basic skills) and the three abilities (computational ability, logical thinking, and spatial sense) were formally made as the key goal of mathematics teaching (Shi and Ma, 2009). In 1992, another new curriculum guide was issued which aim shifted from examination orientation to nurturance of quality citizens. Six sets of mathematics textbook were thus developed in line with the "One curriculum, Diversify textbooks" policy. The policy was replaced by "Diversified curricula, Diversified textbooks" policy in 1997, under which curricula different to the central curriculum was tested in Shanghai and Zhejiang. As time passed by, it was found that the original mathematics curriculum were too "difficult, complicated, prejudiced and obsolete". A new round of mathematics curriculum reform took place in 2001 amid the full-scale implementation of free education and the shifting orientation of mathematics education from elite to universal. Consequentially, the new Mathematics Curriculum Standard (MCS: Ministry of Education, 2001) was issued in July in the same year. In addition, the trial textbook was tested in 38 experimental regions in September, involving 200,000 students. The scale of experiment expanded in yearly basis. After five years of trials and testing, in 2005, the new curriculum was successfully launched. Unfortunately, the reform was accompanied by controversies and reflections.

OBJECTIVE OF THE REFORM

In the MCS, it was stated that "All students should learn mathematics, and school mathematics curriculum should be essential and appropriate for students" (Ministry of Education, 2001, p.1). The overall aim was shifted from the content-based knowledge acquisition to nurturance of a holistic person and laying a firm basis for life long learning.[9]

Constructivism was reflected in different aspects of the MCS including the mathematics learning content, learning methods, mathematics teaching and learning activities and assessment. For instance, it was said that "students' mathematics learning content should be realistic, meaningful and challenging; mathematics learning methods should not rely solely on intimating and memorizing, leaving hands on application, self-exploration, cooperation and exchange; mathematics teaching and learning activities should be established upon student's cognitive development level and pre-acquired knowledge experience foundation; assessment content should focus on students' learning process (learning methods, emotions and attitudes) as well as their learning outcome (knowledge, skills)" (Ministry of Education, 2001, p.2). Thus, the new MCS's targets were not only knowledge and skills based, but also process based emphasizing on student's pre-acquired living experience and learning process experience. All these showed that China's new mathematics curriculum was shifting from the emphasis of the two basics towards a constructivist approach. This was a fundamental change in the mathematics learning and teaching in China.

IMPLEMENTATION AND EFFECTIVENESS OF THE REFORM

To materialize the aforementioned ideologies in the new MCS, various suggestions were raised to ensure the smooth implementation of the new curriculum. For teaching and learning, the MCS stressed realistic simulations as well as cultivating ability of students to self-explore, to cooperate, to discuss, to question and to find solutions to problems. As for assessment, the MCS put forward the methodology of diversified assessment to tab students' higher order thinking abilities. For textbook development, one should take into account of student's experience in daily life, and opportunities should be provided for student to think, present and exchange (mathematical) ideas, utilizing their basic knowledge in mathematics (Ministry of Education, 2001).

---

[9] Details please referred to Liu & Li (2010).

Liu and Li (2010) summarized some prominent changes in classroom teaching over the past decades of curriculum reform, which included changes in learning objectives, teaching method, teacher-student relationships and assessment strategies.[10]

That brought about tremendous change in textbooks as well. As mentioned above, after the establishment of New China, the textbook policy changed from "One curriculum, One textbook" to "One curriculum, Diversified textbooks". But at that time, only a few provinces including Jiangsu, Beijing, Shanghai and Zhejiang developed textbooks for their own use. Others were using the centralized textbook published by the Peoples' Educational Press. The scenario changed with the new curriculum reform. Taking primary mathematics as an example, six different versions of the textbook was developed. Each version had its own characteristics, but all of them focused on student's everyday experience, enhancing students' motivation to learn and boosting their problem solving abilities. Moreover, these textbooks toned down the unreasonably tough requirements on students' manipulation skills; alternatively, more emphasis was paid on students' verbal numerical calculation and estimation skills. Besides, different approaches to a single problem were encouraged; more open problems and application problems were provided. Both numerical and statistical senses were stressed. The new curricula allowed more flexibility for students to think, explore, and manipulate, which emphasized the generating process of knowledge (Jin, 2005; Liu and Li, 2010).

The Ministry of Education carried out two large scale evaluations on the implementation of the new curriculum in 2003 and 2005. The evaluation showed initial success of the new curriculum. Yet the curriculum reform did face a number of challenges, including the differences between urban and rural area, between primary and junior secondary, and the need to strengthen curriculum resources (Ma and Tang, 2004). Half of the teachers surveyed thought that the curriculum content was too difficult or a little bit difficult and the assessment methods did not align with the goals of the curriculum reform (Shi and Ma, 2009).

Ma (2008) analyzed the reasons of problems arisen in Chinese curriculum reform, "at the beginning, the implementation of the new curriculum is relatively slow, the number of national and first-tier provincial experimental regions is limited and more refine work should be done on organization management, experiment design and teachers development. Also, [since] those provinces which participated in the first phrase of experiment are voluntary and [thus] have a better background and preparation" (p.165). Followed by the urge to speed up the curriculum reform, the original ten-year plan of nationwide curriculum reform was shortened to five years, the experimentation was only carried out in larger scales from 2003 and entered into full fletch since 2005. The rapid increase of school and teachers took part into the reform led to the lagging behind of textbook development and teaching education. Other problems have arisen as well.

Ding's (2010) study on the learning environment in mathematics classroom under the new MCS also revealed that the reform did bring about changes. In particular, student's participation, exchange among students, group discussion, sharing of classmates' opinions were increased. Also, teachers gave students more room for exploration and opinion sharing. Students realized that mathematics was no longer limited to the knowledge in textbook, but could be discovered in daily lives. However these also led to various issues. For instance, group discussion was not well suited to all students; some problems for discussion were either

---

[10] Please refer to Liu & Li (2001, pp. 20-21) for more details.

too hard or too trivial. In addition, to increase students' interest, teachers set aside more formal teaching time for games, discussions, and stories which originally aims at motivating student learning, results in a drop of numerical and problem solving skills. This led to the doubt on the effectiveness of new curriculum among mathematics teachers. Although the connection between mathematics and daily lives had been strengthened and student's interests in learning were enhanced, some mathematics teachers questioned whether it was mathematics itself or something unrelated to mathematics that attracted the students. Though the students were expressive, not all the teachers were willing to accept opinions from students. Some teachers even thought that students were too keen on debate while their arguments were incomplete. The most serious problem perceived by the teachers was that the problem solving skills, which was emphasized in the new curriculum, was not detailed systematically in the curriculum. Thus it was difficult for them to teach, as a result, student's problem solving abilities dropped considerably.

DEBATES CIRCLING AROUND THE REFORM

Though the curriculum reform gained some initial success, it faced oppositions from frontline teachers (basically about the pace) and criticisms from scholars like Zheng (2007). The most critical ones came from two world renowned scholars, Wuxi Xiang and Hung-Hsi Wu. The former helped China to develop its experimental mathematics teaching material in the 1980s and the latter was a key figure of the *California Math War* (Jackson, 1997a, 1997b). The debate reached its climax as another renowned mathematician Boju Jiang, Professor at the Peking University and Fellow of the National Science Academy made a petition during National People's Congress and Chinese People's Political Consultative Conference in 2005, calling for a halt of the new mathematics curriculum (Jiang, 2005a). Some called it the *Chinese Math War*, though some hesitated in calling it a "war". While we refer the readers to Ma, Wang, Zhang, Liu, and Guo (2009), Shi and Ma (2009), Su and Xie (2007) and Sun (2008) for a better account of the reform, we will look at various facets of the debate in what follows.

Theoretical Foundation

Naturally, constructivism became one of the focal points of the debate and many doubts on whether it was appropriate to adopt constructivism in the reform (Teng and Zhao, 2005). Incidentally, constructivism was also advocated in the mathematics curriculum reform in Taiwan.[11] Though it is suggested in *The interpretation of "guidelines on basic education curriculum reform* [12] " (Zhong, Cui, and Zhang, 2001) that constructivism was only a reference point in the implementation of quality education, Jin and Ai (2005) queried whether the new MCS was laid on solid theoretical foundation and they suggested the foundation should instead lay upon the Marxist holistic individual development theory. Some others (e.g., Gao, 2005; Ma, 2005) opined that people should not solely rely on the Marxist

---

[11] Please refer to Ding, Wong, Ma, & Lam (2009) for more details.
[12] It is a guideline for curriculum reform across different subjects.

epistemological theories in curriculum development. Liu (2005) tried to offer a more flexible view by saying that not only Marxism, other current educational theories like multiple intelligence should also be incorporated. However, He (2005) believed that constructivism was still a valid reference point, because of that more emphasis has been put on application of knowledge than on theoretical development of knowledge among professional posts in China.

The Subject or the Person?

In sum, the discourse had moved from practical (e.g. implementation strategies) to ideological issues. In sync with the "p (product) – p (process)" issue raised since the 1970s (Wong, Han, and Lee, 2004), the famous *Wang – Zhong Debate* about the relationship between (learning) the subject and (nurturing) the person was heated (Jiang, 2006). The idea that different subject areas were nothing more than an artificial compartmentalization was repeatedly raised in the West (Drake, 1998; Beane, 1997). On one side, Wang (2004) criticized that contemporary education "depreciates subject knowledge and textbook knowledge but emphasizes self-centeredness and everyday experience. This student-oriented approach weakens the role of teachers. Exploration and discovery are advocated while lecturing and inspiration are degraded." On the other, Zhong and You (2004) argued that the nurturance the student should be of the top priority especially in universal education. Moreover, knowledge acquisition was unlimited and one could learn them back in their adult life through self-study if they were equipped with such ability in the first place. This was in concord with the western idea of "learning to learn". However, some pointed out that teacher and student centredness may not necessarily in conflict. There is as possibility of having a *teacher-led yet student-centred* learning environment (Watkins, 2008; Wong, 2009). As for the comments of the traditional school curriculum being too *subject-centred*, Luk (2009) pointed to the difference between subject and discipline; the latter include a set of practices and an entire system of thought. In a sense, learning mathematics was not (just) for learning mathematics' sake.

When the above debate was translated into mathematics and the mathematics curriculum reform in particular, Zhang (2005) called for the clarification of the relationship between *basics* and *creativity*, the relationship among *mathematical knowledge, mathematical abilities* and *mathematical competence*. The *two basics* should not be neglected and should not be dichotomized with abilities. The *two basics*, which scholars like Jiang (2005b) and Zhang (2008) treasured so much and took as a crucial part of Chinese mathematics tradition, should serve as a foundation for students' life long development and nurturance of creativity.

Implementation

Some issues arisen from the implementation process too. For instance, Zhang (2005) reckoned that mathematics was a subject of strict logical sequences so mathematics learning should follow strictly with the logical sequences. Furthermore, there were traditional and difficult topics in school mathematics, but they should not be cancelled, because they could serve as foundations for future learning and they serve as an irreplaceable platform for students' future development of mathematics abilities. Plane (Euclidean) geometry was one example. Cao (2005) concluded that these conflicts laid in subject (content) knowledge versus ability and subject versus person. Those at stake were frontline teachers, mathematics education researchers and mathematicians. Sun (2008, p.81) further summarized the dispute:

- Realistic versus formal: more or less?
- The traditional teaching system: stronger or weaker?
- The speed of implementing: quicker or slower?
- Being scrupulous (*conscientious and exact*) or being active. Can the balance be kept?
- "*Two basics*" (basic knowledge and skills): stronger or weaker?

RECENT DEVELOPMENTS

Nevertheless, China did not call for a halt of the new curriculum but rather involved mathematicians in the revising of MCS. During the process of revision, *receptive learning* and the *two basics* once again earned their regards (Shi and Liu, 2007). Such a move was described by Zhang (2008b) as the *rational return* of the mathematics curriculum reform (i.e. returning to rational discussion after all these emotional debates).

In the process of revising the MCS, about 30 experts, scholars, fellows from the National Science Academy and frontline teachers were recruited into the review panel. The revised MCS was completed in December 2007. Although the revised version was not yet officially published, its basic rationale was widely recognized and some regions had already started studying the revised standard. The *two basics* were once again recognized, in addition, it was further extended to the *four basics*, which included *basic thoughts* and *basic experience on activities* (Shi and Liu, 2007). The long standing "p – p" issue was basically settled. Below were some significant changes in the revised MCS (Ministry of Education, 2009; Revision committee for MCS in Free Education period, 2007):

1. On mathematics. Mathematics was described as the science of quantity and shapes, which was the original intrinsic definition.
2. On curriculum goal. The original goal was "All students should learn mathematics, and school mathematics should be essential and appropriate to students". In the revised MCS, it was amended to "All students should acquire good mathematics education, and school mathematics should be appropriate to different students", indicating that everyone should receive good mathematics education.
3. On teaching and learning activities. The revised MCS suggested that "it is a process that both teachers and students participate, exchange and interact. Effective mathematics teaching and learning activity is a unification of teacher's teaching and student's learning. (Though) the student is the owner of mathematics learning, the teacher is the organizer and facilitator". And it also promoted to nurture students good learning habit.
4. On learning methods. The revised MCS affirmed self-exploration, cooperation and discussions, while also accepted receptive learning as one of the ways of learning mathematics.

From the above, the rationale of the revised MCS did not undergo a drastic change from the original one. Trying to reinforce instead of disregard of the original strengths of Chinese mathematics, it showed respect for traditional ways of mathematics teaching and learning. Meanwhile, new initiatives like inductive reasoning and the utilization of activities in teaching were also clearly promoted. Re-focusing on mathematics *per se* (and not just generic learning aspects) was regarded as the major contribution of including mathematicians in the revision process. What is next in the reform agenda should be the revision of the examination system and the assessment mechanism, without which would make the implementation of reform unsuccessful. In 2009, the Ministry of Education called for the application of projects on reviewing the examination system. This reflected the important role of examinations played in Chinese education.

FACTORS LEADING TO THE SUCCESS OF CURRICULUM REFORM

Political and Economic Factor

China started economic reform in 1978 and implemented market economy in 1992. The National GDP rose steadily and China entered the World Trade Organization in 2001. The new economic system called for a new education system to provide creative elites to facilitate aspects of development in China. The basic education curriculum reform tried to response to the needs of national economic development from all aspects, such as objectives of curriculum, organization of curriculum, standard of curriculum, process of teaching and learning, as well as textbooks development and examination (Feng, 2006).

In this recent curriculum reform, Chinese educators were pressed for providing visible and promising results in limited timeframe. In a word, people thought that the reform should be a revolutionary rather than a gradual process. Shortsightedness of policy makers was one of the crucial factors that led to the various issues sprung out from the curriculum reform (Feng, 2004).

Examination Culture

Examination had a long tradition in China and it had become a sensitive and difficult issue (Wong, 2004). After the curriculum reform, a lot of assessment slogans like formative assessment, performance based assessment, and portfolio assessment emerged. But still, examinations with a selection purpose in China, like college entrance examination, senior/secondary school entrance examination or even secondary/primary entrance examinations were at very high stake. Any change in the formats of these examinations would lead to strong reactions. It was even said that "without changing the advanced level examination, the curriculum reform is difficult to implement" and "without reforming the advanced level examination, the assessment reform is pointless" (Cui, Wang, and Xiao, 2008, pp. 4-5). All in all, the reform of assessment directly affected the curriculum implementation and its effectiveness.

Social Participation

What is encouraging is that in this round of curriculum reform, many mathematicians actively responded. They cited their opinions, participated in discourses, took part both in curriculum reform and the revision of it. Although it is common around the globe that curriculum reform incorporated the views of stake holders (the holistic review in Hong Kong, for instance: Wong, Lam, Leung, Mok, and Wong, 1999), it was first seen in China. Their participation made policy makers realized that following the international trend was just one facet of curriculum development, the views of stake holders, those of subject experts (in this case mathematicians), shouldn't be neglected.

Textbook Development and Teacher Preparation

The development of quality textbooks and teacher continuous professional development are crucial to curriculum reform. The textbook market was opened for the first time but the quality varies. For instance, some textbooks become livelier, but the logical sequence was sometimes not being well taken care of (Li, 2006). Given limited time, some textbooks could not be published on time and teachers had to refer to the original textbooks for the key concepts. As a result, the blending of old and new textbooks brought about confusion in their teaching (Ding, 2010).

China had invested a lot in teacher professional development on the new curriculum, but there still existed a lot of problems. For instance, teachers reflected that some of these courses still laid too much emphasis on the delivery of new curriculum contents, some of which were too theoretical (Lin and Jin, 2005). The teachers were unsure of how to put theories into practices. Also, we should not rely solely on crash courses, and we should have long-term plans for continuous professional development (Ma, 2008). An investigation conducted during a training class showed that short term intensive training was not adequate as a lot of teachers lost their passion and motivation when they returned to their school because they lacked the support of principals and colleagues. In order to meet the requirement of official checking and public lessons, superficial constructivist practices, like holding group discussions in all lessons, are commonplace.

Constructivism concerns the nature of knowledge and its acquisition rather than specific teaching methods (Zheng and Wong, 1997). Therefore, the so-called constructivist teaching with superficial constructivist features was in fact contradictory to constructivism itself. In the MCS and its related documentations, group co-operation, exploration, authentic situation problem solving were stressed, as a result, mathematics lesson merely turned from all-time indoctrination to having the whole lesson filled with "question and answer" sessions, or even having students running around for the whole lesson (Guo, 2003; Wong, 2004). Drilling on algebra and geometry problems had turned to drilling on project report writing. Again, the role of students has shifted from listening attentively to chatting in small group discussions without much independent thinking. Students were over-burdened since they not only had to wrestle with mathematics exercises, but also with a lot of projects.[13] Daily life situations did

---

[13] For more discussions, one is referred to Wong, Han, & Lee (2004).

motivate the students to participate, yet people starts to question whether we were distracting students' attention away from mathematics.[14]

CONCLUSION

Education is a long term investment and hasty implementation of inappropriate policies could create counter-effects (Hargreaves and Shirley, 2009).While seeking for international insights, we should consider to what extent could these foreign experiences fit into local culture (Wong, 2009; Wong, Han, and Lee, 2004). Investigating the reform of primary mathematics curriculum from the 1960s to the 1980s in Hong Kong, Wong and his colleagues (2009) reiterated a fundamental principal of curriculum development: the preparation of various curriculum documents is but one minor milestone in the process (Clarke, Clarke, and Sullivan, 1996). The success of real curriculum reform lies in the continuous professional development of the teachers and other practitioners of related sectors (Wong, Ngan, Fok, Tang, and Wong, 2009).

Commitments of stake holders in the curriculum development process are also vital to its success. A sense of involvement of the curriculum reform could turn passive receivers (or even resistants) into active participators (Fullan, 2010; Hargreaves and Shirley, 2009). Curriculum reform nowadays should no longer take a top-down bureaucratic approach. At the end of day, in addition to supports from policy makers, the administrative system and experts concerned, supports from the school system as well as the public are also of utmost importance.

Examination is another aspect needing reform. Extra care should be given especially in China, where examination-oriented mentality is prevalent. One should explore ways to reform the examination system tactfully to avoid learning be more and more examination driven.

As mentioned above, the role of teachers are important in the implementation of the curriculum. They should not be treated just as technicians who blindly follow the curriculum (Fullan, 2007). Instead, curriculum reform always provides an excellent opportunity for teachers to upgrade their professional knowledge, through pre-service and continuous teacher education. Paradigm shift (from transmission of knowledge to facilitation of learning) is improbable if teachers are trained in an environment which is not conducive to learning (so-called "traditional way of learning"). Therefore, the system of teacher professional development should also be reformed which include the change of teacher's belief and knowledge (Zhang and Wong, 2010).

When we went through these debates, we have found a striking resemblance among the (mathematics) curriculum reform around the world (Wong, Han, and Lee, 2006). In some countries, we find issues pertaining to the mathematics curriculum reform recur over the years (Wong, Ngan, Fok, Tang, and Wong, 2009). Some can be dated back to at least the New Math reform in the 1960s. We do not lack the knowledge of all these (teacher professionalism is crucial to curriculum reform, for instance); what we lack could be a right regard and the courage to take the right step. Jacques Barzun's famous quote: "Teaching is not a lost art, but

---

[14] See Cooper & Dunne (1998) and Wong (1994, 1997) for arguments on realistic situation.

the regard for it is a lost tradition",[15] that was said over half a century ago should call for our deeper reflection.

REFERENCES

Beane, J. A. (1997). *Curriculum Integration: Designing the core of democratic education.* New York: Teachers College Press.

Cao, Y. (2005). Mathematics curriculum reform in compulsory education and its issues of debate. *Bulletin des Sciences Mathematics, 44*(3), 14-16. (in Chinese).

Clarke, B., Clarke, D., and Sullivan, P. (1996). The mathematics teacher and curriculum development. In A. J. Bishop, K. Clements, C. Keitel, J. Kilpatrick and C. Laborde (Eds.), *International handbook of mathematics education* (pp. 1207–1233). Dordrecht, The Netherlands: Kluwer Academic Publishers.

Cooper, B., and Dunne, M. (1998). Anyone for tennis? Social class differences in children's responses to National Curriculum Mathematics Testing. *The Sociological Review, 46*(1), 115-148.

Cui, Y., Wang, S., and Xia, X. (2008). *Standard based student achievement assessment.* Shanghai: East China Normal University Press. (in Chinese).

Ding, R. (2010). *Exploring the primary mathematics classroom environment in the Chinese mainland.* Changchun: Northeast Normal University Press. (in Chinese).

Ding, R., Wong, N. Y., Ma, Y., and Lam, C. C. (2009). *Mathematics curriculum reform in basic education in the Chinese mainland, Taiwan, and Hong Kong: Comparisons and implications.* Hong Kong: Faculty of Education and Hong Kong Institute of Educational Research, The Chinese University of Hong Kong. (in Chinese).

Drake, S. M. (1998). *Creating integrated curriculum: Proven ways to increase student learning.* Thousand Oaks, California: Corwin Press, Inc.

Feng, D. (2004). *Frontier landscapes of educational administration in the U.S., U. K., and Australia.* Beijing: Educational Science Publisher. (in Chinese).

Feng, D. (2006). China's recent curriculum reform: Progress and problems. *Planning and Changing, 37*(1/2), 131-144.

Fullan, M. (2007). *The new meaning of educational change* (4th edition). New York: Teachers College Press.

Fullan, M. (2010). *All systems go: The change imperative for whole system reform.* Thousand Oaks: Corwin and the Ontario Principals' Council.

Gao, T. (2005, August 13). Discussion from a philosophical point of view. *China Education News.* p. 3. (in Chinese).

Guo, Y. (2003, December 27). Handling several relationships in curriculum reform. *China Education News.* Retrieved from http://www.mcyz.com/Article/ShowArticle. asp?ArticleID=697. (in Chinese).

Hargreaves, A., and Shirley, D. (2009). *The fourth way: The inspiring future for educational change.* Thousand Oaks: Corwin and the Ontario Principals' Council.

---

[15] December 5 issue of *Newsweek*, 1955.

He, K. (2005). *Reflection on the educational ideological and philosophical foundation of constructivism.* Retrieved 18 September 2009 from http://www.etc.edu.cn/academist/hkk/jiangoufansi.htm. (in Chinese).

Jackson, A. (1997a). The Math Wars: California battles it out over mathematics reform (Part I). *Notices of the American Mathematical Society, 44*(6), 695-702.

Jackson, A. (1997b). The Math Wars: California battles it out over mathematics reform (Part II). *Notices of the American Mathematical Society, 44*(7), 817-823.

Jiang, B. (2005a, March 16). What does mathematics lesson lose under the New Curriculum Standard, *Guangming Daily.* Retrieved from http://www.gmw.cn/content/ 2005-03/16/content_197119.htm. (in Chinese).

Jiang, B. (2005b). About the basic ideas of secondary school mathematics curriculum standard. *Bulletin des Sciences Mathematics, 44*(8), 1-4. (in Chinese).

Jiang, F. (2006). On the "Wang – Zhong debate" and its three subsequent questions. *Journal of Nanjing Xiaozhuang College*, (2), 55-60. (in Chinese).

Jin, C. (2005). *Curriculum and teaching methodology for primary mathematics.* Nanjing: Nanjing University Press. (in Chinese).

Jin, Y. and Ai, X. (2005, May 28). What are the theoretical foundation of the new curriculum reform. *China Education News.* p. 3. (in Chinese).

Li, J. (2006). *Comparative study between two versions primary mathematics textbooks: The People' Education Press version and the Beijing Normal University Press version.* Unpublished MPhil thesis, Central China Normal University, Wuhan, China. (in Chinese).

Lin, Z., and Jin, Y. (2005). The questions and strategies of teachers' training in the new curriculum. *Curriculum, Teaching Material and Method, 25*(5), 79-83. (in Chinese).

Liu, J. and Li, Y. (2010). Mathematics curriculum reform in the Chinese mainland. In F. K. S. Leung and Y. Li (Eds.), *Reforms and issues in school mathematics in East Asia: Sharing and understanding mathematics education policies and practice* (pp. 9-31). Rotterdam: Sense Publishers.

Liu, P. (2005, September 17). What should be abandoned in the new curriculum reform? *China Education News.* p. 3. (in Chinese).

Luk, B. H. K. (2009). *What price my soul? Global capitalism, education and spirituality.* Hong Kong: Chung Chi College, The Chinese University of Hong Kong.

Ma, F. (2005, August 13). Disagree with some opinions of Jin. *China Education News.* p. 3. (in Chinese).

Ma, Y. (2008). Implementation strategies and characteristics of curricula in the Chinese mainland. In P. K. Fok, Z. Y. Yu., H. X. Xu, and J. Chu (Eds.), *Curriculum and instruction: A journey of research and practice* (pp. 164-171). Chongqing: Chongqing University Press. (in Chinese).

Ma, Y., and Tang, L. (2004). The current status of the new curriculum reform experiment: survey and reflections. *Management of Primary and Secondary School*, (1), 11-15. (in Chinese).

Ma, Y., Wang, S., Zhang, D., Liu, X., Guo, Y. (2009). mathematics curriculum reform in the basic education period in China. In J. Wang (Ed.), *Mathematics education in China: Tradition and reality* (pp. 131-175). Nanjing, China: Jiangsu Educational Press. (in Chinese).

Ministry of Education, People's Republic of China (2001). *Full time free education mathematics curriculum standard (Trial edition)*. Beijing: Beijing Normal University Press. (in Chinese).

Ministry of Education, People's Republic of China (2009). *Full time free education mathematics curriculum standard (Revised edition)*. Internal document. (in Chinese).

Revision committee for MCS in Free Education period. (2007). *Comparison between the trial version and revised version of mathematics curriculum standard*. Retrieved 1 July 2009 from http://guozhuan.net/ReadNews.asp?NewsID=7462.

Shi, N., and Liu, H. (2007). Basic goals and paths of implementation of quality education. *Education Research, 28*(8), 10-14. (in Chinese).

Shi, N. and Ma, Y. (2009). *Mathematics curriculum for basic education: The design, implementation and outlook of the reform*. Nanning: Guangxi Education Publishing House. (in Chinese).

Su, S., and Xie, M. (2007). Review and prospect of mathematics education reform in the Chinese mainland. *Journal of Basic Education, 16*(1), 57-66. (in Chinese).

Sun, X. (2008). mathematics curriculum standards of China. In Z. Usiskin and W. Willmore (Eds.), *Mathematics curriculum in Pacific rim countries – China, Japan, Korea, and Singapore: Proceedings of a conference* (pp. 73-82). Charlotte, New Carolina, U.S.A.: Information Age Publishing.

Teng, F., and Zhao, Q. (2005). Questioning about the suitability of constructivism in basic education curriculum reform. *Education Science Research*, (6), 9-11. (in Chinese).

Wang, C. (2004). The education trend of *looking down on knowledge* should be seriously addressed: Reflecting on the statements on the shift from examination-oriented education to quality education. *Peking University Education Review, 2*(3), 5-23. (in Chinese).

Watkins, D. A. (2008, February). *Learning-centered teaching: An Asian perspective*. Keynote address at the 2nd International Conference on Learner-centered Education, Manila, the Philippines.

Wong, K. M. (1994). Can mathematical rules and procedures be taught without conceptual understanding? *Journal of Primary Education, 5*(1), 33-41.

Wong, K. M. (1997). Do real-world situations necessarily constitute "authentic" mathematical tasks in the mathematics classroom? *Curriculum Forum, 6*(2), 1-15.

Wong, N. Y. (2004). The CHC learner's phenomenon: Its implications on mathematics education. In L. Fan, N. Y. Wong, J. Cai and S. Li (Eds.), *How Chinese learn mathematics: Perspectives from insiders* (pp. 503-534). Singapore: World Scientific.

Wong, N. Y. (2009). Exemplary mathematics lessons: What lessons we can learn from them? *ZDM – The International Journal on Mathematics Education, 41*, 379-384.

Wong, N. Y., Han, J. W., and Lee, P. Y. (2004). The mathematics curriculum: Towards globalisation or Westernisation? In L. Fan, N. Y. Wong, J. Cai and S. Li (Eds.), *How Chinese learn mathematics: Perspectives from insiders* (pp. 27-70). Singapore: World Scientific.

Wong, N. Y., Lam, C. C., Leung, F. K. S., Mok, I. A. C., and Wong, K. M. P. (1999). Holistic reform of the mathematics curriculum – the Hong Kong experience. *Journal of the Korea Society of Mathematical Education (Series D): Research in Mathematical Education, 3*(2), 69-88.

Wong, N. Y., Ngan, M. Y., Fok, P. K., Tang, K. C., and Wong, K. L. (2009). History of mathematics curriculum development in Hong Kong: Reviewing several issues of recent curriculum development and decision. *Journal of Curriculum Studies*, *4*(2), 57-80. (in Chinese).

Zhang, D. (2008a). *"Two Basics" mathematics teaching: Theory and practice*. Nanning: Guangxi Educational Press. (in Chinese).

Zhang, D. (2008b). Chinese mathematics education: Advancing in reform and reflections. *Bulletin des Sciences Mathematics*, *47*(12), 22-26. (in Chinese).

Zhang, J. (2005). Contemplating on several problems in mathematics education reform. *Bulletin des Sciences Mathematics*, *44*(6), 6-10. (in Chinese).

Zhang, Q. P., and Wong, N. Y. (2010). Mathematics teachers' professional knowledge, beliefs and their implications on their teaching. In Y. Shimizu, Y. Sekiguchi and K. Hino (Eds.), *Proceedings of the 5th East Asia Regional Conference on Mathematics Education, Vol. 2* (pp. 849-856). Tokyo, Japan: Japan Society of Mathematics Education.

Zheng, Y. (2007). Reflecting on mathematics education reform in the Chinese mainland – from a pedagogical perspective. *Journal of Basic Education*, *16*(1), 33-44. (in Chinese).

Zheng, Y., and Wong, K. M. (1997). A critical challenge to traditional theories of instructional design: A preliminary analysis of the implications of constructivism for instruction. *Education Journal*, *25*(2), 81-97. (in Chinese).

Zhong, Q., and You, B. (2004). Mouldy cheese: Reading reflections of the article "the education trend of looking down on knowledge should be seriously addressed". *Global Education*, *33*(10), 3-7. (in Chinese).

Zhong, Q., Cui, Y., Zhang, H. (Eds.) (2001). *For the revival of China and for the development of every child: Interpretation of the "Curriculum Reform Guidelines for Basic Education"*. Shanghai: East China Normal University Press. (in Chinese)

In: Curriculum Reform in China
Editors: Hong-Biao Yin and John Chi-Kin Lee

ISBN 978-1-61470-943-5
© 2012 Nova Science Publishers, Inc.

Chapter 7

CHEMISTRY CURRICULUM REFORM IN CHINA: POLICY AND PRACTICE

Bing Wei

ABSTRACT

Since the start of the new millennium, the chemistry curriculum at the level of the secondary school in China has experienced a dramatic change. This chapter reviews the current school chemistry curriculum reform in China in both policy and practice with particular focus on these issues: science curriculum policy, the official chemistry curriculum standards, chemistry textbooks, and curriculum implementation. The changes, both positive and negative, from these two perspectives are analyzed and critically commented upon. The data examined for this chapter mainly came from official documents, research studies, and internally circulated documents. In the last part of this chapter, the problems and challenges identified in the current chemistry curriculum reform have been discussed within the perspective of Confucian cultural tradition.

SCIENCE CURRICULUM POLICY

Since the late 1970s, great social and economic changes have occurred in the People's Republic of China. The enterprise of education, especially, basic education (the equivalent to K-12 grades in the American schooling system), was considered not adaptable to the nation's social and economic development. Against this background, the latest round of curriculum reform was commenced in 1999 after a long period of ferment (Huang, 2004). In fact, the curriculum reform was stimulated by a 1996 national survey of the quality of the nine-year compulsory education system which had been fully implemented since the fall of 1993. Nearly 16 thousand pupils of various grades and more than two thousand principals and practicing teachers at primary and secondary schools in nine provinces and municipalities were involved in this survey, which focused on the fulfillment of the purposes of the curricula, the appropriateness of the teaching contents, the issues involved in the process of teaching and learning, and the issues of examinations and evaluations. The original intent of the survey was to eulogize the virtues and achievements of nine-year compulsory education. Unfortunately, the findings of this survey were very disappointing, as they indicated that there were many problems in the practices of the nine-year compulsory education. The salient problems were: many pupils had little interest in their schooling; teaching and learning styles were very rigid; most of the pupils were unable to use their learned knowledge to solve practical problems, even if these problems are very simple; and some pupils had no sense of social responsibility towards their community and country.

The problems identified gave great impetus to constructing the new curriculum structure of basic education. In subsequent years, several workshops and symposiums, sponsored by the Department of Basic Education of the State Education Commission (SEdC, substituting the Ministry of Education, MoE, from 1985 to 1998) were held to discuss the issues involved in the curriculum reform. By the end of 1998, the guiding philosophy, the new curriculum framework, and the policies and strategies of promoting the new curriculum had been formed (Cui, 2001). In early 1999, the Center for Curriculum Development of Basic Education, attached to the Department of Basic Education of the MoE, was established as the headquarters for this reform. At the same time, more than 40 scholars and researchers in universities were invited to draft the 'Guideline on Basic Education Curriculum Reform', which would incorporate the basic ideas of the new curriculum reform and serve as the practical guidelines in implementing the reform. Two and a half years later, in June 2001, the Guideline was formally issued. The first section of this Guideline (MoE, 2001a), in response to the problems mentioned above, set the goals of this curriculum reform as follows:

- Emphasize the process of learning;
- Change the structure of curriculum and make it adaptable to the various needs of pupils in different regions;
- Strengthen the relevance of curriculum to pupils' lives, society, and the development of science and technology;
- Stress the inquiry of learning;
- Strengthen the function of curriculum evaluation in promoting the development of pupils;
- Realize curriculum management at national, local, and school levels.

According to the Guideline, at junior high school level the science curriculum can take either of two forms - separated curriculum (called 'physics', 'chemistry', and 'biology', etc.) or integrated curriculum (called 'science'). Whatever form was taken, it was intended that science curriculum should deviate from the traditional subject centered mode. Therefore, the concept 'science education' (*kexue jiaoyu*) was advocated to highlight the relationships among science, technology and society rather than the subjects of physics, chemistry, and biology themselves. For example, in the International Symposium of Science and Mathematics Education of Primary Schools held in Beijing in November 2000, Chen (2000), the then Minister of the MoE, pointed out:

> It should be said that science education is a kind of education that is about the interrelationship between science and technology, and the relationship between science, technology and social culture.... But the internal relations among these various subjects, intrinsic and extrinsic impetuses behind the discoveries and invention of these subjects, and

the contributions they made to the development of the human, are what science education should be concerned about. Science education does not equal subject education, it is not simple integration of the knowledge of various subjects.

Such a view of 'science education' meant that chemistry curricula, as well as other individual or integrated curricula, were to be constructed on the basis of the 'common framework' rather than individually and separately as before. The 'common framework' is defined by the three dimensions 'knowledge and skills', 'processes and methods', and 'emotions, attitudes, and values'. It was emphasized that these dimensions were equally important and all of them should be reflected in the teaching contents (Zhu, 2000). It should be noted that the common framework, applicable to both natural science and social science curricula, originally came from the construction of the concept of scientific literacy by the designers of science curricula in this curriculum reform. In fact, as early as the late 1980s, the term 'scientific literacy' was introduced to China by scholars in comparative education (for example, Zhong, 1988). Since then, it had been discussed within science education circles in parallel with the discussions regarding quality education. However, not until the initiation of the most recent round of curriculum reform was this term seriously related to any existing or proposed science curricula.

It was stipulated in the Guideline that the 'national curriculum standards' was used to replace the 'syllabus', that is the link between the national curriculum program ('teaching program') and the textbooks. As with the 'syllabus', the 'national curriculum standards' was to function as the 'basis of the writing of textbooks, practical teaching, teaching evaluation, and examinations' (MoE, 2001a). According to the Guideline, the national curriculum standards should reflect the 'basic requirements' of the nation of students at various stages in terms of 'knowledge and skills', 'processes and methods', and 'emotions, attitudes, and values' (MoE, 2001a). Specifically, the 'national curriculum standards' has been characterized with the following features (Zhong, Cui, and Zhang, 2001):

- It describes learning outcomes over a certain period of schooling rather than specific stipulations of teaching contents (as syllabus or textbooks);
- It offers common and unified basics, rather than highest requirements;
- It ensures that descriptions of the learning outcomes should be understandable, as achievable as possible and able to be evaluated, rather than vague or beyond reach;
- It implies that teachers are not deliverers of textbooks but developers of teaching programs; and
- Its scope covers three fields of individual development - cognition, emotion, and manipulative skill.

Two years after the Guideline was issued, the Ministry of Education promulgated the *Program of the Senior High School Curriculum Reform* (PSHSCR, MoE, 2003a), which served as the guideline of curriculum reform in senior high school. As stipulated in this program, the senior secondary school curriculum is composed of eight fields of study: language and literature, mathematics, humanities and social studies, natural sciences, technology, arts, physical education and health, and practical activities. Each field of study consists of one or more subjects, which are similar in their nature. For instance, the field of natural sciences consists of four science subjects that are physics, chemistry, biology, and natural geography. Each subject consists of several course modules, which are interrelated with each other but have their own structures and emphases. It is required in the PSHSCR that each secondary school student should study all of these eight fields of study within every year. In the case of chemistry, required course modules consist of Chemistry 1 and Chemistry 2 (Chemistry 1 precedes Chemistry 2), and the six selective course modules are: Chemistry and Daily Lives, Chemistry and Technology, Particulate Structure and Properties of Substance, Chemical Reaction Mechanism, Basic Organic Chemistry, and Experimental Chemistry. Each course module is designed for 36 hours and students can obtain two credits. It is required that each student should at least obtain six credits in the subject of chemistry during the period of their senior high schooling. That is to say, students should select at least one selective course module after they finish Chemistry 1 and Chemistry 2. This is called the "4 plus 2" scheme as the minimum requirement. The structure of the new senior high school chemistry curriculum is shown in Figure 1.

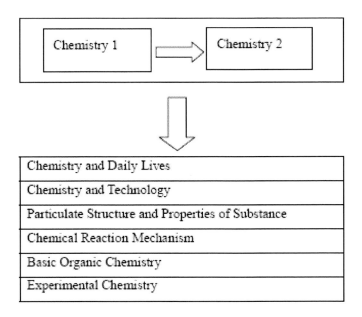

Figure 1. The structure of the new senior high school chemistry curriculum.

THE OFFICIAL CHEMISTRY CURRICULUM

For the design of the official curricula, the chemistry curriculum reform included two stages: the first stage was on the level of junior high schools (seventh to ninth grades) while the second stage was on the level of senior high schools (tenth to twelfth grades). The first stage began at the early 1999 and ended in June 2001 with the national standards of junior high school chemistry curriculum formally issued by the Ministry of Education (MoE, 2001b). The project of designing the national standards of senior high school chemistry curriculum was initiated in the autumn of 2001. This marked the startup of the second stage of the school chemistry curriculum reform. The designers were the same persons involved in producing the national standards of junior high school chemistry curriculum, most of them are young chemistry educators in teachers' universities in the country (Wei and Thomas, 2005). After about two years of work, the 'national standards of senior high school chemistry curriculum' was issued by the MoE for trial use (MoE, 2003b). A notable feature of the new chemistry curricula is that scientific literacy is explicitly stated as the gist of both junior and senior high school chemistry curricula (MoE, 2001b; MoE2003b). This thus has brought about great changes in both purposes and contents of the new chemistry curricula. In this section, I will compare the new chemistry curricula with the previous syllabi in terms of purposes and contents, which constitute the main parts of these two types of official chemistry curriculum documents, in order to discern the features of the new chemistry curricula.

According to Bybee and DeBoer (1994), the intentions of science curriculum can be viewed in two ways. One is focused on the knowledge, methods, and applications that are to be learned while the other is looked at the ends to which the knowledge, methods, and applications apply. In the traditional school chemistry curriculum, it was argued that chemistry "is of paramount importance to the modernization of industry, agriculture, national defense, and science and technology in China" (e.g., MoE, 1978; p.1). Therefore, the provision of chemistry in schools was linked to the fulfillment of so-called socialist construction and training qualified personnel for the development of the nation. The needs for personal, social or cultural purposes, however, were rarely mentioned. Accordingly, the basic knowledge and skills of the subject of chemistry, which were termed by Chinese scholars and practicing teachers as 'double bases' (*shuangji*), were highly valued, while practical applications were given little emphasis. Furthermore, chemical applications were only used to solidify the 'double bases" and their coverage was only limited to 'industrial' and 'agricultural' fields (MoE, 1978). 'Scientific processes' had not been included as a curriculum goal until 1986 (SEdC, 1986). Training students' 'abilities' had been advocated since the late 1970s but for a long time it was confined within the four elements - 'observing', 'experimenting', 'thinking', and 'learning by self' (Wei, 2010). Moral and political education were emphasized but mainly referred to 'dialectic materialism' and 'patriotism' (Wei, 2003).

In the new curricula, the rationale of the junior high school curriculum is described in the preface of the national chemistry curriculum standard as follows (MoE, 2001b, p. 1):

> Chemistry is an important branch of the natural sciences with its focus on the relations among the composition, structure, and properties of matter, and the rules of matter changes and the manner of adjustment of these changes. Today, chemistry has become the fundamental subject that underlies the subjects of materials, lives, environment, and energy, and become an important force that has promoted social development and technological progress, and made enormous contributions to solving a series of crises, such as the energy crisis, the environmental crisis, and the food crisis.

While the above is focused on the relationship between chemistry and society, the following is about the relationship between chemistry and individuals:

> The chemistry curriculum at the stage of compulsory education can help pupils understand the roles played by chemistry in society, recognize the issues related with science, technology, society, and daily lives from the viewpoint of chemistry, understand the influences of chemical products on the health of humankind, and know how to bring environmental pollution under control and exploit chemical resources by using chemical

knowledge and methods. Also, chemistry curriculum can enhance pupils' social responsibility and enable them to make more reasonable and scientific decisions when facing the challenging of social issues related with chemistry (MOE, 2001b, p. 1).

Compared with the general purposes of previous chemistry curricula, it can be seen that the purposes of 'four modernizations' or 'socialist construction' are no longer apparent in the curriculum standards. Of course, this does not mean the new chemistry curriculum is not beneficial for economic development. It is fair to say, however, that the new junior high school chemistry curriculum is mainly argued for from both social and personal perspectives (Wei and Thomas, 2005). As for senior high schooling, it is argued in the national standards of the senior high school chemistry curriculum that chemistry curriculum is an integrated component of science education and plays important roles in further raising the level of scientific literacy of senior high school students. Furthermore, it is asserted that the senior high school chemistry curriculum "should be linked up with the chemistry or science curriculum at the stage of compulsory education and therefore it is, in essence, a kind of curriculum oriented to general education" (MoE, 2003b, p.1). According to this document, the curriculum is intended to help students in the following aspects: (1) to actively learn basic chemical knowledge and skills which are needed for their future development and have a deeper understanding about the physical world; (2) to experience the processes of scientific inquiry, learn scientific research methods and have a deeper understanding about the nature of science; (3) to foster scientific attitudes and have a deeper understanding about the relationships among science, technology, and society (MoE, 2003b).

As mentioned earlier, the curriculum goals are defined by three dimensions of the view of scientific literacy: (1) knowledge and skills; (2) processes and methods; (3) affection, attitudes, and values. For the senior high school chemistry curriculum, for example, in the first dimension, the components are 'basic chemistry concepts and theories', 'nature of chemical phenomena', and 'basic ideas about chemistry', 'basic knowledge and skills of chemical experiments', and 'relationship between and among chemistry and other subjects of science' and so on. The components in the second dimension are 'abilities of scientific inquiry', 'consciousness of problems', 'independent thinking and cooperation with others', and 'abilities of obtaining and treating data and information'. In the third dimension, the components are 'interest in learning chemistry', 'consciousness of applying chemical knowledge', 'appreciation of the contributions of chemistry to human being and social development', 'the world view', and 'scientific attitudes and scientific spirits', etc. (MoE, 2003b). Compared with the previous chemistry curricula, we can say that 'double bases' are still emphasized but their meanings are expanded, at the same time, much attention is paid to personal and social applications of chemistry in the new senior high school chemistry curriculum. This, to some degree, reflects the intention of establishing a balance among competing goals in science education (Bybee and Ben-Zvi, 1998), and also provides a framework for the designers to select and organize curriculum contents for both required and elective course modules.

Traditionally, chemistry subject knowledge was perceived as contents in the chemistry curricula composed of six elements: basic chemistry concepts, chemical terminology, elements and compounds, fundamental chemistry theories, chemistry experiments, and chemistry calculations. While analyzing the 1978 school chemistry curriculum, Liu (1983) described the different roles played by these six elements in this curriculum: "chemistry experiment is the basis, chemistry theories are the main thread, elements and compounds are the skeleton, chemistry calculation is the application and development of the other five, chemical terminology and basic concepts are the thinking tools in learning and understanding various chemical problems" (p. 26). In the traditional school chemistry curriculum, chemical applications were involved in most cases, however, they were marginalized by subject knowledge. In the 1996 senior high school chemistry syllabus, for instance, some 'knowledge points' about chemical applications, such as, 'iodine and personal health', 'recycling metals and environmental protection', 'new types of polymer materials' were given the lowest level of requirements - 'tentatively knowing' or suggested as 'optional studies' (SEdC, 1996). It is obvious that chemistry curriculum contents were dominated by chemistry subject knowledge with little emphasis being given to chemical applications. In the new senior high school chemistry curriculum, this situation has changed: of the 25 themes in both required and the elective course modules in the national standards, there are seven themes that are closely relevant to chemistry applications, or one third of all the themes. These themes are: 'Chemistry and sustainable social development', 'Chemistry and human health', 'Materials in daily lives', 'Chemistry and environmental protection', 'Chemistry and exploitation and applications of natural resources', 'Chemistry and manufacture and applications of materials', and 'Chemistry and industrial and agricultural production' (see Table 1).

Table 1. Themes in the new senior high school chemistry curriculum

Course modules	Themes
Chemistry 1	Knowing chemistry as a science
	Basics to Chemical experiments
	Common inorganic elements and compounds and their applications
Chemistry 2	Particulate structure of substance
	Chemical reaction and energy
	Chemistry and sustainable social development
Chemistry and Daily Lives	Chemistry and personal health
	Materials in daily lives
	Chemistry and environmental protection
Chemistry and Technology	Chemistry and exploitation and application of natural resources
	Chemistry and manufacture and application of materials
	Chemistry and industrial and agricultural productions
Particulate Structure and Properties of Substance	Atomic structure and elements
	Chemical bonds and properties of substances
	Intermolecular forces and properties of substances
	Values of investigating particulate structure of substances
Chemical Reaction Mechanism	Chemical reaction and energy
	Velocity of chemical reaction and chemical equilibrium
	Ionic equilibrium in solution
Basic organic chemistry	Components and structures of organic compounds
	Properties and applications of hydrocarbon and its ramifications
	Saccharide, amino acids, and protein
	Synthesized polymer compounds
Experimental Chemistry	Basics to chemical experiments
	Enquiry by chemical experiments

As in most other countries, practical work has long been regarded as an essential component of chemistry curriculum in China and it has been claimed to be beneficial to achieve cognitive, manipulative and emotional goals. In the 1978 chemistry curriculum, for example, the roles of practical work were identified as "helping students understand chemical concepts, understand and solidify chemical knowledge, inculcating students with abilities to observe phenomena, analyse and solve problems, and acquire experimental skills, thus cultivating scientific attitudes of seeking truth from facts and being serious and conscientious" (MoE, 1978, p.5). These perceived roles of practical work seem to have changed with scientific inquiry being highlighted in chemistry curriculum. In the national standards of junior high school chemistry curriculum, for example, practical work is presented as an "important way for students to learn chemistry and engage in scientific inquiry" (MoE, 2001b, p. 4). At the same time, it proposes that "observing, investigating, collecting data, reading, discussing, debating are also active learning methods" (MoE, 2001b, p. 4). 'Conducting experiments' is treated as one of the 'elements' of scientific inquiry, in parallel with other discrete processes, such as 'posing questions', 'making predictions', 'making a proposal', 'collecting data', etc. (MoE, 2001b). It is also stated in the curriculum standards that "doing experiments can be used as a way of collecting evidence, it can also be served as a basis of posing questions or making hypotheses" (MoE, 2001b, p. 12). Obviously, the role of experiments is shifting from the tools of 'solidifying chemical knowledge' to one of the ways of conducting scientific inquiry.

In the traditional chemistry curricula, practical work was treated more as an integral part of the subject of chemistry than as a teaching strategy. Therefore, it was selected and organized with the logic of subject content. All practical work, both teachers' demonstration experiments and students' experiments, incorporated the logic and content of subject knowledge presented in the texts. Impacted by the idea of scientific inquiry, most of chemistry experiments in the new chemistry curricula are restructured in the form of scientific processes. In the national standards of junior high school chemistry curriculum, chemistry experiment is presented under the theme of 'scientific inquiry', including three clusters – understanding scientific inquiry, developing the abilities of scientific research, and leaning basic experiment skills. Furthermore, in the new chemistry curricula, practical work is not divided into 'demonstrating experiments' and 'students' experiments' any more. According to the designers, more than 80% of chemistry experiments in the junior high chemistry curriculum standards can be classified as students' experiments, and more than half of them are presented in the form of scientific inquiry (Wu, 2002, p. 72). All these changes show that the espoused teaching and learning modes and strategies in the chemistry curricula have shifted to student-centered ones, though constructivist theories have not been explicitly presented in the documents.

CHEMISTRY TEXTBOOKS

Since the 1950s, the People Education Press (PEP) has been designated as the national education press to produce the syllabi and textbooks directly under the leadership of the Ministry of Education (Wu, Chen, and Lv, 1992). For several decades, the nationally unified syllabi and textbooks, which is usually called the system of "one syllabus and one textbook" for a given subject curriculum, was adopted in primary and secondary schools (except the period of Cultural Revolution, 1966-1976). With the implementation of nine-year compulsory education in the late 1980s, however, it became increasingly obvious that this system could not meet the needs of varied regions and schools. For this reason, the system of "one syllabus and multiple textbooks" (*yigang duoben*) was adopted (You, 1990). It meant that individuals and research institutes were allowed to develop textbooks following the guidelines of the nationally unified teaching syllabi. The textbooks needed to pass the examination of the National Committee for Screening Elementary and Secondary School Teaching Materials (NCSESSTM), which was under the leadership of the Ministry of Education, before they could be put into use. In the new curriculum reform, as mentioned previously, it was stipulated in the Guideline that the 'national curriculum standard' should replace the 'syllabus', the link between the national curriculum program ('teaching program') and the textbooks; as with the 'syllabus', the national curriculum standards was to function as the 'basis of the writing of textbooks, practical teaching, teaching evaluation, and examinations' (MoE, 2001b, p.2).

In the case of the subject of chemistry, it is commonly recognized in chemistry education circles that textbooks can be seen as the substantiation of the curriculum, and the ideas of new curriculum are to some extent delivered to practicing teachers through textbooks (Wang, 2010). Both chemistry educators in universities and professional editors in the PEP have enthusiastically involved themselves in writing textbooks to meet the curriculum reform. It is not only because that this endeavor is profitable but also because that they are aware of the fact that curriculum reform will be destined to fail if no suitable textbooks are available for practicing teachers. Therefore, in the whole process of curriculum reform, no effort has been spared to compile and publish the new textbooks. Up to now, there have been five series of junior high school chemistry textbooks and three series of senior high school chemistry textbooks, which were written according to the national chemistry curriculum standards, have passed the examination of the NCSESSTM, and are currently used in schools (Wang, 2010). Although no exact numbers concerning the market shares commanded by varied publishers are available, chemistry textbooks produced by the PEP are commonly used in classrooms. This may be due to several factors but the most obvious one is that the structure, contents, and presentations of knowledge in the PEP textbooks is more like that in previous textbooks, and thus they are more familiar to school chemistry teachers who feel comfortable with them.

Generally speaking, the ideas of curriculum reform have been reflected in the new chemistry textbooks available in the markets. The philosophy underpinning the design of chemistry textbooks from the PEP, for instance, has been articulated as follows: (1) to balance the three dimensions of the goals of chemistry curriculum to achieve scientific literacy for all students; (2) to engage students in scientific inquiry; (3) to make textbooks more flexible to cater for different needs of students; (4) to link the contents with the reality of social development and the growth of science and technology; and (5) to integrate information technology with the curriculum content (Hu, 2002; Wang and Li, 2005). Compared with traditional textbooks, changes which have occurred in textbooks under this curriculum reform are tremendous. When commenting on the current curriculum reform in science in China, Gao (2007) observed that new science (inclusive of chemistry) textbooks featured these characteristics: (1) to integrate nature, science and student' lives in a holistic way; (2) to broaden the scope of scientific knowledge with the difficulty reduced and to reflect the growth of practical application of modern sciences; (3) to give more emphases on the scientific processes and scientific inquiry, and provide students with more opportunities to observe, manipulate, experiment, and think independently; (4) to design varied activities by which to direct students to learn in an initial, independent, cooperative, and investigative way (5) to inspire students' learning interest by making layouts, inscriptions, and words of textbooks more attractive.

As claimed in official curriculum documents, the current chemistry curriculum reform is aimed to raise the level of scientific literacy of all students and the national chemistry curriculum standards specifies that textbooks should be taken as one of instructional resources to support teachers in planning and delivering science instruction to meet students' needs (MoE, 2001b, 2003b). However, an undeniable reality is that textbooks are often used as the sole instructional resource owing to lack of economic support for instruction and the traditional teaching culture that puts textbooks at the centre of study in China, and thus textbooks usually become the curriculum and determine what is taught and learned about chemistry in the larger majority of classrooms in the country. Therefore, we dare to say that chemistry textbooks play a pivotal role in implementing the policy of scientific literacy education. However, thorough examinations of chemistry textbooks revealed that discrepancies exist between the idea of scientific literacy advocated in the national curriculum standards and the contents presented in the textbooks. For example, a graduate student at the University of Macau is conducting a quantitative study to examine the balance of the themes of scientific literacy in the three series of high school chemistry textbooks in China by use of the model proposed by Chiappetta, Fillman, and Sethna (1991), who argue that scientific literacy comprises these four themes: (1) science as a body of knowledge; (2) science as a way of investigating; (3) science as a way of thinking; and (4) the interaction between science, technology, and society. The preliminary findings of this study show that the majority of texts analyzed place most emphases on science as a body of knowledge, followed by a science as a way of investigating, and the interaction between science, technology, and society, with very little content being devoted to science as a way of thinking (Chen, 2010).

IMPLEMENTATION OF CHEMISTRY CURRICULUM

According to Wang (2001), then vice minister of education, the whole curriculum reform can be divided into three phases, ferment and preparation, trial and experiment, and implementation and expansion. For the implementation, a pragmatic policy of 'practicing first and then spreading' was adopted. This meant that the new curriculum would be gradually expanded to a larger and larger audience until it was fully adopted in all primary and secondary schools across the country. Guided by this policy, from the autumn of 2001, the junior high school chemistry was trialed in 38 national experimental zones and it continued to expand to the provincial and local experimental zones in the subsequent year. After three years of experiment, up to the autumn of 2005, all of the junior high schools had adopted the new chemistry curriculum. Since the autumn of 2004, the senior high school chemistry curriculum has been trialed in schools in four provinces (Guangdong, Shandong, Ningxia, and Hainan) and the number of students exposed to the new curriculum accounted for 13% of the population of the same age in these provinces.

Some empirical studies concerning the implementation of new curriculum reform, which are dispersed in Chinese educational journals, demonstrate that new curriculum have brought out positive changes in school practices. As evidenced in their survey study, Lv and Song (2002) claimed that the changes could be summarized as these points: (1) teachers' conceptions of knowledge, learning and teaching have changed to the constructivist orientation; (2) inquiry teaching is accepted by most practicing teachers and the interaction between teachers and students is becoming more effective; (3) students' learning styles are monitored by teachers and attention is given to the cultivation of students' confidence in learning; (4) teaching evaluation multiplies multiplied; and (5) teachers' professionalism is promoted. However, other research studies have disclosed problems and obstacles in the initial stage of the curriculum implementation. According to Tang and Ma (2002), the scarce curriculum resources, the tardy external examination reform, and challenges faced by teachers are three big problems that constrained the expansion of curriculum reform. Specifically, while recognizing the positive changes to teachers, they thought that the new curriculum was constrained by these problems: (1) teachers' work overload; (2) unqualified teachers; (3) the unsatisfactory quality and quantity of teacher training programs (Tang and Ma, 2002). Gao (2004) investigated teachers' conceptions in 11 national experimental zones with 1005 practicing teachers involved in his study and found that these teachers were in favor of student-centered rather than teacher-centered teaching modes in the initial stage of teacher training program when learning the ideas of the new curriculum; however, teachers tended to return to the teacher-centered orientation after one semester of actually experiencing the new curriculum in their classes. Obviously, as argued by Gao, the change of the teaching conceptions is not stable and easily reverts to the traditional orientation.

Although empirical research studies specifically related to implementation of the new chemistry curriculum have not been available, we can learn something from journal papers written by authors of chemistry textbooks. It needs to mention, in order to promote their textbooks, the authors of new chemistry textbooks came close to teaching practices and combined teacher training programs with actual use of textbooks in classrooms. By this chance, they obtained first-hand information about the actual situation of the new chemistry curriculum at school and classroom level. Briefly, similar to the results of those cross-subject studies as mentioned above, some positive changes have been observed in the case of chemistry curriculum. For example, in the report of features and implementation of the senior high school chemistry textbook series, for which she serves as the chief editor, Wang (2005) contended that the changes of chemistry teaching in the national experimental zones can be summed up as follows: (1) teachers' conceptions and understandings have been gradually improved; (2) the modes of teaching and learning have been changed to the student-centered direction; (3) varied kinds students' activities have been developed based on local supports and conditions; (4) diversified evaluation strategies have been tried; and (5) flexible and various management measures in curriculum and instruction have been adopted. The most prevalent problem in the experimental zones, as observed by Wang (2005), is that chemistry teachers cannot understand the intentions of curriculum designers in the curriculum structure and knowledge system and they are used to dealing with the depth and scope of subject knowledge according to their previous teaching experiences. Therefore, some knowledge points have been required to a higher but not proper level and some knowledge points have been taught earlier than expected. These practices, combined with the commercial exercises available in markets, led to the phenomena that "(students) learn with fun but exercise with pain" (Wang, 200, p.16). Wang and Li (2005) observed the same phenomena in the promotion of their PEP textbooks in other experimental zones. In addition, they observed these problems that exist in teaching practice: (1) the new curriculum reform challenges teachers in terms of teaching conceptions, practices, and workload; (2) three dimensions of curriculum goals have not been achieved in a balanced way with the fact that the knowledge dimension has been emphasized and can be easily evaluated while the latter two dimensions are easy to ignore and difficult to assess; (3) provision of students' activities are restrained by the poor conditions in some rural areas, such as large classes, the limited teaching hours, scarce teaching equipment and facilities.

CONCLUSION

This chapter has reviewed the current school chemistry curriculum reform in China in these aspects: the change of science curriculum policy, the official chemistry curriculum standards, chemistry textbooks, and curriculum implementation at the levels of policy and practice respectively. At the policy level, as shown in this chapter, the chemistry curriculum reform was driven by the political and economic factors in China and was influenced by Western thinking about science education in general and science curricula in particular. The problems identified from teaching practice and the goals listed in the Guideline embody the concerns of the central government over the quality of manpower resources in view of economical development. Impacted by the international trends of science curriculum development, the science curriculum in China is featured with these characteristics: Firstly, it has been structured with a holistic view rather than an separate discipline view; Secondly, national curriculum standards have been used to replace the national teaching syllabi; and Thirdly, the science curriculum at senior school level was composed of required and elective course modules. As for chemistry curriculum in particular, the redefined roles of chemistry in education, and the emphasized relationship between chemistry and individuals, and espoused slogan of raising scientific literacy of all students have shown that chemistry curriculum has shifted from being elite oriented to being citizenry oriented. At this point, as I argued elsewhere, science curriculum, including chemistry curriculum in China, has become more 'mature' than ever (Wei, 2010). From this chapter, we can see that this reform has brought out positive changes in the chemistry textbooks, classroom practice, and chemistry teacher development.

For a long time, science textbooks have been criticized as being with 'detached', alienating students from science in their every-day lives. In this curriculum reform, varied series of chemistry textbooks have become available for use and more importantly, textbooks have been designed to engage students in active learning with the contents and presentations being more attractive to students. In classrooms, some empirical studies, though not all of them had been critically designed, have shown that teaching and learning have indeed changed with the student-centered modes adopted in science classrooms, and inquiry oriented instructions tend to be welcomed by both teachers and students. Improving teachers' professional development is an important concern of this curriculum reform and positive changes have been observed: teachers' conceptions of knowledge, learning and teaching are being changed to constructivist orientations; inquiry teaching is accepted by most practicing teachers; teachers are becoming more and more concerned with the needs and interest of their students; the ideas of multiple teaching evaluation are being accepted by many practicing teachers. However, problems still exist. As for the textbooks, the themes of scientific literacy have not been dealt with very well in texts - most of the emphasis is given to the theme of science as a body of knowledge with very little attention devoted to science as a way of thinking. As for teacher development, their conceptions concerning teaching and learning had indeed changed to student-centered orientation in the initial stage of curriculum promotion but they turned back to teacher-centered orientation when they put the new curriculum into practice. Specifically, teachers fail to recognize the intentions of curriculum designers implicated in the curriculum structure and knowledge system and they are used to dealing with the depth and scope of subject knowledge based on their previous teaching experiences.

The gap between intended and implemented curriculum is a widespread phenomena across the world. As recognized by science educators elsewhere, a prominent factor inhibiting the implementation is lack of coherence between what is advocated in science curriculum documents and the assessment regime (Coll and Taylor, 2008). That is to say, there is inherent tension between the development of learner-centered curriculum and the traditional examination, which almost inevitably reward the rote memorization of scientific facts. In China, this case is even more marked. An important reason might be that so called 'examination culture' plays a pivotal role (Gu, 2004). As an ancient Chinese idiom says, 'although studying silently for ten years, once you are successful, you will become well-known in the world' (*shinian hanchuang wuren shi, yiju chengming tianxia zhi*). Young people, especially those that came from average or poor families, were encouraged by this kind of culture to study diligently and consistently to raise their social and economic status. Nowadays, the 'examination culture' still prevails in schooling in China. Success in public examinations, particularly the national university entrance examination, means that one can have a good expectation of high income after graduation from university; students' achievements in public examinations usually serve as an important indicator of schools' reputations; teachers take the responsibility to ensure students to achieve the exam requirements (Gao and Watkins, 2002). In recent years, with the spread of large scale assessment of scientific literacy, like PISA, which is purported to assess students' abilities to use science to solving real problems in social contexts, some changes have occurred in the senior high school admission examination and the national university admission examination. We hope that the change in the external examinations will be helpful to lead the science curriculum reform to the desirable direction of achieving scientific literacy for all students.

REFERENCES

Bybee, R. W., and Ben-Zvi, N. (1998). Science curriculum: transforming goals to practices. In B. J. Fraser, and K. J. Tobin (Eds.), *International handbook of science education* (pp. 487-498). Dordrecht: Kluwer Academic Publishers.

Bybee, R. W., and DeBoer, G. E. (1994). Research on goals for the science curriculum. In D. L. Gabel (Ed.), *Handbook of research on science teaching* (pp. 357-387). New York: Macmillan.

Chen, B. (2010). *An examination of the balance of the themes of scientific literacy in the three series of high school chemistry textbooks in China*. Unpublished Master thesis, The University of Macau, Macua.

Chen, Z. (2000, November). *A speech at the International Conference of Science and Mathematics Education of Primary Schools* (Internally circulated documents). Beijing, China. (in Chinese).

Chiappetta, E. L., Sethna, G. H., and Fillman, D. A. (1991). A quantitative analysis of high school chemistry textbooks for scientific literacy themes and expository learning aids. *Journal of Research in Science Teaching, 28* (10), 939-951.

Coll, K. R. and Taylor, N. (2008). The influence of context on science curricula: Observations, conclusions and some recommendations for curriculum development and implementation. In R. K. Coll and N. Taylor (Eds.), *Science education in context* (pp. 355-362). Rotterdam: Sense Publishers.

Cui, Y. (2001). The new curriculum: Illustrating the outline of curriculum reform of basic education. *Exploring Education Development*, (9), 5-9 (in Chinese).

Gao, L. (2007). Reform and challenge: An review of new science curriculum reform in China. In Y. Sio and M. H. Cheung (Eds.), *The research of science education in Chinese society* (pp. 17-28). Hong Kong: Seedland Publishing Limited (in Chinese).

Gao, L. and Watkins, D. A. (2002). Conceptions of teaching held by school science teachers in P. R. China: Identification and crosscultural comparisons. *International Journal of Science Education, 24*(1), 61-79.

Gao, L. (2004). An investigation on teachers' teaching conceptions under climate of the new curriculum reform. *Journal of South China Normal University (social science edition)*, (1), 116-121 (in Chinese).

Gu, M. (2004). *The cultural foundation to the Chinese education*. Taiyuan: Shangxi Jiaoyu. (in Chinese).

Hu, M. (2002). The philosophy and features of the chemistry textbook according to the curriculum standard of the compulsory education. *Chinese Journal of Chemical Education*, (3), 7-10. (in Chinese).

Huang, F. (2004). Curriculum reform in contemporary China: Seven goals and six strategies. *Journal of Curriculum Studies, 36*(1), 101-115.

Liu, Z. (1983). *Teaching materials and methods of secondary school chemistry*. Beijing: Beijing Normal University. (in Chinese).

Lv, S., and Song, X. (2002). The changes brought by the implementation of the new curriculum. *Curriculum, Teaching Material and Methods, 22*(8), 1-4. (in Chinese).

Ministry of Education (1978). *The chemistry syllabus of secondary schools of full-time and ten-year system (Trial draft)*. Beijing: People's Education Press. (in Chinese).

Ministry of Education (2001a). Guideline on basic education curriculum reform (trial). *Subject Teaching*, (7), 1-5. (in Chinese).

Ministry of Education (2001b). *The chemistry curriculum standard of compulsory education of full-time system*. Beijing: Beijing Normal University. (in Chinese).

Ministry of Education (2003a). *Program of the senior secondary school curriculum reform* (official document). (in Chinese).

Ministry of Education (2003b). *National standards of general senior secondary school chemistry curriculum*. Beijing: People's Education Press. (in Chinese).

State Education Commission (1986). *The chemistry syllabus of secondary schools*. Beijing: People's Education Press. (in Chinese).

State Education Commission (1996). *The chemistry syllabus of senior high schools*. Beijing: People's Education Press. (in Chinese).

Tang, L. and Ma, Y. (2002). A survey on the implementation of the new curriculum: Problems and obstacles. *Theory and Practice of Education*, *22*(7), 52-55.

Wang, J., and Li, D. (2005). The writing and trial use of the new senior high school chemistry textbooks of the PEP series. *Chinese Journal of Chemical Education*, Supplementary issue, 44-47. (in Chinese).

Wang, L. (2005). The features and the implementation of the senior high school compulsory chemistry textbooks of the 'new century' version. *Chinese Journal of Chemical Education*, (3), 13-17. (in Chinese).

Wang, L. (2010). Progress and reflection of secondary chemistry curriculum reform in the past ten years (part A). *Chinese Journal of Chemical Education*, (4), 15-21. (in Chinese).

Wang, Z. (2001). Promoting quality of education and initiating the new phase of the curriculum reform of basic education. In Q. Zhong, Y. Cui and H. Zhang (Eds.), *For the rejuvenation of the Chinese nationality and for development of each pupil: Interpreting the Guideline on basic education curriculum reform* (pp. 1-15). Shanghai: Eastern China Normal University Press. (in Chinese).

Wei, B. and Thomas, P. G. (2005). Explanations for the transition of the junior secondary school chemistry curriculum in the P. R. China during the period from 1978 to 2001. *Science education*, *89* (3), 451-469.

Wei, B. (2003). *A case study of curriculum change in China: The junior secondary school chemistry curriculum - 1978 to 2001*. Unpublished PhD thesis, The University of Hong Kong, Hong Kong.

Wei, B. (2010). The changes in science curricula in China after 1976: A reflective review. In Y. J. Lee (Ed.), *Science education research in Asia* (pp. 89-102). Boston: Sense Publishers.

Wu, L., Chen, H., and Lv, D. (1992). Theories and practices in making teaching materials of primary and secondary schools in new China. In The Chinese Association of International Education Exchange (Ed.), *Curriculum development and social progress: Selected papers in the international symposium on curriculum development and social progress* (pp. 15-22). Beijing: People's Education Press. (in Chinese).

Wu, X. (2002). The content standards of the chemistry curriculum of compulsory education. In Z. Wang (Ed.), *Illustrations of the national standards of junior high school chemistry curriculum* (pp. 61-80). Wuhan: Hubei Education Press. (in Chinese).

You, M. (1990). On the reform and construction of curriculum and teaching materials in compulsory education. *Subject teaching*, (3), 1-5. (in Chinese).

Zhong, Q. (1988). *Advance of contemporary instruction theories*. Beijing: Educational Science Publisher. (in Chinese).

Zhong, Q., Cui, Y., and Zhang, H. (2001). *For the rejuvenation of the Chinese nationality and for development of each pupil: Interpreting the "Guideline on Basic Education Curriculum Reform"*. Shanghai: East China Normal University Press. (in Chinese).

Zhu, M. (2000, October). *A talk on the symposium of the textbook revision*. (Internal documents). Beijing, China. (in Chinese).

In: Curriculum Reform in China
Editors: Hong-Biao Yin and John Chi-Kin Lee

ISBN 978-1-61470-943-5
© 2012 Nova Science Publishers, Inc.

Chapter 8

INTEGRATED SCIENCE REFORM IN CHINA

Shuang Zhang

ABSTRACT

This chapter is about the policy and implementation of integrated science curricula at junior secondary schools in Mainland China. Adopting the framework of John Goodlad's (1979) three levels of curriculum, i.e., intended curriculum, implemented curriculum and attained curriculum, this chapter mainly addresses the intended and implemetented integrated science curricula. It is divided into three parts. First, it provides an overview of the integrated science curricula in China based on related curriculum policy documents. Second, it reports the findings of a research attempting to reconstruct the experiences of teachers in two junior secondary schools who have been involved in implementing the integrated science curricula for six years. Finally, it discusses the implications of the research findings for the future development of integrated science.

INTRODUCTION

The education system of Mainland China has been dominated by the subject-based curricula. Like many other countries, China has launched a massive curriculum reform in the millennium, aiming at fostering students' innovative spirits and practical abilities to meet the demand of the knowledge society and to compete in global economy (Ministry of Education, 2001a). One of the major curriculum reform initiatives is curriculum integration. A new integrated curriculum named "Science" is introduced to integrate the subject-based physics, chemistry, biology and geography (natural geography) and has been implemented in junior secondary schools in experimental zones since September, 2001.

The ideology and teaching approach of the new integrated science curricula differ from teachers' usual classroom practices. From the beginning, the implementation is far from smooth. According to Tang's research, 90% teachers and leaders from experimental zones are unwilling to teach "science" for lack of the capability and prerequisite conditions to implement integrated science. Even in the first 7 experimental zones taking "science" in 2001, many teachers object to selecting "science", and in some experimental zones, parents express their concerns about taking "science" and the representatives of NPC (National

People's Congress) put forward the motion of switching back to the traditional subject-based curricula (Tang, 2003; Wang, 2007). Although there are slow increases in the number of experimental zones, Wuhan city, after other four experimental zones, also declare to stop integrated science reform and switch back to separate science subjects in 2009 (Lei, 2009). Some media also report the strange phenomenon happening in schools taking "science", where two set of textbooks of both "science" and old separate science subjects are taught at the same time (Li, 2005). Recent studies by academics have also reported implementation problems have been encountered. The problems are identified as: teacher knowledge and ideology are not suitable for the reform; lack of curricula resources and time; assessment reform becomes the bottleneck of implementation; old school structure impedes the implementation; lack of cooperation in school culture and so on (Liu, 2002; Wang, Ma, and Fang, 2007; Zhang, 2007).

Then why to introduce the nationwide integrated science curricula? Why has it been so difficult to implement the curriculum? All these are important and interesting questions that should be answered. If we want to answer these questions, it would be essential to understand the policy context and the lives of teachers in this turmoil of curriculum reform.

A BRIEF HISTORY OF INTEGRATED SCIENCE

China has a relatively short history of integrated science curriculum reform. The culture of the middle years of schooling in China, as in many parts of the world, is predominantly discipline based. From 1980s, the UNESCO has been engaged in promoting integrated science curriculum and practice globally. Meanwhile some western innovations of science integration like STS (Science, Technology and Society) education are introduced into China and draw the attention of educators in China (Wang, 2007; Zhang, 2007). Some attempts at offering integrated science curriculum begin to emerge in Chinese schools. The two decade history of integrated science reform is separated by two waves of reform initiatives. The first wave is during 1980s to 1990s. At first it is the grass-roots educational changes initiated by schools or teachers, such as the practice of attached junior secondary school of Northeast Normal University in 1986. Then the reform efforts expand to a city or a province led innovations. In 1988, Shanghai starts the innovation of integrated curriculum including social science and science. Among those efforts, the innovation of integrated science led by Zhejiang province in 1993 has significant influence on the national integrated science curriculum named "science". In this period, these efforts are just sporadic trails in schools in a city or a province. As an alternative to separate science subjects, the integrated science is offered with the intention of lightening student course burden by reducing the number of subjects (Wang, 2007; Wei, 2009). Integrated science in this era is mainly characterized by "integration with subjects" (Wei, 2009) or "multidisciplinary" (Zhang, 2007), with emphasizing the relevance between different subjects while remaining the boundary of subject knowledge (Wang, 2007). Although some of the efforts didn't survive and their experience and result were out documented or studied seriously, these efforts become the herald of the national level integrated science curricula reform in 2001.

The second wave of integrated science reform is the national "science" curriculum in 2001 marked by the issue of "the national standards of science curriculum (Grades 7-9) (trial)

(Ministry of Education, 2001b)". It occurs in the context of globalization and Chinese fast changing society. Compared with previous efforts in integrated science, the new "science" curricula is introduced as part of the large-scale national curriculum reform launched in 2001 and represent the spirit of the new curriculum reform. In response to the challenge of knowledge-based society and globalized competiveness, society needs people with skills that are different from the past. It seeks to cultivate active lifelong learners with innovative spirits and practical ability. Integrated science curricula, as a prevalent western education practice aiming to cultivate student science literacy, is believed as an effective way to achieve those goals.

Meanwhile, the initiative also seeks to address the long-seated problem of examination-driven and subject-based education in China. The curriculum and teaching in schools in China have, for a long time, been characterized by subject-based curricula, competitive assessment system and teacher-centered pedagogy (Zhong, Cui, and Zhang, 2001). Up to early 1990s, schooling and teaching in China was coined as "examination-oriented education" (*yingshi jiaoyu*), and the output of the "examination-oriented education" was criticised as "high scores, low ability". Teachers relied on teacher-centred methodology to impart the curriculum content so that the students would be able to secure good results in public examinations. More and more students lost their interest with increasing course load and difficulty. Realizing these weaknesses and facing the challenge of the globalized, knowledge-based society, the Chinese Government saw the urgency of introducing educational reform in the 1990s to promote quality education (*suzhii jiaoyu*). In 2001, the new curriculum reform was launched with the issue of the policy paper, "Guidelines on Basic Education Curriculum Reform (Trial)". The new basic education curriculum is designed for helping every student to develop their potential rather than imparting subject knowledge. The new curriculum content should also be more related to students' daily life and current technological and societal development. Teachers should abandon the conventional teacher-centred methodology. Enquiry strategies should be used to promote students' IT competency, analytical, problem-solving and communication ability (Ministry of Education, 2001a). In light of this, the new integrated subject, namely science is introduced to replace biology, chemistry, physics, geography and history in junior secondary schools in the new curriculum experimental zones and seen as the breakthrough of the new curriculum reform (Zhu, 2002).

NATIONAL INTEGRATED SCIENCE CURRICULA IN 2001 – SCIENCE

In 2001, Ministry of Education issued the national standards of science curriculum (Grades 7-9) (Ministry of Education, 2001b) to take place of the old subject syllables. Before the curriculum reform, subject syllable has been the standard for teacher teaching. It covers mainly the specific knowledge and skills that student should grasp. The goals of teaching emphasize basic knowledge and basic skills (*shuangji*). "Science" centers the curriculum on science literary rather than on the mastery of fragmented information within the boundaries of subject areas. In the new science curriculum standard, the goal of science literacy is divided into three related dimensions: emotion, attitude and values; learning process and method, knowledge. It is a very obvious move away from the traditional goal of *shuangji* in separate science subjects.

In the aspect of content standard, new "science" curriculum "does not simply synthesize the different subjects; Instead, it aims to render student to understand natural world as a whole and to understand scientific content in the view of basic scientific ideas (Ministry of Education, 2001b, p.5). The content of science curriculum is composed of five themes:

- Scientific inquiry (processes, methods, and abilities).
- The life sciences (living systems, metabolism, homeostasis, continuity and evolution of life, human, health, and environment)
- The physical sciences (common substances, the structure of matter, motion of matter, energy, and energy resources)
- The earth, universe, and space sciences (location of the earth in apace, humans and earth)
- Science, technology, and society (history of science, technology, and social issues).

The standard is the basis for teaching and textbook compiling. In the science textbooks published by Zhejiang Education Publishing House, the content is organized by different themes, such as "water in our life". The themes are divided by different sub-themes like "where does water come from", "the component of water", "the conservation and use of water" (Zhu, 2001). It makes knowledge more accessible or more meaningful by bringing it out of separate subject compartments and placing it in contexts. According to Wei (2009), the model of integration has been adopted in science subject is "integration beyond science subjects". If we see from Drake's continuum of integrated[16], the design of "science" curriculum can also be identified as interdisciplinary (Zhang, 2007).

Besides integrating the subject knowledge, learning-centred strategies should be used by teachers to promote students' development of generic skills and competencies (Ministry of Education, 2001b). Experiential learning and enquiry teaching are preferred. Assessment should not be confined to traditional paper and pencil examination. Continuous formative assessment should be included (Ministry of Education, 2001b).

The key changes in the science curriculum are depicted in Table 1.

Table 1. Differences between separate science subjects and integrated science curriculum

	Separate science subjects	Integrated science curriculum
Curriculum goals	Develop basic knowledge and basic skills	Science literary Emotions, attitudes and values Learning process and method knowledge
Curriculum Content	Fragmented subject knowledge	Knowledge beyond science subjects
Teaching and learning processes	Teacher-centered teaching, receptive learning	Student-centered, inquiry-based teaching and constructivist learning centered process
Assessment	Standard paper and pencil test, subject-based and high stake	Assessment for learning, formative assessment like portfolio assessment

---

[16] According to Drake, there are three levels of integration from multidisciplinary, interdisciplinary to transdisciplinary (Drake, 1993).

The "science" curriculum in 2001 is innovative as it involves a fundamental change in educational values. However, the deep discipline-based structure and process in schooling not easily changed by this policy rhetoric.

As Bean points out "No matter how persuasive argument and evidence may otherwise be, subject-cantered approaches are protected by the interests of a powerful network of educational elites whose symbiotic relationships are based on the dominance of subjects in curriculum organization (Bean, 1997, p75). In 1949, China set up highly centralized and subject-centered basic education system and teacher education system modeling Soviet Union.

The isolation and fragmentation of knowledge is part of the deep structures of schooling. This is evident in the subject-specific textbooks, tests, syllabus, schedules, and other artifacts of schools. Although from 1980s, there are continuous efforts trying to change the rigorous subject-centered system, it remains the same and has been embedded in national education system, school level structure and individuals' minds.

First from the national-level, all the administrative structure is subject-centered. The education bureau is divided with different subject department to supervise school subject teaching. Teachers' hiring and promotion is on the basis of their subjects. Their identity, status, title and salary are connected with their teaching subjects. For example, in the middle school, teacher's career ladder system (*zhicheng zhidu*) is on the basis of subject, such as the senior level of Chinese language teacher, the middle level of physics teacher. Tang noted that since there was no consistent policy on career ladder for science teachers, science teachers' motivation were influenced by unchanged subject-centered career ladder system (Tang, 2003).

On the other hand, the college and university are organized by separate subject and teacher educators use subject cantered approaches to teach prospective teachers. Both of them never have the experience of science integration and don't know how to teach science. In the school level, the entire schooling network is subject-cantered, including test and textbook, teaching schedule, school structure.

At the same time, "science" is not just integration of knowledge, it emphasizes the use of formative assessment to assess student' learning process. But it is quite different from the old way of paper-pencil standardized test. Since science is the test subject in high school entrance examination (HSEE, *zhongkao* in Chinese). "How to assess it" becomes the biggest concern of teachers. With the examination culture, HSEE is a very high stake test which has a great influence on what to teach and how to teach.

From the above analysis, we can see the new science curriculum is a transformational change. To school practitioners, it is a very radical reform which redefines what good teaching is.

It is not just an integration of knowledge. In fact, to teachers, what to teach, how to teach and how to assess students all changed. But the paradox is the powerful conservativeness of the traditional subject-based curricula and examination culture. The assumptions underlying them are inconsistent with the ideology of science curricula. So it is a big challenge to teachers. How they implement the curriculum is the key to science curriculum reform.

IMPLEMENTED SCIENCE CURRICULA:
FINDINGS FROM AN ETHNOGRAPHY STUDY

In order to understand how teachers responded to the call for curriculum reform, two schools in a large booming city in South China were invited to participate in a study in 2007. Ethnographic approach was adopted to develop an in-depth understanding of teachers' life and work. The researcher spent a month in each school to interview teachers, observe lessons, and collect relevant documents and archives such as teachers' reflective journals, curriculum plans, lesson plans and students' work.

The data collected reveal the journey the teachers experienced in the implementation process since the launch of the change in 2001. It should be noted that each single teacher is a unique individual with their own characteristics, values and beliefs and experiences. But they, as a group, were working in the same context and environment. In the following section, the context of their working environment and how they responded to the call for change will be described. From the findings I can construct the six-years lived experiences of teachers during the implementation of science curriculum.

The Dominance of the Reform Discourse

Under the hierarchical education system in China, front-line teachers have little "say" in the top-down reform. They have to follow the instructions from the officials. In the two case schools, the teachers felt obliged to be in line with the view and directives from the officials of district education bureau, who acted as the interpreters of the policy documents issued by Ministry of Education.[17] They dominated the reform discourse.

When the curriculum reform was launched, most of the teachers had neither deep understanding of the ideology of the new curriculum, nor the necessary subject knowledge to teach the integrated subjects. For example, a teacher in School A, described his situation at the early days of the new curriculum implementation:

"I have to make change now; I am used to the old way of teaching, now I don't know how to teach. I face two big difficulties. First is the subject knowledge, I can't teach what I don't know. Second, how to organize learning activities in class. The most difficult thing is how to motivate student's thinking by organizing appropriate activities for them to explore knowledge independently. You see, in the textbook, the text is only 100 words in every lesson. Every time (when I start planning the lessons), I just stare at these words and don't know how to proceed. I feel very tired and stressed out, my hair turned grey in the first two years, at that time I was no more than 40. This is the first time in my teaching career that I had to cram up so many things in such a short time. I was very upset that I didn't know what I should teach the next day and how students would react to my lesson. I had no confidence of my teaching. I went to my class with my head down while in the old days, I went to my geography class with my head up." (S2SC-He).

---

[17] The policy documents are "General guidelines on the Implementation of Basic Education Curriculum Reform (Trial)" and "the national standards of science curriculum (Grades 7-9) (Trial)".

Teachers, having been deskilled, naturally felt threatened and stressed. They did not prefer adopting "Science". However, the district education bureau decided that the subjects be implemented in all junior secondary schools in the district. Although seminars introducing the spirit and content of the new subjects were organized for teachers in the first year, it was far from adequate to equip teachers with the necessary knowledge and skills.

The district education officials, realized the kind of problems teachers were facing, adopted new strategies to improve the effectiveness of the change process. They instructed teachers from different disciplines to cooperate in the lesson preparation work and observe each other's lesson. At the same time, teachers whose teaching beliefs were in line with the ideology of the reform were chosen and honored as teacher leaders. Other teachers were required to learn from them by observing their class teaching and attending the sharing. Moreover, these teacher leaders were entrusted with the influential task of setting examination questions for the whole district. Different from the traditional test items, the new test items emphasized students' enquiry and critical thinking, which somewhat alleviated teachers' concerns about the examination. During the second and third years, more teachers made serious efforts to implement the new integrated subjects as instructed.

In this process, for teachers, the direct influences from the science curriculum were the changes in teaching content and teaching method. Neither of them was easy for teachers. But the study shows that the reform poses both challenges and opportunities for the professional development of teachers, and that schools play an important role in helping teachers cope with the imposed reform imperatives. In a case study school, teachers get the full support from their school. A department of science is constructed to let teachers with different subject background to have time and space preparing lessons together. Teaching schedule becomes more flexible with the needs of teaching and learning. They also get enough resources to carry out experiment and promote inquiry learning. Besides all the actual support from school, the inherent cooperative school culture plays an important role of making teachers change. As a teacher said,

> "Colleagues in our science department are very supportive and helpful. Not like other school, science teachers don't communicate each other, isolated from each other and have to face the reform by themselves. We are different, we often prepare lesson together, argue about teaching problems in the office." (S1HI-Yang).

The Emergence of the Traditional Voice

In the first three years of the implementation, the reformist voice dominated the whole school curricular scene in both case schools. But this does not mean that the traditional voice of stressing the importance of transmission of subject knowledge had totally subsided. When the first cohort of students taking science reached Junior Secondary 3, this traditional voice began to emerge from the carpet again. The reason being that the new science subject was included in the standardized HSEE, a high stake public examination determining which senior high schools the students would go to.

Following the reformists' advocacy for formative assessment, all the teachers in both case schools adopted formative assessment. They spent huge amount of time and effort to prepare portfolio for each single student, organize student peer assessment and self assessment as recommended by the reformists. But after the HSEE, they found that all these efforts were wasted as formative assessment played little role in the final high-stake HSEE, only the ranking of the final pencil-paper test was counted.

"We put so much effort, energy and recourses into making it (portfolio assessment), but it means nothing, it is useless in the *zhongkao* in the end. Then why do we do this? What is it for? It is very time-wasting work, I feel very exhausted doing this…" (S2SC-Li)

After HSEE, the traditional voice re-surfaced as the dominating voice. The district education authority ranked schools according to the performance of their students in the public examination. This not only brought the schools in the same district into competition, but also among districts where science was implemented. Schools with good results were honored while those fell behind lost "face".

Another interesting development was that one year after the HSEE for the first cohort of students was held, the district education authority issued a new policy paper named "Manual on Knowledge Essential in the Linking of Junior Secondary and Senior High Curriculum" to the teachers (In the following, it is called "linking policy" in short). Knowledge that was considered as important and imperative for successful senior high learning was detailed and teachers in junior secondary schools in this education district were required to cover all of these knowledge items in their teaching. Teachers took this as an important turning point in curriculum policy. Mr. Jiang of School B explained their interpretation as,

"This is a signal. It means that the goal of the reform is changed back to knowledge transmission. Now knowledge and students' academic achievement are of higher importance. Education is for fostering students to get into high schools, not for helping all students develop their potentials as they (referring district education officials responsible for reform implementation) previously said." (S2HI-Jiang)

Although the educational officials had not pushed the traditional voice openly, the use of "league table" was powerful enough to show what really mattered. Ball (1999) noted, perfomativity is a form of "non-intervention intervention" that uses targets and performance indicators to drive, evaluate and compare educational "product". The league table placed all schools into surveillance by all stakeholders and drove schools to compete for their survival. Schools became a highly competitive habitat. Parents as the stakeholder in market had the right to choose school for their children, put more pressure to schools to compete for their survivals.

In this situation, the management and administrators in schools had no alternative but to adopt the same managerial culture and transfer the survival pressure for teachers who were the key actors in schools responsible for school effectiveness and student quality.

"The education bureau exerted the pressure on schools. And our principal transferred it to us. He was very anxious about the school ranking and organized a special staff meeting on it. In the meeting, he praised those teachers whose students got most A+, for other teachers like me, we felt very uneasy as this act meant that we were criticized, though anonymously. From that on, our principal started to observe all teachers' class, and all the examination results including mid-term, final-term and HSEE are ranked and released to all staff. This was not the case before 2005. But after HSEE in 2005, this changed and it became very stressful." (S2HI-Shen).

Living with the Two Voices

This study reveals that teachers actually experienced two conflicting policy discourses in the reform process. The assumptions underlying the two discourses are different. The reform voice advocated promoting student-centered classroom teaching and the fostering of student all-around development and the traditional voice viewed students' development as performances in the pencil-paper test. How did teachers manage and respond to such conflicting discourses?

Most of the teachers found it difficult to cope with the reform as they were required to implement the new integrated subjects. Yang, a physics teacher for almost 20 years is a case in point. Before the reform, she was comfortable with her well-established belief that her primary responsibility was to impart subject knowledge for students to secure good scores in the HSEE. She built up her reputation and status as a senior physics teacher through hard work. When the education reform was launched in 2001, she was coerced to meet the new expectations by teaching "science", a new integrated subject, using more exploratory teaching strategies. She had a guilty feeling as she saw that many important subject knowledge and concepts were left out in the new integrated subject. At the first year of implementation, she was assigned to set the final exam paper for students, in which she used the traditional discipline-based test items to assess students. She was criticized by her seniors and colleagues for not being able to embody the reform ideology. She felt very shameful and depressed, and said "after 20 years of teaching, I suddenly felt I'm unable to teach well".

Yang was not the only one who felt deskilled and loss of their traditional professional identity. Nevertheless, the majority of these teachers did try to comply with the new discourse and apply the new teaching and learning methods. They attended classes to learn more about the spirit of the reform and the skills essential for implementing the changes. However, being trapped in the two discourses, even those teachers who upheld beliefs more in line with the new reform ideology found it less difficult to adapt. Han was one of the three teachers who belonged to this group. She shared her experience,

> "I like to teach biology by relating the (curriculum) content to students' life. I teach what I think would be useful to my students. I'm humorous in class and students like my way of teaching. So I think high of the ideology of reform and it is just what I have been expecting for a long time..." (S2SI-Han).

But to this type of teachers, difficulties occurred when the reform voice was suppressed by the traditional voice re-emerged after the HSEE for the first cohort of students taking the new curriculum. They felt trapped and betrayed. Han described her problem,

> "But now although still emphasizing relating knowledge to students' life, I was designated to teach a key point class (zhongdian ban), but I'm not a "professional killer" (a metaphor referring teachers who can make students successful in public exams). Now I have to compete with others with gun (a term used to symbolize powerful means)." (S2SI-Han)

It is difficult for teachers to accommodate both voices in their teaching even if they wanted to. It can be seen from Miss Han's lesson on the respiratory process.

"According to the (new) curriculum standard, we need to cover knowledge about the structure and function of respiration, respiratory movement and air change. But according to the linking policy, you should add the knowledge about four continuous processes of respiration. When I prepare my lesson, I just followed the (new) curriculum standard ignored the linking policy recommendation. I think that is the required standard for examination. However, I did try to cover that knowledge (four continuous processes of respiration) in my class briefly. But I can't teach it clearly within limited time. For you know, another whole lesson is needed if you want to present and make it clear to students. … As what you have seen today, I only use 5 minutes to explain the four processes and students can't understand it at all. So I feel very distressed" (S2SI-Han).

CONCLUSION

The new integrated science curriculum reform is operated in an increasingly complex and confusing environment. The change cannot be isolated from the social-political and economic transformations ongoing in China. The present study points out that the implementation problem is very complicated.

The spirit of reform launched on the Chinese mainland in 2001 deviated so much from the conventional practice that it has been labeled as a "paradigm shift" (Zhong, 2003). Teachers and schools were trained, taught, coerced to adopt the new reform initiatives. But when the students have to face the high stake examination, the reform measures were seen and criticized as impractical. The parents were very concerned and expressed the need of having to switch back to the old curriculum. Such concern was part of the traditional Confucian Heritage Culture. On the school administration side, the municipal education authority adopted the performativity culture and neo-marketization strategies of using students' scores in the HSEE, a high stake examination, to rank order the schools. The combination of these traditional examination culture and managerialism created a voice in conflict with the reformist voice.

Teachers were thus placed in a difficult situation. They were persuaded by the reformists to adopt the "progressive" reform initiatives, but in their work place, they experienced the strong pressure of the need to achieve good examination results. Their teaching experience told them that the traditional didactic teaching method was more effective in securing good examination results. Being caught in this difficult situation, they encountered serious problem with their professional identity. Before the reform was launched, the expected role of teachers was clear: be a subject expert effective in transmitting knowledge to the students. But now, teachers were lost. It seems that there was not much that teachers could do to help themselves out. Those who upheld the conventional practice, would face difficulties when it came to activities like open lessons. These open lessons were usually judged according to the reformists' criteria. The more progressive teachers, on the other hand, found it difficult to survive in the keen competition in the "public examination race".

Both policy makers and educational researchers have acknowledged the pivotal role of teachers in the implementation process (Hargreaves, 2003). However, if the implementation does not go smoothly as planned, can we blame on teachers? If we dig into the crux of the problems, we find teachers actually face conflicting demands and dilemmas. From the study described above, we can summarize some implications for the future development of the integrated science curriculum reform.

The fist implication concerns understanding teachers' dilemmas. For the policymakers and change leaders, they often concern how it is intended to do. One of the reasons why change fails is that change planners or decision-makers are unaware of the situations that potential implementers are facing. They introduce change without providing the means to identify and confront the situational constraints and without attempting to understand the values, ideas and experience those who are essential for implementing any changes (Fullan, 2001, p.96). Policy makers and change leaders must try to understand how people involved in the changes think. Since it is the people in the setting who must live with the change, it is their definitions of the situation that are crucial if change is going to work.

The second implication concerns positive supports to teachers. As Fullan note, the more supports teacher can get form the change, like the continuing learning, cooperation, consistent change objectives, the more capacity system have to implement large-scale reform (Fullan, 2001). It is essential to provide positive support to teachers. It includes the consistency of change policy. From the study's findings, local policy is conflicting with the ideology of policies from Ministry of Education, teachers have to fulfill different demands. It also includes the opportunity of teacher development to help teachers solve the practical problems. In a very complex change, teachers intended to implement it on surface. They need deep professional reflection and continuing learning. "Cooperative problem-solving" approach from the study may be an effective way for teacher professional development.

The third implication concerns cooperation within and beyond schools. Science curriculum is very complex which go beyond individual teacher's capacity. It is critical for teachers to cooperate with colleagues and solve problems together. To create a cooperation culture, the first step is to establish "common culture of teaching". It needs changes from different levels. For school leaders, they should make changes in school structure and teaching time to create opportunities for teachers' cooperation. At the same time, it is very important for leaders to create a collaborative culture in schools instead of competitive culture. In the teachers' level, mutual trust and cooperation is needed, like opening classroom and reviewing each other's lessons.

Beside cooperation within schools, strengthening cooperation beyond schools and creating a learning community are a direction for sustainable development of the change. Since the reform is top-down, the voices from schools and teachers should be heard and paid more attention. Only through this way, teachers can really get empowerment to carry on the reform.

REFERENCES

Ball, S. J. (1999). *Educational reform and the struggle for the soul of the teacher!* (Education Policy Studies Series No.17). Hong Kong: Faculty of Education and Hong Kong Institute of Educational Research.

Fullan, M. (2001). *The new meaning of educational change* (3rd ed.). New York: Teachers College Press.

Goodlad, J. I. (1979). The scope of curriculum field. In J. I. Goodlad and Associates (Eds.), *Curriculum inquiry: The study of curriculum practice*. New York: McGraw-Hill.

Hargreaves, A. (2003). *Teaching in the knowledge society: Education in the age of insecurity*. Maidenhead, Philadelphia: Open University Press.

Lei, Y. (2009, January 9). Wuhan city stop science reform back to separate science subjects. *China Youth Newspaper*. (in Chinese).

Li, Y. F. (2005, October 30). Mom, why I have to learn both new and old textbooks. *Shenzhen Economic Newspaper*. (in Chinese).

Liu, Y. (2002). The implementation and strategies of integrated curriculum in junior secondary school. *Curriculum, Teaching Material and Method, 22*(11), 7-10. (in Chinese).

Ministry of Education (2001a). *General guidelines on the Implementation of Basic Education Curriculum Reform (Trial)*. Beijing: Ministry of Education. (in Chinese).

Ministry of Education (2001b). *The national standards of science curriculum (Grades 7-9) (Trial)*. Beijing: Ministry of Education. (in Chinese).

Tang, J. (2003). The problems and coping strategies of science curricula implementation. *Academic Journal of Hangzhou Senior Medical College, 24*(6), 281-285. (in Chinese).

Wang, X. H., Ma, Y. P., and Fang, X. Y. (2007). Are integrated science teachers ready: An investigation to the teacher's adaptation. *Theory and Practice of Education, 27*(3), 45-48. (in Chinese).

Wang, X. (2007). *The case study on reform and development of integrated science curriculum in Chinese junior middle school*. Unpublished PhD Dissertation, Northeast Normal University, Changchun, China.

Wei, B. (2009). In search of meaningful integration: The experiences of developing integrated science curricula in junior secondary schools in China. *International Journal of Science Education, 31* (2), 259-277.

Zhang, S. (2007). *A study on teachers' beliefs of integrated curriculum in Mainland China: Two case schools*. Unpublished PhD Dissertation, The Chinese University of Hong Kong, Hong Kong.

Zhong, Q. Q. (2003). The transition of curriculum model: The progress and problems in the basic education reform in Chinese mainland. *Comparative Education, 24*(1), 6-10. (in Chinese).

Zhong Q. Q, Cui Y. H., and Zhang, H. (2001). *For the great revitalization of Chinese nation for students' all around development: Interpreting the general guideline of the basic education curriculum reform*. Shanghai: East China Normal University Press. (in Chinese).

Zhu, M. (2002). *Going into new curriculum: Dialogue with practitioners*. Beijing: Beijing Normal University Press. (in Chinese).

Zhu, Q. S. (2001). *Science: Experimental textbook for compulsory basic education (The third volume, Grade 8)*. Hangzhou: Zhejiang Education Press. (in Chinese).

In: Curriculum Reform in China
Editors: Hong-Biao Yin and John Chi-Kin Lee

ISBN 978-1-61470-943-5
© 2012 Nova Science Publishers, Inc.

Chapter 9

TRANSFORMING CITIZENSHIP EDUCATION IN SOCIAL STUDIES CURRICULUM OF PRIMARY SCHOOLS: A TEXTBOOK ANALYSIS

Wenlan Wang, John Chi-Kin Lee and Hong-Biao Yin

ABSTRACT

Citizenship education is an emerging area of study in Mainland China. In this chapter, two sets of social studies textbooks are compared and analyzed to find any transformation of citizenship education in primary schools under the current China' NCR. Based on a frequency comparison and content analysis of these textbooks, results show that citizenship education in social studies curriculum has undergone dramatic transformations, including the depoliticisation of social studies curriculum and the significant increase in content of citizenship education, increase of diverse elements of citizenship education, and the changing nature of content and pedagogies of citizenship education. However, the new social studies curriculum still adopts a relatively passive, obligation-based approach to citizenship education. This chapter concludes that there is still a need to enhance citizenship education in Mainland China.

INTRODUCTION

In the Peoples' Republic of China, the school subject of social studies was established in the 1990s. On August 6, 1992, the State Education Commission (SEC, the predecessor of the Ministry of Education) issued the *Nine-year Plan for Compulsory Education Curriculum* and the *Syllabus of Society for Whole-day Primary Schools in Nine-year Compulsory Education (Trial)*, and required that the subject of Society (*shehui*) should be set up from grade four to grade six. In 1995, the SEC published the revised version of the Society syllabus. In this revised syllabus, it was emphasized that "the establishment of the subject of Society has important implications for the implementation of the principle of all-round development, covering ethics, the intellect and the physique, the cultivation of socialist citizens with lofty ideals, integrity, knowledge and a strong sense of discipline, and the enhancement of the ideological and ethical standards of the entire people" (SEC, 1995, p.1). However, there were some overlapping areas in the objectives and content between the subjects of Moral Education (Grades 1-6) and Society (Grades 4-6).

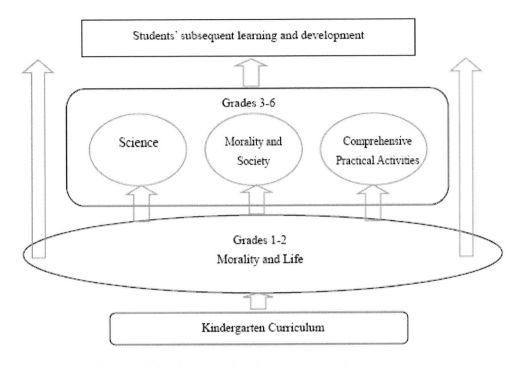

Figure 1. The position of social studies curriculum in primary education.

In 2001, the Chinese Ministry of Education (MOE) issued the *Guidelines on Basic Education Curriculum Reform (Trial)* and initiated a new round of national curriculum reform. Social studies is one of the major subjects undergoing transformation. Under the current curriculum reform, Moral Education (Grades 1-6) and Society (Grades 4-6) are replaced with two integrated courses: *Morality and Life* (*pinde yu shenghuo*, Grades 1-2) and *Morality and Society* (*pinde yu shehui*, Grades 3-6). The National Curriculum Standards for these two subjects were released in June 2002. As specified by the national curriculum standards, *Morality and Life* is "an activity-based comprehensive curriculum aimed at cultivating students' good character, willingness to inquire and love of life" (MOE, 2002a, p.1), while *Morality and Society* is "a comprehensive curriculum based on upper primary students' life experiences, aimed at facilitating students' good moral character and social development" (MOE, 2002b, p.1). Moreover, *Morality and Society* covers the issues of patriotism, collectivism and socialist education, and provides students with an education on history, culture and national conditions, aimed at cultivating students to make them become socialist citizens with the ability to participating modern society (MOE, 2002b, pp.1-2). Figure 1 shows the position of these subjects in the new curriculum system of primary education defined by the national standards (MOE, 2002a, p.6). On the one hand, *Morality and Life* and *Morality and Society* are discrete, coherent and sequential. On the other hand, they are closely related to other subjects in primary education, i.e., *Science* and *Comprehensive Practical Activities*.

CITIZENSHIP EDUCATION AND SOCIAL STUDIES CURRICULA IN MAINLAND CHINA

The significance of a social studies curriculum for citizenship education has been extensively discussed. Social studies education is usually regarded by nation-states as a primary mechanism for accomplishing the task of linking the individual to the collective, with the belief that individuals can be cultivated as citizens (Fairbrother, 2004). The social studies curriculum, in the form of syllabus, guidelines, standards and textbooks, "not only provides political knowledge, but also defines the normative expectations, appropriate attitudes and values and behavior of an ideal citizen" (Tse, 2008, p.62). As such, the social studies curriculum reflects the state's goals and priorities, defining the relationship between citizens and the nation (Fairbrother, 2004).

Citizenship can be defined as "passive and active membership of individuals in a nation-state with certain universalistic rights and obligations at a specified level of equality" (Janoski, 1998, p. 9). China's long and rich history and traditions of moral education have affected Chinese society and citizenship in various ways (Tse and Lee, 2008; Zhu and Feng, 2008). Influenced by Confucian traditions which place the harmony of social relations above the rights of the individual, those elements of citizenship involving individual rights and freedom to engage in constructive criticism in the political field are a foreign concept to traditional China (Tse and Lee, 2008). Since the founding of a socialist regime in 1949, ideologies such as socialism, collectivism and patriotism have been officially advocated in China. Therefore, in the relationship between citizens and the nation in China, the status of nation takes precedence over the status of citizen, and citizenship education emphasizes the individual's obligations to the nation rather than the rights of the individual as a citizen of the nation. As discussed by Lo and Man (1996), "in Chinese societies, the concept of citizenship differs from that in Western nations in that it denotes less of a contractual relationship between the individual and society and more of an inheritance of identity, bound to nationality and loyalty...Patriotism becomes a necessary condition for citizenship" (p. xviii). A study of the ideological beliefs of college students found that social science students in Mainland China were more authoritarian than Hong Kong students, and tended to gain stronger nationalism with an increased duration of study (Cheung and Kwok, 1998).

Although the nation-predominant, obligation-based preference in citizenship education contributes to the stability of the nation, the over-emphasis on the individual's conformity to the nation constrains the individual's active participation in social and political affairs. However, as Fouts and Chan (1995) argued, the long-term success of economic, political and social reform and the integration of China into the world community will depend on a citizenry educated in democratic ideals, and "the most logical place for this education to take place is in the schools and through the social studies curriculum" (p.523).

As Zhong and Lee (2008) observed, the curriculum of citizenship education historically undertook three stages of orientation shifts: political orientation (1949-1978); both political and moral orientations in parallel (1978-1993); and moral orientation (since 1993). Before the current national curriculum reform, it was found that the five-love principles (i.e., love of motherland, love of people, love of labor, love of science and love of socialism) for "socialist modernization construction" is the main feature of the social studies curriculum in China (Tse, 2008). Citizenship education was implemented mainly as "ideological and moral education" in primary schools and as "ideological and political education" in secondary schools (Chen and Reid, 2002). The teaching of social studies has also been criticized for having some major drawbacks. For example, the traditional social studies education stressed the ideological indoctrination, socialist education and information retention in a specific knowledge area, but ignored the development of comprehensive knowledge in the interrelated disciplines (such as society, moral education, political science, history and geography) and students' high order thinking and the ability to apply knowledge and skills to problem solving (Zhao, Hoge, Choi, and Lee, 2007). To improve the implementation of citizenship education in Mainland China, it was suggested that (a) more content and time should be allocated to citizenship education, independent of political interpretation; (b) teaching methods should be made more effective by adopting discussions, interviews, simulations and games, in addition to lecture-based lessons; and (c) assessment methods be improved and citizenship education, as a core theme, should be incorporated into the college entrance examination (Chen and Reid, 2002).

Although some studies have been conducted to explore the characteristics and content of social studies textbooks in different eras in China (e.g., Fouts and Chan, 1995; Fairbrother, 2004; Tse, 2008; Zhao et al., 2007), there is no study to systematically compare the changes to social studies textbooks under the current curriculum reform. In this chapter, using the method of textbook analysis, we compared and summarized the major transformations of citizenship education in social studies curriculum in primary schools under the national curriculum reform. Based on this analysis, the implications for the implementation of citizenship education and social studies curriculum reform will be discussed.

METHODOLOGY

The Textbooks

Textbooks are a salient part of a formal curriculum. The change in textbook content directly reflects the changes of national educational policies, and textbooks often take the role of change agent for curriculum and instructional reform (Ball and Cohen, 1996). For most social studies teachers in China, textbooks are the most important, if not the exclusive, material used for their classroom teaching (Wang and Huang, 2007). Two sets of social studies textbooks published by the People's Education Press were compared and analyzed in this chapter. The main reason for selecting these textbooks is that the People's Education Press is the publishing house directly under the supervision of the Chinese Ministry of Education. Furthermore, the textbooks published by the People's Education Press are the most widely circulated in China.

The first set of social studies textbooks was compiled in accordance with the *Syllabus of Society for Whole-day Primary Schools of Nine-year Compulsory Education (Trail)*(SEC, 1995), named as *Society* (Wu, 2001) which comprised six volumes for Grade four to six students and were published from 1996 to 2001. This set of textbooks is referred to as "S4-6" in this chapter.

The other set of social studies textbooks was written according to the *National Curriculum Standard for Morality and Society* (MOE, 2002b). These textbooks entitled

Morality and Society (Zhao, 2003) were published in 2003 and comprised eight volumes for Grade three to six students. In this chapter, they are referred to as "MS3-6".

Because the two sets of social studies textbooks are used for students in similar grades, analysis of them by comparing and contrasting can provide appropriate information about the transformation of citizenship education in primary schools.

The Framework of Analysis

Considering the characteristics of social studies education in Mainland China, Wang (2006) suggested the framework to analyze the content of social studies textbooks in primary schools be comprised of three categories, namely (a) moral education which implies the transmission of the traditional and modern moral norms or expectations, (b) ideological-political education which deals with the cultivation of some particular political and ideological value, e.g., socialism and communism, and (c) citizenship education which deals with the relationship between nation and citizens.

For the citizenship education curriculum, Tsang (1994) suggested that a balanced citizenship education curriculum should contain three themes, i.e., nation-state education for nurturing individual's national identity, the rights and responsibilities of citizens, and the dialectic relationship between nation-states and citizens. In recent years, it was argued that exercising a citizen's influence on social governance through active participation is an effective way of citizenship formation and citizenship education (Gearon and Brown, 2003). Moreover, impacted by the current trend of globalization, it was also suggested that citizenship education should go beyond the boundary of nation-states, and incorporate the element of cosmopolitan citizenship to cultivate the notion of "citizen of the world" (Isin and Turner, 2002, p. 8).

In this chapter, the framework suggested by Wang (2006) was used to analyze the content of social studies textbooks. The relative proportion of content in relation to the areas of moral, ideological-political and citizenship education in two sets of textbooks were compared. In order to know the transformation of citizenship education under the current curriculum reform, the aspect of citizenship education was further classified into six elements, i.e., national identity, civic responsibility, civil rights (e.g., democracy, liberty and equality), active participation, and global citizenship.

The procedures of analysis consisted of two parts: frequency comparison and content analysis. When two sets of social studies textbooks were compared, first, each lesson was adopted as the unit of analysis. Based on the topic of each lesson, the content of the lesson was classified into different categories and elements, and the frequency of each category and element was then calculated. Second, the content of some representative lessons about citizenship education in the two sets of social studies textbooks was analyzed in detail to reveal the transformations in citizenship education.

FINDINGS

Frequency Comparison: A General Picture

Comparing the Three Categories in Social Studies Textbooks

Table 1 shows the frequency distribution of the three categories in Wang' (2006) framework in the two sets of social studies textbooks.

Table 1. The three categories in the two sets of social studies textbooks

Categories	S4-6		MS3-6	
	No. of lessons	%	No. of lessons	%
Moral education	38	33.9%	87	43.5%
Ideological-political education	43	38.4%	8	4%
Citizenship education	31	27.7%	105	52.5%
Total	112	100%	200	100%

The results in Table 1 indicate that some changes had taken place in the new social studies textbooks. The most dramatic change is concerning ideological-political education. In the *Society* (G4-6) textbooks, there are 43 lessons (38.4%) aiming at inculcating socialist and communalist ideologies into students, but in the *Morality and Society* (G3-6) textbooks, only 8 lessons (4%) are about the inculcation of socialist and communalist ideologies.

Conversely to the decrease of ideological-political education, the proportion of moral education and citizenship education showed an increase in the new textbooks, especially so citizenship. Specifically, in the *Society* (G4-6) textbooks, there are 38 lessons (33.9%) for moral education and 31 lessons (27.7%) for citizenship education. In the *Morality and Society* (G3-6) textbooks, there are 43.5% (87 lessons) and 52.5% (105 lessons) on moral education and citizenship education, respectively.

Comparing the Five Elements of Citizenship Education

In order to identify trends of transformation in citizenship education, the lessons about citizenship education in the two sets of textbooks were compared further according to the five elements of citizenship education mentioned above. Table 2 shows the distribution of these elements in the two sets of social studies curriculum textbooks.

Table 2. The five elements of citizenship education in social studies textbooks

Elements	S4-6		MS3-6	
	No. of lessons	%	No. of lessons	%
National identity	24	77.4%	54	51.4%
Civic responsibilities	2	6.5%	14	13.3%
Civic rights (e.g., democracy, liberty and equality)	5	16.1%	18	17.1%
Active participation	0	0	14	13.3%
Global citizenship	0	0	5	4.8%
Total	31	100%	105	100%

To summarize, there are three distinct changes in citizenship education, namely:

1. the content of national identity decreases from 77.4% to 51.4%;
2. although the content related to civic rights (e.g., democracy, liberty and equality) remains proportionately similar, the element of civic responsibilities increases from 6.5% to 13.3%;
3. the elements of active participation and global citizenship dramatically increase. There are no such elements in the *Society* (G4-6) textbooks, but in the *Morality and Society* (G3-6) textbooks, there are 14 lessons (13.3%) about active participation and 5 lessons (4.8%) about global citizenship, respectively.

Content Analysis: An in-Depth Comparison

In order to show the changes in citizenship education, an in-depth content analysis of some representative lessons was conducted to reveal the transformations in the two sets of textbooks.

National Identity

The two sets of social studies textbooks both have rich content on national identity. These lessons usually feature topics like defending the country against invasion, emphasizing national reunification, praising historical characters, and directly advocating patriotism. The following excerpt is an example of national identity education in relation to the reunification of Taiwan in the fifth volume of *Society* (G4-6).

> Excerpt 1: Taiwan and the mainland are of the same blood (Society, Vol. 5, Grade 6)
> About one million years ago, Taiwan island and the Chinese mainland were geographically linked…Later, large numbers of people from Fujian and Guangdong moved to Taiwan island. The Gaoshan tribe are the original inhabitants of Taiwan, and they have their own language, culture, social customs and habits.
> Taiwan has been an integral part of China since ancient times. To realize the national reunification is the common wish of all people on both sides of the straits.

However, as Table 2 shows, national identity is the dominant element of citizenship education in the *Society* (G4-6) textbooks, with the percentage being 77.4%. But in the *Morality and Society* (G3-6) textbooks, the proportion of national identity decreases a remarkable 26 percentage points to 51.4%. Compared with the old textbooks, the new textbooks provide more room for other elements of citizenship education while preserving the core status of national identity.

Civic Responsibilities

Civic responsibilities include passive obligations and active obligations (Janoski, 1998). The former refers to citizens' responsibility to not violate the national regulations and laws, that is, observing law and discipline. The latter refers to citizens knowing how to enact socially prescribed actions on national, societal and individual levels. On the national level, citizen's active obligations mainly include voting, tax payment and service in the army. On the societal level, citizen's active obligations refer to the participation in community management or voluntary organizations. On the individual level, citizen's active obligations refer to the duties that each citizen undertakes for some specific social roles. The element of civic responsibility is more about citizens' knowledge and understanding of these responsibilities.

Compared with the *Society* (G4-6) textbooks, the content about civic responsibilities in the *Morality and Society* (G3-6) has doubled, from 6.5% to 13.3%. More importantly, the old textbooks only mention passive obligations and teach students they should observe the laws in correspondence, transportation, etc., but seldom use any topics related to citizen's active obligations. However, the new textbooks stress the role of active obligations in community life, and encourage students to enact these responsibilities at national, societal and individual levels. Excerpt 2 provides an example about civic responsibilities in the new textbooks.

> Excerpt 2: I can do it well (Morality and Society, Vol. 1, Grade 3)
> Regardless whether we are in home, school or society, we should meet our own responsibilities...
> Materials and events in the classroom community are also our own things. Sometimes, we need to make lots of effort to participate in or care for these things. We are living in a society, and we need to be responsible for many things ourselves.

Civic Rights

One important function of citizenship education is to enlighten students' ideas of civil rights, including democracy, liberty and equality. Through the internalization of these civil rights, students are encouraged to actively participate in social governance.

Although the proportion of content about civil rights in the old and new textbooks does not significantly change, the nature of the content alters. The content of civil rights in the *Morality and Society* (G3-6) is more related to students' life experience. Using the sense of democracy as an example, the following two excerpts are drawn from the old and new textbooks respectively.

> Excerpt 3: National People's Congress (Society, Vol. 4, Grade 5)
> The National People's Congress (NPC) exercises the supreme power on behalf of the whole nation. It is the highest statutory body of our country. The NPC has the authority to stipulate the national constitution and other laws, to vote for, select and dismiss the leaders of national bodies, to decide the important issues of domestic and foreign affairs, and to exercise supreme supervisory authority...

> Excerpt 4. How to elect a class leader? (Morality and Society, Vol. 3, Grade 4)
> Question: After we joined the Young Pioneers, we took part in many elections for the leaders of the Young Pioneers. How are they elected?
> Figures: Self-recommendation; recommended by other members; anonymous voting; counting the ballots; announcing the results.
> Question: Why do we elect the leaders in this way? Could they be directly appointed by the teacher?

The *Society* (G4-6) textbooks introduce the regime and democratic mechanism in Mainland China, but it is still difficult for primary students to understand the essence of democracy. In contrast, the *Morality and Society* (G3-6) textbooks explain the issue of democracy through the activity of election of a class leader which is more relevant to students' experience, and raises some questions to invite student discussion about democratic participation, election and supervision.

Active Participation

By nature, democracy requires citizens' participation in social affairs. Active participation is necessary for a citizen's sense of democracy, focusing on individuals' actions to put democracy into practice. Through participation in social affairs, social members have the opportunities to exercise their civil rights. Therefore, the cultivation of active participation is of great importance for citizenship education. Active participation includes participation in class and school activities as well as participation in the social affairs and national/political affairs.

There is no lesson about active participation in the *Society* (G4-6) textbooks. However, in the *Morality and Society* (G3-6) textbooks, there are 14 lessons (13.3%) related to students' participation in school activities, community and social affairs. Compared with the old textbooks, active participation is a fresh element of citizenship education in the new textbooks. Excerpt 5 provides an example for this:

> Except 5. Who should do these things? (Morality and Society, Vol. 1, Grade 3)
> In our life, there are always some things which are for the benefit of all people but are seemingly not the responsibilities of any one person. Hence, all of us tend to wait for others to do these things. Who should do these things? What is the consequence if no one takes care of these things?
> (Figures. Water leakage; Snow pack; Street light out of order) Why does nobody deal with this?
> Conclusion: Society is the 'family' of all of us. Some social affairs are also our own personal responsibility. Everyone living in this society should take action for the good of all.

Global Citizenship

Global citizenship is a newly emerged element of citizenship education. This is also the case for the social studies curriculum in Mainland China. There is no such element in the *Society* (G4-6) textbooks, but in the *Morality and Society* (G3-6) textbooks, there are five lessons related to the "global sense", including the study of different cultures in the world, the similarity and difference between cultures, and the interdependence among countries for economic development. Excerpt 6 shows an example of economic globalization in the current world.

> Excerpt 6. Some interesting cultural phenomena
> With the development of scientific technology, the economic linkages among different countries are strengthened. The products of one country are often processed in other countries. For example, a well known home appliances manufacture has 18 oversea design centers and 22 factories abroad...
> Question: Please use the knowledge you have gained to explain the reason for these phenomena.

Although the new textbooks cover issues related to globalization, there is a dearth of content about the relationship between national identity and global citizenship. In a globalized world, people may have multiple identities and need to deal with the place of citizenship in the dynamic relationships between region, state and global society (Isin and Turner, 2002). How to strike a balance among these different identities and still pursue the common interests of people could be an objective of global citizenship education needing to be considered in future curriculum and textbook revision.

CONCLUSION

The textbook analysis conducted in this chapter indicates that the citizenship education in the social studies curriculum of primary schools has undergone dramatic transformations in this round of national curriculum reform. Firstly, at least on the level of formal curriculum and textbooks, contrary to Chen and Reid's (2002) suggestion that citizenship education has been implemented mainly as "ideological and moral education" in primary schools, the proportion of citizenship education has significantly increased and takes up more than half (52.5%) of the new social studies textbooks. By contrast, the proportion of ideological-political education in the new social studies textbooks has markedly decreased to 4%. In Zhong and Lee's (2008) review, they also found that a fundamental change in the new citizenship education syllabi, i.e., the national curriculum standards for *Morality and Life* (MOE, 2002a) and *Morality and Society* (MOE, 2002b), is that the prefix "ideo-" is removed from the title, which implies that the role and functions of citizenship education are disassociated from politics. These findings echo the current depoliticisation trend in Mainland China (Wang, 2008; Zhong and Lee, 2008). It can be inferred that the core of social studies curriculum has moved from ideological-political education to citizenship education, and citizenship education has come to make up an important part of the new social studies textbooks.

Secondly, changes have also happened to the five elements of citizenship education. The decrease of content related to national identity in the new social studies textbooks provides more room for some new elements of citizenship education, i.e., active participation and global citizenship, reflecting some recent trends in citizenship education which highlight global citizenship (Isin and Turner, 2002) and students' active participation in and beyond schools (Gearon and Brown, 2003). However, it must be mentioned that national identity is still the major, if not dominant, component of citizenship education in Mainland China, with a percentage of 51.4% in the *Morality and Society* (G3-6) textbooks. The main characteristic of citizenship education can be defined by Halpin's (2010) observation about China's national curriculum reform, that is, the subjects such as *Morality and Life* and *Morality and Society* are designed to "foster in students an appropriate patriotic spirit and commitment to civil society, including of course an adherence to socialist and democratic ideals" (p. 260).

Thirdly, the nature of the content and the pedagogies of citizenship education suggested in the textbooks have changed, too. To be specific, the content of citizenship education is more relevant to students' life experience in school, as we presented in the comparison of civic responsibilities and civil rights. Meanwhile, as some researchers observed (e.g., Chen and Reid, 2002; Zhao et al., 2007), the teaching of citizenship education in Mainland China was once dominated by information retention of some specific knowledge. This has changed, and by contrast, in the new social studies curriculum the textbook designers deliberately provide some controversial issues or questions to encourage primary students' discussion and reflection. This indicates that some effective teaching strategies such as critical thinking, group discussion and problem solving are advocated by today's citizenship education (See excerpt 4 and excerpt 6 for examples). Recently, Zhao and Fairbrother (2010) also noted the impact of the current national curriculum reform on citizenship pedagogies, trying to move Chinese schools away from teacher- and textbook-centered pedagogies to a more open classroom climate, learning by doing, and attention to students' own thinking, participation, and analytical and communicative skills.

In general, the comparison of the two sets of social studies textbooks, i.e., *Society (G4-6)* and *Morality and Society* (G3-6), reveals that significant differences exist between the old and new textbooks. In the old textbooks, i.e., *Society* (G4-6), citizenship education focuses strongly on national identity and ignores other elements of citizenship education, such as active participation and global citizenship. In the new textbooks, i.e., *Morality and Society* (G3-6), the content of citizenship education is enriched and more diverse, covering all the five elements of citizenship education. However, there are still some challenges in the new citizenship education. First, the national identity and civic responsibilities, reflecting the national and social expectation of the individual citizen, take up 64.7% of the social studies curriculum, while the content related to citizens' rights and active participation is much less (30.4% in total). Second, though the content of the new citizenship curriculum is more relevant to students' experience, these issues and examples are usually confined to students' participation in school life, community affairs and economic activities, seldom extending to participation in the political life and social activities of the state. The content about the state's political life inclines to only list the national policies, laws and institutions. These findings indicate that the new social studies curriculum is still inclined to adopt a relatively passive, obligation-based approach to citizenship education. While this approach can facilitate the stability of the state, it may not be fully conducive to citizen's active participation and political influence on social governance from the western perspective, which will contribute to social cohesion and integration in the long run (Jansen, Chioncel, and Dekkers, 2006). After all, citizenship education is in its infancy in Mainland China (Zhong and Lee, 2008). There is still a long journey of exploration and experimentation of citizenship education in social studies curriculum to be undertaken.

REFERENCES

Ball, D. L., and Cohen, D. K. (1996). Reform by the book: What is – or might be – the role of curriculum materials in teacher learning and instructional reform? *Educational Researcher, 25*(9), 6-14.

Chen, Y., and Reid, I. (2002). Citizenship education in Chinese schools: Retrospect and prospect. *Research in Education, 67*, 58-69.

Cheung, C.-K., and Kwok, S.-T. (1998). Social studies and ideological beliefs in Mainland China and Hong Kong. *Social Psychology of Education, 2*(2), 217-236.

Fairbrother, G. P. (2004). Citizenship education in a divided China, 1949-1995. *Asia Pacific Journal of Education, 24*(1), 29-42.

Fouts, J. T., and Chan, J. C. K. (1995). Confucius, Mao and modernization: Social studies education in the People's Republic of China. *Journal of Curriculum Studies*, *27*(5), 523-543.

Gearon, L., and Brown, M. C. (2003). Active participation in citizenship. In L. Gearon (Ed.), *Learning to teach citizenship in the secondary school* (pp. 203-224). London: RoutledgeFalmer.

Halpin, D. (2010). National curriculum reform in China and England: Origins, character and comparison. *Frontiers of Education in China*, *5*(2), 258-269.

Isin, E. F., and Turner, B. S. (2002).Citizenship studies: An introduction. In E. F. Isin and B. S. Turner (Eds.), *Handbook of citizenship studies* (pp.1-10). London: SAGE.

Janoski, T. (1998). *Citizenship and civil society: A framework of rights and obligations in liberal, traditional, and social democratic regimes.* Cambridge: Cambridge University Press.

Jansen, T., Chioncel, N., and Dekkers, H. (2006). Social cohesion and integration: Learning active citizenship. *British Journal of Sociology of Education*, *27*(2), 189-205.

Lo, L. N. K., and Man, S. W. (1996). Introduction: Nurturing the moral citizens of the future. In L. N. K. Lo and S. W. Man (Eds.), *Research and endeavours in the moral and civic education* (pp. ix-xxix). Hong Kong: Hong Kong Institute of Educational Research, The Chinese University of Hong Kong.

Ministry of Education (2002a). *National curriculum standard for Morality and Life*. Beijing: Beijing Normal University Press. (in Chinese).

Ministry of Education (2002b). *National curriculum standard for Morality and Society*. Beijing: Beijing Normal University Press. (in Chinese).

State Education Commission (1995). *Syllabus of Society for Whole-day Primary Schools of Nine-year Compulsory Education (Trail)*. Beijing: State Education Commission. (in Chinese).

Tsang, W. K. (1994). Non-colonized citizenship education: A conception of the citizenship education in Hong Kong schools after 1997. *Educational Journal*, *22*(2), 237-248. (in Chinese).

Tse, T. K. C. (2008). Images of good citizen: A comparative analysis of the elementary social studies textbooks in Mainland China and Taiwan. In S. T. Hall and M. W. Lewis (Eds.), *Education in China: 21st century issues and challenges* (pp.61-79). New York: Nova Science Publishers, Inc.

Tse, T. K. C., and Lee, J. C. K. (2008). China: Defending socialism with Chinese characteristics. In J. S. Landowe (Ed.), *Education in China* (pp.25-39). New York: Nova Science Publishers, Inc.

Wang, H. (2008). *The politics of depoliticizing politics and the end of China's 20th century* (Working paper series no. 73). Hong Kong: David C. Lam Institute for East-West Studies, Hong Kong Baptist University. (in Chinese).

Wang, W. L. (2006). *Citizenship education in social studies curriculum*. Beijing: China Social Sciences Press. (in Chinese).

Wang, W. L., and Huang, F. Q. (2007). The curriculum development of citizenship education in Mainland China since 1949. In A. R. Liu, J. H. Wang, Y. H. Deng and Q. H. Hong (Eds.), *Citizenship education in cross-strait* (pp.67-83). Taipei: Normal University Press. (in Chinese).

Wu, L. (2001). *Society (Volume 1-6)*. Beijing: People's Education Press. (in Chinese).

Zhao, X. (2003). *Morality and society (Volume 1-8)*. Beijing: People's Education press. (in Chinese).

Zhao, Y., Hoge, J. D., Choi, J., and Lee, S.-Y. (2007). Comparison of social studies education in the United States, China, and South Korea. *International Journal of Social Education, 21*(2), 91-122.

Zhao, Z., and Fairbrother, G. P. (2010). Pedagogies of cultural integration in Chinese citizenship education. In K. J. Kennedy, W. O. Lee and D. L. Grossman (Eds.), *Citizenship pedagogies in Asia and the Pacific* (pp. 37-52). Hong Kong: Comparative Education Research Centre, The Hong Kong University.

Zhong, M., and Lee, W. O. (2008). Citizenship curriculum in China: A shifting discourse towards Chinese democracy, law education and psychological health. In D. L. Grossman, W. O. Lee and K. J. Kennedy (Eds.), *Citizenship curriculum in Asia and the Pacific* (pp. 61-73). Hong Kong: Comparative Education Research Centre, The Hong Kong University.

Zhu, X., and Feng, X. (2008). On the development of citizenship education outlook in China. *Frontiers of Education in China, 3*(1), 1-21.

In: Curriculum Reform in China
Editors: Hong-Biao Yin and John Chi-Kin Lee

ISBN 978-1-61470-943-5
© 2012 Nova Science Publishers, Inc.

Chapter 10

CURRICULUM REFORM OF MORAL EDUCATION IN HIGH SCHOOLS IN CHINA

J. Mark Halstead and Chuanyan Zhu

ABSTRACT

The complexity of Moral Education (*deyu* in Chinese) is illustrated both by the breadth of content of the subject, which combines character education and personal and social development (including mental and physical health) with the academic study of politics, economics, law, ethics and philosophy, and also by the diversity of influences on contemporary Chinese values, which include the socialist, collectivist and patriotic values associated with the ideology of communism, traditional values such as Confucian teaching and contemporary social and economic values that are to some extent influenced by western materialism and individualism. The curriculum reforms seek to bring coherence to this complexity by encouraging teachers responsible for Moral Education to meet the needs of contemporary China by using modern theories and approaches to create future citizens of the highest moral calibre who retain their ideological and political commitments. The chapter reviews existing research on the impact of the reforms and then presents the findings of the authors' own research which examines school responses to the reforms in more detail, focusing on teachers' practice and students' attitudes. A clear tension emerges between the replacement of the old textbooks with their outdated material and the retention of the old system of university entrance examinations which inhibit the full implementation of the reforms. A further tension exists between the natural tendency of teachers to be authoritarian and dominate the whole instruction process and the intention of the reforms to make learning more autonomous and student-centred. These tensions may partly be resolved by more in-service training for teachers, but it is also important that Moral Education should remain in touch with the actual values students are developing in their own lives.

INTRODUCTION

There are three main factors which make moral education in China a much more complex concept than it is in the West. The first is the breadth of content: Moral Education (the phrase will be capitalised to indicate the school subject known as *deyu* in Chinese) combines not only character education and guidance on social and interpersonal values, which has been called 'micro-*deyu*' (Li, Zhong, Lin, and Zhang, 2004, p. 449), but also political, economic, legal and philosophical education and education for mental and physical health, which they call 'macro-*deyu*' (*ibid.*, p. 450). In other words, Moral Education combines many different kinds of learning, from academic to practical and from factual to ideological. The second factor is the diversity of moral values which underpin Moral Education. The values of collectivism, patriotism and socialism occupy pride of place in the Chinese moral education curriculum, with its ideological emphasis on the principles of Marxism-Leninism, the policies of the Communist Party of China and the teachings of its political leaders. However, there are two other major value frameworks operating in schools that do not sit altogether comfortably with socialist ideals. Traditional values such as Confucian teaching about authority, obedience and hierarchical structures are deeply ingrained in many teachers' and parents' consciousness and may colour the moral influence they have on children. In addition, the unprecedented social and economic transformations of the last thirty years have ushered in a new openness to democratic and more individualistic values and to a large extent it is these changes that have provided the impetus for the curriculum reforms discussed in this chapter, as the government is aware that preparing young people to compete in the global economy involves some shifts of emphasis within the domain of values education. The diversity of influences on Moral Education is made more complex by the big differences in values orientation between young and old, between rich and poor, between urban and rural communities and among minority groups within Mainland China. The third factor is the range of teaching and learning methods used in Moral Education. Though Moral Education is a compulsory subject on the curriculum for all Chinese students at all levels, it is also intended to be a cross-curricular theme that permeates other subjects and it is taught through compulsory extra-curricular activities like sport, military training and the activities of the Young Pioneers and the Communist Youth League and through special days like Children's Day and the Party's Day. The *process* of Moral Education is thus highly complex, and it is made more so because students may pick up messages through the hidden curriculum that are at variance with the overt curriculum. The term 'hidden curriculum' in this context includes such things as the example set by teachers, the school's ethos, routines and rituals and learning from peers (Halstead and Xiao, 2010).

Bringing coherence to this complexity and diversity in a way that ensures the compliance of teachers as well as meeting the needs of both students and country is a major challenge for policy makers in China and a major factor in the drive towards curriculum reform. Unsurprisingly, it is Moral Education as a timetabled subject on the curriculum that has received most attention in the reforms. Formal Moral Education courses are taught at all stages of schooling, from the start of primary schooling to the end of Senior High, and indeed at university as well. Ever since the founding of the People's Republic of China in 1949, and even more so during the Cultural Revolution (1966-76), the content of Moral Education has been mainly political. Over the last thirty years, however, a number of reforms have been ushered in, as described more fully below. In 1982 the subject was renamed Education in Ideology and Morality in primary schools (where there was a strong emphasis on patriotism, self-discipline, obedience and hard work) and Education in Ideology and Politics in junior and senior high schools (where the focus shifted more to socialist ideals, civic morals, Marxist theory, adherence to the law and sound personality and psychological traits). The ideological underpinnings of Moral Education at university level have also moved from their exclusive focus on Marxist theory prior to the 1980s to include first the teachings of Mao and more recently Deng's theory of 'socialism with Chinese characteristics' with its emphasis on a market economy combined with socialist reconstruction.

Like any other subject, Moral Education is supposed to be taught by specialist teachers at all stages of schooling, though this is not always the case in rural areas, or even in some major cities. Like other subjects, too, teaching is based on officially approved textbooks; actually, these are chosen at the local level, but there is not much variety because they all have to follow national guidelines. Nie (2008) provides a valuable case study of Moral Education in a secondary school in the south-west of China, which she calls 'Central High School', carried out from September 1998 to March 1999. She outlines both the administrative structure of Moral Education in the school and the nature of the intended moral curriculum. The school's Politics and Ideology Department includes two directors and four teachers, under the control of a vice-principal. Each teacher has special responsibilities; for example, one is responsible for the Communist Youth League and another for problem behaviour and school security. In addition to their teaching of ideology and politics, the team has overall responsibility for sports and students' physical well-being, for the cleanliness of the physical environment, for rituals like the flag ceremonies, for other whole-school activities like field trips and singing contests and for evaluating the class masters (i.e. form tutors), the class collectives and students. However, the Moral Education teachers in this school do not appear so settled or so valued as staff in other departments, and their subject is generally considered low status. Though Moral Education is supposed to be integrated into the lessons of other subjects, it is often squeezed out by more pressing matters like preparation for tests and examinations. Class masters also carry special responsibility for the personal and ideological development of students and for promoting patriotic and collectivist values in their class, but once again they generally pay more attention to the students' academic performance. At the heart of the taught Moral Education curriculum lies a distinctive conception of morality as closely related to ideology, politics and civic virtue, and a distinctive understanding of the purpose of moral education as the ideological shaping (some use the word 'indoctrination': Li, 1990, p. 170) of young people to accept the communist ideal as represented by the Communist Party of China (CPC), based on the values of collectivism, patriotism, socialism and Marxism.

It is these two distinctive underlying features (the conception of morality and the purpose of Moral Education) that represent the biggest difference between Chinese and western moral education. While western moral education is concerned to open students' eyes to different moral perspectives, to give them the tools to make meaningful moral decisions and ultimately to encourage personal and moral autonomy, Moral Education in China has traditionally been seen as the transmission of 'correct' political thoughts, appropriate moral principles and officially accepted ideology to the next generation. Indeed, Moral Education in China is all-encompassing, intended to shape the entire identity, values, attitudes and worldview of young people. Chinese Moral Education differs from western in other respects as well. First, because Moral Education is an examined subject in China, there is a greater emphasis on objectified knowledge and understanding and less on identifying the needs of individual students and helping them to develop their individual worldviews and values. Second, there is no encouragement for students to adopt a critical perspective towards the values to which they are introduced in Moral Education. Third, there is always a 'right answer' to ethical dilemmas, and it is the role of the teacher to pass this on to students. Students are not taught different ethical theories or encouraged to make autonomous rational moral judgments.

In recent years, particularly as a result of the opening up policies, Chinese educationalists and academics have become much more familiar with western theory and practice in the domain of moral education. Some have studied in the West, and many more have engaged in dialogue with western educationalists through international conferences (such as the 37th annual conference of the Association for Moral Education held in Nanjing in October 2011) and collaborative publications (such as the Special Issue of the *Journal of Moral Education* on 'Moral Education in Changing Chinese Societies', Li, Taylor and Yang, 2004). However, it would be a serious mistake to assume that one of the purposes of the curriculum reforms in China is to emulate western approaches, though this may occasionally be an unintended outcome of the reforms. In fact, the reforms are focused much more on the perceived educational needs of Chinese society and on finding solutions that are appropriate to the Chinese context when these needs are not currently being met. Some elements in the reforms can be traced to Confucian thinking, others to western thinking. In fact, it will become apparent as this review of the curriculum reforms of moral education proceeds that though western influence can be detected on the developing methods used in moral education in China, there is very little influence on its aims or content. First, however, we turn in the next section to the need for reform.

NEED FOR CONTINUING REFORM

Many commentators note that in spite of strong official support for Moral Education and its permeation across the curriculum, Moral Education has been less than successful in China (Bakken, 2000; Meyer, 1990). Lu and Gao describe Moral Education as 'the least welcome subject' in the school curriculum and say that it has 'evoked some students' active dislike' (2004, p. 496). While it may be naïve to expect that even good moral education will immediately result in reduced levels of corruption and crime, at least the success of moral education is open to question in a situation where, to use Nie's (2008, p. 3) words, 'there is a confusion of moral standards ... and immoral behaviors have become rampant'. As early as 1990, Deng Xiaoping said that at the time of China's massive economic development the biggest failure of the reforms so far was ideological and political education.

Although there may be general agreement on the need for stronger personal moral values at a time of major social change and thus on the need for the reform of moral education, there is much less agreement on the factors that have contributed to Moral Education's lack of success and therefore on the precise reforms that are needed. The remainder of this section lists eight factors that have been identified by Chinese scholars as areas where there is room for improvement in the provision of Moral Education.

First, Moral Education appears to occupy a comparatively lowly position in the hierarchy of academic subjects (CPC and State Council, 2000). Success in Chinese, Mathematics and English is normally the top priority for parents, teachers and students, because these subjects carry more weight in the University Entrance Examination, and Moral Education is often perceived as one of the least useful and least interesting of the remaining compulsory subjects.

Second, Moral Education is often criticised for not taking adequate account of recent social and economic changes in Chinese society. Qi and Tang (2004) identify five such changes which they consider to be particularly relevant to the provision of Moral Education: the formation of the market economy system; the impact of globalisation, mass media and the Internet; the emergence of cultural diversity and value pluralism; trends towards democratisation in politics; and structural changes in the family (pp. 467-475). These various influences are transforming the way young people view the world; they may have greater environmental awareness than their parents' generation, for example, and though some may be more materialistic, others may be more critical of the materialism and hypocrisy of older people and leaders. The Moral Education curriculum has not kept pace with the new realities of life in China, and the values, ideologies and cultures promoted in schools are increasingly out of touch with young people's everyday experiences and values.

Third, moral educators can no longer rely on indoctrination in order to achieve commitment to moral and political ideals (Ying, 2007). The CPC's control over how people think is in decline and the younger generation is becoming more individualistic and independent-minded. Lu (2004) argues that the market economy is creating 'a new space for the development of independent character' and that Moral Education should be opening up 'the possibility of cultivating self-determined, liberal, democratic, equal and fair individuals' (quoted in Li, Zhong, Lin, and Zhang, 2004, p. 448).

Fourth, because the message of Moral Education lessons is often rigid, abstract and removed from the reality of children's lives, they may find them boring and irrelevant. What they learn does not help them to make moral judgments in real life situations. Students are sometimes blamed for not engaging fully with Moral Education, but the lack of engagement may have more to do with the content of the lessons than with the moral failure of the students. Lu and Gao (2004, p. 496) give an example of the way a school textbook tackles the teaching of the 'ten moral requirements' (National Education Committee, NEC, 1997a): each of the 'requirements' (such as 'show brotherliness to fellow classmates' or 'work hard and live simply') is illustrated first with a picture and a description and then with a story from the life history of a Chinese leader in the past (particularly Mao Zedong). The remoteness of the approach and the growing tension between Moral Education and the students' own social and moral realities may encourage them to dismiss the subject as unimportant, so that they end up throwing out the baby of moral principles with the bathwater of outdated and irrelevant teaching material.

Fifth, two particular issues have been identified with the *structure* of Moral Education. In spite of the rhetoric of integration into other subjects in the curriculum, Moral Education is largely treated in practice as an isolated domain of knowledge, not only having (like other subjects) its own courses, its own teachers, its own departments and its own textbooks, but also failing to involve families and local communities. Also, the way that Moral Education is structured in terms of the logic of the subject pays inadequate attention to the developmental stages of children's moral understanding. Especially for young children, the political aims of the curriculum may exceed their capacity to understand and does not allow them to progress step by step (Lu and Gao 2004, p. 496).

Sixth, the content may be problematic in other ways, in that it consists of a top-down imposition of moral values (Lu and Gao 2004, p. 496) and may encourage the uninformed following of moral guidelines rather than autonomous moral decision-making. There is a strong emphasis on discipline and following moral rules, and comparatively little emphasis on moral motivation, character development, guidance, making moral judgments or developing and practising virtuous behaviour. Ying (2007) suggests that not enough attention is paid to children's need for moral relationships and for personal, social and emotional development.

Seventh, the teaching methods are often old-fashioned and inappropriate. Lu and Gao (2004, pp. 496-497) describe a system that is still heavily dependent on the teacher's total dominance of the class through lecturing, talking, reading and explaining, while the students remain passive recipients trying to memorise the contents of the lessons and the textbook for regurgitation in the Moral Education examination. They comment ironically that this is neither a moral nor an effective way of developing children's personalities. Because of the absence of a more interactive, student-centred pedagogy, students remain unengaged and their initiative, creativity and moral competence under-developed (Zhan and Ning, 2004, p. 512).

Eighth, teachers of Moral Education are sometimes criticised for showing low standards of professional ethics and lacking commitment and sincerity, perhaps because of the lower status and salaries that Moral Education attracts. But there is another side to this - the increasing difficulty of the role of Moral Education teacher. They are traditionally expected to serve as role models to their students, but at the same time they may need to demonstrate new skills (such as facilitating moral discussions) for which they are largely unprepared, and while all this is going on they may have to find some way of coping with a growing tension between their personal values and the values they have to teach (Li, Taylor, and Yang, 2004, pp. 423-424; Nie, 2008, pp. 77-80).

To sum up, there are many areas in the provision of Moral Education that remain problematic, and even where the need for reform is clear there may be uncertainty about what kind of reforms are in the best interests of all parties and what the priorities should be. Change has therefore been slow and cautious, but it is moving forward. The next section examines the curriculum reforms more closely in the period from the end of the Cultural Revolution to the present day.

CURRICULUM REFORMS OF MORAL EDUCATION

Curriculum reform of Moral Education has been an almost continuous process since the early 1980s, with a whole series of proposals, programmes, policies, directives, guidelines, statements of principle and teaching plans being issued by the CPC and the NEC, renamed the Ministry of Education (MOE) in 1997. These documents fall into two main categories. First, even since the great discussion was launched at the Third Plenary Session of the Eleventh Central Committee of the CPC in 1978 about the relation between socialism and capitalism and the need for people to contribute to China's economic development, there have been a string of policy statements issued setting out the framework of national values which provide the foundation for moral education. These include the national policy of 'ruling the country according to the rule of law', launched in 1997, the national policy of 'ruling the country with morality', launched in 2002, and the *Programme for Improving Civic Morality* (CPC, 2001). These have been interpreted as shifting the focus of *deyu* from ideological indoctrination towards citizenship education, with an increased emphasis on public morality, family virtue and professional ethics as well as the more traditional socialist morality (Li, Zhong, Lin, and Zhang, 2004, pp. 458-459). Secondly, many documents specifically set out revised approaches to Moral Education. These include a publication setting out the principles of ideological and political education (NEC, 1996), a series of policies developed by the National Education Committee (NEC, 1997b) setting out regulations for moral education and the standards of daily behaviour in schools, and a whole set of publications from the CPC, such as their proposals for 'reinforcing and improving Moral Education work in primary and high schools under the new situation' (CPC and State Council, 2000), for 'carrying forward and cultivating the national spirit in primary and high schools (CPC and Peoples' Republic of China, 2004) and for 'improving the ethical, ideological and moral standards of children and young people across the country' (CPC and State Council, 2004). Undoubtedly the most important documents, however, are those actually setting out the new curricula for Moral Education, to which we now turn in more detail.

A trial version of the *Guidelines for the Primary School Ideology and Morality Curriculum and the Junior High School Ideology and Politics Curriculum in the Nine-Year Compulsory Education* was produced in 1997 (NEC, 1997b), with an amended version being issued four years later and guidelines for the course Moral Character and Life (which is studied in grades 1 and 2 of primary school) and Moral Character and Society (studied in grades 3-6) being issued in 2002 (MOE, 2002a, 2002b). The main changes in the primary curriculum include a focus on lifelong Moral Education and the use of examples related to the reality of children's everyday lives. The approach is child-centred, collaborative and discussion-based, helping the children to understand their own experiences and emotions and gradually develop empathy, a spirit of sharing, an acceptance of diversity, a rejection of excessive competitiveness and an appreciation of human ecology (Lu and Gao, 2004). The experimental version of the Curriculum Guidelines for Ideology and Morality in Junior High Schools was issued in 2003 (MOE, 2003), with similar guidelines for the Ideology and Politics course in Senior High Schools being issued a year later (MOE, 2004). The Junior High curriculum focuses on issues in morality, law, national conditions and mental health (for a fuller discussion of the aims and theoretical foundations of this course, see Zhang and Ning, 2004), and the Senior High curriculum builds on this with compulsory courses in Economics in Life, Politics in Life, Culture in Life and Philosophy in Life as well of a range of options designed to extend students' understanding of scientific socialism, national and international organisations, scientific thinking and ethics. In 2005, the Ministry of Education announced its decision to further revise the Moral Education curriculum in both primary and high schools, but these documents have not yet been released.

The aims of the reforms of the moral education curriculum are (a) to meet the needs of contemporary China by creating future citizens of the highest calibre while retaining their ideological and political commitments, and (b) to use modern theories and approaches to make learning as efficient and effective as possible. The first of these aims involves combining the old emphasis on developing students' knowledge and skills with a new degree of attention to emotions, attitudes and values; students are to be guided so that they can make the 'right' choice of values, develop a sense of social responsibility, work hard for the people and have lofty ideals (MOE, 2001). The second aim involves new methods and processes of teaching and learning, particularly active learning, discovery learning and learning through experience; making assessment more open, active, creative and multi-dimensional; and leaving teachers free to construct their own resources within the broad boundaries provided by the curriculum guidelines. Students are encouraged to think creatively and to approach questions from different angles and perspectives. The old requirement that a single standardised set of textbooks should be used for Moral Education throughout China has been replaced with an acceptance of different textbooks so long as they meet the basic guidelines set by the Ministry of Education. The regulations for assessment have also been relaxed: there is no compulsory examination in Moral Education at the end of primary school (though some districts have retained it on a discretionary basis), and an open-book examination is the norm at Junior High. Two different systems operate in the College Entrance Examination at the end of Senior High: in Shanghai and Beijing moral education is no longer included, but elsewhere it is.

The reforms have major implications for teachers; in fact, they involve a fundamental re-conceptualisation of the teachers' role. Teachers are no longer to see themselves as 'the authority in a higher status' but as 'the chairman in an equal relationship' (Zhou, 2006, p. 141). Former didactic practices are no longer acceptable, and teachers must adopt a more inter-active, student-centred approach, listening to their students, facilitating discussions and planning activities together, helping them to study and guiding them to think through and learn from their diverse experiences. The teacher can no longer simply rely on repeating what is written in the textbooks, but needs to play a more active part in planning lessons and resources. Since these approaches are new to many teachers, they need to develop new skills if they are to satisfy the requirements of the curriculum reforms, and this points to the need for urgent initial and continuing professional development for Moral Education teachers preparing themselves for this new role (Zhu and Liu, 2004).

RESEARCHING THE IMPACT OF THE REFORMS

In any evaluation of the practical impact of the reforms of the Moral Education curriculum the following questions are central and point to the need for empirical investigation. What demands do the reforms make of teachers and of students? Is real change taking place at the school level? How are the teachers' attitudes changing? How is practice changing? What factors hinder implementation of the reforms? What professional development is being offered to teachers in conjunction with the reforms, and how successful is this professional development in terms of facilitating change? What other influences impact on teachers' practice? How do teachers balance the reforms with other considerations such as the traditional culture of the school, the organisational structure of the school and their own personal values? What are the implications of the reforms for school leadership and management? What impact is all this having on students' moral development and moral attitudes? Do students support the reforms? Is there any correspondence between the moral and ideological values the schools promote and the actual values the students hold? What further reforms would the students like to see?

In fact, very little research has been carried out on the effects of the recent reforms so far, and none (to the best of our knowledge) has included the impact on students. Zhang and Ning (2004, pp. 514-516) provide an overview of some of the main theoretical research that influenced the thinking behind the curriculum reform of Moral Education. Nie's (2008) ethnographic study of 'Central High School' in southwestern China actually includes important and detailed findings about students' attitudes to the Moral Education curriculum, based on observation, in-depth interviews and a questionnaire of students' attitudes, but since this research was carried out in the late 1990s, it was before the latest round of curriculum reform which is the main focus of the current chapter. She found that many students had indifferent or negative attitudes towards the political and ideological content of the Moral Education curriculum at that time, and that they were aware of major tensions between the officially promoted collectivist morality and the reality of the competitive learning environment in school. The students no longer viewed their teachers as convincing role models and admitted that their moral values were more influenced by the media and by current economic realities in China than by the school's Moral Education practices such as the campaign of learning from Lei Feng and the scoring system of conduct evaluation (Nie, 2008, pp. 61-86). Students learned to manipulate the system to their own advantage and subvert the intended goals of formal Moral Education (*ibid.*, pp. 115-116).

Other existing research focuses on teachers' attitudes to the reforms. Li (2008) interviewed the Ideology and Politics teachers in senior high schools in the Zabei District in Shanghai. Teachers said that students did not take their subject seriously because they saved all their energy for subjects that featured in the college entrance examination. One Ideology and Politics teacher said: 'What makes me feel tired is that I have to use all kinds of methods ... to keep them interested in the course. If I didn't work hard on it, they would do something else or sleep in class' (2008, p. 24). Teachers also complained about the new textbooks, saying they had lots of questions about them but no-one to ask. They also resented still being assessed by results, which they thought inappropriate for the kind of work they were doing. Zhang (2008) and his colleagues investigated all the Year 12 Ideology and Politics teachers in the 140 senior high schools in Guangzhou, where experimental approaches to the new curriculum had been introduced in 2004. They found that teachers seemed to prefer knowledge based modules, the older, more comprehensive textbooks and written tests, and felt less comfortable with their newly defined tasks of providing more resources themselves, encouraging students to engage in the autonomous construction of knowledge and providing guidance rather than indoctrination. Apart from these few examples, most writing about the moral education curriculum reforms tends to be little more than a re-iteration or exposition of the principles underpinning the reforms. Thus Wang (2010) expounds the philosophy behind the new textbooks, Zhou (2006) explains some of the implications of the teacher's new role as facilitator, and Zuo (2009) and Yuan (2008) explore what autonomous learning involves in practice in the classroom.

The research described in the next two sections of the present chapter was carried out in the summer of 2010, and is intended to supplement and extend existing findings. Originally, the intention was to rely entirely on on-line interviews with teachers and young people. The first five interviews were carried out between 24 July and 6 August 2010 (two with teachers of Moral Education, two with students and one with a head teacher), but they did not generate very detailed responses. There was also a problem of lack of openness in some replies. While personal opinions were sometimes expressed, there was a tendency to regurgitate official policies and intentions without much critical reflection, as if both teachers and students were reluctant to express their true thoughts unless they had complete anonymity. It was apparent from reading the blogs of some teachers about the curriculum reforms that there was a high level of dissatisfaction with the reforms because teachers had not been consulted in the process and because although they were meant to be promoting learner autonomy they (the teachers) had little autonomy themselves in the classroom. Students also used blogs to express their real thoughts, away from school pressure to conform and put a positive gloss on everything. Further interviews were therefore abandoned in favour of a critical analysis of student and teacher blogs that were already in the public domain (at http://blog.sina.com.cn /lm/edu/index.html). Some 600 blogs written by teachers were read, mainly dating from September 2007 (when most schools in China began to implement to new curricula) to the present and selected on the basis that the bloggers expressed themselves consistently and updated their blogs regularly, together with over 2,000 blogs by high school students who wrote about their values, daily lives, families and teachers. For convenience, all the blogs were drawn from sina.com.cn, the largest blog provider in China. Under the subtitle of 'Education', bloggers are grouped into 'teachers' circle', parents' circle' and 'students' circle', which provide an inclusive sampling frame. Coming from many different locations in China, the blogs represent a much richer source of data than the interviews as well as providing genuine insight into the thoughts of the bloggers. In order to keep the amount of data manageable, the blogs of five students (New Life, Xiaozhiruoyu, Xin Xiaojun, Yan Xiang, and Yu) and five moral education teachers (Bubai Rensheng, Dong Kai, Hetang Tingyu, Rang Xinling Huxi Yangguang, and Xiao Dongfeng) were selected for detailed analysis for the purposes of the present article. They were chosen because the bloggers wrote extensively on the curriculum reforms and educational practices in school, because they updated their blogs frequently and also because they included personal opinions about education, teaching and learning. For example, the blogger Rang Xinling Huxi Yangguang ('Let the spirit inhale sunshine') explains that she uses blogging to gather material for her Ideology and Politics classes, to report on activities like the Ideology and Politics conferences she takes part in and her attempts to improve her own work, and to set these in the context of her daily life and her own opinions on education. Only teachers who confirmed their identity as Ideology and Politics teachers and confirmed their real names and the names of their schools were selected (and similar criteria were used for students), but the detailed blog websites have not been provided, in order to protect their identity. Because of the small numbers (and because bloggers may not be typical of the broader population), no claims are made that these are necessarily representative of the broader student or teacher bodies, though they provide valuable insights into the way some teachers and students think.

RESPONSES FROM TEACHERS TO THE REFORMS

Initial responses to the curriculum reforms were mixed. The first teacher interviewed comments that the new curriculum is easier for students because the teaching is linked to real life situations rather than emphasising 'the integrity of the theory' and also because it encourages students to develop independent study skills. After his first term of teaching the new curriculum, however, one blogger (Bubai Rensheng, 2008) writes that it does not fully match up to expectations, because he expects students to be enthusiastic and co-operative as they develop lifelong learning skills but in fact he finds that his subject has been squeezed by the extra time needed for Chinese, English and Maths. He reports that his students see his Politics lessons as a time to relax and be creative, but is ashamed to find the average examination score of his students is a whole point lower than other classes. The reforms have got rid of the complex and outdated material from the old textbooks and help learning to be more focused on analysis and problem-solving and less on memorisation. However, teachers also point out that the reformed curriculum gives them more work, as they are worried that the new textbooks do not provide enough information to allow the students to perform well, and so they have to spend more time in preparation and supplement the textbooks with materials they produce themselves (Teacher interview 2).

Xiao Dongfeng (2010) writes about the importance of having goals and ideals, and Dong Kai (2009) looks forward with optimism to the 60th anniversary of the founding of the People's Republic of China, noting in particular the economic developments of recent times, the new emphasis on democratic socialist values in politics, the overhaul of the legal system and the growing belief in equality and justice. Bubai Rensheng (2008) recognises that these are the values that underpin the latest curriculum reforms of moral education, but also uses his blog to critique some of the ways these underlying principles are developing in practice in schools. In particular, he questions what the true relationship is between the values of democracy and equality and the processes of teaching and learning. He warns against going overboard and refusing to correct students' work or pick students to answer questions in class in the name of 'equality'. He argues for a balanced approach, and suggests that 'a correct perception of equality' might involve respecting the 'different opinions or ideas the students may have'. He accepts the goals of relating the teaching content to real life and paying attention to the students' emotional development, but advises teachers not to lose sight of other objectives like imparting knowledge and developing competencies. He worries that some of the changes are being implemented only superficially because classroom discussions, independent thinking and collaborative activities are being utilised for their own sake, irrespective of whether they are actually facilitating learning and understanding. There is so much 'activity' going on in some classrooms that lessons may not be brought to a successful conclusion and the learning objectives may not be met. 'Discussion' is a popular classroom activity, but it may not always fit the teaching content, and if the topic under discussion is too easy or too difficult or too abstract, the lesson may not have positive outcomes.

Several teachers are very positive about the student-centred focus in the revised curriculum. One blog describes how this principle permeates the entire provision of one of the schools he visited that serves as a model for the implementation of the curriculum reforms, Dulangkou High School:

> 'Every element from the ideas and principles to the conduct of teaching and learning, the choice of teaching and learning model, the assessment of the students, the management of the teachers, the spirit of the school and the school services reveals the 'student-centred' principle.' (Hetang Tingyu, 2010)

In this particular school, there are no school examinations, no homework, no competitive ranking of students, and there is a stronger emphasis on the personal development of both students and teachers. He is impressed by the students' optimism, co-operation and confidence, and links this to the teachers' progressive approach, professionalism and team spirit. Of course, this school is exceptional, but the principle of student-centredness is changing the approach of many schools. The second teacher interviewed mentions that all activity in the classroom now puts the student first by focusing, for example, on developing the skill of analysing and resolving problems.

The main thing that holds back the full implementation of the principle of student-centeredness and other key principles of the curriculum reforms, in the teachers' view, is the continuing emphasis on test results (in the evaluation of teachers' performance as well as in determining student progression to the next stage of their education). Liu (2008, pp. 139-140) notes that parents may request that their children are transferred to another school if they feel that the school is not helping them to get the best possible result in the university entrance examination, and points out that 'the parents' opportunistic actions hinder the implementation of the new curriculum to some degree'. In a blog written in 2009, Rang Xinling Huxi Yangguang describes how parental pressure forced schools to reinstate extra lessons in the evenings and weekends that had been discontinued as part of the curriculum reforms. Bubai Rensheng notes that the younger teachers tend to adopt the more traditional methods of the older teachers 'out of fear that their students' examination results will fall behind' (2008). On a more positive note, however, he also comments in detail on the way both national and local test papers of the university entrance examinations are starting to reflect the ideas and principles of the new curriculum, by 'using situations from real life to bring the questions closer to reality and to the students' lives', by 'building emotional and moral factors into the questions' and by 'asking open questions' to encourage student creativity and autonomous learning (Bubai Rensheng, 2010). Recently, for example, there have been questions about the problem of over-packaging products, the social phenomenon of 'street stands', the experience of the Olympic Games and the issue of rural migrant workers.

All the teachers agree on the need for more in-service training to prepare them for the curriculum changes. Both interviewees say they received just one week's training before the implementation of the new curriculum, including input from the textbook editors and the sharing of ideas and experiences by teachers from the experimental schools. Of course, the blogs themselves also represent an important way for teachers to share and discuss activities and materials. Xiao Dongfeng (2010) includes a number of detailed lesson plans as well as inspirational thoughts, and Xinling Huxi Yangguang (2009) describes an in-service activity in which the Ideology and Politics teachers in two senior high schools listen to each other's lessons and discuss them together.

RESPONSES FROM YOUNG PEOPLE TO THE REFORMS

The students' blogs and interviews (two bloggers, Xiaozhiruoyu and New Life, were also interviewed) provide significant insights into their personal feelings, values, attitudes and worldviews which allow a fuller understanding of their response to the curriculum reforms of moral education. As one would expect, there is a wide diversity in the values and feelings expressed. For example, the first student interviewed says that her week of military training is the happiest time she has had in Senior High School, whereas Xin Xiaojun (2009) appears to feel quite uncomfortable about military training. The latter's blog mentions her feelings of relief when it was over, though she describes how it made her reflect on her own self-centredness and made her more aware of the value of collectivism. Several students express their patriotism (New Life, for example, writes in 2007 that students should not forget their obligations to China), though there also seems to be a trend to greater individualism, which comes out in different ways. New Life (2008) describes the importance of personal morality in her own framework of values, and expresses regret and puzzlement that not all intelligent people are equally moral. Xin Xiaojun (2010) also writes disapprovingly of a classmate whose ideals relate only to making money. Some students seem to suffer from profound loneliness, in spite of superficial friendships, and Yu (2009) even suggests that 'hoping to die ... is a characteristic of most Chinese students'. Xin Xiaojun (2010) explains, however, that they often put a brave face on things to stop their parents from worrying. She talks wistfully of her own ideals and dreams in the past, and described poetically how she blocks these out as she grows older:

> 'I lock myself in a box named reality ... ignoring the voice from my heart. There is only a ruin of the dreams in my heart, full of scars. I have no desire for tomorrow or the future. I have trained myself to be such a cold person in my journey of growing up.' (Xin Xiaojun, 2010)

Xiaozhiruoyu (2010) mentions that boredom is a universal experience for the students. She recalls sitting by the window and reading a sentence written on the windowsill: 'Life is so boring', followed by a reply written by someone else: 'I agree.' Most of the students seem to be under pressure the whole time. Xiaozhiruoyu (2010), who is in her last year of Junior High School, writes that her teacher asked the students to stop all hobbies like music and sports to focus on the Entrance Examination to Senior High School. Xin Xiaojun (2010) addresses her class master directly in one blog: 'I hope you don't put more pressure on me. Is that OK?' New Life (2006) writes of her struggles throughout the course and describes how she spent all summer studying. She shows that her own framework of values has been directly influenced by what she has been taught in Moral Education, and she applies the principles she has learned in her Ideology and Politics course to her personal friendships and relationships with her classmates.

Some of the students explain in their blogs what they want from the reform of the Moral Education curriculum. New Life (2006) writes of the importance of creativity and of learner autonomy (in other words, self-directed study rather than passively learning from the teacher). Xiaozhiruoyu praises the textbook, which she says covers the content so well that the teacher is not really necessary, particularly because her Ideology and Politics test for the Senior High School Entrance Examination is an open book test, though she also feels that the heavy dependence on the textbook has an inhibiting effect on class discussions and more active learning (Student interview 2). Yan Xiang (2009) writes of his appreciation of his teachers for their hard work, simple kindness, good humour, equal concern for all students and willingness to go the extra mile, though New Life criticises some teachers for not treating the students equally; in student interview 1 she complains that they pay disproportionate attention to the most academic students.

The general impression from the students' blogs and interviews is that they feel the reforms have not got to the root of the problems with the Moral Education curriculum. This is not so much because they feel negative towards the regime-sponsored ideology and values, as Nie (2008) suggests in her study of Central High School. On the contrary, the students demonstrate an acceptance of many of the values they have been taught in their Moral Education classes, both personal and collectivist, and they write extensively about how these values affect their relationships, their attitude to work and their political opinions. Their criticisms sometimes refer to very specific issues, such as the increased costs they incur through needing to buy extra textbooks and other materials from school and the fact that some students have been disadvantaged by the changes because they were unable to repeat the year's study or the Entrance Examination. More generally, the students express their concern that teachers do not always set a good moral example: New Life says that some teachers actually got their jobs by bribery (Student interview 1), and Yu (2006) writes that teachers leak the examination questions in an attempt to raise the scores of their own students. The examination system is at the heart of most of the students' complaints, because they feel that it undermines the reforms. Yu (2007) describes the College Entrance Examination as a 'huge burden for students' that leads 'both students and schools to use all kinds of tricks'. He says that the reforms are intended to 'alleviate the students' burden', but the schools are unwilling to do more than change the textbooks they use. Their decision to retain the examination system, weekend classes, the ranking of student performance and the tight control of the teachers has left the students 'very angry and very helpless' (2008). New Life says that if she were the Minister of Education, she would group students according to their interests and ability to learn and teach them accordingly, and she would encourage autonomous learning rather than passive learning enforced by the teacher (Student interview 1).

CONCLUSION

In conclusion, it is clear that the reforms of the Moral Education curriculum are not yet complete – either geographically, because of the difficulty of implementing them in the more rural areas of China, or educationally, because there are still significant obstacles in the pathway to full reform, notably the examination system, which has a wash-back effect on the way teachers plan their lessons and retain their traditional authority and control in the classroom (Alderson and Wall, 1993). The immediate aim of the reforms is to modernise teaching methods and make them more student-centred, and the longer term aim is to encourage more independent thinking on the part of the students as they take more responsibility for their own learning. Thus the reform of the textbooks involves moving away from the old systematic approach to the transmission of political and moral knowledge and understanding to a new approach that puts students' needs, students' experiences and students' development at the centre of curriculum planning (Wang, 2010). However, autonomy and independent thinking are not yet a reality in many schools, for several reasons. First, the authority of the teacher is still deeply engrained in Chinese culture, and this encourages dogmatic teaching and tends to lead to an indoctrinatory approach. Secondly, teachers find it hard to change their traditional dominance over everything that goes on in the classroom, and anyway they believe that this approach is still needed in order to help their students to achieve their best in the examinations (Zhu, 2010). Thirdly, there is still the concept of the single right answer to moral problems and moral dilemmas, and this restricts the freedom of students to explore values for themselves freely and openly; Lei (2009), for example, writes of the need for Ideology and Politics teachers to 'correct the wrong opinions and help the students to agree on the right opinion'. Finally, there is uncertainty about the actual value of autonomy, and the Chinese concept of 'learner autonomy' is very different from the western notion of personal autonomy as a central goal of liberal education (Halstead and Zhu, 2009). Unless teachers' authoritarianism and control gradually change, it may mean that Moral Education in schools slides further adrift from the realities of life for many

Chinese young people. The need for continuing in-service training for Moral Education teachers remains as urgent as ever.

In spite of the uncertainty about the future direction of Moral Education in schools following the reforms, let us end on a positive note. Several teachers in our research write of their continuing determination to show love for their students. In a blog entitled 'Teach like Your Hair's on Fire', Rang Xinling Huxi Yangguang sets out her belief that 'a teacher's value does not depend on how many years he teaches, but on how many years he teaches with his heart' (2010), and Bubai Rensheng writes that in the case of difficult students 'only the love from teachers can nourish their hearts, give them confidence and improve their personality so that they can embark on an appropriate life track' (2007). There may be some negativity on the part of students, as noted above, but there are also grounds for optimism if teachers are able to stay true to their ideals as they continue the implementation process.

REFERENCES

Alderson, J. C., and Wall, D. (1993). Does washback exist? *Applied Linguistics, 14*(2), 115-129.

Bakken, B. (2000). *The exemplary society: human improvement, social control and the dangers of modernity in China.* Oxford: Oxford University Press.

Communist Party of China (CPC) (2001). *Programme for improving civic morality (Gongmin daode jianshe shishi gangyao).* Beijing: People's Daily Press. (in Chinese).

CPC, and People's Republic of China (2004). *Implementation outlines to carry forward and cultivate the national spirit in primary and high schools (zhongxiaoxue kaizhan hongyang he peiyu minzu jingshen jiaoyu shishi gangyao).* Retrieved from http://www.moe.edu.cn/base/deyu/15.htm. (in Chinese).

CPC, and State Council (2000). *Proposals for reinforcing and improving primary and high school Moral Education (Zhonggong zhongyang bangongting guowuyuan bangongting guanyu shiying xinxingshi jinyibu jiaqiang he gaijin zhongxiaoxue deyu gongzuo de yijian).* Retrieved from http://www.moe.edu.cn/base/deyu/6.htm. (in Chinese).

CPC, and State Council (2004). *Proposals for improving the ethical, ideological and moral standards of children and young people across the country (Zhonggong zhongyang guowuyuan guanyu jinyibu jiaqiang he gaijing weichengnianren sixiang daide jianshe de ruogan yijian).* Retrieved from http://www.ccyl.org.cn/ywdd/files/ ywdd20040323.htm. (in Chinese).

Halstead, J. M., and Xiao, J. M. (2010). Values education and the hidden curriculum. In T. Lovat, R. Toomey and N. Clement (Eds.), *International research handbook on values education and student wellbeing* (pp. 303-318). Dordrecht: Springer.

Halstead, J. M., and Zhu, C. Y. (2009). Autonomy as an element in Chinese educational reform: a case study of English lessons in a senior high school in Beijing. *Asia Pacific Journal of Education, 29*(4), 443-56.

Lei, X. S. (2009). The case teaching and learning model in the new Ideology and Politics in senior high schools (lun gaozhong zhengzhi xin kecheng zhong de anli jiaoxue). *Chinese After School Education,* (8), 214, 139.

Li, H. (2008). Constructing the supporting policies to improve the adaptation of the Ideology and Politics teachers in senior high schools to the second phase of the curriculum reform (Jianli peitao zhidu tisheng gaozhong zhengzhi jiaoshi "er qi kegai" shiyingxing). *The Science Education Article Collection, 9*(2), 24-26.

Li, M. S. (1990). Moral education in the People's Republic of China. *Journal of Moral Education, 18*(3), 159-71.

Li, P., Zhong, M. H., Lin, B., and Zhang, H. J. (2004). *Deyu* as moral education in modern China: ideological functions and transformations. *Journal of Moral Education, 33*(4), 449-64.

Li, M. S., Taylor, M. J., and Yang, S. G. (2004). Editorial: Moral education in Chinese societies: changes and challenges. *Journal of Moral Education, 33*(4), 405-28.

Liu, G. L. (2008). Political transaction cost analysis of the new curriculum policy (xin kecheng zhengce de jiaoyi chengben fenxi). *Journal of Xinxiang University, 22*(3), 138-140. (in Chinese)

Lu, J., and Gao, D. S. (2004). New directions in the moral education curriculum in Chinese primary schools. *Journal of Moral Education, 33*(4), 495-510.

Meyer, J. F. (1990). Moral education in the People's Republic of China. *Moral Education Forum, 15*(2), 3-26.

Nie, H. A. (2008). The dilemma of the moral curriculum in a Chinese secondary school. Lanham: University Press of America.

Ministry of Education (MOE) (2001). *Guidelines for the Ideology and Morality curriculum in primary schools and the Ideology and Politics curriculum in junior high schools in the nine-year compulsory education: Revised version (jiunian yiwu jiaoyu xiaoxue Sixiang Pinde he chuzhong Sixiang Zhengzhi kecheng biaozhun: xiuding ban)*. Beijing: People's Education Press. (in Chinese).

MOE (2002a). *Guidelines for Moral Character and Life in full-time compulsory education in China: Experimental draft (Quanrizhi yiwu jiaoyu Pinde yu Shenghuo kecheng biaozhun: shiyan gao)*. Beijing: Beijing Normal University Press. (in Chinese).

MOE (2002b). *Guidelines for Moral Character and Society in full-time compulsory education in China: Experimental draft (quanrizhi yiwu jiaoyu Pinde yu Shehui kecheng biaozhun: shiyan gao)*. Beijing: Beijing Normal University Press. (in Chinese).

MOE (2003). *Guidelines for Ideology and Morality for junior high schools: Experimental version (Quanrizhi yiwu jiaoyu Sixiang Pinde kecheng biaozhun: shiyan gao)*. Beijing: Beijing Normal University Press. (in Chinese).

MOE (2004). *Guidelines for Ideology and Politics for senior high schools: Experimental version (Quanrizhi yiwu jiaoyu Sixiang Zhengzhi kecheng biaozhun: shiyan gao)*. Beijing: Beijing Normal University Press. (in Chinese).

National Education Committee (NEC) (1996). *The principles of ideological and political education (Sixiang zhenzhi jiaoyuxue yuanli)*. Beijing: Higher Education Press. (in Chinese).

NEC (1997a). *Teaching plan for the nine-year compulsory education (six years primary education and three years junior high school education) in China: Experimental draft (zhongguo jiunian yiwu jiaoyu (liunian xiaoxue he sannian chuzhong) jiaoxue jihua: shiyan gao)*. Beijing: People's Education Press. (in Chinese).

NEC (1997b). *Guidelines for the primary school Ideology and Morality curriculum and the junior high school Ideology and Politics curriculum in the nine-year compulsory education: Trial version (jiunian yiwu jiaoyu xiaoxue Sixiang Pinde he chuzhong Sixiang Zhengzhi kecheng biaozhun: shixing).* Beijing: People's Education Press. (in Chinese).

Qi, W. X., and Tang, H. W. (2004). The social and cultural background of contemporary moral education in China. *Journal of Moral Education, 33*(4), 465-80.

Wang, J. J. (2010). The comparison of the old and the new textbooks of the Ideology and Politics course in senior high schools. *Nanchang Educational Institute Journal, 25*(3), 131-132. (in Chinese).

Ying, Z. Z. (2007). *Moral education courses in schools 2* (xuexiao deyu kecheng 2). Retrieved from http://blog.sina.com.cn/s/blog_4993939b01000e1e.html.

Yuan, W. Q. (2008). What the new curriculum brings to the Ideology and Politics classes (xin kecheng gei zhengzhi ketang jiaoxue zhenzheng dailai le shenme). *Journal of Liaoning Administration College, 10*(2), 114-5. (in Chinese).

Zhan, W. S., and Ning, W. J. (2004). The moral education curriculum for junior high schools in 21st century China. *Journal of Moral Education, 33*(4), 511-32.

Zhang, Y. P. (2008). An investigation of the experiment of teaching and learning of Ideology and Politics in the new curriculum in senior high schools (gaozhong sixiang zhengzhi xin kecheng shiyan jiaoxue xianzhuang de diaocha yanjiu). *Chinese Journal of Moral Education, 3*(10), 44-47.

Zhou, L. J. (2006). Play new roles to adapt to the curriculum reform: An argument on shifting the roles of Ideology and Politics teachers in high schools against the backdrop of the curriculum reform (banyan xin juese shiying xin kegai: qiantan xin kecheng gaige xia de zhongxue zhengzhi jiaoshi juese zhuanhuan). *Journal of Chizhou Teachers College, 20*(2), 141-2 and144. (in Chinese).

Zhu, C. Y. (2011, forthcoming). *Students' understanding of values diversity: An examination of the process and outcomes of values communication in English lessons in a high school in Mainland China.* Unpublished PhD thesis, University of Huddersfield.

Zhu, X. M., and Liu, C. L. (2004). Teacher training for moral education in China. *Journal of Moral Education, 33*(4), 481-94.

Zuo, Y. (2009). The new Ideology and Politics curriculum and the cultivation of habits of independence in students (zhengzhi xin kecheng yu xuesheng zizhu zili xiguan de peiyang). *Research in Teaching, 32*(5), 92-94. (in Chinese)

In: Curriculum Reform in China
Editors: Hong-Biao Yin and John Chi-Kin Lee

ISBN 978-1-61470-943-5
© 2012 Nova Science Publishers, Inc.

Chapter 11

TOWARD A COMPETENCE-BASED VOCATIONAL SENIOR SECONDARY ENGLISH CURRICULUM

Wen Zhao and David Coniam

ABSTRACT

Vocational education (VE) in Mainland China has been undergoing curriculum reform since the new millennium, in tandem with reforms in primary, junior and senior secondary education and higher education. This chapter begins with an introduction of the three types of post-secondary vocational schools in Mainland China, with a focus on vocational senior secondary schools. The chapter then describes the vocational senior secondary English curriculums issued since the late 1980s, in particular the 2000 National Vocational English Syllabus (NVES) and the 2009 NVES. The chapter finally presents a detailed description of the competence-based 2009 NVES, with a critical analysis of its two competence dimensions — the level of scales on the vertical dimension and the descriptive scheme on the horizontal dimension. The purpose of the chapter has been to provide a critical overview of the current competence-based vocational senior secondary English curriculum in Mainland China.

INTRODUCTION

The educational system in Mainland China consists of two parts: basic education and higher education, with basic education consisting of general and vocational education (IQAS, 2005). The term *vocational education* (*zhiye jiaoyu*) was evolved from the term *industrial education* (*shiye jiaoyu*) (Liu, 1997, p. 136). Vocational education incorporates education in vocational schools and vocational training at junior secondary, senior secondary and tertiary levels. Junior vocational education is a part of the nine-year compulsory education, with schools mainly located in rural areas. At the end of nine-year compulsory education, learners in general sit for an exam – the General Senior Secondary Unified Graduation Examination (GSSUGE), the watershed between general and vocational senior secondary education. The general educational structure is demonstrated in Table 1.

Table 1. The basic educational system in Mainland China

...				Skilled Workers Schools
12	General Senior Secondary Schools	Vocational Senior Secondary Schools	Specialized Senior Secondary Schools	
11				
10				
9	Compulsory education			
8				
7				
6				
5				
4				
3				
2				
1				

VE at senior secondary level basically consists of three types of schools: (1) vocational senior secondary schools (*zhongdeng zhiye xuexiao*), (2) specialized senior secondary schools (*zhongdeng zhuanke xuexiao*), and (3) skilled workers schools (*jigong xuexiao*). The main tasks of these schools are to train specialized and technical work force for the service and manufacturing sectors. The three types of post-compulsory vocational education appears similar, but differ in terms of curriculums, links to industry, their orientation towards work, affiliation, and curriculum patterns (Biermann, 1999), as shown in Table 2.

Table 2. Types of vocational school

Types	Establishment	Orientation	Patterns
Skilled workers schools	1950s	Manufacturing sector	Pattern 1 : 3 years Pattern 2: 1-2 years
Specialized senior secondary schools	1950s	Manufacturing, technology and management sectors	Pattern 1: 3-4 years Pattern 2: 1-2 years
Vocational senior secondary schools	1980s	Manufacturing, agriculture and service sectors	Pattern: 3 years

Skilled Workers Schools

Skilled workers schools (*jigong xuexiao*), also referred to as 'technical workers schools', were established in the early 1950s after the former Soviet model to train skilled workers (Biermann, 1999). Unlike the other two types, this mode of educational system is not directly under the jurisdiction of the Ministry of Education (MOE), but under the jurisdiction of the Ministry of Labor and Social Security (MOLSS) – which has been the case since 1978. This type of education mainly specializes in technical skills training for the manufacturing industry. Skilled/technical workers schools involve two patterns, with Pattern One consisting of three-year full time study for junior secondary graduates, and Pattern Two involving one or two year(s) of full time study for senior secondary students. "According to the guidelines jointly published by the Ministry of Personnel and the State Education Commission (now MOE) in 1986, the aim of skilled workers schools is to train mid-level skilled workers" (IQAS 2005, p.60). Upon graduation, learners receive a certificate of graduation, and a mid-level occupational qualification certificate, with technical certification programs incorporated into the school curriculum.

Specialized Senior Secondary Schools

Specialized senior secondary schools (*zhongdeng zhuanke xuexiao*) were also established in the early 1950s after the Soviet model to train technicians, with the objective of preparing intermediate level skilled workers for the manufacturing, technology, and management sectors. Until about 1985, over half of students enrolled at specialized senior secondary schools were graduates from senior secondary schools. This type of education is administered by the regional or local educational authorities. Due to the decrease of student enrollment in recent years, two major patterns are in operation. Pattern 1 consists of three or four years of study for junior secondary graduates in both general and specialty subjects, and part of the courses overlap with the courses for vocational senior secondary schools; Pattern 2 includes one or two year(s) of study in specialty subjects for senior secondary graduates. Upon graduation, learners may receive both a certificate of graduation and a mid-level occupational qualification certificate related to their intended occupation.

Vocational Senior Secondary Schools

Vocational senior secondary schools (*zhongdeng zhiye xuexiao*) were established in the 1980s according to the *Decision On Formulating Vocational Senior Secondary School (Three-Year System) Curriculum (guanyu zhiding zhongdeng zhiye xuexiao kecheng de jueding)*, which was drafted in 1986 and promulgated in 1990 to supply sufficient qualified mid-level technicians and skilled workers in agriculture, manufacturing and service for the fast developing and expanding market-oriented economy. The type of education was mostly converted from poorly performing senior secondary schools (Cooke, 2005; Lumby and Li 1998; Yang, 2006). The educational curriculum is for junior secondary graduates, consisting of three-year full time study. Upon graduation, learners receive a graduation certificate on senior secondary VE, and certain occupational qualification certificate in relation to their intended occupation. This type of VE has been undergoing rapid development and has been on the government's agenda in recent years. The focus of the current chapter is on this type of vocational education.

VOCATIONAL ENGLISH SYLLABUSES

The VE programs in China currently consist of three modules – *general subjects, specialty subjects*, and one year of *practicum* (Xu, 2005).

Unlike general senior secondary education which is more academically oriented, vocational senior secondary education aims at reaching two goals: education for earning a living and education for life (Shi, 2001, 2006). *General subjects* serve to provide students with a broad knowledge base both for life and for earning a living, which further consists of three core learning subjects – Chinese Language, Mathematics and English Language. *Specialty subjects* and the *practicum* are courses to enable students to earn a living.

With regard to the learning of English, three vocational senior secondary English syllabuses have been issued since the late 1990s. In Mainland China, the notion of *syllabus* used to denote a broad sense after the former Soviet influence. In this chapter, the notion of *syllabus* refers to the national English curriculum document, the guiding yardstick of curriculum development, implementation and assessment for vocational senior secondary education. The first National Vocational English Syllabus (NVES) issued in 1998 was simply adapted after the English syllabus for specialized senior secondary schools. The other two English syllabuses, however, were issued since the new millennium, with the features of vocational senior secondary schools taken into account. Table 3 presents the features of the latter two syllabuses.

The 2000 National Vocational English Syllabus (NVES) consists of two modules – *General English* (GE) (i.e., 220-260 hours) and *English for Vocational Purposes* (EVP) (i.e., 60 hours). The *GE* module (220-260 hours) in the 2000 NVES is an essential compulsory course for all vocational senior secondary school students while the *EVP module* (60 hours) is an optional course related to vocational specialization (e.g., manufacturing and service sectors), aiming at promoting and enhancing learners' language competences and career development.

Table 3. Module comparisons between the two NVESs

Syllabuses	Modules and Teaching Hours		
2000 NVES (MOE, 2000)	General English (GE) (220-260 hours)	English for Vocational Purposes (EVP) (60 hours)	
2009 NVES (MOE, 2009)	General English (GE) (128-144 hours)	English for Vocational Purposes (EVP) (54-72 hours)	Extended English (EE) (Not specified)

To keep pace with educational reform both at home and abroad and to better cater for competence diversity which currently exists in vocational senior secondary schools, the MOE issued the *Guiding Principles on Developing Teaching Plans for Vocational Senior Secondary Schools* (*guanyu zhiding zhongdeng zhiye xuexiao jiaoxue jihua de zhidao yuanze*) (MOE, 2009a) in 2009 to enact the implementation of the newly revised National Vocational English Syllabus (NVES) (MOE, 2009b). The 2009 NVES extends the previous two modules into three modules, viz., *General English (GE), English for Vocational Purposes (EVP)*, and *Extended English (EE)*, with the GE module compulsory, EE module optional, and EVP module selective. The teaching hours for both the GE and EVP modules are also specified. As indicated in Table 3, the teaching hours for the *GE* module in the 2009 NVES has been reduced from the original 220-260 teaching hours to 128-144 teaching hours, and the *EVP* module has been changed from its original 60 hours to an elastic 54-72 teaching hours. The teaching hours for the *EE* module, however, is not specified, due to the diversity existing at current vocational senior secondary schools. Given its rationale, the recently issued 2009 NVES is basically a competence-based syllabus.

THE COMPETENCE-BASED VOCATIONAL ENGLISH SYLLABUS

The 2009 NVES as the national yardstick is the result of a four-year process of negotiation and compromise (2005-2009) undertaken by an appointed committee of English inspectors, curriculum developers, and English professionals towards a learner-centered curriculum, as is stated in the aims of the 2009 NVES:

> To enable learners to master essential English knowledge and language skills, to cultivate learners' communicative language competences in daily life and under vocational context, to cultivate learners' cultural awareness, to enhance learners' ethical literacy and cultural literacy, and to lay a foundation for learners' vocational career development, sustainable learning and lifelong learning. (MOE, 2009b, p. 1)

Unlike the 2000 version of the NVES which exhibited a strong society-driven and subject-matter-centered tendency, the 2009 NVES is more learner- and learning-centered, aiming at cultivating learners' language competences for both personal and vocational development. The 2009 NVES takes into account learners' current learning needs as well as future personal and vocational development needs, enabling learners to possess transferable competences to move across vocational ladders. This statement is in line with Tanner and Tanner's (1995) comment that "the changing nature of knowledge, changing conceptions of the learner, and changing demands of social life have called for a changing conception and function of curriculum" (p. 197). According to the 2009 NVES (MOE, 2009b), the communicative language competences are the basic requirements that learners should possess both as individuals and social agents in daily life and vocational context.

In line with the curriculum aims, the curriculum goals, as the more specific descriptions of the intended outcomes of curriculum (Richards, 2001), are stated in the 2009 NVES as follows:

> On the basis of 9-year compulsory education, the vocational senior secondary English curriculum should help learners further expand their essential English knowledge, cultivate such language skills as listening, speaking, reading and writing, so that the curriculum can enable learners to possess basic vocational English competences; stimulate and cultivate learners' English learning interest, enhance their self-confidence in learning, help learners master basic learning strategies, form good learning-habits, improve their self-regulated learning, guide learners to understand and distinguish differences between Chinese and Western culture, and cultivate learners' affective feelings, attitudes, values and ethics (MOE, 2009, p. 1) .

The goal statement matches the learner-oriented aims – the philosophical stance of the curriculum (Eisner, 1992). It is the first time in the NVES that learners' learning interests, self-confidence in learning and learning strategies have been mentioned, which makes the 2009 NVES more relevant to individual needs and individual development than the previous two NVESs (MOE, 1998, 2000). The goal incorporates four dimensions: (1) essential English knowledge, (2) language skills (i.e., listening, speaking, reading and writing), (3) basic learning strategies, and (4) affective attributes (i.e., motivation, feelings, attitudes, values and ethics). The rationale of the 2009 NVES is "employment-oriented, competence-based, and learner-centered" (MOE, 2009b), to cultivate learners' language competences and to build a link between the present and the future needs, that is, to build a school-to-work linkage.

In view of social reconstructivism, "schooling as an agency of social change", demands "that education be relevant both to the student's interests and to society's needs. Curriculum is conceived to be an active force having direct impact on the whole fabric of its human and social context" (Eisner and Vallance, 1974, p. 135), with its focus on both the theoretical and empirical aspects, which are context- and practice-oriented (Connelly and Xu, 2008).

The structural components of the 2009 NVES can be classified into four categories after Tyler's (1949, p. 1) four fundamental curriculum questions:

- What educational purposes does the educational institution seek to attain?
- What educational experiences are provided to attain these purposes?
- How are these educational experiences organized?
- How is the attainment of these purposes or the value of these experiences to be evaluated?

In language education, "the first two questions have to do with syllabus design, the third with language teaching methodology, and the fourth with assessment and evaluation" (Nunan, 2006, p. 55). Table 4 demonstrates the four canonical curriculum starting points and their corresponding language components in the 2009 NVES.

Table 4. The structural components of the 2009 NVES

Curriculum elements	Structural components and sub-components in the 2009 NVES
Aims and goals	(1) The nature of curriculum and tasks
	(2) Curriculum aims and goals
Curriculum content	(3) Teaching content
	Phonological knowledge
	Communicative functions
	Communicative themes
	Grammatical structures
	Glossary
	(4) Skill requirements
	General English (GE) module
	Extended English (EE) module
	English for Vocational Purposes (EVP) module
Curriculum organization	(5) Teaching implementation
Evaluation	(6) Evaluation and assessment

Table 4 indicates that the structural components of the 2009 NVES consist of six parts: (1) the nature of curriculum and tasks; (2) curriculum aims and goals; (3) teaching content, which includes such basic English knowledge as phonological knowledge, communicative functions, communicative themes, grammatical structures, and glossary; (4) skill requirements, incorporating requirements for the three modules – GE, EE, and EVP – respectively; (5) teaching implementation, with five guiding principles for implementing a competence-based learner-centered curriculum – although no specific guidance or examples are provided in the document on how to select and organize the teaching and learning content in terms of situations, social roles, and language functions (van Ek 1975, 1977); and (6) evaluation and assessment, which advocates multiple methods of evaluation by encouraging teaching implementation at different levels to conduct both formative and summative evaluation (Brown, 1988, 2005).

The 2009 NVES, the national yardstick of curriculum guidelines, works as an *intended* curriculum at the societal level for implementation at the institutional and instructional levels (Goodlad and Su, 1992), incorporating four curriculum commonplaces: (1) *learners*, (2) *teachers*, (3) *subject matter*, and (4) *milieu* (Schwab, 1973). These four essential ingredients interact with each other to determine the nature of learning, the *experiential/attained* and *implemented* curriculums at the institutional and the instructional levels (Connelly and Xu, 2008; Goodlad and Su, 1992).

LANGUAGE COMPETENCE DIMENSIONS IN THE 2009 NVES

With regard to language competences in the 2009 NVES, two matrices of competence parameters are discussed with reference to the *Common European Framework of Reference for Languages: Learning, Teaching, Assessment* (CEFR) (Council of Europe, 2001), namely, the level of scales on the vertical axis and the descriptive schemes on the horizontal axis.

The CEFR, also addressed as the *Framework*, is a taxonomic reference tool across languages. It deploys a communicative, action-oriented, learner-centered view of language learning and use, demonstrating in a comprehensive way what language learners, as "social agents" (Council of Europe, 2001, p. 9), have to learn to do in order to use a language for communication and what knowledge and skills they have to develop so as to be able to act effectively in a particular cultural context. Regarding its matrix dimension, it contains the *Common Reference Levels* on the vertical dimension and the *Descriptive Scheme* on the horizontal dimension. The *Common Reference Levels* is a comprehensive system of six ascending levels of proficiency for language skills. The *Descriptive Scheme* is made up of a comprehensive and coherent structure of parameters and categories of communicative language competences, a detailed analytic account of the domains of language use and language learning, communicative language activities and strategies, the nature of texts and tasks. The *Framework* makes it possible to follow first the horizontal level and then ascend on the vertical scale that learners need to develop as competent language users. The discussion of the 2009 NVES also centers on the dimensional competence parameters.

Level of Scales on the Vertical Axis

In recent vocational curriculum development, the competence-based curriculum has moved away from its previous KSA (knowledge, skills and attitudes) typology (Bloom, 1956;

1976; Bloom, Hastings and Madaus, 1971; Bloom, Mesia and Krathwohl, 1964) on language input toward the competence typology (Winterton et al., 2006), with its focus on language output or outcomes. Outcome statements are standards of performance against which learners' progress and achievement can be compared (Brindley, 1998). The competence-based 2009 NVES, together with its levels of scales, forms a three-level grid, as shown in Table 5.

Table 5. Modules and level of scales

Modules	Levels of scales
English for Vocational Purposes (EVP) Module	Specific requirements for service- and manufacturing-oriented sectors
Extended English (EE) Module	Advanced level
General English (GE) Module	Intermediate level Basic level

Table 5 shows three ascending levels of competence requirements: (1) basic level, (2) intermediate level and (3) advanced level, and a non-specified requirement for the EVP module, with each incorporating its own range and scope of competence dimensions. All the skill requirements in the 2009 NVES are stated as behavioral "Can-Do" statements so that the learning outcomes are clear, observable and measurable. The requirements for affective factors and cognitive and meta-cognitive learning strategies are also incorporated into the levels of requirements.

The GE module incorporates two levels of scales: basic requirements and intermediate requirements. The *basic* level in the GE module is the minimum requirements for all learners across the Mainland China while the *intermediate* level is for learners whose language competences are beyond the minimum requirements. The *advanced* level in the EE module is aimed at learners who are expected to receive higher vocational education. There is no specified number of teaching hours for the Extended English (EE) module. It is suggested in the curriculum document that each individual school make its own arrangements according to their own situational exigencies. The EVP module lays down general requirements for two general industry sectors: service and manufacturing. Given the diverse specialties and the vague categorization of specialties, the 2009 NVES recommends that each individual school make its own specific EVP requirements, with its own specialty set-up taken into account. Given the regional diversity and individual differences of senior secondary VE in Mainland China, the levels of classification, however, appear somewhat rigid and inflexible in judging a learner's language learning outcome as different learners' language skills may not develop at the same rate. Even for the same language learner, his/her language skills may develop unevenly at different stages of learning.

Descriptive Schemes on the Horizontal Axis

The horizontal dimension is composed of the three competence categories: (1) cognitive competence (i.e., general and linguistic knowledge), (2) procedural competence (i.e., language skills), and (3) meta-competence and social competences (i.e., learning strategies, behaviors and attitudes). The descriptive scheme is presented in Table 6.

Table 6. The competence dimensions of the 2009 NVES

Cognitive competence (general and communicative language competences)		Procedural competence	Personal competence	Social competence
Communicative language competences	Sub-components	Language skills	Learning strategies	Attitudes and motivation
Linguistic competences	Phonological competence Lexical competence Grammatical competence Semantic competence	Listening Speaking Reading Writing	Within skills requirements	Stated in curriculum goals
Sociolinguistic competences	Linguistic markers of social interaction Politeness conventions Register differences			
Pragmatic competences	Discourse competence Functional competence			

As shown in Table 6, the *cognitive* competence contains both general competences and communicative language competences. According to the CEFR, g*eneral competences* are those not specific to language, but should regard a person in general as an individual and a social agent while *communicative language competences* are accumulation of linguistic experiences, consisting of three dimensions: (1) *linguistic,* (2) *sociolinguistic,* and (3) *pragmatic,* with each comprising its own parameters and categories (Council of Europe, 2001, pp. 108-130). The global general competences, however, are vaguely specified in the 2009 NVES curriculum while the communicative language competences are specified in substantial details in the document.

Concerning communicative language competences, the 2009 NVES incorporates mainly linguistic competences, which are composed of the following four competences: *phonological competence, lexical competence, grammatical competence,* and *semantic competence.* The reason that the 2009 NVES includes phonological competence is that a large stream of vocational senior secondary learners lack essential knowledge concerning phonology and pronunciation. The 2009 NVES requires learners to acquire essential phonetic and phonological knowledge for developing their communicative language competences.

A glossary and grammatical structure list occupy two thirds of the curriculum document (MOE, 2009b). *Vocabulary selection* and *grammar gradation* are two key concepts of syllabus design (Halliday, McIntosh and Strevens 1964; Mackey 1965; Fries 1952; Hornby 1954). The 2009 NVES consists of a glossary list of around 2,200 words and expressions, with the inclusion of vocabulary for the nine-year compulsory education syllabus and other frequently-used vocational vocabulary items. Among the lexical glossary, around 1,700 words and expressions are considered essential, with these viewed as constituting the basic threshold level. On the basis of the required core vocabulary, there are a further 200 words and expressions, indicating lexical requirements for the intermediate level. There are then a further 300 marked words and expressions, indicating lexical requirements for the advanced level. According to the curriculum document (MOE, 2009b), the word list was developed through the comparison of word frequencies from 16 national and international word lists, such as the word list for primary, and junior and senior secondary schools in Mainland China, Taiwan, Hong Kong, Singapore, etc. Some frequently used educational and vocational word lists and corpora were also adopted as a reference, such as the COBUILD and other published vocational word lists. In general, the word list in the 2009 NVES is more empirically-grounded than was that of the 2000 NVES.

In view of grammatical competence, the selection of grammatical items has been organized more concisely in the 2009 NVES than those in the 2000 NVES. Learners at all levels are required to master all unasterisked grammatical items listed in the document, intermediate level learners to master more items with one asterisk, and advanced level learners to master items with two asterisks. The issue of the sequence that items should follow and how the items should be integrated in the learning materials to achieve maximum learning effects (Celce-Murcia, 1985) is not specified clearly in the document. Regarding the sequencing of grammatical contents, Corder (1973) and Martin (1978) have suggested a cyclical and spiral treatment of grammatical items. Given learners' current English level, the 2009 NVES suggests that the selection and gradation of the grammatical items be treated in a cyclical and spiral way in textbook and teaching material development.

From the semantic aspect, the 2009 NVES contains a list of communicative functions and notions, as well as a list of communicative themes. The list of communicative functions cover 16 frequently used functions and notions, with eight stipulated for the basic level: (1) greeting and saying goodbye, (2) introducing oneself and others, (3) expressing thanks and making apologies, (4) making appointments and invitations, (5) expressing wishes and congratu-lations, (6) asking for and offering help, (7) expressing agreement and disagreement, and (8) accepting and rejecting. These notions and functions serve as a guideline for textbook and teaching material development as well as test development in curriculum implementation and assessment.

The list of communicative themes, moreover, contains ten categories: (1) personal information and family, (2) school life, (3) daily life, (4) leisure and entertainment, (5) health, (6) living environment, (7) travel, (8) science and technology, (9) work, and (10) festivals and customs. Each topic further consists of sub-themes or topics, covering learners' personal, public, educational and vocational domains (Council of Europe, 2001). The themes, along with the communicative notions and functions, enable textbooks and learning materials to be organized topically rather than structurally (Tomlinson, 2003). The 2009 NVES suggests that communicative themes related to the world of life and the world of work, with categorized communicative functions and activities be incorporated to cultivate learners' communicative competence (Hymes, 1972; Halliday, 1973; Canale and Swain, 1980; Canale, 1983).

The four linguistic knowledge areas are explicitly marked out in the curriculum document while other two competences – *sociolinguistic* and *pragmatic* – are implicitly indicated in the skill requirements. Given learners' individual and vocational development, the latter two competences should be stressed more saliently in curriculum organization, implementation and assessment.

The *procedural competence*, as shown in Table 6, includes the graded requirements in the form of "Can Do" statements for the four language skills (i.e., listening, speaking, reading and writing), along with interpretation and/or translation at the higher levels: intermediate and advanced. The competence-based curriculum gives a clear and concise description of targets to be attained and ladder-like levels of attainment, although the three graded levels are generally considered too general in coverage, given the learner and learning diversity in Mainland China.

Meta-competence, also referred as personal strategic competence, is incorporated into the skill requirements in the 2009 NVES. It is this competence that enables learners to become self-regulated (Lantolf, 2003, 2005, 2007; Lantolf and Thorne, 2006; Lantolf and Poehner, 2008) in their current study and lifelong learning, and encourages learners' involvement in meaningful language use in real life and workplace situations. Other than the incorporation in the skill requirements, learning strategies are not made salient in the curriculum document whereas curriculums for junior and senior secondary English learners have both given a much heavier weight on cultivating and enhancing learners' learning strategies. Given learners' current language learning habits and rote-learning strategies adopted in their current study, the development of learners' language learning strategies should be made more salient in the national curriculum document.

Social competence, which refers to the competence to become a competent social citizen in the knowledge society, is only stated in the curriculum aims and goals. Although the cognitive competence is highly valued in school education, the target workplace puts a much heavier weight on learners' social competence, such as team work, motivation, work ethics, and inter- or intra-communication at the workplace. Given learners' future life and career success, social competence should be cultivated in the whole process of English language education, with specified standards or requirements in the form of "Can Do" statements for assessing learners' social competence at all levels of academic and vocational performance.

To conclude the competence dimension analysis of the 2009 NVES, Boreham's (2002) comment on what constitutes a curriculum is that "(k)nowledge constituted in a curriculum is more than printed words in a syllabus – it is embodied within teachers and students, and socially constructed in interaction between these and other actors in the curriculum process" (pp. 230-231). The 2009 NVES as the official guideline of the intended curriculum at the macro societal level provides a guiding framework for the school-based intended curriculum – the implemented curriculum at the meso institutional level – and for assessing the learners' attained or experiential curriculum at the micro instructional classroom level.

CONCLUSION

The chapter has introduced the three coexisting post-secondary vocational schools types — skilled workers schools, specialized senior secondary schools and vocational senior secondary schools, with the last school type as the focus of the chapter. The features of vocational senior secondary learners and the two versions of national vocational English syllabuses have been described. The key focus of the current chapter has been on the competence-based 2009 NVES, with its two competence dimensions — levels of scales on the vertical axis and descriptive scheme on the horizontal dimension — further highlighted and described. The purpose of the chapter has been to provide a critical overview of the newly issued competence-based vocational senior secondary English curriculum, which is now being implemented in Mainland China with a series of nationally recommended English textbooks and featured school-based curriculums.

REFERENCES

Biermann, H. (1999). China's vocational education system facing the twenty-first century. *International Journal of Sociology, 29*(1), 21-44.

Bloom, B. S. (1956). *Taxonomy of educational objectives: The classification of educational goals: Handbook 1. Cognitive Domain.* New York: Longman Green.

Bloom, B. S. (1976). *Human characteristics and school learning.* New York: McGraw-Hill.

Bloom, B. S., Hastings, J. T., and Madaus, G. F. (1971). *Handbook on formative and summative evaluation of student learning.* New York: McGraw-Hill.

Bloom, B. S., Mesia, B. B., and Krathwohl, D. R. (1964). *Taxonomy of educational objectives.* New York: David McKay.

Boreham, N. (2002). Work process knowledge, curriculum control and the work-based route to vocational qualifications. *British Journal of Educational Studies, 50*(2), 225-237.

Brindley, G. (1998). Outcome-based assessment and reporting in language learning programmes: A review of the issues. *Language Testing, 15*(1), 45-85.

Brown, J. D. (1988). *Understanding research in second language learning: A teacher's guide to statistics and research design.* Cambridge: Cambridge University Press.

Brown, J. D. (2005). *Testing in language programs: A comprehensive guide to English language assessment.* New York: McGraw-Hill.

Canale, M. (1983). On some dimensions of language proficiency. In J. W. Oller (Ed.), *Issues in language testing research* (pp. 333-342). Rowley, MA: Newbury House.

Canale, M., and Swain, M. (1980). Theoretical bases of communicative approaches to second language teaching and testing. *Applied Linguistics, 1,* 1-47.

Celce-Murcia, M. (1985). Making informed decisions about the role of grammar in language teaching. *TESOL Newsletter, 19*(1), 4-5.

Connelly, F. M., and Xu, S. (2008). The landscape of curriculum and instruction: Diversity and continuity. In F. M. Connelly (Ed.), *The SAGE handbook of curriculum and instruction* (pp. 514-533). Thousand Oaks, CA: Sage.

Cooke, F. (2005). Vocational and enterprise training in China: Policy, Practice and Prospect. *Journal of the Asia Pacific Economy, 10*(1), 26-55.

Corder, S. P. (1973). *Introducing applied linguistics.* Harmondsworth, Middlesex: Genguin Books.

Council of Europe (CoE) (2001). *Common European framework of reference for languages: Learning, teaching, assessment (CEFR).* Strasbourg: Council of Europe.

Alberta Advanced Education (2005). *Country education profile: People's Republic of China.* Alberta, Canada: International Qualifications Assessment Service (IQAS). Retrieved 25 December 2008 from http://employment.alberta.ca/documents/WIA/ WIA-IM_iqas_china_profile.pdf.

Eisner, E. W., and Vallance, E. (1974). *Conflicting conceptions of the curriculum* (National Society for the Study of Education Series on Contemporary Educational Issues). Berkeley, CA: McCutchan.

Fries, C. C. (1952). *The structure of English*. New York: Harcourt Brace.

Goodlad, J. I., and Su, Z. (1992). Organization of the curriculum. In P. W. Jackson (Ed.), *Handbook of research on curriculum: A project of the American educational research association* (pp. 327-344). New York: Macmillan.

Halliday, M. A. K. (1973). *Explorations in the functions of language*. London: Edward Arnold.

Halliday, M. A. K., McIntosh, A., and Strevens, P. D. (1964). *The linguistic sciences and language teaching*. London: Longman.

Hornby, A. S. (1954). *Guide to patterns and usage in English*. Oxford: Oxford University Press.

Hymes, D. (1972). On communicative competence. In J. Pride and J. Holmes (Eds.), *Sociolinguistics* (pp. 269-293). Harmondsworth: Penguin.

Lantolf, J. P. (2003). Intrapersonal communication and internalization in the second language classroom. In A. Kozulin, V. S. Ageev, S. Miller, and B. Gindis (Eds.), *Vygotsky's theory of education in cultural context* (pp. 349-370). Cambridge: Cambridge University Press.

Lantolf, J. P. (2005). Sociocultural theory and SLA: An exegesis. In E. Hinkel (Ed.), *Handbook of second language research* (pp. 335-354). Mahwah, NJ: Erlbaum.

Lantolf, J. P. (2007). Sociocultural theory. In J. Cummings and C. Davison (Eds.), *International handbook of English language teaching* (pp. 693-700). New York: Springer.

Lantolf, J. P., and Poehner, M. E. (2008). *Sociocultrual theory and the teaching of second languages*. London: Equinox Publishing Ltd.

Lantolf, J. P., and Thorne, S. L. (2006). *Sociocultural theory and the genesis of second language development*. Oxford: Oxford University Press.

Liu, G. L. (1997). *The study of perspectives on China modern vocational education (zhongguo jindai zhiye jiaoyu sixiang yanjiu)*. Beijing: Higher Education Press. (in Chinese).

Lumby, J., and Li, Y. P. (1998). Managing vocational education in China. *Compare: A journal of comparative education, 28*(2), 197-206.

Mackey, E. F. (1965). *Language teaching analysis*. London: Longman.

Martin, M. A. (1978). The application of spiraling to the teaching of grammar. *TESOL Quarterly, 12*(2), 151-60.

Ministry of Education (1998). *National vocational English syllabus*. Beijing: Higher Education Press. (in Chinese).

Ministry of Education (2000). *National vocational English syllabus*. Beijing: Higher Education Press. (in Chinese).

Ministry of Education (2009a). *Guiding principle on making teaching plans for vocational senior secondary schools*. Beijing: Author. (in Chinese).

Ministry of Education (2009b). *National vocational English syllabus*. Beijing: Higher Education Press.

Nunan, D. (2006). Syllabus design. In M. Celce-Murcia (Ed.), *Teaching English as a second or foreign language* (pp. 55-66). Beijing: Foreign Language Teaching and Research Press.

Richards, J. C. (2001). *Curriculum development in language teaching*. Cambridge: Cambridge University Press.

Schwab, J. J. (1973). The practical 3: Translation into curriculum. *School Review*, *81*(4), 501-522.

Shi, W. P. (2001). *Comparative study of vocational and technical education (bijiao zhiye jishu jiaoyu)*. Shanghai: Shanghai Educational Press. (in Chinese).

Shi, W. P. (2006). *Modern features and vocational education innovation (shidai tezheng yu zhiye jiaoyu chuangxin)*. Shanghai: Shanghai Education Publishing House. (in Chinese).

Tanner, D., and Tanner, L. N. (1995). *Curriculum development: Theory into practice* (3rd ed.). New York: Macmillan.

Tomlinson, B. (2003). *Developing materials for language teaching*. London: Continuum Press.

Tyler, R. W. (1949). *Basic principles of curriculum and instruction*. Chicago: University of Chicago Press.

van Ek, J. A. (1977). *Threshold level for modern language levels in schools*. London: Longman.

van Ek, J. A. (1975). *Systems development in adult language learning: The threshold level in a European unit credit system for modern language learning by adults*. Strasbourg, France: Council of Europe.

Winterton, J., Le Deist, F. D., and Stringfellow, E. (2006). *Typology of knowledge, skills and competences: Clarification of the concept and prototype*. Luxembourg: Office for Official Publications of the European Communities.

Xu, G. Q. (2005). *The curriculum study of practice-oriented vocational education (shijian daoxiang zhiye jiaoyu kecheng yanjiu)*. Shanghai: Shanghai Education Publishing House. (in Chinese).

Yang, D. P. (2006). Pursuing harmony and fairness in education. *Chinese Education and Society*, *39*(6), 3-44.

In: Curriculum Reform in China
Editors: Hong-Biao Yin and John Chi-Kin Lee

ISBN 978-1-61470-943-5
© 2012 Nova Science Publishers, Inc.

Chapter 12

CHINESE SENIOR SECONDARY ELECTIVE COURSES AND COLLEGE ENTRANCE EXAMINATION SYSTEMS: NON-, DUAL-, OR MULTI-STREAMING?

Shengyao Feng

ABSTRACT

In 2003, China's Ministry of Education (MOE) issued the *General Senior Secondary School Curriculum Program (Experimental version)* which puts forward the idea of potential college-major oriented elective courses. From 2006 onwards, the four pilot provinces or autonomous regions began to promulgate successively their college entrance examination programs, paying no attention to the major-oriented elective courses. In 2010, the MOE issued the *National Outline for Medium and Long-term Education Reform and Development (2010-2020)*, with an emphasis on the dominant position of fostering and assessing comprehensive capacities of students. Clearly, there exist inherent contradictions and conflicts among those documents and policies. It is argued in this chapter that the most preferred option in Mainland China should be "multi-streaming" by which is meant there is major-based curriculum differentiation which flexibly provides elective courses according to the potential college-majors. This chapter suggests that such a multi-streaming option is in line with international trends and also has strong theoretical foundations.

In the early 20th century, with the introduction of a Westernized education system and the establishment of China's modernized education system, the issue of the division of the senior secondary curriculum and college entrance examination between arts and science stream candidates emerged. Since the founding of the People's Republic of China (PRC), this dual-streaming educational system has been the dominant practice. However, moving into the 21st century, under the context of a new wave of curriculum reform of basic education, this issue has once again become the focus of attention.

In 2003, China's Ministry of Education (MOE) issued the *General Senior Secondary School Curriculum Program (Experimental version)*, which was the prelude to the senior secondary curriculum reform. With the purpose of not only offering the students a balanced and well-rounded education, but also providing them with more flexible and diversified learning opportunities, three types of courses are offered in the new national curriculum: common fundamental courses, arts- or science-oriented elective courses, and potential college-major oriented elective courses.

Correspondingly, the new curriculum reform started in 2004 in Guangdong, Hainan, and Shandong Provinces and the Ningxia autonomous region, which took the lead in introducing the new national curriculum up to grade 10, later on influenced and modified their provincial college entrance examination programs accordingly. Surprisingly and disappointingly, none of these programs, either in the very beginning or in their revised edition, pay any attention to major-oriented elective courses. Even more surprisingly, from 2009 onwards, in the process of drawing up the *National Outline for Medium and Long-term Education Reform and Development*, there has been a call for common fundamental courses to be placed in the dominant position so as to improve the students' comprehensive capabilities.

It is argued in this chapter that the system for senior secondary elective courses in China should not be a single route in which common fundamental courses are excessively emphasized and arts and science oriented courses are required to be taken concurrently by students, neither should there be dual-streaming in which students are simply streamed into either the arts or science program. Instead, the most preferred option should be multi-streaming by which is meant there is major-based curriculum differentiation which flexibly places elective courses with the potential college-majors. This chapter puts forward the argument that such a multi-streaming option seems to be in line with international trends and the original preferred pathway for China's senior secondary curriculum reform and college entrance examination reforms.

FROM MULTI-STEAMING TO DUAL-STREAMING: THE 2003-2009 CURRICULUM REFORM AND COLLEGE ENTRANCE EXAMINATION REFORMS

National Curriculum Components

In 2003, the MOE promulgated the *General Senior Secondary School Curriculum Program (Experimental version)*, proposing that the senior secondary curriculum design follow the principles of the common basis and selectivity which were:

> Under the premise of enabling every student to formulate their common basis, a variety of relevant and sequential courses in all subjects are designed and offered for students to choose from, in order to cultivate their potential and meet their needs (MOE, 2003a).

In accordance with that principle, two types of courses are offered to senior secondary students, i.e., the common fundamental courses and the elective courses. The common fundamental courses include the following: Chinese Language, English Language, Mathematics (10 credits, or 180 class hours for each); Politics (8 credits, or 144 class hours); History, Geography, Physics, Chemistry, and Biology (6 credits, or 144 class hours for each).

As for the elective courses, there are different requirements for arts or science candidates' selection of courses. Using Mathematics as an example, with the purpose of differentiating the students between arts and science candidates, in addition to the 10 compulsory credits, the arts candidates are required to take 6 while the science candidates take 10 elective credits. In addition, all students, both arts and science candidates, are still encouraged to select 4 elective credits in math subject according to their interests and characteristics of their intended college majors (MOE, 2003b), for the purpose of curriculum differentiation among different intended major candidates.

College Entrance Examination Programs

From these brief comments on the design of the national curriculum, there arises another question: Did the college entrance examination programs in the four pilot provinces meet the demands of the new curriculum? According to a research conduced by the author of this chapter, only the 2007 examination program in Guangdong sought to respond to the design of potential major-oriented elective courses while the other three programs just emphasized the common fundamental courses and arts- or science-oriented courses.

The 2007 examination program in Guangdong clearly put forward the principle of the common basis, insisting that the examination "must demand the basic knowledge and basic abilities required by higher education as the main examination content" (Admissions Committee of Guangdong Province, 2006). It also advocated the principle of selectivity or student choice within their capability:

> The examination program should include various examination courses and flexible enrollment methods for students' to select in order to meet society's needs of a wide range of talents, the different needs of individual development, and the admission requirements of colleges of different levels and categories. (Admissions Committee of Guangdong Province, 2006).

Clearly, the Guangdong examination reform was compatible with the main ideas of the new curriculum reform.

Specifically, the 2007 examination program in Guangdong covered three types of courses: (a) Common fundamental courses: Chinese Language, English Language, Arts-Oriented Mathematics (or Science-Oriented Mathematics), 150 points for each course. (b) Arts or science oriented courses: All students were supposed to take an integrated examination of 150 points. For arts candidates, this included 108 points in Politics, History and Geography and 42 points in Physics, Chemistry and Biology. For science candidates, the exam included 108 points in Physics, Chemistry and Biology and 42 points in Politics, History and Geography. (c) Major-oriented courses: All students were to choose one course as their major examination subject and get 150 points as a maximum. Arts candidates were supposed to choose from politics, history and geography, while science candidates could choose from physics, chemistry and biology.

Superficially it seems to meet the requirements for student selection, but actually there were serious problems in implementing this program. For example, it was surprising that a

Chinese Literature candidate could not choose Chinese as his major oriented elective course, but would have to choose one from the arts courses such as History, Politics and Geography.

The Guangdong Education Department (2008) promulgated *The Revised Program of Guangdong College Entrance Examination Reform* because the idea of major oriented courses hadn't been widely accepted, and there were still some drawbacks in the 2007 examination program. In this revised program, it was notable that the principles of comprehensiveness override the previous principle of selectivity.

The 2008 revised program in Guangdong covered two types of courses: (a) Common fundamental courses: Chinese Language, English Language, Mathematics for Arts (or Mathematics for Science), 150 points for each course. (b) Arts or science oriented courses: All students were supposed to take a three course combined examination delivering 300 points, representing the comprehensive examination for Arts or Science students (i.e., Politics, History and Geography for arts candidates and physics, chemistry and biology for science candidates). In addition, the content of all examination courses were mainly taken from the compulsory but not selective part of the curriculum.

The 2008 revised program in Guangdong was consistent with the mainstream practices of college entrance examination programs in other areas of China. The MOE pointed out specifically, in all provinces and regions, "examination courses should be Chinese Language, Mathematics, Foreign languages and related courses. In general, related courses are referred to as Arts comprehensive examination or Science comprehensive examination" (MOE, 2008).

In a nutshell, even under the new curriculum reform, bipolar division of examination courses for Arts or Science candidates is still the main characteristic of nationwide and various provincial college entrance examination systems, just as it was for decades before this curriculum reform.

College Admission Policy

In China, the college admission is decided by the MOE or the provincial governments instead of colleges themselves. The process of enrollment usually includes the following steps:

Firstly, the MOE allocates the number of places for each university in different provincial areas.

Secondly, the MOE or some authorized provincial governments develop and organize the college entrance examination.

Finally, each university admits students according to their ranking of arts or science total scores within their respective provincial areas.

Therefore, the current college admission policies broadly follow nationwide or sometimes a specific areas' college examination system. However, neither of these are in line with the major-oriented course elective system in senior secondary schools and diversified requirements of various college degree programs.

FROM DUAL-STREAMING TO NON-STREAMING: THE 2009-2010 POLICY TREND

The curriculum reform and college entrance examination programs faced great challenges in 2009, at which time the idea of major-oriented courses was not yet widely accepted. The dual-streaming system into the arts or science program was widely questioned so a heated debate broke out.

The Origin of the Debate

In January 2009, the Task Force Group of the *National Outline for Medium and Long-term Education Reform and Development* put forward 20 major issues for public comment. Among them there was one about "the necessity and feasibility of abolishing the streaming system for arts or science-program", which raised a storm of controversy.

As the most important policy advisory body for the *National Outline*, the Investigation Panel of the China National Institute for Educational Research (CNIER) made an extensive survey regarding the 20 major issues. Here came the conclusion and suggestion of the survey:

> We should gradually abolish the system of streaming for arts or science programs in senior secondary schools. Adhering to the principles of basics, balance and comprehensiveness of basic education, we should first launch a pilot project in the eastern cities to gain the necessary experiences, and then gradually extend it to other areas. (The Investigation Panel of CNIER, 2009, p.13).

The Process of the Debate

It is quite interesting that while the policy consultation report clearly supports the non-streaming system, great controversy occurred among members of the public. According to a www.tencent.com survey of about 26 million internet voters, nearly 54% supported taking arts and science oriented courses concurrently while about 40% advocated the dual-streaming system, and the rest voted "hard to say" (Zhou, 2009). Actually, these two main points of view had equal support and it was hard to tell which side would win. In addition, *Educational Research* (*jiaoyu yanjiu*), one of the most authoritative academic journals in China, published two papers about this issue in 2009, one each representing the two above mentioned main stances.

The Result of the Debate

The debate, did not in fact, sway all policymakers' resolution to abolish the dual-streaming system. In July 2010, the *National Outline for Medium and Long-term Education Reform and Development (2010-2020)* was officially issued, which recommended taking both arts and science courses concurrently.

The *National Outline* pointed out:

(Article 12) Completely improving the comprehensive abilities of senior secondary students.

(Article 36) Improving the admission examination and enrollment system of higher education institutes. Deepening the reform of examination content and form, and focusing on examining the comprehensive abilities of students. (China's State Council, 2010)

Zhengguo Yuan, Director of the CNIER, a member of the drafting group of the *National Outline*, summarized the debate as follows:

This controversy, in which both viewpoints are almost equally supported, is very fiercely contested so now simply isn't the right time to make a decision. But the National Outline clearly demands that senior secondary schools should put emphasis on promoting students' all-round development, encouraging concurrently taking of arts and science courses, and opposing one-sided development. (Zhou, 2010a)

Li Zhang, Director of the National Educational Development Research Center, one of the members of the drafting group of the *National Outline*, clearly pointed out that "worldwide, no country divides senior secondary students into arts or science oriented programs like China does". He considered that "the college entrance examination courses in 2020 will definitely not be streamed into arts or science oriented ones" (Zhou, 2010b). It seems that non-streaming is regarded not only as an international trend but also the direction of the curriculum reform in China.

MULTI-STREAMING UNDER THE MAJOR ORIENTED ELECTIVE SYSTEM: AN INTERNATIONAL TREND

So is there really no other viable alternative to dual-streaming or non-streaming? After researching the situation in other regions or countries, this article argues that almost all western countries or regions provide opportunities for senior secondary students to flexibly choose courses of study and examination according to their intended college majors.

The United States

In the United States, course requirements for high school students not only depend on the individual states, local school districts and the schools, but also on colleges and the degree programs that the student applies for.

In American high schools, degree-program oriented courses mainly include Advanced Placement (AP), International Baccalaureate (IB), dual enrollment, and other advanced coursework elements. Among them, AP courses are the most representative. Highly selective colleges require candidates to take 3 to 5 AP courses according to their intended college majors.

From the column *Major and Career Profiles* on the College Entrance Examination Board website, it can be found how various college major candidates purposefully take helpful courses (The College Board, 2011):

> Comparative literature candidates: AP English Literature, AP European History, AP World History, Foreign languages.
> Classics candidates: AP English Literature, AP Latin Literature, AP Latin: Vergil, World History.
> Natural Resources Management and Policy candidates: AP Biology, AP Calculus, AP Environmental Science, AP U.S. Government and Politics, Economics, Precalculus.
> Archaeology candidates: AP Biology, AP Human Geography, Chemistry, Foreign language, History, Sociology.

For many years, those elective courses, rather than common compulsory courses have become the most important factor of admission requirements of well-known colleges. "Strength of curriculum—and particularly grades in college prep courses—are better indicators of a student's likelihood of succeeding in college" (Smith, Hoganson, Gill, and Mudge, 2008, p. 38.). Fitzsimmons, Dean of Admissions and Financial Aid Harvard University, also pointed out that "One of the best standard predictors of academic success at Harvard is performance on AP Examinations" (The College Board, 2004, p. 3).

England and Wales

Following the Education Reform Act 1988, England and Wales introduced the National Curriculum into primary and secondary state schools. The National Curriculum Key Stage 4 (age 14 to 16, US 10th to 11th grade is equivalent to senior secondary 1st and 2nd grade in Mainland China) comprised the following compulsory subjects: English, Mathematics and Science as the core subjects; Design and technology, Information and Communication Technology; A modern foreign language; Citizenship; Physical education as the foundation subjects. The Education Act 2002 created a legislative distinction between Key Stages 1 to 3 (5- to 14-year-olds) and Key Stage 4 with the purpose to facilitate opportunities to tailor education to the needs of individual students between 14 and 16 years old. As a result, since September 2004, the study of design and technology and a modern foreign language has no longer been compulsory at Key Stage 4. These are minimum course requirements.

Institutions of higher learning and Sixth Form Colleges (age 17 to 18) have also had a profound impact on the Key Stage 4 curriculum. All major higher education institutions are autonomous bodies and each determines its own admission policy. However, applicants are generally required to have obtained at least three General Certificate of Secondary Education (GCSE) passes at grade C or above. For London University, candidates must hold a minimum of five GCSE passes or above.

In addition, English, Mathematics and Science, as common compulsory subjects of the National Curriculum and college admissions, are also made up of a large amount of elective courses. For example, from 2010, if students sit GCSE qualification examination administered by Oxford Cambridge and RSA Examinations (OCR, one of the five UK examination boards), they can choose from Applications of Mathematics (Pilot), Mathematics

A, Mathematics B, or Methods in Mathematics (Pilot). In a word, students at Key Stage 4 begin to differentiate according to their interests and future college majors.

Table 1. Options for UK Key Stage 4 students for GCSE examinations administered by OCR (English and Mathematics)

Subjects	Previous Courses	Courses for 2010
English	English English plus English Literature	English English Language plus English Literature But not: English plus English Literature
Mathematics	Mathematics A Mathematics B (MEI) Mathematics C (Graduated Assessment)	Applications of Mathematics (Pilot) Mathematics A Mathematics B Methods in Mathematics (Pilot)

Note: The data summarized in this table is derived from the OCR official website.

In Sixth Form, major-based curriculum differentiation is further diversified. For example, King's College London requires three A-levels (*GCE Advanced qualification)* and one AS-level (*GCE Advanced Subsidiary qualification)* pass from candidates. Specific courses are decided by colleges and departments. The following are some examples (King's College London, 2011):

Comparative Literature candidates: A-level in English Literature and a relevant modern or ancient language required;
Mathematics and Physics candidates: Grade A in A-level Mathematics; and grade B at A-level Physics;
Molecular Genetics candidates: A-level Chemistry, plus one science A-level, preferably Maths, Physics or Biology.

In conclusion, the introduction of the National Curriculum at Key Stage 4 and *GCE AS qualification* at Sixth Form tries to broaden the range of studies, but are not intended to change the core aim of seeking selectivity, diversity and academic depth. From the very beginning of Key Stage 4 through to Sixth Form, students explore and develop their own interests and abilities through elective courses, and prepare themselves to smoothly gain admission to intended college majors.

Hong Kong Special Administration Region

In recent years, the Hong Kong Special Administration Region (Hong Kong SAR) Government has been implementing the new "334" academic system. This system provides a three-year junior secondary and a three-year senior secondary education followed by a four-year undergraduate program. The first cohort of students under the new system started working to the New Senior Secondary (NSS) curriculum in September 2009, and will take the

Hong Kong Diploma of Secondary Education (HKDSE) examination as the basis of college admission and recruitment in 2012.

It is clear that the NSS curriculum is intended to pursue the combination of whole-person development and diversification, to make the New Senior Secondary syllabus provide a smooth transition zone towards higher education and the workplace.

Under the new system, the course and examination requirements for students provided by the NSS, the HKDSE examination or the tertiary institutions are as follows (Education and Manpower Bureau, 2005): (a) Four core courses are to be taken by all students: Chinese Language (12.5~15% of total effort, 338~405 class hours), English Language (12.5~15%, 338~405 class hours), Mathematics (10~15%, 270~338 class hours) and Liberal Studies (10%, 270 class hours). (b) 20 elective courses, students being expected to take two or three (each course 10%, 270 class hours) according to intended-college-major or future career: Chinese Literature, Literature in English, Calculus and Statistics, Algebra and Calculus, Economics, Geography, History, Tourism and Hospitality Studies, Geography, Biology, Chemistry, Physics, Combined Science, Integrated Science etc.

By so doing, students will not be narrowly streamed into arts, science, commercial or technical studies as before but will be encouraged to choose from a wide range of courses that develop their interests and abilities, and that open up multiple pathways into further college studies and careers. Therefore, it is a flexible multi-stream system, and most certainly not a single stream with all students following a similar curriculum.

Admission requirements of the 8 tertiary institutions in Hong Kong are also coordinated with the NSS and the HKDSE examination. For example, general entrance requirements for the University of Hong Kong will include 4 cores plus 2 electives pass or above in the HKDSE examination. Specific elective courses are prescribed by each faculty or department. The College of Science requires one of the following: Biology, Chemistry, Physics, Combined Science, Integrated Science; and prefer (but not insist on) Calculus and Statistics, or Algebra and Calculus for Mathematics and Physics majors. The College of Engineering requires one of the following: Physics, Combined Science with Physics component; and requires Calculus and Statistics, or Algebra and Calculus. Clearly, the intended college major is the decisive factor of the NSS elective system.

The experience of the Hong Kong SAR, the USA, and England and Wales shows that the practice of major-based differentiation seems to be an international trend, and it should be consistently reflected in the senior secondary curriculum, college entrance examination and admission requirements.

MULTI-STREAMING UNDER THE MAJOR-ORIENTED ELECTIVE SYSTEM: THEORETICAL FOUNDATIONS AND CONCEPT CLARIFICATION

Theoretical Foundations

The idea of major-based differentiation also has strong theoretical foundations. From a psychological perspective, both John Holland's (1973) theory of vocational personalities and Howard Gardner's (1983) multiple intelligences theory show that there exist enormous differences in individual aptitudes and intelligences. Only when pupils' education and careers are congruent with their aptitudes and intelligences, are they most likely to maximize their potential and smoothly develop and grow in their careers. If you like something you are good at it and if you are good at something you like it. Multiple intelligences and personalities call for multiple streaming under the major-oriented elective system.

The theory of division of labor also lays a theoretical foundation for major based differentiation. In the first sentence of The Wealth of Nations, Adam Smith (1776, p. 13.) wrote that "the greatest improvement in the productive powers of labor, and the greater part of the skill, dexterity, and judgment with which it is anywhere directed, or applied, seem to have been the effects of the division of labor." Adam Smith spoke highly of a major role of division of labor in personal development and social development. In the meanwhile, we should also recognize that division of labor in modern society includes both demarcation into specialized single sub-task and also comprehensive of multi-task jobs, which are congruent with specialized or comprehensive degree programs in colleges.

Is the opinion of major based differentiation contrary to the social justice theory? The answer is "no". John Rawls, one of the most influential Western political philosophers of the 20th century, in his milestone book A Theory of Justice, raised his famous "difference principle" as one of the cornerstones of justice. That is, social and economic differences are to be arranged so that they are both (a) reasonably expected to be to the greatest benefit of everyone, especially the least advantaged, and (b) attached to positions and offices open to all under conditions of fair equality of opportunity (Rawls, 1999, p. 266.). Similarly, on the premise of equality of educational opportunity, differences in the actual results of schooling are acceptable (Lo, 1999). The open and flexible system of major based differentiation helps all students, not just a privileged few, to realize their maximum potential, and thus is fair and acceptable.

In respect of developmental trends of disciplines, on the one hand, interdisciplinary, cross-sectional, multi-disciplinary fields become important sources of innovation. On the other hand, the developmental pace of sub-fields or "specialization" within disciplines is equally amazing. For example, in just one specialized field of small particles physics, since 1935, physicists have discovered neutron, positron, π mesons, J/ψ particle, anti-protons and neutrinos, etc., and thus effectively promoted the development of related fields of study and industry. In the era of knowledge explosion and rapid expansion of disciplines, senior secondary students should consider their future plans to determine their college majors, and lay either comprehensive or in-depth knowledge foundations.

Concept Clarification

The principle of major-based differentiation means that apart from certain common requirements, the various colleges or departments at universities put forward specific enrollment requirements according to the characteristics of their degree programs. In line with that approach, in addition to appropriate required courses, senior secondary students can carefully select courses of study and therefore examinations according to their intended college majors. As a result, senior secondary students "stream themselves" into a wide range of courses combinations.

Lingbiao Gao (2008) has designed a straight forward but broadly acceptable college entrance examination program. In his view, the college entrance examination should be divided into two parts. One is a foundation level examination covering senior secondary required curriculum content, and the other examines the two specialized courses in accordance with students' intended college majors. This program may require further development or "fine tuning", but it does reflect and accommodate the principle of major-based differentiation.

To better understanding this principle, it is necessary to clarify certain areas, especially what appear to be some existing misunderstanding of major-based differentiation in Chinese academic circles.

First, the system of intended-major-based differentiation in senior secondary schools is not the equivalent of that of a college major. This means that in addition to the appropriate common fundamental curriculum, senior secondary students are encouraged to choose courses for in-depth study and subsequent university entrance examination that will prepare them for the admission requirements of their intended colleges and departments. The latter relates to the college degree curricula program of higher education which itself includes not only electives, but compulsory courses.

Second, students in senior secondary schools gradually differentiate according to their intended, but not declared majors. The intended major is flexible and changeable. As love is the foundation for the stability of marriage, intended major-based elective courses are the foundation which may guarantee the students can determine their majors in college.

Third, neither the learning of an academic major in college nor major-based courses in senior secondary schools imply a one-sided development of students. The academic major, as the learning field and direction of undergraduate students, might be a comprehensive one such as General Studies and Humanities major. It might also be an in-depth one such as Classics, Statistics or Computer Programming. Therefore, under the system of major-based differentiation, senior secondary students are cultivated to be many kinds of generalists or specialists.

Fourth, the justifiability of major-based differentiation depends not on the breadth or depth of students' knowledge and abilities, but rather on the degree of congruence between individual students' aptitudes and various colleges' major requirements. Meanwhile, enrollment requirements of specific majors should reflect and be relevant to the needs of different occupations and developmental trends of different disciplines.

Fifth, major-based differentiation emphasizes individualized basics, which is also part and parcel of basics like common basis. Therefore, it does not lead to a fragile foundation of students' knowledge but rather a robust one. Shing-Tung Yau, a Chinese American mathematician, pointed out that "the foundations of American students are not inferior to Chinese counterparts'. On the contrary, they are a lot stronger". In the U.S., "in some good schools, eleventh and twelfth grade students have acquired a lot of knowledge of calculus", but Chinese students "seldom learn infinitesimal calculus at all, and the college entrance examination does not cover it either (Liu, 2003). The so-called basics by Shing-Tung Yau are the individualized ones, which are the result of major-based differentiation.

Sixth, there is not conflict between a major-based differentiation system in senior secondary schools and general education or delayed declaration of major in colleges. For example, in the U.S., undergraduates may declare a major on the application for admission to colleges or after taking specialized examinations administered by various degree programs at the very beginning of the first semester, or after meeting the entry requirements for a particular degree program before the end of the second year in college. In any case, American students in high schools or in the foregoing two years in college may take many major-based elective courses.

In conclusion, reconstruction of China's future senior secondary elective courses, college entrance examination courses, and college admission requirements in accordance with the viewpoint of major-based differentiation has become a top priority. Only in this way, can a diversified educational system and personalized student development become possible. The fundamental question remains: "Why do our schools always fail to nurture outstanding talents", asked by many including Xuesen Qian, the father of Chinese missile technology and one of the founders of the Jet Propulsion Laboratory at the California Institute of Technology. It will get a satisfactory answer.

ACKNOWLEDGMENTS

This research is one of the Chinese Department of Education key projects in 2010 "A Comparative Research on Major-Oriented Elective Systems with the Purpose of Fostering Outstanding Talents" (DDA100216) from whence it received its funding. I would like to express my most heartfelt thanks to Dr. Hongyu Wang from School of Teaching and Curriculum Leadership at Oklahoma State University, and Dr. Dongmei Chen from the Centre of Curriculum Studies at South China Normal University, for their careful, comprehensive correction of English written expressions in this article. I also owe a great debt of gratitude to the two editors of this book, John C. K. Lee and Hong-Biao Yin, for their valuable comments and suggestions.

REFERENCES

Admissions Committee of Guangdong Province, Guangdong Department of Education (2006). *Guangdong province in 2007 implementation measures of general college entrance examination program for students under senior secondary new curriculum experiment*. Guangzhou: Admissions Committee of Guangdong Province, Guangdong Department of Education. (in Chinese).

Ministry of Education, PRC. (2003a). *General senior secondary school curriculum program*. Beijing: Ministry of Education. (in Chinese).

Ministry of Education, PRC. (2003b). *General senior secondary mathematics curriculum standards*. Beijing: People's Education Press. (in Chinese).

Ministry of Education, PRC. (2008). *The recommendation about deepening the reform of college entrance examination in provinces and regions of being implementing senior secondary new curriculum reform*. Beijing: Ministry of Education. (in Chinese).

State Council, PRC. (2010). *National outline of medium and long-term education reform and development (2010-2020)*. Beijing: State Council. (in Chinese).

Education and Manpower Bureau (2005). *The new academic structure for senior secondary education and higher education: Action plan for investing in the future of Hong Kong.* Hong Kong: Education and Manpower Bureau.

Gao, L. B. (2008). College entrance examination and the new curriculum. *Examination Research*, *4*(1), 25-29. (in Chinese).

Gardner, H. (1983). *Frames of mind: The theory of multiple intelligences.* New York: Basic Books.

Guangdong Department of Education (2008). *The revised program of Guangdong college entrance examination reform.* Guangzhou: Guangdong Department of Education. (in Chinese).

Holland, J. (1973). *Making vocational choices: A theory of careers.* Englewood Cliffs, NJ: Prentice-Hall.

King's College London (2011). King's college London online prospectus: *Undergraduate programmes.* Retrieved 05 January 2011 from http://www.kcl.ac.uk/prospectus/undergraduate/search/browse/bysubject.

Lo, L. N. K. (1999). Quality and equality in the educational development of Hong Kong and the Chinese mainland. *Educational Research Journal*, *14*(1), 13-48.

Liu, S. Q. (2003, November 7). Is the foundation of Chinese Students more solid than American counterparts? Shing-Tung Yau pours cold water on our basic education. *China Youth Daily.* (in Chinese)

Rawls, J. (1999). *A theory of justice* (Revised Edition). Cambridge, MA: Belknap Press of Harvard University Press.

Smith, A. (1981). The wealth of nations. In R. H. Campbell and A. S. Skinner (Eds.), *Glasgow edition of the works and correspondence of Adam Smith.* Indianapolis: Liberty Classics.

Smith, J., Hoganson, M. L., Gill, P., and Mudge, J. (2008). *Guiding the way to higher education: Step-by-step to college workshops for students (Early High School Curriculum).* Virginia: National Association for College Admission Counseling.

The College Board (2004). *AP and higher education.* Retrieved 15 January 2011 from http://www.collegeboard.com/prod_downloads/ipeAPC/04884aphigheredbro_36745.pdf.

The College Board (2011). Major and career profiles. Retrieved 15 January 2011 from http://www.collegeboard.com/csearch/majors_careers/profiles/.

The Investigation Panel of the China National Institute for Educational Research (2009). All learning needs should be met: Sixty suggestions for the making of "National Outline for Medium and Long-term Education Reform and Development". *Educational Research*, *30*(3), 3-25. (in Chinese).

Zhou, Y. M. (2009, February 9). More than half of internet users advocate abolishing the streaming system of arts- or science-program. *Beijing Times.* (in Chinese).

Zhou, Y. M. (2010a, March 1). The National Outline doesn't deal with the issue about the streaming system of arts- or science-program because of fierce controversy. *Beijing Times.* (in Chinese).

Zhou, Y. M. (2010b, March 3). It is expected to realize in 2020 to abolish the streaming system of Arts- or Science-candidates in college entrance examination programs. *Beijing Times.* (in Chinese).

PART IV. TEACHER PROFESSIONAL DEVELOPMENT IN CURRICULUM REFORM

In: Curriculum Reform in China
Editors: Hong-Biao Yin and John Chi-Kin Lee

ISBN 978-1-61470-943-5
© 2012 Nova Science Publishers, Inc.

Chapter 13

EMOTION AS A LENS TO UNDERSTAND TEACHER DEVELOPMENT IN CURRICULUM REFORM[18]

Hong-Biao Yin, John Chi-Kin Lee and Edmond Hau-Fai Law

ABSTRACT

Teacher emotion provides a lens, through which we can understand the characteristics of teacher development in large-scale educational change. However, compared with the rich exploration of teachers' emotional geographies in the West, only a few studies have adopted Hargreaves' emotional geographies to analyze human interactions in education in Chinese societies. This chapter aims at exploring the nature of emotions felt by teachers in their interactions with teacher trainers during a period of the national curriculum reform in Mainland China. Three kinds of emotional geographies were evident: professional, political, and moral. The implications for teacher emotion research and teacher development in curriculum reform are discussed.

INTRODUCTION

Since the mid-1990s, increasing attention has been given by educational researchers to the role of emotions in teaching (Zemblys, 2005), leadership (Crawford, 2009; Leithwood and Beatty, 2008), educational change (Day and Lee, 2011), and education in general (Schutz and Pekrun, 2007; Schutz and Zembylas, 2009). In contrast with the remarkable scarcity of such exploration in East Asia, especially in Mainland China, studies on teacher emotion have been conducted largely in the West. Employing the conceptual framework of emotional geographies of teaching suggested by Hargreaves (2000, 2001a, 2001b), this chapter attempts to address this gap by analyzing teachers' emotional interactions with teacher trainers in the context of the national curriculum reform in Mainland China, that is, the senior secondary

---

[18] Parts of this chapter are taken from Yin, H. B., & Lee, J. C. K. (2011). Emotions matter: Teachers' feelings about their interactions with teacher trainers during curriculum reform. *Chinese Education and Society*, *44*(4), 84-100.

school (SSS) curriculum reform. Through the lens of teacher emotion, the nature of teacher development and the role of teacher trainers are thus reconceptualized.

Emotional Geographies of Teaching

In the past decade, a significant theoretical shift has appeared in research focused on teacher emotions. Rather than using well-established psychometric instruments to measure aspects of teachers' emotions, such as job satisfaction, concerns with educational change and stress and burnout in the workplace, researchers have begun to study teachers in the context of social interaction so as to understand more clearly the processes involved in "being emotional" (Carlyle and Woods, 2002, p.xiv), because "emotions are located not just in the individual mind; they are embedded and expressed in human interactions and relationships" (Hargreaves, 2000, p.824). Findings from empirical studies have repeatedly suggested that teachers' emotions are rooted in their selves, identities, and relationships with others, thereby affecting them as well (Hargreaves, 1998a; Zembylas, 2003; Lasky, 2005; Lee and Yin, 2011).

It has been asserted that emotion lies "at the heart of teaching" (Hargreaves, 1998b, p.835). Teaching is a form of emotional practice and emotional labor, embedded in situations that constitute emotional understanding between teachers and the people around them—be it students, colleagues, and parents. Drawing on symbolic interactionism and postmodern geography, Hargreaves (2000, 2001a, 2001b) has coined the term "emotional geographies of teaching" to illustrate the proximity and distance of human relationships and their impact on the emotional understanding between teachers and others in teaching and educational change. He defined emotional geographies of teaching as "the spatial and experiential patterns of closeness and/or distance in human interactions and relationships that help create, configure and color the feelings and emotions we experience about ourselves, our world and each other" (Hargreaves, 2001a, p.1061). Specifically, five forms of emotional geographies were examined by Hargreaves (2001a, 2001b): (1) socio-cultural geographies, in which differences of culture, race, gender, and class can create distance between people and lead them to be treated as stereotypes; (2) moral geographies, in which either people pursue common purposes and share a sense of accomplishment together, or they are defensive about their own purposes and unconcerned about the purposes of others; (3) professional geographies, in which teacher professionalism either sets professionals apart from their colleagues and clients, or opens them up to exploring professional issues together; (4) political geographies, in which hierarchical power relationships distort the emotional communication between teachers and those around them; and (5) physical geographies of time and space that can bring and keep people in proximity over long periods so that relationships might develop.

In fact, the idea of "emotional geographies of teaching" reflects the convergence of research trends emerging in two different fields. One is the "emotional turn" in geography, which acknowledges the presence of emotions in our understandings of the world and attempts to understand emotion in terms of its socio-spatial mediation and articulation (Bondi, Davidson, and Smith, 2005). The other is the recognition of "social geographies" of educational change, which emphasizes the importance of social spaces in understanding how people produce and react to educational change, because the process of change and its human landscapes are created by the actors (or agents) operating within a specific social context and structure (Hernández and Goodson, 2004).

For analyzing the human interactions in teaching and educational change, the framework of emotional geographies is helpful in identifying the supports for and threats to the emotional understanding of schooling, resulting from forms of distance or closeness in human relationships between teachers and others. Using this framework, Hargreaves and his colleagues have conducted a series of studies to analyze the emotional interactions between teachers and students (Hargreaves, 2000), leaders (Schmidt, 2000), colleagues (Hargreaves, 2001b), and parents (Hargreaves, 2001a; Hargreaves and Lasky, 2005; Lasky, 2000). Recently, Dowling (2008) has used this framework to understand gender relations in physical education teacher education (PETE). He found that negative emotions about gender issues are hegemonic on account of today's configurations of human relations in PETE, because the feeling rules of physical education construct "negative emotions" as being reasonable (p.247). At a symposium held at the London Institute of Education in 2008, issues related to emotional geographies of education, including the emotional landscape of class relationships in inner city schools (Reay, 2008), the emotional geography of contemporary classrooms (Watkins, 2008), and how the physical spaces of different types of schools are implicated in creating recognizable student subjectivities and demarcating belonging and exclusion (Nairn, 2008), were extensively discussed.

Compared with the relatively rich exploration of teachers' emotional geographies in the West, very few studies adopting Hargreaves' emotional geographies have been undertaken to analyze human interactions in education in Chinese societies. For example, Jiang (2004) has analyzed the interactions between intern teachers and mentors in Taiwan and summarized the five emotional distances caused by role identity, hierarchical power, organizational culture, working competition, and interpersonal attitude. Yin (2009) has explored the emotional landscape, in which teachers are situated in curriculum reform in Mainland China, and found that teachers worked in a highly complex emotional landscape in the context of reform; in addition, Yin also found that that teachers had to pay a great deal of emotional labor to manage their feelings and emotions.

Teacher Development in Educational Change

Just as pointed out by Fullan and Hargreaves (1992), when researchers talk about specific educational changes, "teacher development and implementation go hand in hand" (p.1). At present, the educational changes in many Asian countries adopt a decentralized approach, which allows teachers and schools to make their own professional decisions and advocate many new practices for curriculum, teaching, and learning, such as curriculum integration, inquiry-based learning, and formative assessment. Teachers have had to fulfill the multiple roles of being active curriculum-makers, innovators of teaching strategies, and gatekeepers of student academic achievement (Chan, 2010). Therefore, training them to be an independent professional who can make proper judgments in complex situations and developing them to be responsible for their own professional growth are critical to the successful implementation of educational change. As Borko, Elliot, and Uchiyama (2004) have suggested, the success of current reform initiatives is dependent upon "creating opportunities for teachers' continual learning and providing sufficient professional development resources to support these opportunities" (p. 971).

The connections among educational change, teacher development programs, and teacher growth have been explored by researchers. On the one hand, the significance of teacher development for implementing and sustaining educational change has been recognized by scholars for a long time (e.g., Borko et al., 2004; Lieberman, 1995; Little, 1993; van Driel, Beijaard, and Verloop, 2001). Under today's reform context, the conventional view of teacher development as "a transferable package of knowledge to be distributed to teachers in bite-sized pieces" needs radical rethinking (Lieberman, 1995, p.591). The once dominant training-and-coaching model, which emphasizes on expanding an individual repertoire of well-defined classroom practice, is already viewed as inadequate in terms of satisfying the requirements of present reform initiatives (Little, 1993). Teacher training should focus on the appropriateness of teaching decisions, and effective teacher development programs must engage them in practical tasks and provide opportunities to observe, assess, and reflect on the new ideas and practices being implemented (Darling-Hammond and McLaughlin, 1995). On the other hand, the positive role of professional development programs for teacher growth is supported by the empirical findings from some longitudinal studies. In England, Boyle and his colleagues' study has found that the majority of participants who take part in longer-term professional development change one or more aspects of their teaching practice; they also found that even badly delivered professional development can be helpful (B. Boyle, While, and T. Boyle, 2004). In the United States, Desimone and her colleagues have found that professional development focused on specific instructional practices increases teachers' use of those practices in the classroom, and specific features can increase the effect of the professional development on teacher's instruction (Desimone, Porter, Garet, Yoon, and Birman, 2002).

To make the teacher development programs more effective for teacher growth and educational change, some studies have summarized the characteristics of effective teacher development programs. For example, Garet and his colleagues' study found that three core features of professional development activities have significant and positive effects on teachers' self-reported increased knowledge and skills and changes in classroom practice. These core features are focus on content knowledge, opportunities for active learning, and coherence with other learning opportunities. Moreover, the structural features that significantly affect teacher learning include the form of the activity (e.g., workshop vs. study group), collective participation of teachers form the same school, grade, or subject, and the duration of the activity (Garet, Porter, Desimone, Birman, and Yoon, 2001). Penuel, Fishman Yamaguchi, and Gallagher (2007) have confirmed the significance of teachers' perceptions about how coherent their professional development experiences for teacher learning and curriculum implementation, and they found that the incorporation of time for teachers to plan for implementation and provision of technical support are significant in promoting the implementation of a curriculum innovation. Nonetheless, after an examination of 13 lists of characteristics of "effective professional development," Guskey (2003) has found that the lists vary widely, and the research supporting them is inconsistent and often contradictory. Hence, he suggested that researchers focus on the contextual factors of teacher development activities and the criteria for effectiveness.

Although the design or structural features of effective teacher development have been extensively investigated, policy and research on teacher development and educational change usually ignores or minimizes the emotional significance of teachers' work (Hargreaves,

1998a). Studies on teacher development in educational change have typically focused either on teachers' skills and practices or on their cognitive processes, such as teachers' conception, belief, reflection, and knowledge-building (e.g., Chitpin and Evers, 2005; Lloyd, 1999; Spilková, 2001; Swan, 2007; van Driel et al., 2001). Therefore, researchers may be familiar with "what teachers do" or "how they think," but know little about "how teachers feel" in teaching or educational change, and know little about the emotions that facilitate teachers to engage in their job (Hargreaves, 1994, p.141). The significance of teacher emotion in understanding teacher development has seldom been investigated in previous studies, especially under the context of large-scale educational change.

Recently, it has been suggested that emotion is a lens exploring teachers' identity, commitment, and sense-making in educational change (van Veen and Lasky, 2005). Although the human relationships between teachers and others (e.g., students, colleagues, parents, and leaders) and their impact on teachers' emotions have been investigated in teaching or educational change, the interactions between teachers and teacher trainers in curriculum reform is still an underexplored topic. We thus sought to address this issue through the lens of teacher emotion in the context of the national SSS curriculum reform in Mainland China. To be specific, this chapter aims at exploring these two principal questions: What emotions were felt by teachers during their interactions with teacher trainers in the SSS curriculum reform? What kinds of social factors, including professional, political and moral factors, influenced teachers' emotional interactions with teacher trainers in the reform? Based on this exploration, the implications for teacher emotion research and teacher development in curriculum reform are discussed in subsequent sections.

CONTEXT

Currently, national curriculum reform is high on the Ministry of Education's (MOE) central agenda regarding the reform of basic education in Mainland China. In June 2001, the MOE initiated the eighth round of national curriculum reform by releasing the *Guidelines on Basic Education Curriculum Reform (Experimental Draft)*. In 2003, the new SSS curriculum guideline and the national curriculum standards for 15 subjects were published in succession. Accordingly, experiments in SSS curriculum reform were initiated in four selected locations (i.e., Guangdong, Shandong, Hainan, and Ningxia) in 2004, and these have gradually been extended to other provinces, such as Jiangsu, Fujian, Liaoning, and Zhejiang. By September 2009, 24 of the 31 provinces, municipalities, and autonomous regions in Mainland China were participating in the reform. As planned by MOE, all the other seven provinces (municipalities and autonomous regions) must have adopted the new SSS curriculum by September 2010.

In this round of national curriculum reform, the MOE attempted to bring about systemic change to the SSS curriculum, especially with regard to the following aspects (MOE, 2003): (a) replacing the existing subject-based curriculum structure with a three-level structure consisting of learning fields, subjects and modules; (b) adopting an elective course and credit system; (c) granting students the opportunity to choose courses, thereby improving students' generic skills of independent inquiry, cooperation, communication and problem-solving; (d) establishing a formative student evaluation system and connecting students' academic performance to their growth portfolio; and (e) decentralizing the educational system and encouraging school-based curriculum development.

Not surprisingly, for teachers, implementing such a large-scale curriculum reform is a very complex and difficult task, making their existing knowledge and expertise insufficient for the requirements of reform. Cognizant of this fact in the SSS curriculum reform, various teacher development activities, including lectures and seminars, short-term workshops, demonstration lessons, cross-district/province school visits and school-based teaching research, were arranged by the central and local governments as well as the schools. In these activities, teaching research officers (TROs, *jiaoyanyuan*) and university specialists (USs, *daxue zhuanjia*) in subject content, teacher education, or curriculum studies typically assumed the responsibility for teacher training. Although these activities had some positive influence on the implementation of SSS curriculum reform, researchers also found that both the content and forms of teacher training could be improved further (Ma, Yin, Tang, and Liu, 2009), and that the professional support that teachers obtained was far from adequate (Ma, 2009). Apart from TROs and USs, expert teachers experienced in implementing the reform initiatives were also probably selected by local educational departments to be the trainers in some exceptional cases. They were invited to share their experiences in using the new textbooks, teaching methods, or assessment strategies with other teachers.

METHODOLOGY

The study introduced in this chapter is part of a three-year qualitative research project (2005-2008) that focused on teacher emotion in curriculum reform in Mainland China. In this project, the researchers sought to explore teachers' emotional experiences during the implementation of the SSS curriculum reform in Guangzhou, the provincial city of Guangdong, one of the four pilot locations engaged in the first round of SSS curriculum reform.

The embedded case study method used in this work is one, in which both schools and teachers are considered as units of analysis (Scholz and Tietje, 2002; Yin, 2003). In Guangzhou, all senior secondary schools were classified into five levels according to the students' academic achievements in the enrollment examination. In order to detect teachers' emotional experiences in schools with different backgrounds, the researchers selected two schools belonging in the upper and middle levels, respectively. The one in the upper level (S1) was one of the six key schools in Guangzhou, and the other (S2) was an ordinary school with a lower academic level. In each school, one school administrator with responsibility for teaching matters and several teachers from different genders, subjects, and teaching experience were investigated. Table 1 summarizes the background information about these schools and teachers.

In order to gain some understanding of the perceptions of teacher trainers, three other informants were deliberately invited to participate in this study: one US in curriculum studies in Guangzhou, one TRO in the Guangdong Provincial Teaching Research Office, and one expert teacher who played the role of trainer in teacher development activities during the SSS curriculum reform. In total, 18 informants participated in the present study.

Table 1. Background information about the school informants

School	School background		Informants involved	
	Key school	Level	School personnel	Subject teachers
S1	Yes	Level 1	One teaching affair director	Six
S2	No	Level 3	One grade master teacher in charge of the whole grade teaching affair	Seven

The researchers employed semi-structured interviews to collect information about teacher emotion. Each interview, conducted in a private space within each school, lasted at least one hour and concentrated on eliciting teachers' feelings or emotional episodes experienced during their interactions with teacher trainers in the SSS curriculum reform as well as their opinions about the roles of emotion in teaching and curriculum reform. Following Hargreaves' (2001a) suggestions, the teachers were deliberately asked to describe particular incidents that highlighted their positive or negative emotions. The main interview questions included: Were there any incidents which made you feel joyful (or happy, excited...)/sad (or anxious, worried...) in your interactions with the teacher trainers? Why did you have these feelings about your interactions with the teacher trainers? What were your perceptions of the effectiveness of teacher development in the SSS curriculum reform?

Considering the privacy of teacher emotion, all the interviews were conducted individually by one or both of the authors in some quiet places, such as the playground, staff room, meeting room, or restaurants. The interviews were recorded and then transcribed, after which the transcriptions were sent to the informants for cross-checking. During the data analysis process, NVivo software was used to code, classify, and cluster the data.

FINDINGS

Mixed Emotions: The Emotional Interactions between Teachers and the Group of TROs and USs

Professional Geographies

Professional geographies concern the closeness or distance caused by competing forms of professionalism that help or handicap emotional understanding between teachers and others (Dowling, 2008; Hargreaves, 2001a). Many studies have shown that teachers' attitudes toward curriculum reform (as well as their behavior) follow the "practicality ethic," highlighting the importance of instrumentality of the reform initiatives or training programs (Lee, 2000; Ma et al., 2009). In the teacher development programs of the SSS curriculum reform, different types of teacher trainers (i.e., TROs and USs) had different professional orientations, mirrored reflected in both the teacher interviews and the narrations of the teacher trainers themselves. In general, TROs usually had abundant teaching experience in primary or secondary schools. They could provide teachers with useful, practical guidance for their classroom teaching. However, USs, by and large, were inclined to provide clear interpretation of some kinds of educational theory or updated knowledge in some disciplines. Generally, TROs followed an experience-based, practice-oriented approach, while USs adhered to a knowledge-based, theory-oriented approach, a distinction reflected in these quotations from our interviews with a TRO and a US:

> "I came to the Teaching Research Office after over 20 years as a teacher. I am very clear about how tired a frontline teacher is. [What teachers need most] are lesson demonstrations, discussion of lesson cases. For the subject Geography, it concerns field study....Teachers are most interested to know: How to guide students? How to operate?" (I-TRO-M)
> "I could only talk from a theoretical perspective—this is our responsibility as a theory researcher...I think that it is necessary to have theory before the integration between theory and practice. There is not a lack of practice...What is lacking is theory and so it is essential to develop theories." (I-US-M)

Due to the proximity between the professional orientations of teachers and TROs, in some degree, teachers had positive feelings about their interactions with TROs and had some positive evaluations about the effect of the training programs initiated by TROs.

> "We are quite satisfied with our Teaching Research Officers. They come to advise us about our teaching and help build a platform to facilitate communication between schools....Frankly, these activities are useful." (I-S1-TF-5)

However, because the SSS curriculum reform advocated many new educational ideas and practices, such as constructivism, multiple intelligences and inquiry-based learning, TROs, like the SSS teachers, also lacked thorough knowledge about the theory and practice of these initiatives. As a result, the practical guidance they could provide for teachers was limited.

> "Although teaching research activities offer great support, these activities have little impact. It is because Teaching Research Officers in charge of teacher training do not know how to deal with the New Curriculum themselves. If they don't know, how could they train us? In every teaching research activity, we come across a variety of experimental lessons. They do not give us an overall evaluation: How to conduct a good lesson? How to realize the essence of the New Curriculum? They only say, "This attempt is good"—they also give us this answer. We do not know where our direction is." (I-S2-TM-2)

For the training programs provided by USs, teachers considered that the content of these programs was too abstract and too far away from their teaching practice, so these programs were useless. They even suspected that what the USs told them were merely empty words.

> "The university offers too strong a theoretical aspect and these theories are very hollow—not [really] matching the realities of secondary school teaching. Do they, the so-called expert scholars, really understand the new curriculum?" (I-S1-TM-3)
> "In fact, I think, do university teachers themselves understand or not? They haven't practiced before. They only dig into these theories and talk to teachers after adaptation. After listening, you are taken aback and then they feel that 'Wow, I am so sophisticated.'" (I-S2-TF-3)

If some USs totally ignored the needs of teachers in curriculum reform, the teacher training would be irrelevant to teachers' practice, and the interactions between teachers and these trainers would collapse. A teacher described the breakdown of the interaction between teachers and USs.

> "The university professor before he lectured said, 'You are assigned by different Teaching Research Offices and we are forced by our superiors to offer training. Our professional knowledge does not match the needs of the new curriculum, so what I talk about today may not be something you need. Please excuse me. If you have any problem, please find our leaders.' This professor started to lecture on his expertise in history. [Exclamation] Another professor comes next and...lectures on a similar topic...A teacher stands up and says "Professor, we already know what you have taught. Can you talk about something we wish to know such as what findings you have discovered in the research on the implementation of the new curriculum. Are there any examples? What will the College examination assess? He responds with, 'I am not sure about these issues and it is not the business of our training. This is the business of the examination center'...Under this sort of training, we are all frigid. We get nothing out of this and does it fool the frontline teachers?" (I-S1-TF-4)

In this case, the teacher expressed her anger about the irresponsible USs. The two USs did not pay any attention to teachers' needs in the reform and completely ignored the distance between their professional orientation and that of the teachers, thus, igniting the teachers' fury and not meeting the teachers' expectations in the training programs.

Political Geographies

Political geographies are concerned with the teachers' position in the hierarchical power structure. This structure can have a strong influence on teachers' feelings because emotion is bound with people's experiences of power and powerlessness (Dowling, 2008; Hargreaves, 2001a). As one teacher said, teachers were relegated to a low status in terms of the decision-making hierarchy for curriculum reform in China. Ironically, although teachers might be active agents of change, they had no power to change many elements.

> "Curriculum reform is a grand engineering. However, what are our leverages? It is our teachers who are the weakest part of this educational system, which includes such components as the official agency (the Education Bureau), [the] people designing teaching materials, parents, society, students, schools and teachers...What has curriculum reform chosen?...Teachers. [Although] the teacher is the most active factor, it is the weakest because it does not have the capacity to change other things." (I-S1-TF-4)

In China, teaching research offices (*jiaoyanshi*) have been established within government education departments at the district/county and provincial/municipal levels. The functions of these institutions include helping teachers understand the curriculum standards and teaching materials, coordinating the subject tests in local areas, and providing pedagogical support to teachers. For teachers, the TROs function as educational administrators in the local area. Hence, in various teacher development programs regarding the SSS curriculum reform, although the TROs' guidance about the implementation of ideas advocated by the reform might be limited, teachers still attached great importance to the TROs' advice.

"We often meet the Teaching Research Officers. When we meet, we grasp the chance to express our confusion. It is because they stand in a higher position than us." (I-S1-TF-5)

Meanwhile, teachers had complex feelings about the USs. On the one hand, they felt a sense of envy toward the higher social status enjoyed by the USs; on the other hand, teachers did not trust the training provided by these USs. Moreover, compared with the USs, teachers considered themselves as a disadvantaged group because they were more vulnerable to being blamed for any education failure of the curriculum reform.

"Secondary school teachers really admire university teachers. They [university teachers] work at a higher level, but we feel that they are not doing realistic things. They guide us based on their imagination." (I-S1-TF-1)

"Secondary school teachers form weak communities…but university teachers form strong communities…So when there are problems, they blame basic education: 'You see, it is secondary school teachers who teach students poorly.'" (I-S2-TF-3)

One of the teachers said, in the effective teacher development programs, the relations between teachers and the trainers should be equal rather than hierarchical. If not, the power distance between teachers and trainers would cause emotional misunderstanding between them.

"If real development is to take place, [trainers] should talk to teachers on an equal basis instead of his standing on the podium and us sitting on the benches. In this way, you will look down upon us and we will not listen to you. I have tons of things to do and a heap of assignments for marking. We don't have time to hear your fabrication of tales, right?" (I-S2-TM-2).

Moral Geographies

Moral geographies refer to the distance between teachers' moral purpose and that of the trainers. When they have a common purpose in curriculum reform, emotional understanding between teachers and trainers is more likely to be established (Dowling, 2008; Hargreaves, 2000). Many teachers in our study were excited about the implementation of the SSS curriculum reform because they thought it was the right time to correct the long-standing malpractices of the educational system in China, such as passive learning and the tradition of teaching for examinations.

"Having such a reform makes every teacher feel thrilled.…When we look at surveys on the defect of the old curriculum and hear about the conception of new curriculum reform, I feel that 'Well, this reform is good!'" (I-S2-TF-1)

Prior to the implementation of the SSS curriculum reform, the textbooks used in schools were all compiled and published by the People's Education Press, an official publishing institute under the MOE. However, one significant transformation in the reform was the decentralization of textbook writing and publishing. Many local publishing institutes obtained the authority to publish textbooks once the drafts of the textbooks have been approved by the MOE. As a result, some TROs and USs were invited to compile textbooks for these publishing institutes. In the teachers' opinion, the quality of some new textbooks was really poor; however, some TROs still voted for the use of these textbooks.

> "According to our situation, the new teaching material is still crude. Obviously, the arrangement of exercises does not hang well together with the content of teaching materials and sometimes incoherently gets in a muddle." (I-S1-TM-4)
>
> "What democracy means is using voting to say that, 'We all agree to use the Guangdong version'—we secondary school teachers have no voting right. The people in the *jiaoyanshi* vote together on selecting one out of the five versions. Since some people who vote are also involved in designing the textbook, they will vote for themselves, right!" [knocking the table] (I-S2-TM-5)

These aspects related to the selection of new textbooks led teachers to suspect that the motive of the textbook writers, and also of the teacher trainers, was more about commercial profit rather than education. This was also supported by the US interviewed by the researchers in the present study. Thus, the distance between teachers' moral purpose and that of the trainers weakened the emotional relationship between them.

> "Sometimes, I cannot help thinking whether this reform is really a reform or is it an economic plunder of the educated? The teaching materials have made some contribution to the GDP. It makes people feel that there is an economic element in it and it is not purely for reforming education." (I-S2-TM-1)
>
> "The curriculum reform in Guangdong province in its journey of change cannot resolve the problem of the interest arising from teaching materials...There is also an issue of corruption. Some people use the flag of 'curriculum reform' and extort the wealth of primary and secondary schools." (I-US-M).

A Successful Story: The Emotional Interactions between Teachers and the Expert Teacher

Although teachers felt complex emotions about their interactions with TROs and USs in most teacher development activities, sometimes they did have positive feelings toward the teacher-trainer interactions. When the teacher trainers were "expert teachers" who had similar status as the ordinary teachers and could resolve teachers' difficulties in implementing the new SSS curriculum, the emotional interactions between teachers and the trainers were likely to be successful. Ms. Shen, the expert teacher interviewed in the present study, was one such teacher trainer.

Ms. Shen taught biology in a low-level school (Level 4). At the beginning of this round of national curriculum reform, she was selected to participate in the demonstration lesson competition in Guangzhou, which required the participants to teach following the ideas advocated by the new curriculum. In order to prepare for this demonstration lesson, she exerted a great deal of effort in learning the new curriculum standards. When she performed well in the competition, she was selected to take part in the competition of Guangdong province and then the national demonstration lesson. After these rounds of competitions, she found that the ideas and initiatives of the reform could be unconsciously implemented in her teaching and really make a difference in the teaching and learning effect. Thus, she believed the SSS curriculum reform was worthy of implementation.

"Going through a series of deep learning activities and several rounds of competitions, I feel my lessons have automatically used those things, unconsciously infusing [them]. I think the new curriculum standards are correct, the concepts of those curriculum standards have been transformed into the feeling in my bones. Surprisingly, I discovered [that] the lessons, students, the quality of teaching and my own development have slowly been enhanced, and I feel this curriculum reform should become an essential part of my work." (I-ET-F)

Due to her outstanding performance, she was appointed as the Director of the Office of Teaching Research Affairs in her school. Her responsibility was to mobilize and organize teachers in exploring method that can be used to implement the initiatives of the SSS curriculum reform, such as cooperation learning, inquiry-based teaching, and portfolio assessment. Moreover, she was invited to train teachers in Guangdong or in other provinces (e.g., Jiangsu). She thought she had to learn more and try more because the work of training teachers brought more challenges. As a result, she gradually improved her professional competence. She felt thankful for the curriculum reform and the opportunity of being a teacher trainer.

"I thank the new curriculum. I feel the training work in these few years...pushed me to progress. I have to force myself to improve substantially, or I cannot have the guts to train other people. Then I try many ways to use a new angle, to reflect and try from an angle that teachers find difficult to approach...I feel I am growing, yes, I am very grateful with the implementation of the curriculum reforms." (I-ET-F)

After the training, she often received teachers' appreciation messages or questions about classroom teaching. She felt very please when she received teachers' positive feedback on her training. She mentioned a message sent by a teacher through mobile phone. In this message, the teacher summarized the shortcomings of the training provided by other TROs and USs:

"Reading an email from a teacher: 'Thank you! I attended many training programs, but yours had the deepest impact on me, great help and stimulation. Hope to receive your help and advice regularly,...the previous training invited university professors, pure theories...or inviting leaders of the pedagogical research departments, empty and general talk, but yours helped us greatly, very practical, concrete, being the integration between spirit and practice, showing us the orientation of work.' I feel happy to see the feedback and response from the teachers, very happy, and then I told him we work hard together." (I-ET-F)

The smooth emotional interactions resulted in some desirable emotional geographies between teachers and Ms. Shen. Like other teachers, she respected the instrumentality of reform initiatives, but she knew the significance of continuous teaching inquiry for teacher development. For teachers, she was an experienced and knowledgeable teacher rather than someone with an official title or higher social status. Moreover, she had the same moral purpose as the teachers — to facilitate the effective implementation of the SSS curriculum reform. In summary, a successful teacher development program, which is supposed to be conducted in a democratic rather than hierarchical environment, should be concrete, practical, and consistent with the essence of curriculum reform. To achieve this effect, just as Ms. Shen said, the trainer needs to be prepared to "go together with teachers."

CONCLUSION

Emotional Geographies and Teachers' Feelings about Their Interactions with Trainers

This chapter focuses on exploring teachers' feelings about their interactions with teacher trainers in the SSS curriculum reform in Mainland China. The results showed that teachers experienced various emotions when they interacted with TROs, USs and the expert teacher, and had different evaluations on the teacher development programs provided by the experts. Table 2 presents teachers' perceptions concerning the teacher-trainer interactions in curriculum reform.

Table 2. Teachers' perceptions concerning teacher-trainer interactions

Interaction partners	Feelings	Professional orientation	Power relationship	Moral purpose	Perceived support
TROs	Mixed	Experience-based, practice-oriented	Higher in administrative hierarchy	Possibly eroded by commercial profit	Medium
USs	Mixed	Knowledge-based, theory-oriented	Higher in social status	Possibly eroded by commercial profit	Low
The expert teacher	Positive	Experience-based, research-oriented	Equal	Consistent with the essence of curriculum reform	High

As shown in Table 2, the results of the present study suggested that the framework of emotional geographies is helpful in investigating the social factors impacting teachers' emotions. In this chapter about teachers' feelings of their emotional interactions with teacher trainers, three kinds of emotional geographies were evident: professional, political, and moral.

Although the interactions with the trainers can elicit joy, envy, confusion, anger and other complex emotions in teachers, our findings indicate that teachers' feelings about their interactions with the trainers are mixed rather than pure in most cases, because these feelings are consequences of the interplay between professional, political, and moral geographies. The proximity of one of them alone is not sufficient in developing strong emotional understanding between teachers and trainers. The expert teacher's story showed that only when the three conditions are satisfied at the same time—the desirable professional orientation of the trainer, the equal power relationship between teachers and the trainer, and the consensus on moral purpose between teachers and the trainer — can positive feelings be developed. Compared with other studies on emotional geographies (e.g., Dowling, 2008; Hargreaves, 2000, 2001a, 2001b; Hargreaves and Lasky, 2004) that emphasize the effect of individual emotional geographies on teacher emotion, this chapter highlights the interrelations of different emotional geographies and their comprehensive impact on teachers' feelings.

Understanding Teachers' Voice about Their Professional Development through Emotion

In contrast to the traditional approach of minimizing the significance of teacher emotion in their professional development (Hargreaves, 1998a), the findings of our study suggests that trainers, administrators, and researchers should re-examine the emotional geographies of teacher-trainer interactions and make emotion a core rather than a peripheral part of teacher development.

Emotion reflects teachers' needs and expectations with regards their own professional growth. Teacher trainers who come from Teaching Research Offices, universities, and schools could act as instructional coaches and positive agents of change. Knight (2009, p.131-132) has suggested some tactics that instructional coaches can adopt to enhance change: walking on solid ground, clarifying your message, being ambitious and humble, confronting reality, understanding school culture, and taking care of yourself. It is important for teacher trainers to "do all you can to ensure that your teachers know what is expected of them and have what they need to implement the teaching practices you share with them," (p.132) as well as to maintain their innocence, curiosity, and compassion. Through the lens of teacher emotion, it is possible to know the reason why teachers like or dislike some specific teacher development programs. In essence, teachers' emotions articulate the teachers' voice about their professional lives, moral purpose, and career development (Goodson, 1991). Failure to understand teachers' emotions is failure to understand teachers' teaching and their needs for professional development.

Trainers as Learners: Rethinking the Role of Teacher Trainers in Reform Context

At present, Mainland China is in the process of experimenting with the national curriculum reform of basic education. Teacher professional development has become an imperative because teachers' work is changing, responding to the curriculum reform and its embedded notions of good teaching (Paine and Fang, 2006). The findings from the present study bring some implications for teacher trainers and teacher development in the SSS curriculum reform.

Previous studies have repeatedly recognized the importance of the form and content of teacher development programs (Boyle et al., 2004; Garet et al., 2001; Ma et al., 2009; Penuel et al., 2007). The findings of the present study support the claims of these studies that effective teacher development should focus on improving subject content knowledge, providing guidance for teachers' classroom practice, offering opportunities for active learning, and maintaining coherence with teachers' other learning activities. Meanwhile, it is also suggested that teacher trainers should rethink their understanding of the nature of teacher development and the role of teacher trainers in the context of curriculum reform.

Darling-Hammond and McLaughlin (1995) have argued that in today's climate of reform, teachers need to be involved in teacher development activities as both learners and teachers, because the success depends on how teachers are able to learn the new skill and unlearn previous beliefs and practices. This claim can be extended to reconsider the role of teacher trainers in systematic curriculum reform. The new understanding maintains that teacher trainers should be seen as both trainers and learners. Usually, trainers are reputed to be mentors or supervisors of teachers. However, due to the uncertainties brought by systematic change, even the teacher trainers do not have sufficient knowledge to answer the question, "What is good teaching?" Considering trainers as learners is also important for effective teacher development programs that emphasize mutual and interactive learning and professional development of both the trainers and the frontline teachers, a manifestation of what Knight (2009) meant by referring to the "personal humility" of the coaches (p.132).

REFERENCES

Bondi, L., Davidson, J., and Smith, M. (2005). Geography's 'emotional turn'. In J. Davidson, L. Bondi, and M. Smith (Eds.), *Emotional geographies* (pp.1-16). Aldershot: Ashgate.

Borko, H., Elliot, R., and Uchiyama, K. (2002). Professional development: A key to Kentucky's educational reform effort. *Teaching and Teacher Education, 18,* 969-987.

Boyle, B., While, D., and Boyle, T. (2004). A longitudinal study of teacher change: What makes professional development effective? *The Curriculum Journal, 15*(1), 45-68.

Carlyle, D., and Woods, P. (2002). *The emotions of teacher stress*. Stoke-on-Trent: Trentham Books.

Chan, J. K. S. (2010). Teachers' responses to curriculum policy implementation: Colonial constrains for curriculum reform. *Educational Research for Policy and Practice, 9,* 93-106.

Chiptin, S., and Evers, C. W. (2005). Teacher professional development as knowledge building: A Popperian analysis. *Teachers and Teaching: Theory and Practice, 11*(4), 419-433.

Crawford, M. (2009). *Getting to the heart of leadership: Emotion and educational leadership.* Los Angles: Sage.

Darling-Hammond, L., and McLaughlin, M. W. (1995). Policies that support professional development in an era of reform. *Phi Delta Kappan, 76,* 597-604.

Day, C., and Lee, J. C. K. (2011). *New understandings of teacher's work: Emotions and educational change.* Dordrecht: Springer.

Desimone, L. M., Porter, A. C., Garet, M. S., Yoon, K. S., Birman, B. F. (2002). Effects of professional development on teachers' instruction: Results form a three-year longitudinal study. *Educational Evaluation and Policy Analysis, 24*(2), 81-112.

Dowling, F. (2008). Getting in touch with our feelings: The emotional geographies of gender relations in PETE. *Sport, Education and Society, 13*(3), 247-266.

Fullan, M., and Hargreaves, A. (1992). Teacher development and educational change. In M. Fullan and A. Hargreaves (Eds.), *Teacher development and educational change* (pp. 1-9). London: The Falmer Press.

Garet, M. S., Porter, A. C., Desimone, L., Birman, B. F., and Yoon, K. S. (2001). What makes professional development effective? Results from a national sample of teachers. *American Educational Research Journal, 38*(4), 915-945.

Goodson, I. (1991). Sponsoring the teacher's voice: Teachers' lives and teacher development. *Cambridge Journal of Education, 21*(1), 35-45.

Gronn, P. and Lacey, K. (2004). Positioning oneself for leadership: Feelings of vulnerability among aspirant school principals. *School Leadership and Management, 24*(4), 405-424.

Guskey, T. R. (2003). What makes professional development effective? *Phi Delta Kappan, 84*, 748-750.

Hargreaves, A. (1994). *Changing teachers, changing times: Teachers work and culture in the postmodern age*. London: Cassell.

Hargreaves, A. (1998a). The emotional politics of teaching and teacher development: With implications for educational leadership. *International Journal of Leadership in Education, 1*(4), 315-336.

Hargreaves, A. (1998b). The emotional practice of teaching. *Teaching and Teacher Education, 14*(8), 835-854.

Hargreaves, A. (2000). Mixed emotions: Teachers' perceptions of their interactions with students. *Teaching and Teacher Education, 16*(8), 811-826.

Hargreaves, A. (2001a). Emotional geographies of teaching. *Teachers College Record, 103*(6), 1056-1080.

Hargreaves, A. (2001b). The emotional geographies of teachers' relations with colleagues. *International Journal of Educational Research, 35*(5), 503-527.

Hargreaves, A., and Lasky, S. (2004). The parent gap: The emotional geographies of teacher-parent relationships. In F. Hernández and I. F. Goodson (Eds.), *Social geographies of educational change* (pp.103-122). Dordrecht: Kluwer Academic Publishers.

Hernández, F., and Goodson, I. F. (2004). Social geographies of educational change: Drawing map for curious and dissatisfied travellers. In F. Hernández and I. F. Goodson (Eds.), *Social geographies of educational change* (pp. xi-xxi). Dordrecht: Kluwer Academic Publishers.

Jiang, W. C. (2004). The emotional map of intern teachers: A social-constructivist perspective. *Bulletin of Educational Psychology, 36*(1), 59-83. (in Chinese).

Knight, J. (2009). Coaches as leaders of change. In M. Fullan (Ed.), *The challenge of change: Start school improvement now!* (2nd ed., pp.105-133). Thousand Oaks: Corwin.

Lasky, S. (2005). A sociocultural approach to understanding teacher identity, agency and professional vulnerability in a context of secondary school reform. *Teaching and Teacher Education, 21*(8), 899-916.

Lee, J. C. K. (2000). Teacher receptivity to curriculum change in the implementation stage: The case of environmental education in Hong Kong. *Journal of Curriculum Studies, 32*(1), 95-115.

Lee, J. C. K., and Yin, H. B. (2011). Teachers' emotions and professional identity in curriculum reform: A Chinese perspective. *Journal of Educational Change, 12*(1), 25-46.

Leithwood, K., and Beatty, B. (2008). *Leading with teacher emotions in mind*. Thousand Oaks: Sage.

Lieberman, A. (1995). Practices that support teacher development. *Phi Delta Kappan*, *76*, 591-596.

Little, J. W. (1993). Teachers' professional development in a climate of educational reform. *Educational Evaluation and Policy Analysis*, *15*(2), 129-151.

Lloyd, G. M. (1999). Two teachers' conceptions of a reform-oriented curriculum: Implications for mathematics teacher development. *Journal of Mathematics Teacher Education*, *2*, 227-252.

Ma, Y. P. (2009). The implementation process, characteristics and promotion strategies of curriculum reform of basic education. *Curriculum, Teaching Material and Method*, *29*(4), 3-9. (in Chinese)

Ma, Y. P., Yin, H. B., Tang, L. F., and Liu, L. Y. (2009). Teacher receptivity to system-wide curriculum reform in the initiation stage: A Chinese perspective. *Asia Pacific Education Review*, *10*(3), 423-432.

Ministry of Education, PRC. (2003). *The curriculum compendium of the senior secondary education (Experimental draft)*. Retrieved 31 August 2004 from http://www.moe.edu.cn/edoas/website18/level3.jsp?tablename=1162andinfoid=737. (in Chinese).

Nairn, K. (2008, November). *Understanding alienation from school: Reading spaces, reading emotions*. Paper presented at the Emotional Geographies of Education Symposium, London, UK.

Paine, L. W., and Fang, Y. (2006). Reform as hybrid model of teaching and teacher development in China. *International Journal of Educational Research*, *45*, 279-289.

Penuel, W. R., Fishman, B. J., Yamaguchi, R., and Gallagher, L. P. (2007). What makes professional development effective? Strategies that foster curriculum implementation. *American Educational Research Journal*, *44*(4), 921-958.

Reay, D. (2008, November). *'Too close for comfort?': The white middle classes in multi-ethnic inner city schooling*. Paper presented at the Emotional Geographies of Education Symposium, London, UK.

Schutz, P. A., and Pekrun, R. (2007). *Emotion in education*. Burlington: Elsevier Academic Press.

Schutz, P. A., and Zembylas, M. (2009). *Advances in teacher emotion research: The impact on teachers' lives*. Dordrecht: Springer.

Spilková, V. (2001). Professional development of teachers and student teachers through reflection on practice. *European Journal of Teacher Education*, *24*(1), 59-65.

Swan, M. (2007). The impact of task-based professional development on teachers' practices and beliefs: A design research study. *Journal of Mathematics Teacher Education*, *10*, 217-237.

van Driel, J. H., Beijaard, D., and Verloop, N. (2001). Professional development and reform in science education: The role of teachers' practical knowledge. *Journal of Research in Science Teaching*, *38*(2), 137-158.

van Veen, K., and Lasky, S. (2005). Emotions as a lens to explore teacher identity and change: Different theoretical approaches. *Teaching and Teacher Education*, *21*(8), 895-898.

Watkins, M. (2008, November). *Teachers' tears: Affects and the emotion geography of the classroom*. Paper presented at the Emotional Geographies of Education Symposium, London, UK.

Yin, H. B. (2009). Teachers' emotional landscape in curriculum reform. *Education Journal*, *36*(1/2), 23-51. (in Chinese).

Zembylas, M. (2003). Emotions and teacher identity. *Teachers and Teaching: Theory and Practice*, *9*(3), 213-238.

Zembylas, M. (2005). *Teaching with emotion: A postmodern enactment*. Greenwich: Information Age Publishing.

In: Curriculum Reform in China
Editors: Hong-Biao Yin and John Chi-Kin Lee

ISBN 978-1-61470-943-5
© 2012 Nova Science Publishers, Inc.

Chapter 14

BELIEF AS THE PREREQUISITE TO ACTION: CURRICULUM REFORM AND THE TRANSFORMATION OF TEACHING CONCEPTIONS IN RURAL CHINA

Tanja Sargent

ABSTRACT

The Chinese New Curriculum reforms that began in primary schools in 2001 aim for the transformation of teachers' beliefs as the prerequisite to the transformation of teaching practices from traditional teacher-centered approaches to more progressive student-centered approaches. This chapter draws on classroom observation and in-depth interview data to investigate the relationship between the New Curriculum reform implementation and the beliefs about teaching and learning held by primary school teachers in rural northwest China. My findings suggest that teachers who are more familiar with, and have more positive attitudes about, the New Curriculum reforms also have more "progressive" beliefs about teaching.

INTRODUCTION

In the past decade, education reforms in China, known as the New Curriculum reforms have been implemented with the goal of transforming examination-centered approaches to education to more student-centered approaches that make education more relevant and engaging for students and focus on the cultivation of well-rounded individuals who are imbued with creativity and a spirit of innovation and are also characterized by the capacities of moral virtue, intellectual strength, physical health, and artistic sensibility (*de zhi ti mei*) ((Dello-Iacovo, 2009; Guan and Meng, 2007; Ministry of Education, 2001, 2002; Sargent, 2009; Shi and Ou, 2004; Wang, 2005). An important emphasis of reform implementation has been teacher training and programs of professional development with the aim of transforming the way that teachers think about teaching and learning (Sargent and Hannum, 2009). What are the beliefs about teaching and learning that are held by teachers in rural primary schools in Gansu province? Given the policy emphasis on the transformation of educational concepts, is there any evidence of a relationship between implementation of the New Curriculum reforms and the nature of teachers' beliefs about teaching and learning?

Lynn Paine (1992) studied teacher education programs in China in the 1990s when the 9 year compulsory education law had just been enacted.[19] The policy rhetoric at the time emphasized the important role of education in China's grand modernization. All the emphasis and focus was placed on addressing the severe lack of teachers and on investment in infrastructure such as school buildings and facilities. Paine (1992) argued that in order for China to achieve its modernization goals, the underlying assumptions that teachers held about teaching and learning were even more important than the physical and human capital infrastructure. She argued that creativity and independent thinking in students were important capacities for China's drive towards modernization and that, in order for these to be cultivated in students, teachers needed to gain the ability to engage in transformational types of teaching. According to Paine (1992), the approaches to the preparation of teachers in China at the time supported a view of teaching that was "text-driven and teacher-dominated" and conveyed a consistent message: teachers have authority because of their deep and correct knowledge of accepted texts. From this perspective, "teaching involves transmitting—in precise, elegant but intellectually orthodox ways—knowledge to students, and hence it is more of a performance than an interaction" (Paine, 1992, p. 193).

The goal of the New Curriculum reforms has been to supplant teacher-centered examination oriented teaching practices with student-centered teaching practices that focus on the all-round development of the whole child (Dello-Iacovo, 2009; Guan and Meng, 2007). Policy reform literature in the US presents a highly skeptical view of the extent to which policy reforms can have an impact on classroom practices (Bidwell, 1965; Cohen, 1988, 1990; Cohen and Ball, 1990; Cuban, 1990; Lortie, 1975; Meyer and Rowan, 1978; Spillane and Zeuli, 1999). Stigler and Hiebert (1999), on the other hand, postulate that cross national differences in institutional and cultural environments may affect the degree to which reforms and innovations can be successfully implemented and that the education systems in Asia may be more conducive to the spread of innovations. In China, teachers have frequent opportunities to interact and observe each other teaching (Sargent and Hannum, 2009), which may allow for innovation and learning to be disseminated efficiently and effectively throughout the education system. Teachers who observe and interact with other teachers get new ideas about how to teach and have opportunities to see these approaches implemented in practice and this causes them to reflect on their own teaching and on their own beliefs about teaching and learning (Sargent and Hannum, 2009). Evidence so far suggests, however, that response to the New Curriculum reforms has varied greatly by region in China (Dello-Iacovo, 2009).

The New Curriculum reforms have been implemented in primary schools gradually, beginning in 2001, starting first with national pilot counties, then provincial pilot counties and, finally, all counties were to begin implementation by 2005. In each county, implementation of the new reforms also began gradually, in some cases with a few schools starting ahead of the other schools. In addition, implementation within each school was also gradual, beginning first with Grade 1 of primary school and Grade 1 of junior middle school.

---

[19] The Law on Nine-Year Compulsory Education, which took effect on July 1, 1986, established requirements and deadlines for attaining universal education and guaranteed school-age children the right to receive at least nine years of education.

In this chapter, I draw on qualitative classroom observation data that is linked to post-observation teacher in-depth interview data that were collected in 2004 in rural primary schools in Gansu province to investigate the extent to which implementation of the New Curriculum reforms is correlated with teachers' beliefs about teaching and learning. In 2004 it was still possible to compare classrooms that had already begun reform implementation with classrooms that had not yet begun reform implementation. Several overviews of New Curriculum reforms are available in the literature (Dello-Iacovo, 2009; Huang, 2004; Liu and Maxey, 2005; Zhong, 2006). So far, empirical investigations of the New Curriculum reform implementation reveal much regional variation in implementation success (Dello-Iacovo, 2009). My study contributes empirical data about the New Curriculum reforms from schools that are remote from the centers of policy and prosperity. For this reason, my findings may provide a conservative estimate of the impact of educational reform implementation. On the other hand, it could also be that it is in remote rural primary schools where teachers are more enthusiastic about the reforms and where they have greater freedom to innovate due to the lower intensity of exam competitiveness in rural areas as compared with urban areas. Furthermore, Gansu province is unique in that it was the site of the Gansu Basic Education Project, a successful development project funded by the UK Department for International Development (DFID) which supported the government's New Curriculum reforms especially with regards to investment in teacher training and development (Brock, 2009).

Findings from my study suggest that teachers in rural Gansu who are more familiar with, and have more positive attitudes about, the New Curriculum reforms also have more "progressive" beliefs about teaching and this is reflected in their teaching practice as well.

TEACHING CONCEPTIONS

An extensive body of work in the educational literature, both empirical and theoretical, has considered the relationship between teachers' beliefs and thought processes and the practices they use in their classrooms (Briscoe, 1991; Clark and Peterson, 1986; Eisenhart, Cuthbert, Shrum, and Harding, 1988; Fang, 1996; Kagan, 1992; Nespor, 1987; Pajares, 1992; Prawat, 1992; Thompson, 1992; Yerrick, Parke, and Nugent, 1997). Theorists in the philosophy of knowledge have also considered the relationship between inner subjective worlds and the myth or reality of the external objective world. Beliefs and perceptions of individuals can coalesce into the intersubjectivies of groups of actors which subsequently become institutionalized and legitimated into wider social norms (Berger and Luckmann, 1966). The metaphors that we employ for understanding reality have an impact on our language and behaviors (Lakoff and Johnson, 1980). The philosophy underlying Paolo Freire's (1993) transformative education is fundamentally a theory that an individual's beliefs can be harnessed to reconstruct daily realities not just for individuals but for entire societies.

Fullan (1982) places great importance on the alteration of teacher beliefs in the process of educational change. He states that teachers can use new teaching materials without altering their teaching approach or a teacher could use the materials and alter some teaching behaviors without coming to grips with the conceptions or beliefs underlying the change. According to Fullan (1982), real change comes only with a transformation of subjective realities. He conceptualizes educational change on a continuum from no change, to surface change to change in the deep structure of thought. Spillane and Zeuli (1999) refer to this as transformation at the level of "epistemological belief". Cohen (1990) provides the classic illustration of failed reform in his description of Mrs. O, a teacher who implements a new mathematics curriculum in her California classroom but there is no evidence of any transformation at the epistemological level.

Teacher epistemologies have been conceived of in terms of traditional vs. progressive (Chall, 2000; Dewey, 1938/1997; Labaree, 2004; Macdonald, 1974), traditional vs. constructivist teaching (Prawat, 1992) or transmissional vs. transformational forms of teaching (Freire, 1993; Paine, 1992; Yerrick et al., 1997). Teachers who hold transmissional or traditional ideas of teaching see knowledge as a group of facts to be delivered, whereas teachers who hold transformational beliefs about teaching see knowledge as something that is constructed and transformed during the process of teaching and learning. Traditional beliefs about teaching lead to practice that depends heavily on texts and teachers and that fosters "docility, receptivity, and obedience" in students (Macdonald, 1974). Constructivist, progressive and transformational views on the other hand posit disciplines as "living entities, bodies of knowledge that are in constant flux, growing and changing" with the understanding that "what is accepted as knowledge varies depending on the particular historical-cultural context" (Prawat, 1992, p. 356). Progressive education focuses on the expression and cultivation of individuality, learning through experience, purposeful activity, acquaintance with a changing world, and the development of thinking.

DATA AND METHODS

Classroom observation and in-depth interview data were collected in 15 rural primary schools in six different rural counties across Gansu. The six counties in the sample were purposefully selected to obtain diversity along the dimensions of wealth, geographic location around the province, and whether or not they had already begun implementing the new curriculum reforms. Within the counties, schools were purposefully selected to achieve diversity with regard to school type (central school, village school or teaching point school)[20] and also by remoteness from the county seat. Within each school, the research team requested to observe classes in both mathematics and Chinese, and at a range of grade levels. We made a special request to include the early grades if they were already using the new curriculum materials, but we were flexible according to the school's schedule on the day we arrived and the classes that the principal chose to have us observe.

Observation data consist of 30 classroom observations: 20 Chinese lessons and 10 mathematics lessons,[21] and both new curriculum and old curriculum classes. Corresponding in-depth interviews with teachers were conducted immediately following each observed

---

[20] There are three general types of primary schools at the township and village level: central schools, village schools and teaching point schools. In general, each township has one central school that has access to greater financial and human resources and some responsibilities for supporting the other schools in the township. Village primary schools are usually complete schools with grades from 1-6 and teaching point schools generally provide the first two to four years of schooling in the village so that young children do not have to travel long distances to the village or central schools.

[21] The greater number of Chinese lessons selected reflect the greater number of lessons devoted to language than to mathematics in primary schools in China. According to Wang Xiufang (2003), primary school students in Gansu take an average of 9 lessons per week in Chinese language and only 5 in mathematics.

lesson. [22] As my fieldwork was carried out in the early years of curriculum reform, implementation can only be observed in the early grades. Of the thirty classes that were observed, twelve were already officially implementing the new curriculum reforms. Of the 15 schools that were visited, 9 had begun implementation and 6 schools had not yet begun. Thus, as can be expected, fieldwork revealed that there was a variation in the extent to which teaching methods reflected the reform policy ideals. Some classes that had not yet begun official implementation had already begun to be influenced by new curriculum ideologies and some classrooms that had already begun implementation continued to employ traditional approaches.

The teacher in-depth interviews were conducted immediately following the classroom observations, and this enabled teachers to reflect on the concrete specifics of the lesson they had taught, yielding rich data on their beliefs about teaching and learning. The usefulness of having teachers "think aloud" about actual and specific events in their teaching has been demonstrated by other scholars of teacher beliefs (Clark and Peterson, 1986; Nespor, 1987). All interview data were tape recorded and transcribed. Table 1 illustrates characteristics of the classroom observation and interview data.

Table 1. Number of classroom observations by grade level, subject, curriculum implementation and school type

	Grade 1	Grade 2	Grade 3	Grade 4	Grade 5	Grade 6	Total
Total	8	5	9	4	3	1	30
Subjects							
Mathematics	2	1	3	1	2	1	10
Chinese	6	4	6	3	1	0	20
Curriculum implementation							
Old curriculum	1	3	6	4	3	1	18
New curriculum	7	2	3	0	0	0	12
School type							
Teaching point (4)	3	2	2	0	0	0	7
Village (5)	4	3	3	3	3	1	17
Central (2)	1	0	4	1	0	0	6

DATA ANALYSIS

Classroom observation and teacher in-depth interview data were analyzed for teachers' beliefs about knowledge, that is their "epistemology", and their measures of successful teaching. Teachers' opinions of the New Curriculum reforms reflect the degree of teacher buy-in and allow for an examination of the extent to which teachers' beliefs about teaching correlate with degree of exposure to the New Curriculum ideals. In order to avoid drawing

---

[22] There are 28 interviews for the 30 classroom observations as in one case we observed two classes taught by one teacher and only conducted one interview and the recording for one of the interviews was of such poor quality as to render it unusable.

conclusions about teachers' beliefs from abstract ideals and theories, teachers are not asked directly about their beliefs.

Rather, I draw conclusions about the teachers' beliefs from their actual practices in the classroom and from the ways that they speak about concrete aspects of their teaching. Drawing on both classroom observations and teacher in-depth interviews allows for triangulation by providing two sources of data from which to draw conclusions.

Based on whether or not teachers were using the New Curriculum materials and on the observation and interview data, teachers were categorized according to the level of reform implementation. In some classrooms teachers had not yet begun using the New Curriculum textbooks. Analysis of teacher interviews reveals that some of these teachers were not at all familiar with the goals and ideals of the New Curriculum reforms and observation data showed that these teachers teach in very traditional ways. Some teachers using the old materials, however, had already begun to be influenced by the New Curriculum ideals and this influence was evident in their teaching and in the way that they talked about teaching and learning.

Of the teachers who had begun to use the New Curriculum materials, some teachers were like Cohen's Mrs. O (Cohen, 1990) – they were using new materials but there was no evidence of epistemological shift. A few teachers, however, seemed to have really bought in to the progressive ideologies of the New Curriculum reforms and these teachers also had progressive approaches to thinking about teaching. Thus, there are four categories of teachers in this analysis: 1) old curriculum, no influence (12 teachers); 2) old curriculum, surface influence (6 teachers); 3) new curriculum, surface influence (6 teachers); 4) new curriculum, progressive (5 teachers).[23]

The interview and observation data were analyzed using a matrix to examine the correlation between extent of reform implementation and teachers' conceptions of teaching and learning (See Table 2).

Two aspects of teacher beliefs were examined:

1. Epistemology—Teachers' views of knowledge and the main source of knowledge in the classroom are revealed through their practices, their stated focus in lesson planning, and their lesson objectives. These range from practices and statements that reveal a belief in knowledge as static and mainly residing in texts, to notions of knowledge as being dynamic and co-constructed by teachers and students in the classroom.

2. Measures of successful teaching and learning—Teachers talk about what they were most satisfied with in the teaching of the observed lesson and in so doing reveal their goals for the lesson and measures of successful teaching and learning. These range from content mastery, to satisfaction with student questioning and participation in discussion.

---

[23] One classroom observation was excluded from the analysis: a new "substitute" (*daike*) teacher, a 16 year old middle school graduate who had only been teaching for one month. She was using the new curriculum textbook materials. The first grade class she taught consisted of having the children repeat the sounds for pinyin Romanization for the entire lesson. The students were disengaged and unruly.

Table 2. Analytical matrix: Reform implementation status and indicators of teacher conceptions

Reform implement-action status	Classroom practices	Opinions of New Curriculum reforms	Epistemology	Measures of successful teaching	N
Old curriculum, no influence	Textual reproduction is central to the lesson, heavy use of choral response, and emphasis on teaching how to take the test and on the "one right answer," memorization of rules and procedures, individual students at blackboard while the rest work in their exercise books practicing a problem or writing a sentence using newly learned characters.	Little awareness of the new curriculum reform policies or a lack of buy-in. Skepticism that New Curriculum ideals could work for rural students.	Textbook as main source of knowledge. Knowledge as fixed and unchanging.	Student mastery of textbook content. Exam scores.	12
Old curriculum, surface influence	Introduction of games, songs and activities, technology in the classroom as an aid to the text, use of praise and encouragement to foster a relaxed and pleasant classroom environment. Focus of the class is still on textual reproduction, memorization of rules and procedures and the one right answer.	Familiarity with, and a positive attitude towards, the ideals of the new curriculum.	Textbook as main source of knowledge but students can also generate knowledge from their own experiences	Textbook mastery and student engagement.	6
New curriculum, surface influence	In these classes that were allegedly implementing the new curriculum reforms the teachers still retained a focus on the one right answer, choral response, memorization and drill while introducing some surface changes from the new curriculum including games, hands on activities, discussion and the use of praise.	Awareness of the new curriculum ideals but not at a very deep epistemological level.	Textbook as main source of knowledge but students can also generate knowledge from their own experiences. Application of knowledge is important.	Student engagement and participation.	6
New curriculum, progressive	Students are encouraged to express their own ideas and understandings, different responses to the same question are valued, varied activities, small group work and lively classroom discussion. Use of praise, relaxed but orderly classroom atmosphere.	Understanding, strong buy-in, concern that some teachers don't understand the goals of New Curriculum reforms well.	Knowledge can be generated in the interaction between teachers and students, and between students and students.	Authentic discussion and inquiry activities. Quality of student questions.	5

OLD CURRICULUM, NO INFLUENCE

Classroom Practices – Centrality of Textbook and Techniques for Teaching to the Test

In these classrooms, classroom observations reveal the centrality of textual reproduction in the classroom practice. There is an explicit focus on preparation for the examination. For example, one teacher in a remote village school, who I will call Teacher Li (all names of teachers, schools and counties are pseudonyms), begins the lesson that I observed by clearly identifying the type of examination problem that is the subject of the day's lesson: applied problems with fractions and learning when to divide and when to multiply. He asks the class to recite a rule about when you should turn a division problem with fractions into a multiplication problem. The class recites the rule in rather messy unison and the teacher restates it clearly as he has taught it to them and asks them to repeat it once again. This time the class is able to parrot the rule back with military tidiness. During the lesson, all questions originate with the teacher and all are closed ended questions with a clear answer. Some of Teacher Li's questions elicit choral responses; others require individual responses, in which case the students raise their hands in accordance with a fixed and formal classroom ritual, with elbow on the desk and palm neatly extended. No choices or options are available to students in the interchange between teacher and student. The constant refrain of the question "Is that correct?" (*dui bu dui?*) reinforces an attitude and respect for the one right answer that is required by the examination. The world is neatly subdivided into the correct and the incorrect. Teacher Li copies the entire text of the lesson onto the blackboard even though all the students have the textbook open on the desks in front of them (See Figure 1). This reinforces the central role of the text as the ultimate source of knowledge.

Figure 1. Mastering textbook content and learning how to prepare well to succeed in examinations in a fifth grade math class.

In general, across the classrooms that we observed and placed in the traditional category of the teaching typology, extensive use was made of techniques for drilling the students in the textbook content including choral response, teaching to the test, emphasis on the one right answer, memorization of rules and procedures, and practice of the concepts learned using textbook exercises. Classroom discussion is focused on mastery of the texts and getting the students to grasp correct understandings fully. All activity was directed by the teachers and a tense disciplined atmosphere and regularity of the student posture and ritualized gestures revealed the expectation of adherence to a strict code of classroom interactions.

Opinions about the New Curriculum Reforms

Teachers in this group generally displayed little awareness of the new curriculum reform policies.

> Interviewer: Do you think that the ideas of the new curriculum have influenced your teaching? Teacher: They haven't influenced my teaching at all. (Male fourth grade Chinese teacher, Caizi village school)
> Interviewer: Could you tell us what you know about the new curriculum reforms such as the general content of the new reforms or the overall objectives.
> Teacher: I am not able to say anything about them.
> Interviewer: … Just say whatever you know about them.
> Teacher: Aiyah…I don't know this either." (Male fourth grade Chinese teacher, Jiangan teaching point school)

Other teachers, who knew something about the new curriculum, voiced a lack of buy-in and expressed the sentiment that it was not possible to adapt new curriculum methods to their classes because the conditions in rural schools did not allow for it. For example they mentioned that they did not have PowerPoint available or the resources with which to make teaching aids. One teacher focused his skepticism on the abilities of the rural students themselves and their family circumstances:

> "…Our students have such a bad foundation. When you are in class you ask them questions, they don't know, some won't even raise their hands for you…the family education in the cities is so good. Show me which parents in the rural areas pay attention to their children's education (nongcun jiazhang shei guan ne?) When the children go home who pays attention to their education at home? When the children go home if anyone speaks to them it is: go and do your chores well. The students can't even get their homework finished, the parents want them to go home and first get the household chores done and then they can think about their homework." (Male third grade Chinese teacher, Caizi village school)

An analysis of the teacher epistemologies and measures of success in teaching from the in-depth interviews among this group of teachers match the lack of familiarity with the New Curriculum ideals and also the practices observed in the classroom.

Epistemology – Textbook as Main Source of Knowledge, Knowledge as Fixed and Unchanging

For these teachers knowledge is something that resides in textbooks and through careful preparation the teacher can transmit this knowledge to the students. Knowledge is also something fixed and unchanging.

For example, when asked to describe his lesson planning procedures, one teacher teaching in a remote teaching point school in one of the nationally designated poverty counties in Gansu mentioned that there weren't enough textbooks that year so he didn't have a textbook but he had done all the planning before and was completely familiar with the text. During class he borrowed one of the students' books and that was sufficient.

Another teacher belied the same view that knowledge from the textbook was sufficient and was fixed and unchanging when he noted that the light is so bad in the classroom that he can't read the textbook very well so he has to rely on his memory. He goes on to say,

> "Because I have taught this lesson quite a lot and for many years…I already know the order of all the problems. I have them memorized… I have done all the planning before and so I don't need to do much more because it is pretty much fixed by now." (Male fifth grade math teacher, Xishan village school)

Measures of Successful Teaching and Learning – Content Mastery in Preparation for the Examinations

Among this group of teachers, a lesson is deemed successful if a large percentage of the students have achieved mastery over the textbook content.

> "I think what I was most satisfied with about the lesson was that basically I achieved the objective of the lesson and, I can't say one hundred percent of the students mastered the lesson, but it should be over 95 percent of the students already don't have any problem with division calculations." (Female third grade math teacher, Caizi central school)

Traditional teaching is notoriously examination oriented. One of the teachers expressed the importance of teaching to the test and the extent to which the examination results were the only measure of successful teaching to which he was held accountable.

> "At the moment, generally speaking, whether or not you are doing a good job is mainly decided by the examination results…So, to tell the truth, when I prepare my lessons, the main thing I consider is how I can cope with the exams. For example, today when I was teaching synonyms and near synonyms I did my best to focus on the parts of the text that I thought could potentially be on the examination, and do some exercises related to these …" (Male third grade Chinese teacher, Jiangan village school)

Old Curriculum, Surface Influence

Classroom Practices – Textbook Still Central, Introduction of Games and Activities

In the classrooms that were still using the old curriculum but showed some surface influence of the new curriculum ideologies, classroom observations revealed that the teachers in this group attempted to introduce games, songs, and activities into the classroom. More use was made of praise and encouragement, in line with the new curriculum call to foster a more relaxed and pleasant classroom environment. However, the focus of the lessons was still overwhelmingly on textual reproduction, memorization of rules and procedures and the one right answer.

All the influences of the new curriculum were channeled in the service of more effectively drilling the students in the textbook content.

Opinions of the New Curriculum Reforms – Some Familiarity, Positive Attitude Toward Reforms

The attitudes of these teachers towards the New Curriculum set them apart from the first group of teachers. Generally, all the teachers in this group expressed both a familiarity with, and a positive attitude towards, the ideals of the new curriculum. There was an appreciation of the extent to which the new curriculum ways of teaching stimulate students to think and to be active participants in their own learning.

> "Even though I haven't taught a new curriculum class yet, I have already seen the books that have been distributed and I think that it is really strange...there is very little content in the books and yet the students can learn so much because, first the content makes the students think (*dong naojin*), second, because mostly the focus is on action, from engaging in real activity we can acquire the knowledge that we want to teach and we want to learn." (Male third grade Chinese teacher, Xishan village school)

Another teacher in a small teaching point school was using the new curriculum materials in teaching first and second grade, although we observed his teaching of his third grade class which was still using the old materials. In our classroom observation of his class, that has a total of three students in it, he engaged all the students in continuous questioning and the solving of mathematical problems (See Figure 2):

> "In the past the teaching was all really just the teacher speaking. Now, as a result of the new curriculum reform, and through experimentation, our new curriculum, and new way of learning has really stimulated students' enthusiasm, made students try to learn, try to speak. After they learn they try to digest it on their own..." (Male teacher who teaches grades 1-3 all subjects, Xuenan teaching point school).

Figure 2. A teacher watches as all three of the students in his third grade class solve problems at the board.

Epistemology – Textbook as the Main Source of Knowledge, Students Also Capable of Generating Knowledge

Four out of six of the teachers in this group mentioned the centrality of mastery of textbook content. However, the interview excerpt below reveals also an emphasis on relevance to students and the desire to meet other goals of well-rounded education such as ability to express oneself. The teacher believes in the importance of students own experiences and tentatively contemplates the use of student-generated material "perhaps in the next class":

> "Then, through understanding the content of the picture they can learn the assigned text, that is, it is learning through an integration of pictures and text but the whole time the textbook is still central. ...It is autumn now and the lesson is about autumn...and so the lesson can be directly perceived through the senses by the students...Because the text of this lesson is very easy to understand, if the students have time they should draw their own autumn pictures...and then perhaps in the next class I will ask them to show their pictures and tell a

story about their picture. Of course that will be different from the text book. After all it will be their own content and they will talk about it how they like, but this will allow students to practice their oral expression ability, and it is also a foundation for their writing; at least that is what I think." (Female second grade Chinese teacher, Chaoyang village school).

Measures of Successful Teaching and Learning – Mastery of Content Still Central But Relevance and Enthusiastic Student Participation Are Important Too

While textbook mastery was central for all of these teachers, they also all expressed a desire to bring about a higher level of student engagement and participation. One teacher said that fostering student initiative through use of discussion methods was important although he seemed a little uncertain as to whether or not this is really possible and his responses seem suspiciously abstract. Classroom observation data reveal he did attempt to organize a whole class discussion during the observed lesson but was unable to successfully stimulate student participation.

Another teacher organized games and competitions in her class using the new vocabulary that they were to learn from the textbook. Her rationale suggests that she has bought into the new curriculum ideology of a relaxed classroom environment but may have taken this goal further than the policy intended--she claims she now puts play at the center!

"I just want to let them relax for a while, just be happy and have some fun for a while...so I use games as a method...playing is the most important natural instinct of children...so I try hard to put play at the center." (Female fourth grade Chinese teacher, Xuenan village school).

NEW CURRICULUM, SURFACE INFLUENCE

Classroom Practice – Texts Still Central, Introduction of Games and Activities

In some classrooms that were already using the new curriculum materials, teachers still used teaching practices that had vestiges of a traditional teaching style. Classroom observations revealed that these teachers still retained a focus on the one right answer, the extensive use of choral response, and memorization and drill, while introducing some surface changes from the new curriculum such as a song, a few minutes of classroom discussion, a game, and the use of praise and encouragement.

For example, Teacher Zhang, a middle aged female teacher in a central school, begins the class by asking students about the research that they did for homework on the topic of war. One student stands up to say that he learned that the United States was at war with Iraq. Another student reports that he learned about the Nanjing Massacre. A third student says that there is war between Israel and Palestine. After each student speaks the teacher repeats what the student has said. There is no evaluation of the comment on the part of the teacher but the tone of voice used by the teacher affirms the comment as a valuable and meaningful contribution to the class discussion.

> Student: Afghanistan and Iraq are at war
> Teacher: Oh, Afghanistan is at war and Iraq is also at war.

This initial discussion is striking as compared with old-curriculum classrooms to the extent to which students have been encouraged to carry out their own inquiry and to the extent to which self-expression and student generated content are valued. However, after the first five minutes of classroom discussion, the main activity of the lesson then consisted of different permutations of the students reading and rereading the text out loud. In total, I counted that the students reread the text 13 times during the lesson. Finally, with less than five minutes of class time remaining, the teacher asked the students for their ideas on the theme of the text which was international peace. She also asked the students what they could do to make the world a more peaceful place. About six students volunteered their ideas, which included not saying mean things to people, helping each other, and taking care of their families.

The amount of time spent drilling students in the textbook content in this classroom indicated a continued belief in the importance of textbook mastery. The discussion activities were just an add-on activity rather than a well-integrated transformation in teaching approach. However, a key difference between this classroom and the more traditional classrooms is the increased openness to hear students' own understandings and interpretations of the content being learned.

Opinions of the New Curriculum Reforms – Generally Positive But Some Concerns

There is a diversity of opinion about the new curriculum reforms represented among the teachers in this group. Some of the teachers in this group exhibited strong buy-in to the ideals of the new curriculum. One of the teachers described his appreciation of the extent to which the new curriculum materials look deceptively simple but are in fact quite profound:

> "The advantage of the new curriculum is that it is very broad, the materials look like they are very simple but actually they are very deep. They require that you fully develop the students imagination…and also so many of the questions have no answers so teachers can develop and elaborate on the ideas fully…because the topics are so broad there is a great deal of space to develop and elaborate." (Male first grade Chinese teacher, Xishan village school)

One of the teachers in this group, however, expressed concern and skepticism. She had just graduated and she mentioned that she was not very familiar with the new curriculum materials and ideologies even though she was teaching the new curriculum in the first grade. She voiced her concern that mastery learning was being sacrificed under the New Curriculum reforms. However, in spite of her inexperience and her concerns about the new curriculum, her ideas and methods reveal that she has already been socialized into the new ideologies and she spoke ardently about the need to have children apply their learning. This ambiguity may be revealing of the extent to which the new curriculum ideologies are becoming permanently institutionalized in the Chinese education system.

Analysis of the in-depth interviews among this group of teachers reveals that the continued focus on student mastery appears to subtly suggest a more conceptual mastery rather than merely content mastery. Also, in talking about their planning, all the teachers in this group discussed trying to find ways to get students thinking for themselves, introducing choice for the students according to their own interests and discussion, or raising student awareness of the world around them.

Epistemology – Evidence of an Interest in Cultivating Conceptual Understandings and a Belief in Learning through Interaction with Other Students

These teachers wanted to enhance students' ability to apply the concepts they were learning more broadly, to try to use the concepts as they learned them. For example, a first grade teacher teaching children phonetics in Chinese wanted children to choose which of the letters p, q, b, and d they wanted to construct with sticks and semi-circles and then read the sound they had constructed:

> In this class my main objective was to review and consolidate the six *yunmu* [vowel sounds that make up a Chinese syllable) and the 23 *shengm*u [consonants in the Chinese syllables], and I wanted to make students apply their learning (*dongshou*), because if you relate all the knowledge to be learned to the students lives then it will be more relevant to them... The most difficult letters to distinguish are d, b, p, and q because they are all composed of a stem and a semi-circle and it is just the position of the semi-circle that is different. Through asking the students to pronounce the letters they make themselves, whatever they are able to pronounce you know that they have mastered that letter. It is only through putting it into practice that the student will actually grasp it (Male first grade Chinese teacher, Longkou teaching point school).

Another teacher made much of the fact that she allowed her students to choose which new characters to learn. When called upon they could tell her any character that they recognized as opposed to her calling on a student to test them to see if they had learned a particular character. The students could also choose which character they wanted to use to make words out of. This teacher also held a belief that students can learn from each other and not just from the teacher and text.

> I asked them to choose the characters they wanted to recognize, the things they liked. The students are really interested in the things that they like or the things they are able to recognize... For example, if I told them to make some words out of the first character (*yu*) of language (*yuwen*) they won't be able to do it, but if I ask them to choose a character, choose any character they would like to make words out of, then they have a lot of leeway and you will have students willing to raise their hand and the teacher feels so happy, and the students' excitement rises...students know many words and they have mastered them at different levels. Some of them they are not so sure of and others they know well. They can say the ones they know well and then for the others they can listen to the words that their friends know...so I let

them learn from each other (Female second grade Chinese teacher at Tangyang village school).

Measures of Successful Teaching – Active Student Participation is Key

In contrast to teachers in the old curriculum classrooms, the teachers in this group tend to focus their self-evaluations on the quality of the classroom interactions. They are much more adamant about the need for successful student participation in the class as a measure of the success of their teaching. When asked what she was most satisfied with in the lesson that had just been observed one teacher responds:

> "I think the cooperation in this class between the teacher and the students was very good. I think they mastered the content pretty well because I arranged it so that the teacher teaches something and then the students cooperate together in groups to learn it by themselves, then they are a little more conscious of what they are doing. In this way there are many methods used in many formats and the students are happy. When the teacher is teaching they learn from the teacher, when they are cooperating in the small groups they discuss things together…and at the same time they are learning the spirit of cooperation and also other dimensions…the relationship between the students improves…and I think that is great…and from when they are little they develop the ability to learn by themselves." (Female second grade Chinese teacher at Tangyang village school).

NEW CURRICULUM, PROGRESSIVE

Classroom Practices – Student-Centered, Varied Activities

In the classrooms that I deemed to be fully implementing the progressive ideals of the New Curriculum reforms, teachers encouraged students to express their own ideas and understandings, valued different responses to the same question, used varied classroom activities related to the lesson objectives, and stimulated lively classroom discussion. Classrooms in this category were also characterized by use of praise and a relaxed but orderly classroom atmosphere.

For example, Teacher Du, a second grade math teacher in a small teaching point school, did not use a textbook even once in the lesson that I observed. At the start of the class he asked students to construct shapes of their choice using small pieces of straw that each student has brought with them from home. Some children choose to make a series of triangles, some make squares and some make "pine trees." Teacher Du asked the children to tell him what they had made and then went on to ask his students to come up with a formula for how to calculate the number of sticks that they used. The students take out their small notebooks and write things like 3+3+3+3+3+3 or 4+4+4+4+4+4+4 based on the pictures they had built (See Figure 3). Teacher Du gives them about 1-2 minutes to complete the task and then he calls on the students to tell him their answers. He proceeds to write these formulae on the blackboard and this student-generated information then becomes the basis for the lesson. Throughout the lesson there were opportunities for students to discuss ideas with their classmates and to express ideas and ask questions of the teacher. The structure of the lesson symbolized a collective process of investigation and knowledge construction.

Figure 3. Exploring the concept of multiplication in a New Curriculum second grade math class.

Opinions of the New Curriculum Reforms – Deep Understanding and Strong Buy-in

The teachers in this group exhibited understanding of and strong buy-in to the New Curriculum ideologies. A couple of them also expressed some of the new challenges that had arisen in the implementation of the new curriculum reforms. Teacher Du, while asserting his position that the New Curriculum ideologies are essentially sound, raised the concern that misunderstandings of the deeper purpose of the new curriculum implementation can devolve into a focus on performance (similar to the concern mentioned by one of the teachers in the previous group).

> "All aspects of the New Curriculum reforms from the design, the ideas, all of it is extremely good. Because they put people at the center, make the all-round development of the individual become the main focus, and also emphasize the cultivation of students' capacities. But in the actual implementation, some teachers have perhaps misunderstood. They think that the fancier you do things the better, the whole class you just feel that the students are engaged in so many activities, all kinds of activities and plans but otherwise not very meaningful or completely divorced from any knowledge…perhaps in the process it is easier for teachers to organize activities." (Teacher Du, male second grade mathematics teacher, Longkou Teaching Point School).

Another teacher noted the new challenges that face teachers as a result of the effects of the new curriculum reforms on students. In unleashing the curiosity of students and empowering the students in self-expression, the teacher can be left feeling very vulnerable and this requires entirely new attitudes towards the students on the part of the teacher.

"The greatest challenge [in teaching] now is that since the new curriculum reforms started I feel that my own knowledge is far too narrow. The new curriculum has already been implemented for three years [in this school], and if I compare these students with the previous cohorts, the thinking abilities of these students…whatever kind of new information they learn they become so cunning and discerning that sometimes some of the students' questions leave me hanging at the podium with no way to respond…" (Female third grade Chinese teacher, Xishan Central School).

Epistemology – Students and Teachers as Co-Conceptualizers

Teachers in this group emphasized lesson objectives of getting students thinking and coming up with their own ways to do things. There is a notion of cooperation between teacher and student in the conceptualization of ways to think about things and coming up with new and better ways to do things. One teacher describes her lesson objective as to exercise her first grade students' thinking abilities and engage them in coming up with the best ways to do subtraction. She admires all the different ways that students found to do this:

"Mainly [my objective] was to exercise students thinking abilities through looking at pictures, and getting students to use their own hands to do things, and make them figure out how best to calculate things. Students have all kinds of ways, all of them are great, we just compare whose method provides the quickest answer, whose method works out the best." (Female first grade math teacher, Chaoyang village school)

Teacher Du linked students to "mathematicians" through their engagement in the mathematical activities, namely the devising of mathematical representations. He emphasizes the cooperative role of teachers and students in the investigation of mathematical concepts.

"Through the students' questions and trying to solve the problem together with the teacher, working together, we were able to get the students to understand multiplication." (Teacher Du, male second grade mathematics teacher, Longkou Teaching Point School).

Measures of Successful Teaching – Stimulating Student Inquiry and Self-Expression

In reflecting on what had made them most pleased about the lesson they had just taught, teachers in this category emphasized the students' abilities in asking questions, expression of personal opinions, and in exchange with other students.

"I think what I like most about how the class went today was the students' questions, they asked such great questions: 'what is the name of the symbol in the middle?' and I said 'that is the multiplication sign' and there was a 4x7 and they asked 'where did the seven come from?' and then we counted and we found 'Oh the seven comes from the number of numbers that were added together.' And so from the questions that the students asked and just a little guidance from me they understood..." (Teacher Du, male second grade mathematics teacher, Longkou Teaching Point School)

"In the class I was rather pleased that the students' observation skills were so good, they are able to observe the details and for most of the students their thinking is very realistic...these things made me happy...from Grade 1 to Grade 3 they like to speak, it doesn't matter if they say it right or wrong, they dare to speak out their own opinions and they like to exchange their ideas with their classmates. This is another point that I am pleased about." (Male third grade mathematics teacher, Xishan central school)

Teachers whose lessons were placed in this category spoke in concrete terms about their participatory teaching practices. For these teachers, teaching and learning extended beyond the classroom and there was a heavy emphasis on students putting learning into practice through application, self expression, and investigation and questioning originating with the students. Interviews also revealed the extent to which teachers designed their own lesson plans, as opposed to depending heavily on the set teachers' guide, and felt that is was legitimate and proper for them to be doing this.

CONCLUSION

In this chapter, I have argued that there is a strong correlation between teacher beliefs and practices and the implementation of the New Curriculum reforms in China. Familiarity and buy-in to the curriculum generally increases across the four categories in the direction of the "progressive" teachers, suggesting a strong correlation of teacher awareness of the new curriculum ideologies and the teachers' conceptions of teaching and learning.

Epistemologically, the views expressed by teachers who are not yet familiar with the New Curriculum reform ideologies indicate a strong preoccupation with texts as the almost exclusive sources of knowledge.

At the other end of the spectrum, "progressive" teachers reveal a strong interest in engaging students in thinking and conceptualization and a belief that students can learn from each other and can also be creators of knowledge. Among these New Curriculum teachers, there is support for the idea that even young children can be engaged in inquiry activities and asking their own questions.

For "traditional" old curriculum teachers, success in teaching is measured by content mastery and examination results. New Curriculum teachers, on the other hand, speak about their success as teachers in terms of the extent to which they are able to engage their students in thinking, inquiry and self-expression.

While it is difficult to make any causal arguments from a cross-sectional study, this study suggests that, if it is possible to influence the ways that teachers think about the goals of education and the source and nature of knowledge, it might indeed be possible to effect change at the classroom level.

REFERENCES

Berger, P. L., and Luckmann, T. (1966). *The social construction of reality: A treatise in the sociology of knowledge*. New York: Anchor Books.

Bidwell, C. (1965). The school as formal organization. In J. March (Ed.), *Handbook of organizations*. Chicago, IL: Rand McNally.

Briscoe, C. (1991). The dynamic interactions among beliefs, role metaphors, and teaching practices: A case study of teacher change. *Science Education, 75*(2), 185-199.

Brock, A. (2009). Moving mountains stone by stone: Reforming rural education in China. *International Journal of Educational Development, 29*(6), 454-462.

Chall, J. S. (2000). *The Academic Achievement Challenge: What Really Works in the Classroom?* New York: The Guilford Press.

Clark, C., and Peterson, P. L. (1986). Teachers' thought processes. In M. Wittrock (Ed.), *Handbook of research on teaching* (3rd ed., pp. 255-296) New York: MacMillan.

Cohen, D. (1988). *Teaching Practice: Plus ca change*. East Lansing: National Center for Research on Teacher Education.

Cohen, D. (1990). A revolution in one classroom: The case of Mrs. Oublier. *Educational Evaluation and Policy Analysis, 12*(3), 311-329.

Cohen, D., and Ball, D. L. (1990). Policy and practice: An overview. *Educational Evaluation and Policy Analysis, 12*(3), 233-239.

Cuban, L. (1990). Reforming again, again, and again. *Educational Researcher, 19*(1), 3-13.

Dello-Iacovo, B. (2009). Curriculum reform and "quality education" in China: An overview. *International Journal of Educational Development, 29*, 241-249.

Dewey, J. (1938/1997). *Experience and education*. New York: Touchstone.

Eisenhart, M., Cuthbert, A., Shrum, J., and Harding, J. (1988). Teacher beliefs about their work activities. *Theory into Practice, 27*(2), 137-144.

Fang, Z. (1996). A review of research on teacher beliefs and practices. *Educational Research, 38*, 47-65.

Freire, P. (1993). *Pedagogy of the oppressed* (New rev. 20th-Anniversary ed.). New York: Continuum.

Fullan, M. (1982). *The meaning of educational change*. New York: Teachers College Press.

Guan, Q., and Meng, W. (2007). China's new national curriculum reform: Innovation, challenges and strategies. *Frontiers of Education in China, 2*(4), 579-604.

Kagan, D. M. (1992). Implications of research on teacher belief. *Educational Psychologist, 27*(1), 65-90.

Labaree, D. F. (2004). *The trouble with ed schools*. New Haven: Yale University Press.

Lakoff, G., and Johnson, M. (1980). *Metaphors we live by*. Chicago: University of Chicago Press.

Lortie, D. (1975). *Schoolteacher*. Chicago: University of Chicago Press.

Macdonald, J. (1974). *A new look at progressive education*. Alexandria, VA: ASCD.

Meyer, J., and Rowan, B. (1978). The structure of educational organizations. In J. Meyer (Ed.), *Environments and organizations*. San Francisco, CA: Jossey Bass.

Nespor, J. (1987). The role of beliefs in the practice of teaching. *Journal of Curriculum Studies, 19*(4), 317-328.

Paine, L. (1992). Teaching and modernization in contemporary China. In R. Hayhoe (Ed.), *Education and modernization: The Chinese experience*. Oxford, UK: Pergamon Press.

Pajares, M. F. (1992). Teachers' beliefs and educational research: Cleaning up a messy construct. *Review of Educational Research, 62*(3), 307-332.

Ministry of Education, PRC. (2002). *The concept of quality education: Key points for study (suzhi jiaoyu guannian: xuexi tiyao)*. Beijing: Ministry of Education.

Prawat, R. S. (1992). Teachers' beliefs about teaching and learning: A constructivist perspective. *American Journal of Education, 100*, 354-395.

Sargent, T. (2009). Revolutionizing ritual interaction in the classroom: Constructing the Chinese renaissance of the 21st century. *Modern China, 35*(6), 662-691.

Sargent, T., and Hannum, E. (2009). Doing more with less: Teacher professional learning communities in resource constrained primary schools in rural China. *Journal of Teacher Education, 60*(3), 258-276.

Spillane, J. P., and Zeuli, J. S. (1999). Reform and teaching: Exploring patterns of practice in the context of national and mathematics reforms. *Educational Evaluation and Policy Analysis, 21*(1), 1-27.

Stigler, J., and Hiebert, J. (1999). *The teaching gap*. New York: Free Press.

Thompson, A. (1992). Teachers' reliefs and conceptions: A synthesis of the research. In D. A. Grouws (Ed.), *NCTM handbook of research on mathematics teaching and learning* (pp. 127-146). New York: MacMillan.

Wang, J. (2005). *Curriculum reform of elementary education in China*. Embassy of the People's Republic of China in the United Kingdom of Great Britain and Northern Ireland. Retrieved 9 March 2010 from http://www.chinese-embassy.org.uk/eng/zt/Features/t214562.htm.

Wang, X. (2003). *Education in China since 1976*. Jefferson: McFarland and Company, Inc.

Weiss, R. S. (1994). *Learning from strangers*. New York: The Free Press.

Yerrick, R., Parke, H., and Nugent, J. (1997). Struggling to promote deeply rooted change: The "filtering effect" of teachers' beliefs on understanding transformational view of teaching science. *Science Education, 81*, 137-159.

In: Curriculum Reform in China
Editors: Hong-Biao Yin and John Chi-Kin Lee

ISBN 978-1-61470-943-5
© 2012 Nova Science Publishers, Inc.

Chapter 15

TEACHER LEARNING THROUGH TEACHING REFLECTION IN THE CONTEXT OF CURRICULUM REFORM

Mingren Zhao

ABSTRACT

State-sponsored teacher training for the New Curriculum reforms has often been based on "deficit approaches" leaving teachers as passive participants in the process. This is ironic given that the theoretical core of the New Curriculum is based on constructivism and progressivism. School-based teaching reflection, on the other hand, can be situational and target-oriented. In this chapter, the reflection and learning of teachers with different levels of teaching competence are examined. Findings suggest that teaching reflections vary significantly by teaching competence. Teachers with average teaching competence usually learn superficially from reflection following a "point-by-point summary", producing gradual teacher change. Veteran teachers achieve authentic learning by reflection based on "systematic inquiry", resulting in a fundamental teacher change. However, when teachers doubt the value of curriculum reform, following any reflection, they prefer not to express their doubts in case it is viewed as a lack of commitment to the reform, thus diminishing public discussion of problems and reducing constructive critical reflection and action.

INTRODUCTION

In the past ten years, constructivist learning theory and progressive education philosophy have played an important role as the core theoretical basis for the national curriculum reform in Mainland China (Ministry of Education, 2001; Huang, 2004), which advocates that teachers and students re-examine and reconstruct their understanding about knowledge during the implementation of the new curriculum. Generally, it has been recognized that there is reciprocal relationship between the curriculum and teachers in the transaction of curriculum (Connelly and Ben-Peretz, 1980). However, people tend to discuss the importance of the teacher and the strategy of professional development accepting a precondition of instrumentalism, ignoring the subjectivity of the teacher. In fact, a teacher should research his/her own practice during the implementation of the curriculum, have an authentic understanding of the schooling context, develop a conscious understanding of the design of the curriculum and teaching, and cultivate an ability to think critically and then convert these conceptions into action (Stenhouse, 1975, pp. 156-157). In other words, the reflection and learning of teachers is the key impetus for both their professional growth, and the success of the curriculum reform.

POLICIES AND PRACTICES OF TEACHER LEARNING IN THE CURRICULUM REFORM: A MACROSCOPIC VIEW

In Mainland China, in-service teacher training and learning are given much emphasis by the state. For instance, the *Regulations of Continuing Education for Primary and Middle School Teachers* (Ministry of Education, 1999) requires that new teachers should participate in 120 hours of job-specific pre-service training, and all teachers need to participate in 240 hours of in-service training which repeats in a 5-year cycle. In the context of the national curriculum reform, teacher training is regarded as a precondition for implementing the new curriculum. It is required that all schools have to follow the principle of "training before implementation and no implementation without training". All teachers have to receive at least 60 hours of training before they implement the new curriculum in their classrooms (Ministry of Education, 2004).

So how effective has the New Curriculum teacher training been? As Clarke and Hollingsworth (2002) observed, teacher training activities initiated or led by the government are usually based on the following model: in-service teacher training → change in knowledge and beliefs → change in teachers' classroom practice → change in student learning outcomes. Although this type of training activity may be economical and efficient, it mainly reflects the viewpoint of teacher educators rather than teachers themselves (Putnam and Borko, 1997). After participation in these training activities, teachers may to some extent change their espoused theory, but their "theory-in-use" is hardly ever changed (Argyris and Schön, 1974).

Recently, Zhao, Zhou, and Zhu (2009) conducted a survey of 5,255 teachers, primary and secondary, in Beijing to find their opinions of the effectiveness of teacher training activities. The results, shown in Table 1, reveal that teachers have a high level of satisfaction (85.7%) with the state-level elite teacher training organized by colleges or universities. However, less than one-quarter of teachers (1,176) have the opportunity to take part in these training activities. As for school-based teaching research and the training activities specific to the curriculum reform, though most teachers can access these activities, they show only a moderate level of satisfaction with the activities. As for the continuing education training in which all teachers participate, indeed are required to participate, teachers' evaluation of the effectiveness is quite low (18%).

Zhao et al. (2009) also conclude the factors influencing the effectiveness of teacher training, which include:

- heavy workload;
- unreasonable schedule of the training activities;
- impractical content of the training activities;
- no continuous guidance;
- incapable teacher trainer; and
- inappropriate training method.

Table 1. Teacher Learning Activities Satisfied and Expected by Teachers (n = 5,255)

Training activities		Teacher Participators	
Type	Popularity	Headcount	Level of satisfaction (%)
State-level elite teacher training	Low	1,176	85.7
Curriculum reform training	Relatively high	3,561	54.3
School-based teaching research	Relatively high	4,372	56.0
Continuing education training	Compulsory for all teachers	4,249	18.0

TEACHER LEARNING THROUGH TEACHING REFLECTION: FINDINGS FROM A CASE STUDY

Teaching reflection is a process of seeking improvement in instructional technique through on-going, careful self-deliberation on teaching practice. Teacher's self-reflections are sparked by the problems and confusion which occur in complex teaching situations. The process of teaching reflection can be viewed as composed of three stages: problem identification, situation description, and reconstruction after analysis (Dewey, 1933; Grimmett, MacKinnon, Erickson, and Riecken, 1990; Jay and Johnson, 2002).

Research Method

The case study method was adopted for this research as it is well-suited to an exploration of the rich contextual factors that affect teaching reflection as well as being capable of capturing the on-going process of teaching reflection. In order to investigate the reflective process of teachers with different levels of teaching competence, four teachers from the same primary school in a south China city, which was in one of the first areas for experimenting the national curriculum reform were invited to participate in this study. The four teachers were identified by a combination of principal's recommendation and the researchers' judgment. Two, Song and Li, were rated as average level teaching competence, and two, Zhang and Tian, were veteran teachers rated as high level teaching competence.

The investigation in this primary school was carried out in December 2005. During the process of data collection, all the self-reflection notes written by the four teachers in the past 15 months (i.e., September 2004 - December 2005) were collected, resulting in a collection of 78 separate teaching reflection notes. Four classroom observations were conducted of each teacher (a total of 16 observations). Each observation was followed by an in-depth semi-structured interview.

Two Types of Teaching Reflection: Point-by-Point Summary and Systematic Inquiry

The reflective practice adopted by the four teachers can be divided into two basic types and these are shown in table 2. The methods are point-by-point summary and systematic inquiry.

Point-by-point summary refers to a general description of various teaching and learning phenomena about a certain theme rather than identifying specific problems. This kind of reflective practice produces a perception or summary of the surface features of the phenomena rather than the rationale behind them. The two teachers rated as having average teaching competence, conducted their teaching reflection through the practice of point-by-point summary.

Systematic inquiry refers to a detailed investigation and deliberation over some specific problems in complicated teaching situations, and the causes and consequences of the relevant events in these situations. This is to reveal the reasons for the problems and the rationale for identifying such reasons. The two teachers rated at a high level of teaching competence conducted their teaching reflection by systematic inquiry.

Table 2. The proportions of the four teachers' reflection practices (%)

Type of teaching reflection	Teachers		Problem identification			Situation description			Analysis and reconstruction				
			Problems		Feelings	No description	Summarized description	Factual description	Changes in espoused theory	Changes in theory-in-use	Mutual confirmation	Conclusion	
	Level of teaching competence	Code	Answering	Discovering									
Point-by-point summary	Average	Song	30.2	12.5	57.3	12.5	25.0	62.5	6.3	0	6.3	87.5	
		Li	33.3	6.7	60.0	13.3	20.0	66.7	0	20.0	20	60.0	
Systematic inquiry	High	Zhang	61.5	38.5	0	0	46.2	53.8	23.1	30.8	30.8	15.3	
		Tian	38.2	61.8	0	14.7	8.8	76.5	14.7	0	58.8	26.5	

As previously mentioned, the process of teaching reflection usually comprises three stages: problem identification, situation description, and reconstruction after analysis. In the following sections, the process of the two types of teaching reflection will be described in detail.

Reflection by the Process of Point-by-Point Summary

(1) Problem identification: Feelings instead of problems

The problematic situations causing teachers to reflect can be divided into two categories: "feelings" and "problems". Feelings refer to teachers' reflection being caused by their emotions being aroused by some difficulty they meet in their teaching practice. Though the situations may be comparatively difficult to cope with, there is no resultant conflict. Problems refer to teachers' reflection caused by an occurrence due to a specific and serious conflict in their classroom practice. Furthermore, the action teachers initiate upon discovery of a problem is used to classify problems into two types: "answering problems" and "discovering problems". Answering problems are those where teachers do not recognize a problem until an interruption occurs in their classroom teaching, for example, student feedback. Teachers cannot continue their teaching until these problems are resolved. Discovery problems refer to those occurrences teachers discover in their routine teaching activities due to their self-conscious attitude and critical examination of their teaching. In general, "problems" can lead teachers to more authentic reflection than "feelings".

At the stage of problem identification, the two average competence teachers, Song and Li had more "feelings" than "problems". Among Song's 16 and Li's 15 reflection notes, for each, nine were caused by their "feelings". These reflections usually only describe the procedures of their teaching practices, without digging into the meanings of these procedures for their teaching practice. The reflections of Song and Li, showing the "answering problems" are much more than the "discovering problems", is in line with the notion that "problems" help teachers to have further improvements through the examination of their own teaching practices.

(2) Situation description: Focusing on factual description

At the stage of describing situations, the reflections of the four teachers can be divided into three types: no description, summarized description, and factual description. In Song's 16 reflection notes, there are two without any description, four using summarized description, and ten using factual description. In Li's 15 reflection notes, there are two with no description, three with summarized description, and ten with factual description. The notes without description start the analysis and offer strategies for improvement right after posting the problems of interest. In such reflections without description of the problematic situation, the analysis becomes too vague because there is no clear definition of the specific problem. This type of reflection is limited in improving teachers' teaching practice. In the summarized description, teachers describe the problems of interest in simple words. Such oversimplified description is one of the reasons why the analysis becomes discursive and cannot connect to the practices of classroom teaching.

(3) Analysis and reconstruction: More description of the phenomena than authentic inquiry of subjective theories

According to action theory (Argyris and Schön, 1974), there are two types of analysis and reconstruction shown in four teachers' reflection. The first type is only to describe the actions taken by teachers and students and their consequences for in classroom teaching, ignoring the analysis of the underlying rationale. The second one not only describes the actions and consequences but also uncovers the espoused theory and theory-in-use embedded in these actions which reflect teachers' own subjective theories about teaching and learning. If teachers realize the weaknesses in their teaching performance, and find out that the cause of these weaknesses is an improper adoption of the theory-in-use, they will try to change their interpretation to improve their teaching. If teachers encounter a surprising situation in their teaching and become aware of their underlying theory-in-use, they may consider changing the espoused theory, hoping to replace the existing teaching methods with some better strategies. If teachers have a clear idea of how to improve their teaching practice before teaching and harvest positive feedback after their actions, teaching reflection will confirm the effectiveness of espoused theory and theory-in-use, and the teacher will thus be able to achieve coherence between the two.

Among Song's reflection notes, 14 describe problematic phenomena and belong to the stage of analysis and reconstruction. Among them, there are only two notes unveiling the subjective theory embedded in the relevant events, indicating that Song's reflections mostly focus on the perceptual description of events instead of rationally inquiring into the essence of his teaching practices. In Li's reflection notes, there are nine in the category of phenomenon description, three on the change of theory-in-use, and three on the confirmation of the espoused theory from the theory-in-use. In other words, the model is to change the idea first. After some practical attempts at implementing espoused theory, teachers reflect on the viability of the ideas. If the actions expected in the espoused theory happen in the classroom and the students show a desirable change in performance, teachers will then discover the theory-in-use, and confirm the viability of the espoused theory.

The Reflection Process of Systematic Inquiry

(1) Problem identification: "Problem" as the starting point

Among the reflection notes of the two teachers who are identified as highly competent teachers, Zhang's and Tian, there is no reflection merely starting from their feelings. Both of them have a strong sense of problem seeking, and their reflections usually start from a specific conflicting situation, leading to a central problem with clear definition for their inquiry. Eight of Zhang's 13 notes and 13 of Tian's 34 notes start from answering problems. Some of the problems have already been the theme of their continuous thinking, and have been put forward again when they encounter a related situation. Although it seems that these problems are put forward incidentally, they are actually the certain result of their long-term thinking. Moreover, five pieces of Zhang's notes and 21 of Tian's are derived from discovering problems.

(2) Situation description: More factual description than simplified description

At the stage of situation description, the two teachers with average level of teaching competence are similar to the two with high competence. All of them focus on factual description rather than simplified description. However, in general, Zhang's and Tian's descriptions are more elaborated than Song's and Li's.

(3) Analysis and reconstruction: More authentic inquiry of subjective theories than description of phenomenon

Generally, Zhang's teaching reflection can be considered a typical process of teaching inquiry. The basic structure of Zhang's reflection is firstly to define the problems of interest, and then to describe the background and process of the problematic situations. Finally, the causes and consequences of the problems are questioned and analyzed. This is a systematic process of teaching reflection in order to clarify and change subjective theories. In Chen's (1998) words, the teachers place themselves in a continuous interaction between the theory-in-use and espoused theory. They continually examine the conflicts existing among various phenomena in their teaching practices, and seek out the causes of these conflicts, in order to integrate the originally conflicting phenomena into a dynamic balanced system. These exercises make the essentials of the existing teaching problems, such as educational ideas, values and ideologies, more obvious.

More than 60% of Tian's reflection notes are to confirm the espoused theory with the theory-in-use. In most cases, Tian has already formed clear espoused theories through conscious and continuous thinking before action, and he keeps experimenting with these espoused theories in his classroom teaching. He achieves more changes of theory-in-use in his teaching reflections. Through in-depth reflective inquiry, Tian gradually summarizes his own subjective theories about teaching and learning.

Teacher Learning in the Process of Teaching Reflection

Thompson (2001) classified teacher change into three levels: changes of materials and activities, changes of teaching practices, and changes of pedagogical values, beliefs and ethics. The first two levels are surface change while the last one is authentic change. In the case studies of the four teachers discussed above, the reflections that were characterized by "point-by-point summary" remained only at the level of surface learning, while the reflections characterized by "systematic inquiry" facilitated authentic teacher learning and authentic professional development.

Point-by-Point Summary and Surface Teacher Learning

Teaching reflection empowers teachers by providing an opportunity to let them stand back from their routine work and conduct systematic reflective thinking about their own practices. Through individual reflection or communication with others, teachers can bring problematic situations into the range of their conscious consideration, and analyze these unusual incidents using their original cognitive schema as a reference. This process of analysis solves the disequilibrium brought by these incidents to the original schema. If the analysis is simple and shallow, the disequilibrium will be easily filtered by the original cognitive schema. This latter kind of reflection cannot change teachers` mindset, and their actions will remain the same.

If teachers perform a conscious analysis of their cognitive imbalance, they may further enrich instead of fundamentally change their original schema. In this case, the imbalance will be eliminated by the effect of assimilation while a new meaning of the teaching incidents will be added into the original schema. Generally, this type of reflection does not focus on the consequences of the teaching practice and the subjective theories embedded, but only attempts to analyze the professional practice through the phenomena. Through this reflection, teachers can accumulate effective teaching experiences, but that is not enough to trigger their authentic changes in mind or significant changes in action. It is a kind of "incremental change" which is a continuation of the past actions and practices instead of a fundamental reconstruction. Therefore, it may be reversed, and teachers' practices may return to the past state (Cao, 2006).

Systematic Inquiry and Authentic Teacher Learning

If the inquiry into the cognitive imbalance is more in-depth and radical enough to cause a strong cognitive conflict, the reflection will lead to a change of teachers' espoused theory as well as theory-in-use, and thus a "revolution" in mind. In this type of reflection, teachers can start from a dilemma situation where they are forced to gradually dig out the underlying theoretic significance of the problem, so a theoretical theme will be formed in the teacher's reflection. The formation of this theoretic theme is usually a process of the teacher's gradual and careful analysis. This process will then bring the teacher a more authentic perception of his/her professional practices and provide these practices with a more solid theoretical base.

The influence of this type of reflection, i.e., systematic inquiry, is that teachers get in touch with the theories embedded in their own mind. These ideas are usually placed at the core level of their subjective theories. Once these core theories change, their principles of action, explanations of daily work, and specific teaching actions will be influenced and transformed. However, this type of reflection only happens infrequently, and usually can not be triggered by some ordinary events. When teachers have continuous observation and consideration on these "critical incidents" in their teaching practices, they can reconstruct and integrate these accumulated observations into a meaningful storyline with some theoretical significance. The fundamental change brought by this type of teaching reflection means not only a deeper level of change, but also an irreversibility of the change, indicating a fundamental reconstruction of the teacher's past experiences (Cao, 2006).

TEACHER LEARNING THROUGH TEACHING REFLECTION: TOWARDS A CONSTRUCTIVIST PERSPECTIVE

Teachers teach according to their own methods of learning (Brooks and Brooks, 1996, p. 35). If teachers are expected to constructively teach, they should constructively learn by themselves first (Falk, 1996, p. 28). In the view of constructivism, teacher learning is both an attitude and a process of teachers' active discovery and inquiry. It is a developmental process in which teachers can gradually enrich their ideals and knowledge, enhance their professional understanding and skills, and keep refreshing themselves by cultivating creativeness.

Cognitive constructivism advocates a "growth approach", rather than "deficit approach", to teacher learning which cherishes teachers' reflection on their own experiences. Through their active inquiry, teachers improve their professional knowledge and competence step by step. This national curriculum reform is characterized with a salient outside-in feature in its organization and implementation (Fullan, 2000). Except for a few teachers who can explore the way of implementing the new curriculum based on their own experiences, the majority consider the curriculum reform as a complete unknown. Moreover, many reform initiatives are mainly transplanted from exotic theories instead of derived from teachers' past experiences. The teacher training conducted by the state usually adopts a defect approach (Eraut, 1985). For example, the training on reform issues and teachers' continuing education are mostly based on the lecturing and listening model. The prevailing assumption of these training activities is that teachers' existing knowledge and skills is out-dated or ineffective. Teachers need to be filled up with new knowledge and abilities to implement the curriculum. This approach ignores teachers' existing reservoir of experience and the constructivist nature of teacher learning. Even in school-based research which usually features contextual and practical teacher learning, teachers are still passive in the reflection of point-by-point summary.

From the perspective of social constructivism, the depth of teacher learning is co-constructed through inter-personal collaborations, and then internalized as part of the development of the teachers' cognitive schema. In Mainland China, the teaching research system (*jiaoyan xitong*) from the central administration to the provincial, municipal, county, school districts and school is a professional organization in charge of teachers' communication about and inquiry on their teaching practices. Based on this teaching research system, the curriculum reform in Mainland China is carried out through various teacher communication activities, including inter-school visitations, peer observations, teaching competitions, and school-based research. Rooted in a unique tradition of "teaching research" in China, the curriculum reform has built a huge learning community among teachers which provides teachers with opportunities for learning from each other as well as emotional support for teachers' growth in reform situations (Zhao, 2009, pp.187-197).

Critical constructivism focuses on the issues of power and equality in teacher learning, considering teacher learning not as an external imposed activity but a process of self-conscious emancipation. Under the centralized educational administration system in Mainland China, teachers are accustomed to following the official will of the superior administrators. Teachers can seldom use their own interpretation of the reform policies. Instead, they are subjected to the dominating viewpoints of the state and follow the orders of the government, presenting a characteristic of "limited professionalism" (Lai and Lo, 2005). Therefore, the typical characteristic of teacher reflection is that they put most attention on perfection of their teaching skills for imparting knowledge, and ignore reflection on the aims, beliefs and values underpinning their teaching.

In summary, in the context of the curriculum reform, although various teacher training activities provide teachers with opportunities of learning and communication, the motivation for and cognitive process of teacher reflection are not active enough. Due to the lack of critical teacher reflection, even if teachers have doubts about the rationale and feasibility of the reform initiatives, they prefer to give vent to their opinions by reticence or lack of commitment to the reform, instead of public debate or constructivist reflection and action.

REFERENCES

Argyris, C., and Schön, D. A. (1974). *Theory in practice: Increasing professional effectiveness*. San Francisco: Jossey-Bass.

Brooks, M. G., and Brooks, J. G. (1996). Constructivism and school reform. In M. W. Mclaughlin and I. Oberman (Eds.), *Teacher learning: New policies, new practices* (pp.30-35). New York: Teachers College Press.

Cao, T. S. (2003). *Teacher professionalism in university-school partnership: A comparative study of cases in Hong Kong and Shanghai.* Unpublished PhD Thesis, The Chinese University of Hong Kong, Hong Kong.

Chen, H. P. (1998). *Educational action research.* Taipei: Taiwan Normal University Press.

Clarke, D., and Hollingsworth, H. (2002). Elaborating a model of teacher professional growth. *Teaching and Teacher Education, 18*(8), 947-967.

Connelly, F. M., and Ben-Peretz, M. (1980). Teachers` roles in the using and doing of research and curriculum development. *Journal of Curriculum Studies, 12*(2), 95-107.

Dewey, J. (1933). *How we think: A restatement of the relation of reflective thinking to the educative process.* Boston: Heath.

Eraut, M. (1986). Inservice teacher education. In M. J. Dunkin (Ed.). *The international encyclopedia of teaching and teacher education* (pp.730-743). Oxford: Pergamon Press.

Falk, B. (1996). Teaching the way children learn. In M. W. McLaughlin, and I. Oberman (Eds.), *Teacher learning: New policies, new practices* (pp. 22-29). New York: Teachers College Press.

Fullan, M. (2000). The three stories of education reform. *Phi Delta Kappan, 81*(8), 581-584.

Grimmett, P. P., MacKinnon, A. M., Erickson, G. L, and Riecken, T. J. (1990). Reflective practice in teacher education. In R. T. Clift, W. R. Houston and M. C. Pugach (Eds.), *Encouraging reflective practice in education* (pp. 20-28). New York: Teacher College Press.

Huang, F. Q. (2004). Curriculum reform in contemporary China: Seven goals and six strategies. *Journal of Curriculum Studies, 36*(1), 101-115.

Jay, J. K., and Johnson, K. L. (2002). Capturing complexity: a typology of reflective practice for teacher education. *Teaching and teacher education, 18*(1), 73-85.

Lai, M. H., and Lo, N. K. (2005). Teacher professionalism in educational reform: Experiences of Hong Kong and Shanghai. *Education Journal, 33*(1-2), 63-87.

Ministry of Education (1999). *Regulations of continuing education for primary and middle school teachers.* Beijing: Ministry of Education.

Ministry of Education (2001). *Outline for basic education curriculum reform.* Beijing: Ministry of Education.

Ministry of Education (2004). *Instructions from ministry of education on further strengthening the teacher training for the new elementary education curriculum.* Beijing: Ministry of Education.

Putnam, R. T., and Borko, H. (1997). Teacher learning: Implications of new views of cognition. In B. J. Biddle, T. L. Good and I. F. Goodson (Eds.), *International handbook of teachers and teaching* (pp.1222-1295). Netherlands: Kluwer Academic Publishers.

Stenhouse, L. (1975). *An introduction to curriculum research and development.* London: Heinemann Educational Books Ltd.

Thompson, M. D. (2001, July). *Teachers experiencing authentic change: The exchange of values, beliefs, practices and emotions in interactions.* Paper presented at the Experiencing Change, Exchanging Experience Virtual Conference.

Zhao, M. R. (2009). *Reflective teaching and teacher development in curriculum reform.* Beijing: Beijing Normal University Press. (in Chinese).

Zhao, M. R., Zhou, J., and Zhu X. D. (2009). A Survey on the participation and needs of primary and secondary school teachers' professional development. *Teacher Education Research*, *21*(1), 62-67. (in Chinese).

In: Curriculum Reform in China
Editors: Hong-Biao Yin and John Chi-Kin Lee

ISBN 978-1-61470-943-5
© 2012 Nova Science Publishers, Inc.

Chapter 16

QUALITIES OF GOOD TEACHERS IN CHINA: A COMPARATIVE PERSPECTIVE

Shujie Liu and Lingqi Meng

ABSTRACT

Since the 1920's many researchers have conducted studies exploring the qualities of good teachers. However, a limited number of empirical studies have been conducted in the People's Republic of China (hereafter called China). The current study has two objectives. The first one aimed to compare a good teacher's characteristics in China and the USA. To achieve this, qualitative data of a good teacher's characteristics were collected in China. The results obtained from China were then compared to those reported in the USA. The second objective was to test whether or not there are differences among teachers', students' and parents' perceptions of a good teacher's characteristics in China. To achieve this, questionnaires were administered, and then statistical analyses were conducted. The qualitative data analyses have revealed four themes about the characteristics of good Chinese teachers: teacher ethics, professional skills, professional development, and students' test scores. This study helps readers better understand good teachers in a Chinese context and provides a framework for future comparative study between China and the USA regarding the qualities of good teachers.

INTRODUCTION

A number of empirical studies have been conducted since the 1920s exploring the qualities of good teachers (Askew et al., 1997; Beishuizen et al., 2001; Brophy and Good, 1986; Campbell et al., 2003, 2004; Corbett and Wilson, 2002; Kutnick and Junes, 1993; Kyriakides and Campbell, 2003; Murphy et al., 2004; Polk, 2006; Reynolds and Teddlie, 2000; Rosenshine and Stevens, 1986; Shulman, 1987, 2000; Stronge, 2007; Stronge and Hindman, 2003; Weinstein, 1989). While quite a few researchers have focused on good teaching, some have extended this to factors beyond the classroom (e.g., Kyriakides and Campbell, 2003; Stronge, 2007). A review by Reynolds and Teddlie (2000) concluded that effective teaching processes included (1) management of time; (2) classroom organization, such as preparing lessons in advance, clarity both in explaining the purpose of the lesson and in the actual curricular and content, and the structure of the lesson; (3) the use of effective teaching practices, such as questioning strategies, maintaining a task orientation in the classroom, and a warm and accepting classroom climate; and (4) adaptation of practice to the particular characteristics of the learners (pp. 146-147).

A synthesis from a meta-review of extant research by Stronge (2007, pp. 110-114; Stronge and Hindman 2003, p. 50) provided a comprehensive list of qualities of effective teachers with six dimensions: (1) prerequisites of effective teachers (e.g., verbal ability, knowledge of teaching and learning, certificate status, content knowledge, teaching experience), (2) the teacher as a person (e.g., caring, shows fairness and respect, interactions with students, enthusiasm, motivation, dedication to teaching, reflective practice), (3) classroom management and organization (e.g., classroom management, organization, discipline of students), (4) planning and organizing for instruction (e.g., importance of instruction, time allocation, teachers' expectations, instruction plan), (5) implementing instruction (instructional strategies, content and expectations, complexity, questioning, student engagement), and (6) monitoring student progress and potential (e.g., homework, monitoring student progress, responding to student needs and abilities).

Regarding research methodology, most studies explored the qualities of good teachers by interviewing or observing only teachers, and a few studies have been conducted from the perspectives of students (Beishuizen et al., 2001). Few, if any, studies have been conducted from perspectives of parents about the qualities of good teachers. For example, one of the limited comparative studies by Murphy, Delli, and Edwards (2004) used an adapted version of the Tuckman Teacher Feedback Form (Tuckman 1995) to measure second graders', preservice teachers' and inservice teachers' beliefs about effective teaching. The results of the study revealed a great deal of agreement across all the three groups. Among the 12 items, being caring, patient, not boring, polite, and organized were rated by all the three groups as more important characteristics of good teachers while being soft-spoken, ordinary, or strict were less important.

In contrast to the numerous studies on good teachers conducted in Western countries, a limited number of empirical studies have been conducted in China (e.g., Cortazzi and Jin, 1996; Ling, 2001; Shao and Hao, 2002; Shi, 2005; Zhu, 2004). This makes the current study more important for two reasons. First, this study looks at the qualities of good teachers not just from the perspective of teachers or students, but from the perspectives of teachers, students, and parents. Second, as one of the few empirical studies of good teachers conducted in China, this chapter will contribute new knowledge to the field of teacher effectiveness research.

Despite the fact that only a few empirical studies on good teachers have been conducted in China, there have been numerous studies of teacher evaluation (For more in-depth coverage of teacher evaluation in China, see Liu and Teddlie, 2003, 2005) which help provide a picture of good Chinese teachers since teacher evaluation systems and teacher qualities are closely related. As Stronge and Tucker (2003) stated, "...without high quality evaluation systems, we cannot know if we have high quality teachers" (p. 3).

Traditionally a teacher evaluation system in China has four components: (1) morality (e.g., political stands and vocational morality as a teacher), (2) diligence (e.g., attendance rate), (3) ability (e.g., teaching ability, research ability), and (4) student performance (based on student test scores) (Feng, 2002; Jiang and Zhang 2003; Li, 2002; Li and Xuan, 2003;

Ying and Fan, 2001). Within the teacher evaluation system, the effective teaching indicators in China are usually divided into three, four, or five major domains. For example, Jiang (2001) provided a five-domain teaching evaluation system in a Chinese middle school: (1) teaching objectives (e.g., present clear objectives of the lesson), (2) teaching contents (e.g., present a proper quantity of content information, present the content of the lesson in a logical sequence), (3) teaching methods (e.g., demonstrate a clear and complete design of instruction, create contexts and promote interests of students, provide timely feedback), (4) teaching processes or skills (e.g., deliver accurate knowledge, communication is clear, demonstrate a natural and elegant gesture while teaching, appropriately allot teaching time), and (5) teaching effects (e.g., Has secured students strong interests and attention to the lesson). These teacher evaluation indicators will be used for questionnaire construction at the Stage-Three study of the current study.

This chapter had two objectives. The first one aimed to investigate a good teacher's qualities in China. The second objective was to test whether or not there are differences among teachers', students' and parents' perceptions of a good teacher's qualities in China. The theoretical perspective underlying our approach is that we regard the notion of a good teacher as a socially constructed concept. We adopted Sawyer's (2001) methodological individualism which holds that "social properties can be fully explained in terms of properties of individuals and their interactions" (p. 561). Therefore, individual perspectives from students, teachers, and parents in terms of the qualities of good Chinese teachers can be treated as social properties of the qualities of good Chinese teachers. The following two research questions guided this chapter: (1) What are the perceived qualities of good teachers by teachers, students, and parents in China? (2) Are there differences among teachers', students' and parents' perceptions of the qualities of good teachers in China?

Not only is there no universal agreement about good teachers, but there are different terms for good teachers. Cruickshank and Haefele (2001) identified ten versions of good teachers (e.g., ideal teachers, competent teachers, expert teachers, effective teachers). In this paper, good teachers, ideal teachers and effective teachers are used interchangeably due to our data sources. One of the sources is from Liu's project (2006) which aimed to identify the processes of effective schooling and teaching in China. Thus terms such as effective teachers, effective teaching, and teacher effectiveness were used in the project. Meanwhile one of the teacher interview questions for that project was asking teachers to describe the "ideal teacher" at their schools.

RESEARCH METHODOLOGY AND RESULTS

Three-stage data collection was conducted to achieve the research objectives. The Stage-One data were collected in Chinese elementary schools during late 2005 and early 2006 as part of Liu's project (2006) to identify the processes of effective schooling and teaching in China. The Stage-Two data were collected from a Chinese middle school in March, 2008. The qualitative data from these two stages were integrated to establish a complete profile of a good Chinese teacher and answer the first research question.

The second objective was to test whether or not there are differences among teachers', students' and parents' perceptions of a good teacher's qualities in China. To achieve this, the

Stage-Three data collection was collected in late April at the same Chinese middle school as sampled in the second stage to obtain quantitative data by administering questionnaires to teachers, students and parents and thus answer the second research question.

Stage-One Study

Participants and Data Collection

The sampling for the Stage-One data collection included two steps. First, stratified purposeful sampling was used to select 12 elementary schools in a northwestern city of China with school effectiveness classification and socio-economic status as the strata. Secondly, at each school 40 students and 30 parents were randomly selected for questionnaires, so that a total of 480 (40 × 12=480) students and 360 (30 × 12=360) parents were involved in the questionnaires. Also, at each school intensity and maximum variation sampling techniques were used to select five teachers for interviews. Thus a total of 60 (5 × 12=60) were purposefully selected from the teachers who had been observed, based on their demonstration of diverse classroom behaviors.

The student and the parent questionnaires were based on those developed by Brookover and Lezotte (1979) and used in both the Louisiana School Effectiveness Study (LSES) and in the Louisiana School Effectiveness and Assistance Program (SEAP) (Teddlie 1999). Both questionnaires included the following open-ended item: List three best things about the school. The teacher interview protocol was specifically developed for Liu's study (2006) to secure teachers' opinions regarding their schools. Two of the interview questions were pertinent to the current study: How would you describe the "ideal teacher" at your school? What kinds of characteristics does that teacher have?

Six Chinese researchers from a northeastern university in China were involved in the data collection. These members formed three two-person teams. For the first site visit, all the members worked together at one school in order to develop consistent and standardized implementation procedures, increasing the inference quality of the results. In order to increase the transferability, thick descriptions of each school were developed. Three techniques were used to determine the credibility of the qualitative results in the study: (1) triangulation technique (Patton, 2002, p.556), which involved both methods triangulation (qualitative and quantitative data collected at the same time) and triangulation of sources (the qualitative data collected from observations, interviews, and documents); (2) member checks (Tashakkori and Teddlie, 1998, p.92). One teacher from each school who was involved in this study was invited to check the analyses, conclusions, and interpretations; and (3) peer debriefing (Tashakkori and Teddlie, 1998, p.91). One Chinese professor in education was invited to review the analyses and interpretations.

Data Analysis

Constant comparative analysis (e.g., Glaser and Strauss, 1967) was used to analyze the qualitative data obtained from teachers, students and parents as described above. The analysis involved four steps: First, all the transcriptions were read for a general idea of the data. Second, phrases in the data were underlined, and each phrase was assigned a code (e.g., being patient, respecting students, or caring about students). Third, similar codes were grouped together. Fourth, these groups were combined and reduced to several themes.

Results

A constant comparative analysis of the data obtained from teacher interviews revealed three themes: (1) teacher ethics, which included being patient, respecting students, caring about students, being responsible for students, being fair to each student, having a good relationship with students and peers, being dedicated to teaching (e.g., spending time outside of school to prepare lesson plans or grade students' homework); (2) professional skills, which included being knowledgeable and creative, and having great teaching skills (e.g., fostering students' abilities according to their individual characteristics, employing different teaching methods to arouse students' interest in studying, creating a comfortable classroom atmosphere); and (3) professional development, which included continuing in-service learning, and keeping abreast of new educational theories.

The themes revealed in the open-ended question of the student questionnaire (i.e., list three good things about your school) also included three aspects of a good teacher. The first two were the same as those revealed in teacher interviews (described above): teacher ethics and professional skills. The last theme was teaching effects, indicated by students' good test scores. As one student said, "One of the good things about my school is my teachers are great. For example, my math teacher often gives me extra help, and my test scores have greatly improved."

The analysis of the data from the parent questionnaire revealed two themes: teacher ethics and students' academic achievement. One parent mentioned students' test scores when asked to list good things about the school: "This school has good teachers, and, consequently, the students' test scores at this school are much higher than those in other schools." Table 1 was a summary of the themes from teachers, students and parents.

The above results showed that elementary teachers, students and parents shared consensus opinions about the qualities of a good teacher on one factor: teacher ethics. In addition, both students and parents thought that students' test scores was a very important characteristic of a good teacher. This is understandable given the exam-driven education system in China where students' test scores are so closely related to a child's future (e.g., whether or not to enter an excellent next-level school, what level college to enter, etc.). Surprisingly, the teachers did not mention test scores. One possible reason is that they do not like people to use students' test scores to judge how good a teacher is, since this would put pressure on teachers. Studies (e.g., Meng and Liu, 2008) showed that the pressure from the teacher evaluation system, in which students' test scores play a very important role, is the main source of teacher stress in China.

Table 1. Themes revealed at stage-one study regarding characteristics of a good teacher

From Teachers	From Students	From Parents
1. Teacher Ethics 2. Professional Skills	1. Teacher Ethics 2. Professional Skills	1. Teacher Ethics
3. Professional Development	3. Teaching Effects	2. Students' Academic Achievement

Integrating the opinions of teachers, students and parents, the qualities of good teachers can be classified into four categories: (1) teacher ethics, (2) professional skills, (3) professional development, and (4) teaching effects (e.g., students' test scores). These categories were used as the predetermined themes of the data obtained from the second stage study.

Stage-Two Study

At Stage One, all the data were collected in Chinese elementary schools. Moreover, only indirect responses were obtained from students and parents about the qualities of good teachers since they were asked to list three good things about the school rather than specifically about the teacher. The purpose of the Stage-Two study was to secure responses from middle school teachers, students and parents about qualities of a good teacher.

Participants and Data Collection

The three groups (30 teachers, 55 students, and 25 parents) of participants were from an urban middle school in a northeastern city. The 30 teachers consisted of seven males and 23 females, and their ages ranged from 25 to 54. All of the 55 students were seventh graders with their ages ranging from 13 to 15. 25 of them were boys and 30 were girls.

The teachers, students, and parents were asked to write a free essay about a good teacher. The question was given by a teacher in that school to teachers and students on a school day and returned on the same day. The question papers for parents were taken home by students and returned the following day. All the participation was voluntary, and students' participation was permitted by their parents.

The free-essay question was: What kinds of characteristics do you think a good teacher has? The instructions included the following: Please list characteristics of good teachers, and write about good teachers in general without mentioning any particular teachers. There was no restriction of the essay length.

Data Analysis

The qualitative analyses were organized around the four predetermined themes obtained from the Stage-One study: teacher ethics, professional skills, professional development, and students' test scores.

Results

The responses from teachers, students and parents were presented in Table 2 using the predetermined four categories: (1) teacher ethics, (2) professional skills, (3) professional development, and (4) teaching effects (e.g., students' test scores). From the table we could also see what items were shared by all the three groups, what items were shared by two groups, and what items only emerged from one group for each category.

Results from the middle school teachers, students and parents at this stage were consistent with those obtained from elementary teachers, students and parents at stage-One of the current study. For example, regarding teacher ethics, all the sampled teachers, students and parents (both at Stage-one and Stage-two) thought that teacher ethics included the following characteristics: Be responsible, treat all students equally, care about all students, and have a good relationship with students.

Table 2. Responses from teachers, students and parents regarding characteristics of a good teacher at stage-two study

	From Teachers	From Students	From Parents
Teacher ethics	Be responsible Treat all students equally Care for all students, especially low performing students Maintain good relationships with students, parents, and peers Respect individual differences Be patient Set a good model for the student Grade students' papers at home	Be responsible Treat all students equally Care for students Maintain close and friendly relationship with students Be humorous Be considerate of students Be strict with students Often communicate with students and parents Do not ridicule students Control temper	Be responsible Treat all students equally Care for students Maintain good relationship with students Accommodate individual differences Be patient Be humorous Be considerate of students Be strict with students Respect students
Professional skills	Be knowledgeable Have excellent teaching skills Design lesson plans based on students' actual levels Present the lesson content in a logical sequence Use flexible teaching methods Encourage student participation in class Communicate well in class Offer timely praise for student progress Apply the textbook appropriately to real life Demonstrate a clear and complete design of instruction Efficiently use class time	Be knowledgeable Have excellent teaching skills Create active classroom atmosphere	Be knowledgeable Have excellent teaching skills Communicate well in class Arouse students' learning interest Manage classroom well
Professional development	Keep abreast of new content knowledge and pedagogy knowledge by continuing in-service learning		Continue to improve their professional development (e.g., inservice training)
Test scores		Focus on students' test scores	Teach in such a way that enables students to achieve good test

Also, being knowledge and having excellent teaching skills were reported by all the groups (both at Stage-one and Stage-two) as important professional skills. Same as with the results from Stage-One, both teachers and parents emphasized professional development as important qualities of good teachers. For example, several teachers mentioned, "A good teacher should keep abreast of new content knowledge and pedagogy knowledge by continuing in-service learning."

Once again, good students' test scores were regarded by students and parents as a very important indicator to evaluate a good teacher. One parents responded as follows, "A good teacher is the one whose students have very good test scores compared to other teachers; a good school is one which has teachers who can make students' scores higher than those in other schools. What my son needs is a good score to compete with other students to enter an excellent high school which could ensure a high probability of entering a good university in the future."

Stage-Three Study

The teachers, students, and parents questionnaires used at this stage were developed based on the results from the first two stages of the current study as well as on the literature review of good teachers or teacher evaluation in China (e.g., Feng, 2002; Jiang, 2001; Jiang and Zhang, 2003; Li, 2002; Li and Xuan, 2003; Ying and Fan, 2001). Although the sampled teachers at the first two stages did not mention students' test scores, it was still included in the Stage-Three questionnaires because many sections of society (e.g., parents and school administrators) appear to evaluate teachers by student test scores.

Teachers, students and parents were asked to rate each characteristic according to its importance on a scale from 1 to 5. Then statistical analyses were conducted to see whether or not there are differences among teachers, students and parents regarding qualities of good teachers in China and thus answer the second research question. The teacher and the student questionnaires were distributed on a school day and returned on the same day. The parent questionnaires were brought home by students and returned the following day.

Participants and Data Collection

The teacher, student, and parent questionnaires were administered to the same groups as those at Stage Two, but one male teacher, three female students and five parents did not return the questionnaires. Thus the participants at Stage Three consisted of 29 teachers (6 males and 23 females), 52 students (25 boys and 27 girls), and 20 parents.

The parent questionnaire included 10 items about qualities of good teachers in general (e.g., Knowledgeable, Patient, Creative). Parents were asked to rate how important each item was for good teachers using a five-level Likert scale with "1" indicating "not important at all" and "5" indicating "very important."

The teacher and the student questionnaires consisted of 18 items. In addition to the 10 items described above, both the teacher and the student questionnaires included eight more items about good teaching in particular (i.e., Demonstrate a clear design of instruction, Teaching methods are flexible and appropriate, Uses available teaching materials and aids to

Qualities of Good Teachers in China

achieve lesson objectives, Demonstrates ability to communicate effectively with students, Accommodates individual differences, Relates homework to the content under study and to student capacity , Encourages student participation in class, and Provides timely feedback to students regarding their progress) using the same five-level Likert scale as above, given that teachers and students know more about the teaching processes.

Data Analysis

Ten one-way ANOVAs were performed to compare the mean differences among teachers, students, and parents on qualities of good teachers in general. The independent variable was group (teacher, student, parent), and the dependent variables were qualities of good teachers (e.g., knowledgeable, patient). These analyses used the Bonferroni adjustment (i.e., $\alpha = .05/10 = .005$) to reduce risk of Type I error.

Table 3. Means, standard deviations, of the qualities of good teachers by group

	Teacher (N=29)		Student (N=52)		Parent (N=20)	
	M	SD	M	SD	M	SD
Knowledgeable	4.45	.74	4.40	.75	4.20	.89
Patient	4.31	.66	4.56	.64	4.75	.44
Creative	4.03	.68	4.27	.63	4.25	.72
Excellent teaching skills	4.48	.63	4.58	.64	4.40	.94
Dedication	4.55	.57	4.67	.65	5.00	.00
Care about students	4.45	.63	4.69	.54	4.70	.47
Responsible	4.52	.63	4.69	.61	4.82	.37
Have a good relationship with students and peers	3.90	.62	4.02	.87	4.10	.91
Treat all students equally	4.45	.51	4.73	.56	4.25	1.02
His/her students have good test scores	3.69	.76	3.73	1.10	3.80	1.10
Demonstrate a clear design of instruction	4.28	.70	4.40	.70		
Teaching methods are flexible and appropriate	4.10	.62	4.40	.73		
Uses available teaching materials and aids to achieve lesson objectives	3.79	.62	3.98	.83		
Demonstrates ability to communicate effectively with students	3.69	.81	4.31	.94		
Accommodates individual differences	4.24	.58	4.33	.92		
Relates homework to the content under study and to student capacity	3.76	.87	3.96	1.12		
In class encourages student participation	4.28	.53	4.40	.89		
Provides timely feedback to	4.34	.55	4.42	.94		

	students regarding their progress

Eight t-tests were conducted to examine the differences between teachers and students about the eight qualities of good teaching in particular. The independent variable was group (teacher, student), and the dependent variables were qualities of good teaching (e.g., a clear design of instruction, flexible teaching methods). These tests also used the Bonferroni adjustment (i.e., $\alpha = .05/8 = .006$) to reduce risk of Type I error.

Results

Table 3 presented the means and standard deviations for the qualities of good teachers by group. Overall the respondents reported that all the listed characteristics were important for good teachers and good teaching. Among them, "responsible" and "dedication" were regarded by all the groups as the most important qualities of good teachers while items of "creativity," "have a good relationship" and "good test scores" were ranked at the bottom across the groups.

Table 4 presented the ANOVAs results. It can be seen from the table that there were no significant differences among the three groups on any of the ten qualities of good teachers after applying the adjusted probability value of $p = .005$.

Table 5 presented the t-tests results. It can be seen from the table that a significant difference was found between teachers and students only on one (Demonstrates Ability to Communicate Effectively with Students), $t(79) = -2.97$, $p < .006$, with students ranking it higher ($M = 4.31$, $SD = .94$) than teachers ($M = 3.96$, $SD = .81$).

Table 4. One-way ANOVAs for qualities of good teachers among teachers, students and parents

	F	df (between group, within group)	p
Knowledgeable	0.68	(2, 98)	.51
Patient	3.30	(2, 98)	.05
Creative	1.25	(2, 98)	.29
Excellent teaching skills	0.50	(2, 98)	.61
Dedication	3.96	(2, 98)	.02
Care about students	2.02	(2, 98)	.14
Responsible	2.01	(2, 98)	.14
Have a good relationship with students and peers	0.40	(2, 98)	.67
Treat all students equally	4.31	(2, 98)	.02
His/her students have good test scores	0.07	(2, 98)	.93

Table 5. T-tests for qualities of good teachers between teachers and students

	$t_{(79)}$	p
Demonstrate a clear design of instruction	-1.03	.31
Teaching methods are flexible and appropriate	-2.12	.04
Uses available teaching materials and aids to achieve lesson objectives	-1.06	.29
Demonstrates ability to communicate effectively with students	-2.97	.00
Accommodates individual differences	-0.45	.65
Relates homework to the content under study and to student capacity	-0.84	.40
In class encourages student participation	-0.71	.48
Provides timely feedback to students regarding their progress	-0.41	.68

CONCLUSION

One of the main objectives of the current study was to compare a good teacher's qualities in China and the USA. Combining the qualitative results of the current study, we picture a good Chinese teacher as someone who has the following characteristics: good teacher ethics, excellent professional skills, continuous professional development, and great teaching effects indicated by their students' good test scores. In spite of the different categories found in the current study and in the USA, most of the characteristics of good Chinese teachers are consistent with those identified in the USA, such as the six dimensions by Stronge (2007) and Stronge and Hindman (2003) (i.e., prerequisites of effective teachers, the teacher as a person, classroom management and organization, planning and organizing for instruction, implementing instruction, and monitoring student progress and potential).

In the current study, teacher ethics was regarded as one of the most important qualities in China. A teacher with good ethics was defined by teachers, students and parents as someone who is patient, strict with students, humorous, considerate of students, respectful of students, and dedicated (e.g., spending time outside of school to prepare lesson plans or grade students' homework, using lunch break to help students with their studies). A teacher with good ethics also cares about students, treats all students equally, grades fairly and has a good relationship with students and peers, and takes responsibility for students' academic performance as well as other aspects of their school experience (e.g., escorting students to the gate after dismissal and waiting until their parents pick them up). The Chinese teacher ethics described here is in fact similar to Stronge's category for the teacher as a person which includes caring, showing fairness and respect, interactions with students, enthusiasm, motivation, dedication to teaching, and reflective practice.

Stronge's other five categories (prerequisites of effective teachers, classroom management and organization, planning and organizing for instruction, implementing instruction, and monitoring student progress and potential) are similar to the excellent professional skills category revealed in the current study. For example, Stronge (2007) defined prerequisites of good teachers as verbal ability, knowledge of teaching and learning, certificate status, content knowledge, and teaching experience. These were classified in the current study under the category of excellent professional skills which identifies a teacher as someone who is knowledgeable (e.g., has a high level of content knowledge and pedagogy knowledge).

Furthermore, the category of excellent professional skills in the current study also includes teaching skills such as designing a lesson plan based on students' actual levels, using flexible teaching methods, encouraging student participation, effectively communicating with students in class, providing timely praise to students whenever they make progress, efficiently using class time, and having good classroom discipline. All these were classified as four characteristics by Stronge (2007): classroom management and organization (e.g., classroom management, discipline of students), planning and organizing for instruction (e.g., importance of instruction, time allocation), implementing instruction (instructional strategies, student engagement), and monitoring student progress and potential (e.g., monitoring student progress, responding to student needs and abilities).

Such kind of consistent findings between countries is supported by other studies (e.g., Hiebert et al., 2005; Liu and Teddlie, 2003, 2005). Liu and Teddlie found that the typical classroom observation components used in the USA are very similar to the indicators of traditional classroom teaching evaluation in China.

However, the sampled Chinese students and parents in the current study revealed one further characteristic of good teachers – that of students' test scores - which appears to be unique to the Chinese context. While many studies have explored the relationship between teacher qualities and student achievement (e.g., Creemers, 1997; Scheerens and Bosker 1997; Stronge et al., 2007), students' test scores have not been listed as one of the teacher qualities identified in Western countries. There are several possible reasons for test scores being regarded as a characteristic of a good Chinese teacher: The first reason might be the Chinese examination system. Over the past decades the National Uniform College Entrance Exam (NUCEE) has been the main route by which students are accepted by colleges in China. Entering a college means a person will become a professional; otherwise, this person will probably become a laborer. Therefore, the NUCEE exerts a powerful influence on the primary and secondary education systems across the country. In this situation, good test scores are of course extremely important for students and parents. In recent years, as the college acceptance rate increases, Chinese high school students have more opportunities to go to a college; however, they still compete for top universities since they are more likely to be employed if they graduate from one of the reputable top universities.

Students' test scores are also important to American students and parents; however, the role that teachers play in preparing students for the college entrance exams is different in China and USA. Unlike American teachers' role in SAT or ACT preparation, Chinese teachers play a very important role in preparing high school seniors to earn an excellent NUCEE score because the NUCEE is more course-specific than American tests. Thus there is a demand for skillful teachers. Teaching high school seniors reflects a teacher's status in the school. A reputable teacher who has a higher percentage of former students accepted by top universities is likely to teach seniors again. In fact, successful preparation of students for the college entrance examination appears to be a characteristic of award-winning teachers at the national, regional, and local levels.

The second research objective of this study was to test whether there are differences among teachers, students and parents regarding qualities of good teachers in China. Both the ANOVAs and the t-tests from the third stage have found no differences among the teachers, students and parents on the qualities of good teachers except on one item: Demonstrates ability to communicate effectively with students. This implies that Chinese teachers, students and parents have for the most part consensus opinions about the qualities of good teachers (e.g., knowledgeable, patient, responsible, a clear design of instruction, flexible teaching methods). This consistency among groups has also been found in Western countries. For example, Murphy, Delli and Edwards (2004) concluded in the USA that "second graders, preservice teachers, and inservice teachers seem to agree easily on the requisite characteristics for being a good teacher, as well as on those characteristics that good teachers do not need to possess" (p. 87).

As mentioned earlier, only the students and parents (but not teachers) listed students' test scores as one of the qualities of good teachers at the first two research stages, but it was still included in the Stage-Three questionnaires, given the fact that many sections of society (e.g., parents and school administrators) appear to evaluate teachers by students' test scores. The statistical analysis did not find significant differences among the teachers, students and parents on this item; however, we can see from Table 3 that both the mean and the standard deviation of the teachers' rating of item 10 (students test scores) were lower than those of the other two groups. The smaller mean from the teachers' responses implies that teachers do not think students' test scores are as important as parents and students think they are since many factors (e.g., students' motivation and efforts, parents' support) may influence students' test scores. A good teacher with excellent teaching skills cannot guarantee his/her students' good test scores. Thus teachers do not want to use students' test scores to judge whether a teacher is good or not. The smaller standard deviation from the teachers' responses might be because the teachers participating in this study worked in the same school and thus shared the same school culture and similar educational philosophy, which may make their responses more consistent than the students and parents whose backgrounds are diverse (e.g., high- and low-performing students). Future studies may address how students' and parents' background influence their perception of a good teacher.

As one of the few empirical studies exploring qualities of good teachers from perspectives of teachers, students and parents in China, this study helps audiences better understand the qualities of good teachers in a Chinese context. In addition, the current study's implications are important for educational administrators in China as well as in other countries. Hiring and retaining highly qualified teachers have been major focuses of educational reforms in many countries (OECD, 2005). This study has provided evidence that characteristics of a good Chinese teacher are similar to those identified in Western countries, which implies that countries might be able to learn from each other regarding how to attract and retain good teachers. However, assimilating a good practice from another country is complex. Culture and a national system of education can make the same individual factors work differently as a whole. As researchers (e.g., Hiebert et al., 2005; LeTendre et al., 2001) indicated, the difference between the countries in student academic achievement mainly lies in the system of teaching and the cultural roles of teachers in different countries rather than individual teaching beliefs and behaviors. Thus, how culture influences teacher effectiveness in different countries certainly merits further exploration.

REFERENCES

Askew, M., Rhodes, V., Brown, M., William, D., and Johnson, D. (1997). *Effective teachers of numeracy: Report of a study carried out for the Teacher Training Agency*. London: King's College London, School of Education.

Beishuizen, J. J., Hof, E., Putten, C. M., Bouwmeester, S., and Asscher, J. J. (2001). Students' and teachers' cognitions about good teachers. *British Journal of Educational Psychology*, *71*, 185-201.

Brookover, W. B., and Lezotte, L. W. (1979). *Changes in school characteristics coincident with changes in student achievement*. East Lansing: Institute for Research on Teaching, College of Education, Michigan State University.

Brophy, J. E., and Good, T. L. (1986). Teacher behavior and student achievement. In M. C. Wittrock (Ed.), *Handbook of research on teaching* (pp. 328-375). New York: MacMillan.

Campbell, R. J., Kyriakides, L., Muijs, R. D., and Robinson, W. (2003). Differential teacher effectiveness: Towards a model for research and teacher appraisal. *Oxford Review of Education*, *29*, 347-362.

Campbell, R. J., Kyriakides, L., Muijs, R. D., and Robinson, W. (2004). *Assessing teacher effectiveness: Developing a differentiated model*. London: RoutledgeFalmer.

Cheng K. M. (2004). China: Turning the bad master into a good servant. In I. C. Rotberg (Ed.), *Balancing change and tradition in global education reform* (pp. 3-19). Oxford: ScarecrowEducation.

Cheng, K. M., and Wong, K. (1996). School effectiveness in East Asia: Concepts, origins and implications. *Journal of Educational Administration*, *34*(5), 32-49.

Corbett, D., and Wilson, B. (2002). What urban students say about good teaching? *Educational Leadership*, *60*(1), 18-22.

Creemers, B. P. M. (1997). *Effective schools and effective teachers: An international perspective*. Warwick, UK: University of Warwick.

Cruickshank, D. R., and Haefele, D. (2001). Good teachers, plural. *Educational Leadership*, *58*(5), 26-30.

Feng, Z. (2002). On the transition of teacher evaluation mechanism in the context of quality education. *Journal of Shenyang Teacher College*, *26*(2), 10-12. (in Chinese).

Glaser, B. G., and Strauss, A. L. (1967). *The discovery of grounded theory: Strategies for qualitative research*. Chicago: Aldine.

Hiebert, J., Stigler, J. W, Jacobs, J. K., Givvin, K. B., Garnier, H., Smith, M., Hollingsworth, H., Manaster, A., Wearne, D., and Gallimore, R. (2005). Math teaching in the United States today (and tomorrow): Results from the TIMSS 1999 video study. *Educational Evaluation and Policy Analysis*, *27*, 111-132.

Jiang, F. H. (2001). *Modern educational evaluation: Theory, technology and methods*. Guangzhou, China: Guangdong People's Press. (in Chinese).

Jiang, F. H., and Zhang, Q. L. (2003). Some thoughts on teacher evaluation in the context of the curriculum reform for basic education. *Educational Guiding Journal*, (5), 40-43. (in Chinese).

Kutnick, P., and Junes, V. (1993). Pupils' perceptions of a good teacher: A developmental perspective from Trinidad and Tobago. *British Journal of Educational Psychology*, *63*, 400-413.

Kyriakides, L., and Campbell, R. J. (2003). Teacher evaluation in Cyprus: Some conceptual and methodological issues arising from teacher and school effectiveness research. *Journal of Personnel Evaluation in Education, 17*, 21-40.

LeTendre, G., Baker, D., Akiba, M., Goesling, B., and Wiseman, A. (2001). Teachers' work: Institutional isomorphism and cultural variation in the U.S., Germany, and Japan. *Educational Researcher, 30*(6), 3-15.

Li, R. (2002). New ideas on teacher evaluation. *Modern Elementary and Secondary Education*, (6), 53-55. (in Chinese).

Li, R., and Xuan, L. (2003). Limitation and transcendence on teacher evaluation. *Educational Science Research*, (3), 22-24. (in Chinese).

Ling, R. (2001). Exploration of professional development of excellent middle school teachers in China. *Journal of Changshu College*, (6), 26-30. (in Chinese).

Liu, S. (2006). *School effectiveness research in the People's Republic of China.* Unpublished PhD thesis, Louisiana State University, Louisiana, LA.

Liu, S., and Teddlie, C. (2003). Teacher evaluation and curriculum reform in the People's Republic of China: Ongoing developments. *Journal of Personnel Evaluation in Education, 17*, 243-261.

Liu, S., and Teddlie, C (2005). A follow-up study on teacher evaluation in the People's Republic of China: Historical analysis and latest trends. *Journal of Personnel Evaluation in Education, 18*, 253-272.

Meng, L., and Liu, S. (2008). Mathematics teacher stress in Chinese secondary schools. *Journal of Educational Enquiry, 8*, 73-96.

Murphy, P. K., Delli, L.A., and Edwards, M. N. (2004). The good teacher and good teaching: Comparing beliefs of second-grade students, preservice teachers, and inservice teachers. *The Journal of Experimental Education, 72*, 69-92.

Organization for Economic Co-operation and Development (OECD) (2005). *Teachers matter: Attracting, developing and retaining effective teachers*. Paris: Author.

Polk, J. A. (2006). Traits of effective teachers. *Arts Education Policy Review, 107*, 23-29.

Reynolds, D., and Teddlie, C. (2000). The processes of school effectiveness. In C. Teddlie and D. Reynolds (Ed.), *The international handbook of school effectiveness research* (pp. 135-159). London: Falmer Press.

Rosenshine, B., and Stevens, R. (1986). Teaching functions. In M. C. Wittrock (Ed.), *Handbook of research on teaching* (3rd ed., pp. 376-391). New York: Macmillan.

Sawyer, R. K. (2001). Emergence in sociology: Contemporary philosophy of mind and some implications for sociological theory. *American Journal of Sociology, 107*, 551-585.

Scheerens, J., and Bosker, R. (1997). *The foundations of educational effectiveness*. Oxford: Pergamon.

Shao, G., and Hao, D. (2002). A study of young teachers' knowing about excellent teachers. *Teacher Education Research, 14*(5), 22-27. (in Chinese).

Shi, K. (2005). A comparative study of psychological qualities of excellent teachers from the perspectives of middle school students, preservice teachers and inservice teachers. *Theory and Practice of Education, 25*(8), 55-59. (in Chinese).

Shulman, L. S. (1987). Knowledge and teaching: Foundations of the new reform. *Harvard Education Review, 57*, 1-22.

Shulman, L. S. (2000). Teacher development: Roles of domain expertise and pedagogical knowledge. *Journal of Applied Developmental Psychology, 21*, 129-135.

Stronge, H. J. (2007). *Qualities of effective teachers* (2nd ed.). Alexandria, VA: Association for Supervision and Curriculum Development.

Stronge, H. J., and Hindmean, J. L. (2003). Hiring the best teachers. *Educational Leadership, 60*(8), 48-52.

Stronge, H. J., and Tucker, P. D. (2003). *Handbook on teacher evaluation: Assessing and improving performance.* Larchmont: Eye On Education.

Stronge, H. J., Ward, T. J., Tucker, P. D., and Hindman, J. L. (2007). What is the relationship between teacher quality and student achievement? An exploratory study. *Journal of Personnel Evaluation in Education, 20*, 165-184.

Teddlie, C. (1999). *Report on the psychometric properties of the attitudinal and behavioral instruments used in the SEAP-II site visits, SY 1996-97 and SY 1997-98.* Baton Rouge: Louisiana Department of Education.

Tuckman, B. (1995). Assessing effective teaching. *Peabody Journal of Education, 70*, 127-138.

Weinstein, C. (1989). Teacher education students' perceptions of teaching. *Journal of Teacher Education, 40*(2), 53-60.

World Bank (2003). *World development report 2003.* Washing, DC: World Bank.

Ying, P. C., and Fan, G. R. (2001). Case study on teacher evaluation patterns: On the limitations of traditional pattern of teacher evaluation and exploration of a new pattern. *Theory and Practice of Education, 21*(3), 22-25. (in Chinese).

Zhu, S. (2004). Analysis of forming cause of excellent teachers' competence and the discussions on teachers' training. *Journal of Hunan First Normal College, 4*(4), 121-124. (in Chinese).

INDEX

A

abolition, 48
academic learning, 39
academic performance, 65, 139, 190, 247
academic success, 175
access, 29, 52, 65, 68, 70, 71, 206, 226
accommodation, 16
accountability, 5, 42, 54
acquaintance, 206
action research, 23, 234
adaptability, 34, 40
adaptation, 6, 7, 16, 24, 34, 122, 152, 192, 238
adjustment, 65, 99, 245, 246
administrators, 7, 16, 19, 24, 73, 118, 193, 198, 233, 244, 249
adults, 168
advertisements, 53
advisory body, 173
advocacy, 53, 117
aesthetic, 32, 38
Afghanistan, 216
age, 5, 9, 76, 104, 122, 175, 200, 204
agencies, 54, 55, 65, 70
agriculture, 99, 156, 157
alienation, 201
align curriculum, 57
alters, 130
amino, 101
amino acid, 101
amino acids, 101
anger, 193, 197
appointments, 164
articulation, 186
Asia, xiv, xv, xvi, 6, 7, 8, 9, 27, 28, 29, 45, 75, 76, 109, 133, 135, 151, 166, 201, 204
Asian countries, 5, 187

assessment, vii, xiii, 3, 4, 6, 9, 13, 14, 15, 16, 17, 19, 24, 28, 33, 35, 41, 42, 43, 53, 57, 75, 82, 83, 87, 90, 107, 112, 113, 114, 115, 117, 126, 143, 147, 158, 160, 161, 164, 166, 187, 190
assimilation, 231
atmosphere, 18, 209, 211, 218, 241, 243
authoritarianism, 150
authorities, 17, 51, 66, 69, 81, 157
authority, 34, 72, 75, 118, 120, 130, 138, 144, 150, 195, 204
autonomy, xvi, 21, 54, 55, 139, 145, 149, 150
awareness, viii, 38, 41, 61, 62, 66, 159, 209, 211, 217, 221

B

background information, 190
ban, 119, 152
barriers, 22, 76
base, 4, 6, 23, 37, 38, 49, 151, 158, 232
basic education, vii, viii, 1, 2, 3, 5, 6, 7, 9, 14, 27, 29, 30, 45, 46, 61, 84, 87, 90, 91, 92, 95, 96, 108, 109, 113, 115, 122, 155, 156, 169, 173, 181, 189, 194, 198, 201, 234, 250
behaviors, 140, 163, 205, 240, 249
Beijing, xiii, 9, 10, 13, 17, 19, 20, 21, 22, 23, 25, 28, 29, 30, 33, 45, 58, 63, 72, 75, 76, 83, 90, 91, 92, 96, 108, 109, 122, 134, 135, 144, 151, 152, 153, 167, 180, 181, 223, 226, 234
benefits, 25, 54
blame, 121, 194
blogger, 146
blogs, 24, 145, 148, 149
blood, 129
blueprint, 2, 15, 18, 19
bonds, 101
bones, 196

254 Index

bonuses, 69
boredom, 149
Borrowing, 24
brain, 69
brain drain, 69
Brazil, 15
breakdown, 193
Britain, 72
British National Curriculum, 41
bureaucracy, 48
burnout, 186
businesses, 65

C

calculus, 179
candidates, 169, 171, 172, 174, 175, 176, 181
capitalism, 91, 142
career development, 158, 159, 198
career success, 165
case studies, 64, 66, 71, 72, 231
case study, 10, 46, 66, 67, 70, 71, 72, 73, 75, 109, 117, 122, 139, 151, 190, 222, 227
categorization, 162
category a, 127
certificate, 157, 238, 248
certification, 157
challenges, viii, ix, 1, 7, 8, 9, 14, 16, 17, 19, 24, 25, 27, 31, 32, 45, 48, 49, 57, 68, 75, 76, 83, 95, 105, 106, 117, 133, 134, 152, 173, 196, 219, 220, 222
cheese, 93
chemical, 54, 99, 100, 101, 102
chemical reactions, 54
Chicago, 28, 45, 168, 222, 250
child development, 15
childhood, 22
children, 18, 20, 76, 90, 118, 138, 141, 142, 143, 148, 151, 204, 206, 208, 211, 215, 216, 217, 218, 221, 234
Chinese government, vii, 1, 31
cities, 18, 22, 48, 139, 173, 211
citizens, ix, 1, 123, 124, 125, 129, 134, 137, 143
citizenship, ix, xv, 8, 38, 123, 125, 126, 127, 128, 129, 130, 131, 132, 133, 134, 135, 142
Citizenship education, ix, 123, 125, 128, 133, 134
City, 22, 40
civil rights, 127, 130, 131, 132
civil society, 132, 134
clarity, 238
class size, 21
class teaching, 117

classes, 21, 105, 106, 119, 146, 149, 153, 206, 207, 209, 211
classification, 162, 166, 240
classroom, viii, x, xiii, 4, 16, 18, 20, 21, 25, 27, 31, 32, 33, 37, 39, 40, 41, 42, 43, 44, 46, 57, 70, 83, 90, 92, 105, 106, 111, 119, 121, 126, 130, 133, 145, 147, 150, 165, 167, 188, 191, 196, 199, 201, 203, 204, 205, 206, 207, 208, 209, 210, 211, 212, 213, 215, 216, 218, 221, 222, 223, 226, 228, 229, 230, 231, 237, 238, 240, 241, 243, 247, 248
classroom activity, 147
classroom environment, xiii, 90, 209, 213, 215
classroom management, 238, 247, 248
classroom teacher, 4, 33, 39, 40, 41, 43
classroom teachers, 4, 33, 39, 40, 41, 43
clients, 186
climate, 108, 133, 199, 201, 238
clusters, 57, 102
coaches, 198, 199
coastal region, 69
cognition, 97, 234
cognitive development, 82
cognitive process, 189, 233
coherence, ix, 107, 137, 138, 188, 199, 230
collaboration, xvi, 15, 26, 27, 28, 63, 73
collectivism, 2, 124, 125, 138, 139, 148
College entrance examination, 181
College Entrance Examination, vi, 144, 150, 169, 170, 171, 172, 175
college students, 125
colleges, 76, 171, 172, 174, 175, 176, 178, 179, 226, 248
Colombia, 28
commercial, 105, 177, 195, 197
communication, 6, 15, 16, 17, 24, 113, 153, 161, 165, 167, 186, 189, 192, 231, 233, 239
Communicative language competence, 163
communism, ix, 127, 137
Communist Party, 19, 72, 138, 139, 151
communities, vii, 13, 17, 19, 21, 23, 24, 26, 27, 29, 65, 66, 67, 72, 138, 141, 194, 223
community, 23, 28, 39, 65, 66, 70, 75, 96, 121, 125, 130, 131, 133, 233
community service, 39
comparative analysis, 45, 134, 240, 241
comparative education, xiii, xiv, xvi, 27, 97, 167
compassion, 198
competition, 42, 53, 68, 118, 120, 187, 195
competitiveness, 2, 48, 143, 205
complexity, viii, ix, 31, 32, 137, 138, 234, 238
compliance, 16, 138
composition, 99

Index

255

compounds, 100, 101

compression, 4

compulsory education, 2, 3, 5, 15, 16, 17, 35, 38, 39, 67, 90, 95, 99, 100, 103, 108, 109, 152, 153, 155, 159, 163, 204

Compulsory education, 16, 156

computer, xiii, xvi

conception, 37, 134, 139, 159, 189, 194

conceptualization, 220, 221

conference, 19, 52, 75, 92, 140

configuration, 74

conflict, vii, 6, 13, 85, 120, 179, 229, 232

conformity, 125

Confucian, ix, xv, 20, 95, 120, 125, 137, 138, 140

Confucianism, 20, 29

Confucius, xvi, 58, 134

congruence, 179

consciousness, 100, 138

consensus, 53, 54, 65, 66, 198, 241, 249

conservation, 114

consolidation, 14

construction, 39, 97, 99, 100, 109, 125, 145, 219, 239

constructivism, xi, 5, 84, 88, 91, 92, 93, 192, 225, 232, 233

Constructivism, 46, 82, 88, 234

constructivist learning, 114, 225

content analysis, ix, 123, 127, 129

controversial, 133

controversies, 82

convention, 49

convergence, 6, 186

conviction, 71

cooperation, 5, 16, 34, 82, 86, 100, 112, 121, 189, 196, 218, 220

cooperative learning, 18, 39

coordination, 16, 34

coping strategies, 10, 122

correlation, 208, 221

corruption, 140, 195

cost, 68, 152

cost accounting, 68

cost minimization, 68

Council of Europe, 161, 163, 164, 166, 168

counseling, 72

course work, 72

covering, 2, 15, 123, 133, 164, 179

CPC, 139, 140, 141, 142, 151

creative thinking, 57

creativity, 15, 16, 18, 25, 38, 39, 47, 48, 51, 62, 85, 142, 149, 203, 204, 246

crises, 99

critical analysis, x, 146, 155

critical thinking, 6, 39, 48, 117, 133

criticism, 125

cross-sectional study, 221

cultivation, 2, 5, 6, 48, 105, 123, 127, 131, 153, 203, 206, 219

cultural beliefs, 43

cultural differences, 73

cultural influence, 20

cultural literacy, 159

cultural tradition, ix, 4, 8, 95

cultural transformation, 25

culture, viii, xv, 4, 7, 8, 9, 19, 25, 27, 29, 37, 40, 43, 56, 58, 62, 81, 89, 96, 104, 107, 112, 115, 118, 120, 121, 124, 129, 144, 150, 159, 186, 200, 249

curricula, ix, 2, 3, 8, 15, 18, 33, 40, 45, 46, 48, 81, 83, 91, 95, 97, 98, 99, 100, 102, 106, 108, 109, 111, 112, 113, 115, 122, 143, 146, 179

Curriculum change, 10

curriculum development, 7, 16, 17, 21, 33, 40, 42, 69, 85, 88, 89, 90, 92, 106, 108, 109, 134, 158, 161, 190, 234

Curriculum development, 109, 168

Curriculum implementation, 207

Curriculum making, 37

Curriculum planning, 32

Curriculum reform, vii, x, 1, 10, 30, 44, 45, 46, 47, 48, 59, 77, 89, 108, 142, 193, 203, 204, 205, 207, 208, 209, 216, 218, 219, 221, 222, 223, 225, 227, 234

cycles, 14

Cyprus, 251

D

data analysis, 191

data collection, 228, 239, 240

decentralisation, 72

decentralization, 5, 6, 8, 38, 42, 48, 195

decision-making process, 70, 73

deep learning, 196

deficit, x, 225, 232

Delta, 9, 199, 200, 201, 234

democracy, 38, 127, 128, 129, 130, 131, 135, 147, 195

democratisation, 141

demonstrations, 70, 192

Department of Education, xiv, xv, 63, 180, 181, 252

dependent variable, 245, 246

depth, vii, x, 13, 14, 18, 19, 50, 105, 107, 116, 129, 144, 176, 178, 179, 203, 205, 206, 207, 208, 211, 217, 228, 231, 232, 233, 238
designers, 97, 98, 100, 102, 105, 107, 132
developing countries, 5
developmental process, 232
deviation, 249
dialogues, 40
dichotomy, 29
didactic teaching, 120
diffusion, xvi
directives, 116, 142
directors, 139
disequilibrium, 231
dissatisfaction, 145
distance education, 29
distribution, 65, 69, 128
diversification, 177
diversity, ix, 4, 7, 26, 67, 137, 138, 141, 143, 148, 153, 158, 162, 165, 176, 206, 216
division of labor, 178
dominance, 115, 142, 150
donations, 51, 68
draft, 3, 18, 19, 35, 96, 108, 152, 201
drawing, 73, 170, 207
drug abuse, 32

E

earnings, 40
East Asia, xv, 9, 91, 93, 185, 250
ecology, 143
economic change, 95, 141
economic development, 38, 87, 95, 100, 131, 140, 142, 147
economic progress, 19
economic reform, 87
economic status, 107, 240
economic transformation, 120, 138
economic values, ix, 137
economics, ix, 66, 137
editors, 7, 103, 148, 180
education reform, xv, 1, 7, 9, 23, 29, 44, 45, 50, 71, 76, 119, 180, 203, 234
Educational administration, 58
educational experience, 36, 160
educational institutions, 71
educational objective, 166
educational policy, 9
educational practices, 69, 146
educational programs, vii
educational research, 65, 71, 120, 167, 185, 223

educational system, vii, 6, 13, 45, 155, 156, 169, 180, 190, 193, 194
educators, vii, 4, 5, 7, 8, 36, 42, 62, 87, 99, 103, 107, 112, 115, 141, 226
Egypt, 15
elaboration, 37
election, 131
electives, 16, 177, 179
elementary school, 239, 240, 242
elementary teachers, 241, 242
embassy, 223
emotion, x, xv, 57, 59, 97, 113, 185, 186, 189, 190, 191, 193, 198, 201, 202
emotional experience, 190
Emotional geographies, 199, 200
empathy, 143
empirical studies, xi, 49, 50, 105, 106, 186, 237, 238, 249
employees, 54
employment, 69, 76, 160, 166
empowerment, 121
encouragement, 139, 209, 213, 215
energy, 42, 47, 51, 99, 101, 114, 118, 145
engineering, 74, 193
England, viii, xiii, 5, 6, 9, 45, 61, 63, 64, 67, 70, 74, 75, 134, 175, 177, 188
English curriculum, x, xvi, 8, 155, 158, 159, 166
English Language, 158, 170, 171, 172, 176, 177
enrollment, 58, 171, 172, 174, 178, 179, 190
environment, 4, 50, 61, 70, 72, 73, 89, 99, 114, 116, 120, 197
environmental awareness, 2, 141
environmental crisis, 99
environmental protection, 38, 101
epistemology, 4, 207
equality, 125, 127, 128, 129, 130, 147, 178, 181, 233
equilibrium, 101
equipment, 106
equity, 29, 65
essay question, 242
ethical standards, 124
ethics, ix, xi, 123, 137, 142, 143, 159, 160, 231, 237, 241, 242, 243, 247
ethnographic study, 144
Europe, 9, 166
European Union (EU), 6
evidence, viii, 3, 6, 47, 48, 50, 55, 69, 73, 75, 76, 102, 115, 204, 206, 208, 249
evolution, 114
examinations, ix, 17, 19, 42, 48, 53, 58, 62, 81, 87, 95, 97, 103, 104, 107, 113, 137, 139, 147, 148, 150, 176, 178, 179, 194, 210

Index

257

exclusion, 187
execution, 36
exercise, 6, 105, 130, 131, 209, 220
Experiential learning, 114
expert teacher, 3, 190, 195, 197, 239
expertise, 25, 69, 70, 71, 190, 193, 251
exploitation, 101
exposure, 207
external relations, 76
extra help, 241

F

fabrication, 194
factories, 131
fairness, 168, 238, 247
families, 107, 141, 146, 216
farmers, 40
fear, 148
federal government, 33
feelings, 53, 148, 159, 160, 185, 186, 187, 191,
    192, 193, 194, 195, 197, 199, 229, 230
fidelity, 16
financial, 7, 17, 19, 21, 22, 50, 51, 52, 53, 54, 62,
    63, 64, 65, 66, 67, 68, 69, 73, 74, 206
financial capital, 64, 65, 67, 68, 69, 73, 74
financial resources, 17, 19, 53
financial support, 51, 53, 54, 63
financial system, 7
fine tuning, 179
fingerprints, 27
Finland, viii, 5, 61, 63, 64, 67, 70
first dimension, 100
flexibility, 83
food, 99
force, 36, 38, 99, 156, 160, 196
foreign affairs, 130
foreign language, 39, 167, 175
formation, 58, 68, 127, 141, 232
formula, 218
foundations, x, 66, 85, 143, 169, 177, 178, 179,
    251
framing, 37
France, 168
freedom, 33, 125, 150, 205
frequency distribution, 128
funding, 22, 51, 52, 65, 67, 68, 69, 74, 180
funds, 52, 67, 68, 69

G

GCE, 176
GDP, 87, 195
general education, 100, 155, 179
geography, 39, 98, 111, 113, 116, 126, 171, 186,
    187, 201
geometry, 85, 88
Germany, 15, 251
gestures, 211
global economy, 38, 111, 138
global education, viii, 61, 250
globalization, vii, xiv, xvi, 1, 4, 5, 6, 7, 8, 9, 10,
    31, 76, 113, 127, 131
Globalization, xiii, xiv, xvi, 8, 9, 10, 74
governance, viii, xiv, 38, 42, 44, 52, 61, 62, 63,
    64, 65, 66, 67, 69, 72, 73, 74, 127, 130, 133
government funds, 52
government policy, 48
governments, viii, 26, 31, 34, 47, 54, 55, 172
grades, 17, 18, 35, 95, 98, 127, 143, 175, 206,
    207, 213, 247
grass, 112
Great Britain, 223
group work, 24, 25, 209
growth, 4, 19, 103, 188, 190, 232, 233
Guangdong, 3, 15, 17, 23, 104, 129, 170, 171,
    172, 180, 181, 189, 190, 195, 196, 250
Guangzhou, xiii, xv, 22, 145, 180, 181, 190, 195,
    250
guidance, 138, 142, 145, 161, 191, 192, 193, 199,
    221, 227
guidelines, 15, 17, 33, 41, 84, 96, 103, 116, 122,
    125, 139, 141, 142, 143, 156, 161
guiding principles, 161
guilty, 119

H

habitat, 118
hair, 116
harmony, 125, 168
health, 39, 97, 99, 101, 114, 164
heterogeneity, 6
high school, 8, 16, 17, 35, 39, 53, 55, 57, 58, 69,
    75, 76, 97, 98, 100, 101, 103, 104, 105, 107,
    108, 109, 115, 117, 118, 138, 143, 145, 146,
    148, 151, 152, 153, 174, 180, 244, 248
higher education, x, 155, 171, 174, 175, 177, 179,
    181
hiring, 115
historical character, 129

history, xv, 5, 39, 40, 112, 113, 114, 124, 125, 126, 141, 171, 193
homeostasis, 114
homework, 147, 211, 215, 238, 241, 245, 247
homogeneity, 5, 6
Hong Kong, xiii, xiv, xv, xvi, 15, 27, 45, 58, 88, 89, 90, 91, 92, 108, 109, 121, 122, 125, 133, 134, 135, 164, 176, 177, 181, 200, 234
House, 58, 92, 114, 166, 168
human, x, 97, 100, 101, 114, 143, 151, 160, 185, 186, 187, 189, 204, 206
human capital, 204
human health, 101
human interactions, x, 185, 186, 187
human resources, 206
Hungary, 75
hybrid, vii, 13, 24, 28, 201
hybridization, 6
hypocrisy, 141

I

ideal, 16, 20, 125, 139, 239, 240
ideals, 20, 37, 123, 125, 132, 138, 141, 143, 147, 149, 151, 207, 208, 209, 211, 213, 216, 218, 232
identification, 227, 228, 229, 230
identity, 55, 74, 115, 119, 120, 125, 128, 129, 132, 133, 139, 146, 187, 189, 200, 201, 202
ideology, ix, 14, 15, 111, 115, 116, 117, 119, 121, 137, 139, 149, 215
imagination, 194, 216
Imperial Examination, 48
imports, 19, 27
improvements, 18, 56, 65, 229
income, 51, 107
independence, 153
independent variable, 245, 246
India, 15
individual character, 241
individual characteristics, 241
individual development, 84, 97, 159, 171
individual differences, 162, 243, 245, 247
individual rights, 125
individual students, 139, 175, 179, 209
individualism, ix, 137, 148
individualistic values, 138
individuality, 206
individualization, 74
individuals, 19, 23, 26, 38, 65, 99, 103, 106, 115, 125, 131, 141, 159, 203, 205, 239
indoctrination, 88, 126, 139, 141, 142, 145
industry, 65, 99, 156, 162, 178

infancy, 133
inflation, 65
information technology, 39, 103
infrastructure, 204
ingredients, 161
inheritance, 2, 125
initiation, 28, 97, 201
innocence, 198
insecurity, 122
inspections, 52
inspectors, 159
instinct, 215
institutions, 65, 66, 70, 133, 175, 177, 193
instructional design, 93
instructional materials, 35
instructional practice, 188
Integrated science, 112, 113, 114
integration, 5, 6, 97, 111, 112, 114, 115, 122, 125, 133, 134, 135, 141, 187, 192, 196, 214
integrity, 2, 72, 123, 146
intellect, 123
intellectual capital, 65, 68, 69, 71, 73
intelligence, 85
interdependence, 131
interest groups, 41
intermediaries, 41
internalization, 130, 167
Internationalisation, xiv, xv
internationalization, 45
interpersonal attitude, 187
interrelations, 198
intervention, 48, 118
investment, 18, 52, 89, 204, 205
iodine, 101
Iraq, 215, 216
isolation, 65, 115
Israel, 215
issues, viii, 9, 14, 15, 16, 17, 19, 22, 24, 28, 35, 38, 40, 49, 52, 58, 62, 67, 71, 76, 83, 85, 87, 89, 90, 91, 92, 95, 96, 99, 114, 124, 130, 131, 133, 134, 141, 143, 149, 166, 186, 187, 193, 233, 251
iteration, 145

J

Japan, 5, 15, 21, 92, 93, 251
job satisfaction, 186
junior high school, 96, 98, 99, 100, 102, 103, 104, 109, 152, 153
jurisdiction, 156

Index

K

kindergartens, 58
knowledge acquisition, 82, 85
knowledge economy, 62
Korea, 5, 15, 92

L

landscape, 166, 187, 202
landscapes, 44, 90, 187
language proficiency, 166
language skills, 159, 160, 161, 162, 163, 165
languages, 49, 161, 166, 172, 175
Large-scale reform, 9
laws, 32, 38, 129, 130, 133
lead, viii, 26, 47, 50, 87, 107, 150, 170, 179, 186, 206, 229, 232
leadership, viii, xiv, xv, 2, 9, 21, 24, 26, 30, 47, 48, 49, 50, 56, 57, 58, 59, 67, 70, 72, 73, 74, 76, 102, 144, 185, 199, 200
leadership development, xv
leakage, 131
learners, 4, 8, 9, 14, 45, 56, 113, 155, 157, 158, 159, 161, 162, 163, 164, 165, 199, 238
learning activity, 86
learning environment, 83, 85, 145
learning outcomes, 97, 162, 226
learning process, 82, 113, 114, 115
learning styles, 96, 105
legislation, 4
leisure, 164
lending, 73
lens, x, 8, 185, 186, 189, 198, 201
lesson plan, 70, 116, 148, 208, 212, 221, 241, 243, 247, 248
liberal education, 150
liberty, 127, 128, 129, 130
life experiences, 124
life sciences, 114
lifelong learning, viii, 38, 61, 62, 146, 159, 165
lifetime, 27
light, 43, 113, 131, 212
linguistics, xiii, xvi, 166
literacy, xv, 2, 44, 97, 99, 100, 103, 104, 106, 107, 108, 113, 159
living environment, 164
local community, 44, 68, 71
local government, 33, 51, 53, 54, 55, 68, 190
localization, 74
logical reasoning, 49
loneliness, 149

longitudinal study, 199
Louisiana, 240, 251, 252
love, 2, 38, 124, 125, 151, 179
loyalty, 54, 55, 125
Luo, 48, 58, 76

M

magnitude, vii, 13
Mainland China, ix, x, xvi, 3, 50, 111, 122, 123, 125, 126, 127, 130, 131, 132, 133, 134, 138, 153, 155, 156, 158, 162, 164, 165, 166, 169, 175, 185, 187, 189, 190, 197, 198, 225, 226, 233
major issues, 173
majority, 38, 66, 70, 104, 119, 188, 232
management, vii, 2, 3, 13, 33, 68, 72, 83, 96, 105, 118, 130, 144, 147, 156, 157, 237, 238, 248
manipulation, 83
manpower, 106
manufacturing, 156, 157, 158, 162
market economy, 29, 38, 87, 139, 141
market share, 103
marketing, 53
marriage, 179
mass, 141
mass media, 141
materialism, ix, 99, 137, 141
materials, 2, 33, 37, 41, 99, 101, 108, 109, 133, 147, 148, 149, 164, 168, 193, 195, 205, 206, 208, 213, 215, 216, 231, 244, 245, 247
mathematical knowledge, 85
mathematics, viii, xiii, xv, 5, 7, 8, 39, 75, 81, 82, 83, 84, 85, 86, 87, 88, 89, 90, 91, 92, 93, 97, 180, 201, 206, 219, 220, 221, 223
Mathematics curriculum, 90, 91, 92
mathematics education, viii, 8, 81, 82, 86, 90, 91, 92, 93
matrix, 161, 208, 209
matter, iv, 35, 40, 99, 114, 115, 159, 161, 185, 221, 251
media, 19, 53, 112, 145
mediation, 186
membership, 125
memorizing, 43, 82
memory, 212
mental health, 42, 143
mesons, 178
messages, 6, 51, 54, 55, 138, 196
metabolism, 114
metals, 101
metaphor, 54, 119
methodological individualism, 239

methodology, xiii, 82, 91, 113, 160, 238
middle class, 201
military, 70, 138, 148, 210
Ministry of Education, vii, x, xvi, 1, 2, 3, 9, 10,
 14, 18, 28, 33, 42, 45, 76, 81, 82, 83, 86, 87,
 92, 96, 97, 98, 102, 108, 111, 113, 114, 116,
 121, 122, 123, 124, 126, 134, 142, 143, 144,
 152, 156, 167, 169, 180, 189, 201, 203, 223,
 225, 226, 234
minority groups, 138
misunderstanding, 179, 194
mixing, 6
mobile phone, 196
models, xiv, 6, 8, 17, 21, 23, 25, 26, 74, 142, 145
modern science, 103
modern society, 16, 124, 178
modernity, 151
modernization, 2, 99, 125, 134, 204, 223
modifications, 43
modules, 98, 100, 101, 106, 145, 157, 158, 161,
 189
Mongolia, 21, 22, 23
moral development, 48, 144
Moral education, 77, 128, 152, 153
moral judgment, 140, 141, 142
moral standards, 140, 143, 151
morality, 139, 142, 143, 145, 148, 151, 238
motivation, 16, 18, 38, 68, 83, 88, 115, 142, 160,
 163, 165, 233, 238, 247, 249
multicultural education, xiv
multi-ethnic, 34, 201
multiplication, 210, 219, 220, 221
music, 39, 149
mutual respect, 23, 26

N

NAFTA, 6
national borders, 4
national culture, 25
national identity, 127, 129, 131, 132, 133
national policy, 142
nationalism, 125
nationality, 109, 125
natural resources, 101
natural science, 97, 99
natural sciences, 97, 99
negative attitudes, 145
negative emotions, 187, 191
negativity, 151
Netherlands, xiv, 27, 58, 74, 75, 90, 234
neutrinos, 178
next generation, 139

No Child Left Behind, 5
North America, 6
Northern Ireland, 223
Norway, 5, 31, 41
nurturance, 81, 82, 85

O

Obama, 5
obedience, 138, 206
obstacles, 58, 105, 109, 150
officials, 40, 52, 55, 56, 116, 117, 118
Oklahoma, 180
openness, viii, 61, 62, 138, 145, 216
opportunities, 36, 38, 40, 43, 67, 71, 82, 104,
 117, 121, 131, 170, 174, 175, 187, 188, 199,
 204, 218, 233, 248
optimism, 147, 151
organ, 2
organic compounds, 101
organizational behavior, xv
organizational culture, 187
organize, 5, 49, 100, 116, 117, 161, 172, 196,
 215, 219
overlap, 157

P

Pacific, xiv, xv, xvi, 6, 7, 8, 9, 27, 28, 29, 75, 76,
 92, 133, 135, 151, 166, 201
pain, 106
paradigm shift, 120
Paradigm shift, 89
parallel, 97, 102, 125
parental pressure, 148
parents, viii, xi, 24, 41, 43, 47, 51, 52, 53, 56, 65,
 68, 70, 73, 111, 120, 138, 140, 141, 146,
 148, 149, 186, 187, 189, 193, 211, 237, 238,
 239, 240, 241, 242, 243, 244, 245, 246, 247,
 248, 249
participants, x, 16, 19, 23, 30, 50, 188, 195, 213,
 225, 242, 244
pathways, 177
patriotism, 2, 99, 124, 125, 129, 138, 139, 148
peace, 216
pedagogy, 14, 16, 44, 113, 142, 243, 244, 248
peer assessment, 24, 117
peer support, 17, 21
PEP, 102, 103, 106, 109
performance indicator, 118
permeation, 140
personal autonomy, 150

personal development, 19, 147, 178
personal responsibility, 52, 131
personal values, 142, 144
personality, 138, 151
Philadelphia, 122
Philippines, 92
phonology, 163
physical education, 32, 39, 97, 187
physical environment, 139
physical health, ix, 38, 137, 138, 203
physical sciences, 114
physical well-being, 139
physics, 96, 97, 111, 113, 115, 119, 171, 172, 178
PISA, 107
platform, 85, 192
playing, 215
pluralism, 141
policy, vii, viii, ix, xiv, xvi, 4, 5, 6, 7, 8, 9, 13, 14,
        32, 37, 39, 41, 42, 43, 44, 45, 48, 49, 50, 54,
        55, 59, 61, 62, 74, 81, 83, 87, 88, 89, 95,
        104, 106, 111, 112, 113, 115, 116, 118, 119,
        120, 121, 138, 142, 152, 173, 175, 188, 199,
        204, 205, 207, 215
policy initiative, 48, 50
policy makers, 4, 49, 87, 88, 89, 120, 138
policy reform, 204
policymakers, 43, 121, 173
political leaders, 138
politics, ix, 41, 75, 132, 134, 137, 139, 141, 147,
        171, 200
pollution, 99
polymer, 101
polymer materials, 101
population, 36, 48, 104, 146
portfolio, 24, 27, 87, 114, 117, 118, 190, 196
portfolio assessment, 87, 114, 118, 196
positive attitudes, x, 203, 205
positive feedback, 196, 230
positive relationship, 71
positron, 178
poverty, 212
power relations, 186, 198
practical activity, 39
practical knowledge, 40, 201
PRC, 169, 180, 201, 223
preparation, iv, 24, 42, 76, 83, 89, 104, 117, 139,
        147, 204, 210, 212, 248
preschool, 2
preservice teachers, 238, 249, 251
president, xv
President, xvi, 18, 19, 27

primary school, ix, x, 29, 35, 58, 76, 123, 126,
        127, 132, 138, 143, 144, 152, 203, 204, 205,
        206, 223, 227, 228
primary sector, 14
principles, xiv, 43, 44, 45, 81, 125, 138, 139, 141,
        143, 145, 147, 149, 152, 168, 170, 172, 173,
        232
private education, 19, 74
probability, 244, 246
probe, 50
problem solving, 22, 39, 83, 84, 88, 126, 133
problem-solving, 15, 113, 121, 146, 189
professional development, vii, xi, xv, 4, 8, 13, 14,
        16, 17, 18, 19, 20, 21, 23, 27, 28, 29, 32, 36,
        39, 41, 42, 43, 69, 70, 71, 88, 89, 106, 117,
        121, 144, 188, 198, 199, 200, 201, 203, 226,
        231, 235, 237, 241, 242, 243, 244, 247, 251
professional growth, 187, 198, 226, 234
professionalism, 89, 105, 147, 186, 191, 233, 234
professionals, 34, 55, 159, 186
profit, 68, 195, 197
project, viii, 13, 14, 20, 21, 22, 23, 24, 25, 26, 27,
        29, 30, 39, 46, 61, 62, 63, 64, 65, 66, 72, 88,
        98, 167, 173, 190, 205, 239
pronunciation, 163
prosperity, 19, 205
protection, 101
protons, 178
prototype, 168
psychological health, 135
psychometric properties, xiv, 252
public domain, 146
public employment, 69
public interest, 45
public sector, 74
public service, 29
publishing, 126, 195

Q

qualifications, 22, 69, 166
qualitative research, 190, 250
quality assurance, 17
Quality education, 42
quality improvement, 5
quantitative research, 24
Queensland, xiv, 44
questioning, 40, 208, 213, 221, 238
questionnaire, 29, 144, 239, 241, 244
quotas, 51

R

race, 120, 186
reactions, 87
reading, 27, 32, 102, 142, 145, 149, 159, 160, 165, 201, 216
reality, 49, 91, 103, 104, 141, 143, 145, 148, 149, 150, 198, 205, 222
reasoning, 87
recall, 17
recognition, 16, 21, 53, 186
recommendations, iv, 73, 108
reconstruction, 139, 180, 227, 228, 229, 230, 231, 232
recycling, 101
reflective practice, 45, 228, 234, 238, 247
reformers, 36, 42, 43
reforms, viii, ix, x, 4, 5, 6, 10, 16, 18, 19, 22, 25, 48, 56, 57, 61, 62, 64, 67, 69, 71, 137, 138, 140, 142, 143, 144, 145, 146, 147, 148, 149, 150, 151, 155, 170, 196, 203, 204, 205, 206, 207, 208, 209, 211, 216, 218, 219, 220, 221, 223, 225, 249
regulations, 5, 32, 39, 129, 143, 144
rejection, 143
relevance, 2, 15, 96, 112, 214
relief, 148
religious beliefs, 66
renaissance, 2, 223
reproduction, 209, 210, 213
reputation, 54, 119
requirements, 3, 4, 32, 38, 42, 49, 54, 57, 81, 83, 97, 101, 107, 141, 144, 159, 160, 161, 162, 163, 164, 165, 171, 172, 174, 175, 177, 178, 179, 180, 188, 190, 204
research institutions, 71
researchers, xi, 4, 8, 14, 16, 23, 25, 26, 49, 62, 86, 96, 132, 186, 187, 188, 189, 190, 191, 195, 198, 227, 237, 240, 249
resistance, vii, 13, 18, 19, 20, 27
resolution, 173
resources, vii, viii, 13, 17, 18, 19, 21, 22, 40, 47, 51, 52, 61, 62, 63, 65, 68, 69, 83, 99, 104, 105, 106, 112, 114, 117, 143, 144, 145, 188, 211
respiration, 120
response, 1, 24, 31, 64, 71, 81, 87, 96, 113, 148, 196, 204, 209, 211, 215
responsiveness, 40
restaurants, 191
restrictions, 18
restructuring, 42
revenue, 67

rhetoric, 6, 51, 54, 115, 141, 204
risk, 54, 55, 245, 246
root, 149
roots, 112
routes, 7
routines, 138
rule of law, 142
rules, 92, 99, 141, 187, 209, 211, 213
rural areas, 17, 18, 19, 21, 22, 106, 139, 150, 155, 205, 211
rural counties, 206
rural schools, 211
Russia, 15

S

scarcity, 7, 67, 185
schema, 231, 233
scholarship, 29, 30
school activities, 70, 131, 139
school community, 72
school culture, 112, 117, 198, 249
school improvement, 75, 200
school learning, 166
School-based teaching research, 227
schooling, viii, 4, 9, 15, 18, 37, 38, 39, 41, 43, 45, 61, 62, 67, 71, 76, 95, 97, 98, 107, 112, 113, 115, 138, 139, 160, 178, 187, 201, 206, 226, 239
science, viii, ix, xv, 2, 5, 8, 16, 30, 39, 86, 95, 96, 97, 99, 100, 101, 103, 104, 106, 107, 108, 109, 111, 112, 113, 114, 115, 116, 117, 118, 119, 120, 121, 122, 125, 164, 169, 170, 171, 172, 173, 174, 176, 177, 181, 201, 223
Science education, 97, 108, 109
scientific knowledge, 103
scope, 14, 19, 97, 103, 105, 107, 122, 162
second language, 166, 167
secondary education, x, 2, 3, 14, 45, 155, 158, 176, 181, 201, 248
secondary school students, 158
secondary schools, viii, ix, x, xiii, 8, 36, 49, 58, 61, 62, 63, 64, 65, 66, 67, 68, 71, 95, 103, 104, 108, 109, 111, 113, 117, 118, 122, 126, 155, 156, 157, 158, 164, 165, 167, 172, 173, 174, 179, 190, 191, 195, 251
secondary students, 156, 170, 174, 178, 179
security, 139
seedlings, 40
selectivity, 170, 171, 172, 176
self-confidence, 159
self-discipline, 138
self-evaluations, 218

Index

self-expression, 216, 220, 221
self-reflection, 227, 228
self-study, 85
seminars, 15, 17, 36, 64, 117, 190
semi-structured interviews, 191
senses, 83, 214
sequencing, 164
shape, 39, 61, 65, 139
shortage, 17, 19
showing, 7, 25, 142, 196, 229, 247
signals, 32, 39
signs, 57
simulations, 82, 126
Singapore, xv, 5, 31, 92, 164
skeleton, 101
skilled workers, 156, 157, 165
skills base, 82
skills training, 156
social activities, 133
social capital, xiv, 65, 66, 70, 71, 73
social change, 29, 140, 160
social competence, 163, 165
social construct, 14, 222, 233
social constructivism, 233
social context, xv, 107, 160, 187
social control, 151
social development, ix, 2, 3, 72, 99, 100, 101, 103, 124, 137, 178
social justice, 178
social life, 159
social norms, 38, 205
social participation, viii, 81
social relations, 125
social responsibility, 38, 96, 100, 143
social roles, 130, 161
Social Security, 156
social status, 194, 196, 197
socialism, 2, 7, 38, 125, 127, 134, 138, 139, 142, 143
society, 2, 9, 37, 51, 53, 72, 96, 99, 100, 104, 108, 111, 113, 114, 122, 125, 126, 130, 131, 132, 135, 140, 141, 151, 159, 160, 165, 171, 193, 244, 249
sociology, 222, 251
software, 191
solution, 101
South Korea, 135
Soviet Union, 115
specialists, 35, 45, 179, 190
specialization, 158, 178
specific knowledge, 113, 126, 132
speech, 108
spending, 241, 247

spin, 49
spirituality, 91
stability, 76, 125, 133, 179
staff members, 52, 73
stakeholders, 4, 34, 54, 73, 74, 118
standard deviation, 245, 246, 249
state, vii, viii, 10, 30, 31, 32, 38, 40, 41, 42, 43, 44, 48, 54, 57, 69, 125, 127, 132, 133, 175, 226, 232, 233
state laws, 38
state schools, 175
State-based curriculum making, 43
states, 6, 20, 33, 41, 46, 125, 127, 174, 205
statistics, 166
stereotypes, 186
strategy use, 68
Streaming, vi, 169, 170, 173, 174, 177
stress, 2, 3, 31, 39, 130, 186, 199, 241, 251
structural changes, 141
structure, viii, 2, 3, 14, 15, 31, 32, 33, 35, 39, 41, 96, 98, 99, 101, 103, 105, 107, 112, 114, 115, 120, 121, 139, 141, 144, 155, 161, 163, 167, 181, 187, 189, 193, 206, 219, 222, 231, 238
student achievement, 64, 75, 90, 248, 250, 252
student creativity, 148
student development, viii, 48, 56, 61, 71, 180
student enrollment, 157
student motivation, xv, 17
student teacher, 201
style, 3, 215
subjectivity, 226
subtraction, 220
succession, 189
summer program, 36
Sun, 84, 86, 92
supervision, 126, 131
supervisor, 49
supervisors, 199
surveillance, 118
survival, 118
sustainable development, 121
Sweden, 15
synthesis, 223, 238
systemic change, 35, 189
Systemic reform, 45

T

tactics, 198
Taiwan, xvi, 15, 84, 90, 129, 134, 164, 187, 234
talent, 2, 75
target, xi, 165, 225

teach to the test, 42
Teacher belief, 222
Teacher development, 200, 251
Teacher education, 252
teacher effectiveness, xiv, 238, 239, 249, 250
Teacher emotion, x, 185
Teacher epistemologies, 206
Teacher evaluation, 251
Teacher learning, 234
teacher preparation, viii, 41, 81
Teacher professional development, 198, 199
Teacher trainers, 198
teacher training, x, 2, 3, 16, 21, 105, 190, 192, 193, 203, 205, 225, 226, 227, 233, 234
Teacher training, 153, 188
teacher-student relationship, 83
teaching evaluation, 97, 103, 105, 107, 239, 248
teaching experience, 70, 105, 107, 120, 190, 191, 232, 238, 248
Teaching reflection, 227, 231
teaching strategies, 4, 21, 23, 29, 119, 133, 187
team members, 24, 70
teams, 16, 64, 69, 70, 72, 73, 240
technical support, 188
techniques, 4, 211, 240
technological progress, 99
technology, xvi, 2, 4, 5, 16, 40, 68, 96, 97, 99, 100, 103, 104, 114, 131, 156, 157, 164, 175, 180, 209, 250
tension, ix, 4, 56, 107, 137, 141, 142
tensions, ix, 4, 6, 10, 20, 25, 50, 59, 137, 145
term plans, 68, 88
territory, 5
test items, 117, 119
test scores, xi, 237, 238, 241, 242, 243, 244, 245, 246, 247, 248, 249
testing, 17, 24, 76, 82, 166
theoretical approaches, 201
think critically, 226
third dimension, 100
thoughts, 58, 86, 139, 145, 148, 250
threats, 187
threshold level, 164, 168
Tibet, 22
time allocation, 238, 248
traditional authority, 150
traditions, vii, 2, 4, 6, 13, 16, 25, 33, 40, 125
training, ix, 8, 15, 17, 22, 36, 76, 88, 91, 99, 105, 137, 138, 148, 151, 153, 166, 187, 188, 190, 191, 192, 193, 194, 196, 226, 227, 233, 243, 252
training programs, 191, 192, 193, 196
traits, 138

trajectory, 26
transcendence, 251
transformation, viii, ix, x, 15, 37, 41, 61, 62, 63, 64, 65, 66, 73, 74, 75, 123, 124, 127, 128, 195, 203, 204, 205, 216
translation, 165
transmission, 2, 19, 39, 89, 117, 118, 127, 139, 150
transplantation, 5
transportation, 130
treatment, 164
trial, 82, 92, 99, 104, 108, 109, 112, 143
triangulation, 208, 240
Trinidad, 250
Trinidad and Tobago, 250
tuition, 76
Tyler Rationale, 36
Type I error, 245, 246

U

UNESCO, 112
unification, 86
uniform, 34
unique features, 62
United, viii, 5, 6, 9, 61, 64, 65, 67, 70, 74, 135, 174, 188, 215, 223, 250
United Kingdom (UK), 15, 24, 36, 58, 75, 175, 176, 201, 205, 223, 250
United States (USA), viii, 5, 6, 8, 9, 61, 64, 65, 67, 70, 74, 135, 174, 188, 215, 249, 250
universe, 114
universities, xiii, xv, 14, 15, 16, 22, 27, 45, 53, 65, 71, 96, 99, 103, 178, 198, 226, 248
updating, 4, 19
urban, 19, 69, 83, 138, 205, 242, 250
urban areas, 205
urban schools, 69

V

validation, 64
veteran teachers, 227
Vice President, xiv
vision, 15, 16, 31, 33, 34, 35, 37, 38, 39, 41, 45
vocabulary, 163, 215
vocational education, 155, 156, 157, 162, 166, 167, 168
vocational performance, 165
vocational training, 155
voluntary organizations, 130
vote, 130, 195

voters, 173
voting, 129, 130, 195
vulnerability, 200
Vygotsky, 167

W

wages, 69
Wales, viii, 61, 63, 64, 67, 70, 75, 175, 177
walking, 198
war, 84, 215, 216
Washington, 45, 76
watches, 214
water, 114, 181
watershed, 155
wealth, 181, 195, 206
websites, 55, 146
welfare, 51
well-being, 53, 73
Western countries, 5, 70, 73, 238, 248, 249
western education, 113, 140

WIA, 166
work activities, 222
work ethic, 165
workers, 148, 156
workforce, 61
working conditions, 69
workload, 15, 106, 227
workplace, 165, 177, 186
World Bank, 22, 29, 252
World Trade Organization, 38, 87
worldview, 38, 139
worldwide, vii, 13, 41, 67, 174
worry, 52

Y

Yale University, 44, 222
yield, 33
young people, 138, 139, 141, 143, 145, 151
young teachers, 251
yuan, 51, 53